Cultural Anthropology

MARVIN HARRIS
UNIVERSITY OF FLORIDA

HARPER & ROW, PUBLISHERS, New York
Cambridge, Philadelphia, San Francisco,
London, Mexico City, São Paulo, Sydney

1817

CULTURAL ANTHROPOLOGY

Copyright © 1983 by Harper & Row, Publishers, Inc.

Major portions of this work previously appeared in Culture, People, Nature: An Introduction to General Anthropology, Third Edition. Copyright © 1980 by Harper & Row, Publishers, Inc.

Library of Congress Cataloging in Publication Data

Harris, Marvin, 1927–
    Cultural anthropology.

    Includes index.
    1. Ethnology. I. Title.
GN316.H36 1983   306   82-21322
ISBN 0-06-042668-3

PHOTO CREDITS

Front cover: Kenneth R. Good
Chapter openings: (1) United Nations; (2) Baron Hugo Van Lawick, National Geographic Society; (3) United Nations; (4) United Nations; (5) United Nations; (7) Thomas Gregor; (8) UPI; (9) Kroll, Taurus; (10) Baldwin, Leo de Wys, Inc.; (11) American Museum of Natural History; (12) American Museum of Natural History; (13) Leo de Wys, Inc.; (14) Sidney, Leo de Wys, Inc.

Sponsoring Editor: Alan McClare
Project Editor: Cynthia L. Indriso
Designer: Gayle Jaeger (Chapter opener design by Helen Iranyi)
Production Manager: Jeanie Berke
Photo Researcher: Mira Schachne
Compositor: Progressive Typographers
Printer and Binder: R. R. Donnelley & Sons Company
Art Studio: Vantage Art, Inc.

Contents

Contents   v

Preface

About two thirds of the materials in the present volume derive from *Culture, People, Nature: An Introduction to General Anthropology*, Third Edition. But these materials have been extensively reworked, reorganized and updated. In addition there are two largely new chapters, Applied Anthropology (Chapter 13) and The Anthropology of the USA (Chapter 14). I have also written a new brief summary of the history of anthropological theories and included it as an appendix for optional assignment.

In writing this book my objective has been to produce a text which is short enough to be used in a one-semester course while remaining both readable and comprehensive. The task is not an easy one and I have had to make many difficult choices concerning what to keep in and what to leave out. Yet I am satisfied by the knowledge that students can get through the entire book on a chapter-a-week basis during a typical academic semester without sacrificing the coverage of any fundamentally important topics.

As in previous texts, I have tried to make the chapters unfold in a logical and substantively coherent fashion. The careful reader will find that the unity of the book is enhanced by frequent cross-references to related matters identified by chapter or page number. In order to sustain the student's interest I have tried to make the book as a whole address not only the essentials of cultural anthropology but also the concerns and anxieties of young people in an age of rapid cultural change.

In order to make the text as readable as possible, I have stepped up the attack against complicated sentences and unnecessary jargon. Of course, technical terms cannot be avoided if a discipline is to retain its authenticity. So I have tried to ease the student's burden by defining each new technical term as it appears for the first time.

Finally, a word about the illustrations. I have tried to enliven the text with photos of the specific people and places discussed. I am especially grateful to the many anthropologists who have made their photographs available for this purpose.

Marvin Harris

1

Anthropology and the Study of Culture

This chapter tells what anthropology is, how anthropologists make a living, and what anthropology is good for. It also provides a definition of culture and of certain general features of cultures that are useful for explaining cultural differences and similarities.

Anthropology is the study of humankind, of ancient and modern people and their ways of living. Since this subject is large and complex, different branches of anthropology focus on different aspects or dimensions of the human experience. Some anthropologists study how our species, known scientifically as *Homo sapiens*, evolved from earlier species. Other anthropologists study how *Homo sapiens* came to possess the uniquely human facility for language, how languages evolved and

1.1 ANTHROPOLOGISTS AT WORK

Below, archaeologist Ralph Solecki at Nahr Ibrahim, Lebanon, where excavations have reached Middle Paleolithic, Levalloiso-Mousterian levels (see Ch. 8). Right, linguist Francesca Merlin with the speakers of a previously unknown language near Mt. Hagen, New Guinea. Facing page top, physical anthropologist Richard Leakey and assistant Kimayou inspecting a fossil jaw near Lake Turkana, Kenya (see Ch. 4). Facing page bottom, ethnographer Margaret Mead among the Manus Islanders. [Ralph Skinner—below; DeVore, Anthro-Photo—right; Walker, Anthro-Photo—facing page top; Wide World—facing page bottom]

diversified, and how modern languages serve the needs of human communication. Still others concentrate on the learned traditions of human thought and behavior known as *cultures*. They study how ancient cultures evolved and diversified and how and why modern cultures change or stay the same.

Within departments of anthropology at major universities in the United States, the different perspectives of anthropology are usually represented by four fields of study (Fig. 1.1): cultural anthropology (sometimes called social anthropology), archeology, anthropological linguistics, and physical anthropology (Fried, 1972; Goldschmidt, 1979).[1]

Cultural anthropology deals with the description and analysis of the cultures—the socially learned traditions—of past and present ages. It has a subdiscipline, *ethnography*, that systematically describes contemporary cultures. Comparison of cultures provides the basis for hypotheses and theories about the causes of human life-styles. Although this book is primarily concerned with the findings of cultural anthropologists, the findings of the other kinds of anthropologists are essential for many of the topics to be discussed.

Archeology adds a crucial dimension to the work of cultural anthropologists. By digging up the remains of cultures of past ages, ar-

[1] See page 331 for an explanation of the system of citations used in this book.

cheologists are able to study long sequences of social and cultural evolution under diverse natural and cultural conditions. The contribution of archeologists to the understanding of the present-day characteristics of human existence, and to the testing of theories of historical causation, is indispensable.

Anthropological linguistics provides another crucial perspective: the study of the great variety of languages spoken by human beings. Anthropological linguists attempt to trace the history of these languages and of whole families of languages. They are concerned with the way language influences and is influenced by other aspects of human life, with the relationship between the evolution of language and the evolution of *Homo sapiens*, as well as with

Anthropology and the study of   **3**
culture

the relationship between the evolution of languages and the evolution of different cultures.

Physical anthropology grounds the other anthropological fields in our animal origins and our biologically determined nature. Physical anthropologists seek to reconstruct the course of human evolution by studying the fossil record. Physical anthropologists also seek to describe the distribution of hereditary variations among contemporary populations and to sort out and measure the relative contributions to human life made by heredity, environment, and culture.

Why anthropology?

Many disciplines other than anthropology are concerned with the study of human beings. Our animal nature is the subject of intense research by biologists, geneticists, and physiologists. In medicine alone, hundreds of additional specialists investigate the human body; and psychiatrists and psychologists, rank upon rank, seek the essence of the human mind and soul. Many other disciplines examine our cultural, intellectual, and esthetic behavior. These disciplines include sociology, human geography, social psychology, history, political science, economics, linguistics, theology, philosophy, musicology, art, literature, and architecture. There are also many "area specialists" who study the languages and lifestyles of particular peoples, nations, and regions: "Latin Americanists," "Indianists," "sinologists," and so on. What, then, is distinctive about anthropologists?

The work of anthropologists is distinctive because of anthropology's global coverage and comparative perspective. Other people-focused disciplines tend to study only a particular segment of human experience or a particular time or phase of our cultural or biological development. But the findings of anthropology are never based upon the study of a single population, race, tribe, class, nation, time, or place. Anthropologists insist first and foremost that conclusions based upon the study of one particular human group or civilization be checked against the evidence of other groups or civilizations. In this way the findings of anthropology transcend the interests of any particular tribe, race, nation, or culture. In anthropological perspective, all peoples and cultures are equally worthy of study. Thus anthropology is opposed to the view of those who would have themselves and no one else represent humanity, stand at the pinnacle of progress, or be chosen by God or history to fashion the world in their own image.

Anthropologists believe that a sound knowledge of humankind can be achieved only by studying distant as well as near lands and ancient as well as modern times. By adopting this broad view of the totality of human experience, perhaps we humans can tear off the blinders put on us by our own lifestyles and see ourselves as we really are.

Because of its biological, archeological, linguistic, cultural, comparative, and global perspective, anthropology holds the key to many fundamental questions. Anthropologists have made important contributions to understanding the significance of humankind's animal heritage and hence to the definition of what is distinctively human about human nature. Anthropology is strategically equipped to study the significance of race in the evolution of cultures and in the conduct of contemporary life. It also holds the key to the understanding of the origins of social inequality in the form of racism, sexism, exploitation, poverty, and international underdevelopment.

Why study anthropology?

Most anthropologists make their living by teaching in universities, colleges, and junior colleges, and by carrying out university-based research. But a substantial and increasing proportion of anthropologists finds employment in nonacademic settings. Museums, especially museums of natural history, archeology museums, and museums of primitive art and folklore have long relied on the expertise of anthropologists. In recent years, anthropologists have been welcome in a greater variety of public and private positions: in government agencies concerned with welfare, drug abuse, mental health, environmental impact, housing, education, foreign aid, and agricultural development; in the private sector as personnel and ethnic relations consultants and as management consultants for multinational firms; and as members of the staffs of hospitals and foundations.

In recognition of the growing importance of these nonacademic roles as a source of employment for anthropologists, many university departments of anthropology have started or expanded programs in *applied anthropology* (see Ch. 13). These programs supplement traditional anthropological studies with training in statistics and computer languages and other skills suitable for solving practical problems in human relationships under a variety of natural and cultural conditions.

Despite the expanding opportunities in applied fields, the study of anthropology remains valuable not so much for the opportunities it presents for employment, but for its contribution to the basic understanding of human variations and relationships. Just as the majority of students of mathematics do not become mathematicians, so too the majority of students of anthropology do not become anthropologists. For human relation fields, such as law, medicine, nursing, education, government, psychology, economics, and business administration, anthropology has a role to play that is as basic as mathematics. Only by becoming sensitive to and by learning to cope with the cultural dimensions of human existence can one hope to be optimally effective in any of these fields.

In the words of Frederica De Laguna, "Anthropology is the only discipline that offers a conceptual schema for the whole context of human experience. . . . It is like the carrying frame onto which may be fitted all the several subjects of a liberal education, and by organizing the load, making it more wieldy and capable of being carried" (1968, p. 475).

The definition of culture

Culture is the learned, socially acquired traditions and life-styles of the members of a society, including their patterned, repetitive ways of thinking, feeling, and acting (i.e., behaving). This definition follows the precedent set by Sir Edward Burnett Tylor, the founder of academic anthropology in the English-speaking world and the author of the first anthropology textbook:

Culture . . . taken in its wide ethnographic sense is that complex whole which includes knowledge, belief, art, morals, law, custom, and any other capabilities and habits acquired by man as a member of society. The condition of culture among the various societies of mankind, in so far as it is capable of being investigated on general principles, is a subject apt for the study of laws of human thought and action. (1871, p. 1)

Some anthropologists, however, restrict the meaning of culture exclusively to the mental *rules* for acting and speaking shared by the members of a given society. These rules are seen as constituting a kind of grammar of behavior. Actions are then regarded as "social" rather than "cultural" phenomena. It is this distinction that some anthropologists seek to make when they write about social anthropology as distinguished from cultural anthropology (Goodenough, 1970). No confusion can result from the more inclusive definition used in this book if care is taken to indicate whether the culturally determined ideas inside peoples' heads or the culturally determined activities of their bodies, or both, are being discussed.

There is one other kind of distinction between "social" and "cultural" that is also quite common. Some sociologists and anthropologists employ the term "social" to refer to the relationships among the groups within a society. For these social scientists, culture consists of the lifeways of the members of a society apart from the society's group structure. In the usage we will follow in this book, social groups and the relation of one social group to another will be regarded as aspects of culture (mental and behavioral). The family, for example, is a social group that conforms to and exhibits a particular society's culture of domestic life.

What then is the definition of society? A *society* is a group of people who share a common habitat and who are dependent on one another for their survival and well-being.

In recognition of the fact that many large societies are made up of classes, ethnic groups, regions, and other significant subgroups, it is often convenient to refer to and study *subcultures*. One may, for example, refer to the subculture of American blacks, or the suburban subculture, or the subculture of peasants in Brazil.

Enculturation and cultural relativism

The culture of a society tends to be similar in many respects from one generation to the next. In part this continuity in lifeways is maintained by the process known as *enculturation*. Enculturation is a partly conscious and partly unconscious learning experience whereby the older generation invites, induces, and compels the younger generation to adopt traditional ways of thinking and behaving. Thus, Chinese children use chopsticks (Fig. 1.2) instead of forks, speak a tonal lan-

1.2 TECHNIQUES OF EATING
Power of enculturation is vividly apparent in diverse eating practices. Below, Chinese girls eating rice. [FAO]

1.3 PASSING CULTURE ON

In Bali (above left), a man reads to his grandchildren from a script on narrow bamboo strips. In Afghanistan (above right), father with son reading from Koran. In Moscow (below left), a ballet class. In Taos, New Mexico (below right), father teaching child to dance. [UPI—above left; Eugene Gordon—above right; UPI—below left; Museum of the American Indian, Heye Foundation—below right]

Enculturation and cultural relativism

guage, and dislike milk because they have been enculturated into Chinese culture rather than into the culture of the United States. Enculturation is primarily based upon the control that the older generation exercises over the means of rewarding and punishing children. Each generation is taught not only to replicate the behavior of the previous generation, but to reward behavior that conforms to the patterns of its own enculturation experience and to punish, or at least not reward, behavior that does not so conform (Fig. 1.3).

The concept of enculturation (despite the limitations discussed below) occupies a central position in the distinctive outlook of modern anthropology. Failure to comprehend the role of enculturation in the maintenance of each group's patterns of behavior and thought lies at the heart of the phenomenon known as *ethnocentrism*. Ethnocentrism is the belief that one's own patterns of behavior are always normal, natural, good, beautiful, or important, and that strangers, to the extent that they live differently, live by savage, inhuman, disgusting, or irrational standards. People who are intolerant of cultural differences usually ignore the following fact: Had they been enculturated with another group, all those supposedly savage, inhuman, disgusting, and irrational life-styles would now be their own.

All cultural anthropologists are tolerant of and curious about cultural differences. Some, however, have gone further and adopted the viewpoint known as *cultural relativism*, according to which each cultural pattern is as intrinsically worthy of respect as all the rest. Although cultural relativism is a scientifically acceptable way of relating to cultural differences, it is not the only scientifically admissible attitude. Like everybody else, anthropologists make ethical judgments about the value of different kinds of cultural patterns. One need not regard cannibalism, warfare, human sacrifice, and poverty as worthy cultural achievements in order to carry out an objective study of these phenomena. Nor is there anything wrong with setting out to study certain cultural patterns because one wants to change them. Scientific objectivity does not arise from having no biases—everyone is biased—but from taking care not to let one's biases influence the result of the research process (see Jorgensen, 1971).

Limitations of the enculturation concept

Under present world conditions, no special wisdom is required to realize that enculturation cannot account for a considerable portion of the life-styles of existing social groups. It is clear that replication of cultural patterns from one generation to the next is never complete. Old patterns are not always faithfully repeated in successive generations, and new patterns are continually being added (Fig. 1.4). Recently the rate of innovation and nonreplication in the industrial societies has

reached proportions alarming to adults who were brought up to expect cross-generational continuity. This phenomenon has been called the *generation gap*. As explained by Margaret Mead:

Today, nowhere in the world are there elders who know what the children know; no matter how remote and simple the societies are in which the children live. In the past there were always some elders who knew more than any children in terms of their experience of having grown up within a cultural system. Today there are none. It is not only that parents are no longer guides, but that there are no guides, whether one seeks them in one's own country or abroad. There are no elders who know what those who have been reared within the last twenty years know about the world into which they were born. (1970, pp. 77–78)

Clearly enculturation cannot account for the generation gap; rather, it must be assumed that there has been a breakdown in enculturation and that increasing numbers of adults have not been effective in inducing their children to replicate their own patterns of thought and behavior (Fig. 1.5). Enculturation, therefore, accounts only for the continuity of culture; it cannot account for the evolution of culture.

Even with respect to continuity, enculturation has important limitations. Every replicated pattern is not necessarily the result of one generation being programmed by another. Many replicated patterns are the result of the response of successive generations to similar conditions of social life. The programming received may even be different from the actual patterns; in other words, people may be enculturated to behave in one way but be

---

1.4 CULTURE, PEOPLE, AND THE SUN
Relationship between people and the sun is mediated by culture. Sunbathing (below) is a modern invention. On the beach at Villerville in 1908 (facing page), only "mad dogs and Englishmen went out in the midday sun" . . . without their parasols. [Johnson, DeWys—below; Jacques Henri Lartique/Museum of Modern Art—facing page]

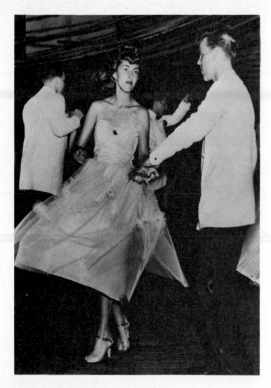

1.5 THE GENERATION GAP
Above, high school prom, 1953—dusk to dawn with chaperones. Below, disco—not what the couple in the photo above expected of their children. [UPI—above; Wide World —below]

obliged by conditions beyond their control to behave in another way. For example, enculturation is responsible for replicating the patterns of behavior associated with driving a car. Another replicated pattern consists of stalled traffic. Are automobile drivers programmed to make traffic jams? On the contrary, they are programmed to keep moving and to go around obstacles. Yet traffic jams are a highly patterned cultural phenomenon.

Poverty requires a similar analysis, as we will see in a later chapter. Many poor people find themselves living in houses, eating food, working, and raising families according to patterns that replicate their parents' subculture not because their parents wanted them to follow these patterns, but because they confront similar political and economic conditions (see Ch. 9).

Diffusion

Whereas enculturation refers to the passing of cultural traits from one generation to the next, *diffusion* refers to the passing of cultural traits from one culture and society to another (Fig. 1.6). This process is so common that the majority of traits found in any society can be said to have originated in some other society. One can say, for example, that much of the government, religion, law, diet, and language of the United States was "borrowed" or diffused from other cultures. Thus the Judeo-Christian religions come from the Middle East; parliamentary democracy comes from Western Europe; the food grains in our diet— rice, wheat, corn—come from ancient and distant civilizations; and the English language comes from the amalgam of several different European tongues.

Early in this century (see p. 323), diffusion was regarded by many anthropologists as the most powerful explanation for sociocultural differences and similarities. The lingering effects of this approach can still be seen in pop-

1.6 DIFFUSION

Can you reconstruct the diffusionary history of the objects and activities shown in these scenes? Mongolian metropolis (left); Brazilian woodsman (above); headman in Arnhem, Australia, summoning his clanspeople to a meeting with a solar-powered portable radio (below). [Cartier-Bresson, Magnum—left; UPI—above; DeVore, Anthro-Photo—below]

ular attempts to explain the similarities among major civilizations as the result of the derivation of one from another—Polynesia from Peru, or vice versa; lowland Meso-america[2] from highland Mesoamerica, or vice versa; China from Europe, or vice versa; the New World (the Americas) from the Old, and so forth. In recent years, however, diffusion has lost ground as an explanatory principle. It is true that, in general, the closer two societies are to each other, the greater will be the cultural resemblance between them. But these resemblances cannot simply be attributed to some automatic tendency for traits to diffuse. It must be kept in mind that societies close together in space are likely to occupy similar environments; hence the similarities between them may be caused by the effects of similar environmental conditions (Harner, 1970). Moreover, there are numerous cases of societies in close contact for hundreds of years that maintain radically different ways of life. For example, the Incas of Peru had an imperial government while the nearby forest societies lacked centralized leadership of any kind. Other well-known cases are the African Ituri forest hunters and their Bantu agriculturalist neighbors; the "apartment house" Pueblos and their marauding, nomadic Apache neighbors in the American Southwest. Resistance to diffusion, in other words, is as common as acceptance. If this were not the case, there would be no struggle between Catholics and Protestants in Northern Ireland; Mexicans would speak English (or Americans Spanish), and Jews would accept the divinity of Jesus Christ. Furthermore, even if one accepts diffusion as an explanation, there still remains the question of why the diffused item originated in the first place. Finally, diffusion cannot account for many remarkable instances in which people who are known never to have had any means of contact invented similar tools and techniques

[2] Mesoamerica is Mexico plus Central America.

and developed similar forms of marriage and religious beliefs.

In sum, diffusion is no more satisfactory as a mode of explanation of similar cultural traits than is enculturation. If nothing but diffusion and enculturation were involved, we should expect all cultures to be the same and to stay the same. This is clearly not the case.

It must not be concluded, however, that diffusion plays no role in sociocultural evolution. The nearness of one culture to another often does influence the rate and direction of change as well as shape specific cultural details, even if it does not shape the general features of the two cultures. For example, the custom of smoking tobacco originated among the native peoples of the Western Hemisphere and after 1492 spread to the remotest regions of the globe. This could not have happened if the Americas had remained cut off from the other continents. Yet contact alone obviously does not tell the whole story, since hundreds of other native American traits, like living in wigwams or hunting with bow and arrow, were not taken up even by the colonists who lived next door to native American peoples.

Mental and behavioral aspects of culture

By talking with people, anthropologists learn about a vast inner mental world of thought and feeling. This inner world exists on different levels of consciousness. First, there are patterns that exist far below consciousness. The rules of grammar are an example of such "deep structures." Second, there are patterns that exist closer to consciousness and that are readily formulated when the proper questions are asked. People can usually formulate values and norms and proper codes of conduct for activities such as weaning babies, courting a mate, choosing a leader, treating a disease, entertaining a guest, categorizing kin, worshipping God, and thousands of additional commonplace activities. But such rules, plans, and values may not ordinarily be formalized or completely conscious. Finally, there are equally numerous, fully conscious, explicit and formal rules of conduct and statements of values, plans, goals, and aspirations that may be discussed during the course of ordinary conversations, written in law codes, or announced at public gatherings (i.e., rules about littering, making bank deposits, playing football, trespassing, and so on).

But conversations are not the only source of anthropological knowledge about culture. In addition, anthropologists observe, measure, photograph, and take notes about what people do during their daily, weekly, or annual rounds of activities. They watch how births take place, attend funerals, go along on hunting expeditions, watch marriage ceremonies, and attend thousands of other events and activities as they actually unfold. These actual events and activities constitute the behavioral aspect of culture.

The relationship between the mental and behavioral aspects of culture is highly complex and the subject of considerable disagreement. Cultures not only have rules for behavior, but rules for breaking the rules for behavior—as when one parks in front of a

1.7 RULES FOR BREAKING RULES
Cultural behavior cannot be predicted from the knowledge of a simple set of rules. [Albertson, Stock, Boston—top; Zimbel, Monkmeyer—below; Hamlin, Stock, Boston—bottom]

13

sign that says "No Parking" and gambles on not getting a ticket (Fig. 1.7). To make matters worse, there is the problem of distinguishing between the culture's own version of its mental rules and behavioral events and the mental rules and behavioral events as they appear to the scientific observer.

Emic and etic aspects of culture

The distinction between mental and behavioral events does not resolve the question of what constitutes an adequate description of a culture as a whole. The problem is that both the thoughts and behavior of the participants can be viewed from two different perspectives: from the perspective of the participants themselves and from the perspective of the observers. In both instances scientific, objective accounts of the mental and behavioral fields are possible. In the first instance the observers employ concepts and distinctions that are meaningful and appropriate to the participants; in the second instance they employ concepts and distinctions that are meaningful and appropriate to the observers. The first way of studying culture is called *emics* and the second way is called *etics* (see Box 1.1 for the derivation of these terms from *phonemics* and *phonetics*). The test of the adequacy of emic descriptions and analyses is whether they correspond with a view of the world natives accept as real, meaningful, or appropriate. In carrying out emic research, anthropologists attempt to acquire a knowledge of the categories and rules one must know in order to think and act as a native. They attempt to learn, for example, what rule lies behind the use of the same kin term for mother and mother's sister among the Bathonga; or when it is appropriate to shame house guests among the Kwakiutl; or when to ask a boy or a girl out for a date among U.S. teenagers.

The test of the adequacy of etic accounts, however, is simply their ability to generate scientific theories about the causes of sociocultural differences and similarities. Rather than employ concepts that are necessarily real, meaningful, and appropriate from the native point of view, the anthropologist now uses categories and rules derived from the data language of science, which are often unfamiliar to the native. Etic studies often involve the measurement and juxtaposition of activities and events that native informants find inappropriate or meaningless.

Emics, etics, and cattle sex ratios

The following example demonstrates the importance of the difference between emics and etics in nonlinguistic aspects of culture. In the Trivandrum district of the state of Kerala in southern India, farmers insisted that they would never deliberately shorten the life of one of their animals—that they would never kill it or starve it to death—thereby affirming the standard Hindu prohibition against the slaughter of cattle. Yet among Kerala farmers the mortality rate of male calves is almost twice as high as the mortality rate of female calves. In fact, male cattle 0–1 year of age are outnumbered by female cattle of the same group in a ratio of 67:100. The farmers themselves are aware that male calves are more likely to die than female calves, but they attribute the difference to the relative "weakness" of the males. "The males get sick more often," they say. When asked to explain why male calves get sick more often, some farmers suggest that the males eat less than the females. Finally, some farmers even admit that the male calves eat less because they are not allowed to stay at the mother's teats for more than a few seconds. But none could say that since there is little demand for traction animals in Kerala, male cattle are culled and female cattle are reared. The emics of the situa-

BOX 1.1 PHONEMICS AND PHONETICS

The terms etics and emics are derived from the concepts of phonetics and phonemics. Human speech behavior involves the formation of sounds called *phones*. A listener who does not know a language can record the phones and decribe them in terms of their physical properties. Thus the [t] sound in *tick* and *stick* are two different kinds of phones. In forming the [t] in *tick* a little puff of air is released, while in forming the [t] in *stick* no puff of air is released. (Try it.) Phonetically these two phones are different, one being an *aspirated unvoiced alveolar stop*, the other being an *unaspirated unvoiced alveolar stop*. (Voicing refers to whether or not the vocal cords vibrate during the production of a phone; an alveolar stop is produced by placing the tip of the tongue against the alveolar ridge behind the upper teeth.) The *phonetic* differences between an aspirated and unas-pirated [t], however, do not constitute a *phonemic* difference to the native speaker of En-glish. That is, the substitution of an aspirated for an unaspirated [t] in any combination of phones will never make a difference in the meaning of an English utterance, and most speakers of English are not aware of the difference between the two phones. Other equally slight phonetic differences, however, are perceived by native speakers of English as constituting a difference in the meaning of utterances that are otherwise identical. For example, the only difference between the [t] in *ten* and the [d] in *den*, which are both al-veolar stops, is that [t] is unvoiced while [d] is voiced. Thus, the phones [t] and [d] are English *phonemes*—that is, a class of phones which when substituted for another class of phones changes meanings in otherwise identical settings, as in ten/den, tip/dip, till/dill, and so on.

For the purpose of defining the emic and etic aspects of culture, the important point to be kept in mind about phonetics and phonemics is that each language has its own sys-tem of phonemic contrasts which can only be described by asking native speakers whether the substitution of one phone for another changes the meaning of an utterance.

Phones that regularly occur in one language may not occur at all in another. When the same phone does occur in two languages, it may be phonemic in one but not the other.

In Chinese, for example, the nonphonemic aspirated and nonaspirated [t] of English *tick* and *stick* are phonemic. Also, Chinese uses sing-song tonal differences for phonemic contrasts in ways that English does not. On the other hand, in English the initial sound difference in *luck* and *rat* are phonemic, whereas in Chinese they are not (in an initial po-sition). Hence "rots of ruck" sounds the same as "lots of luck" to a Chinese learning En-glish.

The distinction between emics and etics is not only basic to the study of language, but to the study of all cultural phenomena.

tion are that no one knowingly or willingly would shorten the life of a calf. Again and again farmers affirm that every calf has the "right to live" regardless of its sex. But the etics of the situation are that cattle sex ratios are systematically adjusted to the needs of the local ecology and economy through preferential male "bovicide." Although the unwanted calves are not slaughtered, many are more or less starved to death. In other parts of India, where different ecological and economic conditions prevail, etic "bovicide" is practiced more against female rather than male cattle, resulting in some states in an adult cattle sex ratio of over 200 oxen for every 100 cows (see Ch. 10 for more discussion on the emics and etics of cattle in India).

The universal pattern

In order to compare one culture with another, the anthropologist has to collect and organize cultural data in relation to cross-culturally recurrent aspects or parts of the social and cultural whole. The structure of these recurrent aspects or parts is called the *universal pattern*.

Most anthropologists would agree that every human society has to have cultural provisions for behavior and thoughts related to making a living from the environment, having children, organizing the exchange of goods and labor, living in domestic groups and larger communities, and for the creative, expressive, playful, esthetic, moral, and intellectual aspects of human life. However, there is no agreement on how many subdivisions of these categories should be recognized nor on what priority they should be given when it comes to the conduct of research.

A universal pattern consisting of three major divisions—infrastructure, structure, and superstructure—will be used in this book.

1 *Infrastructure* Consists of the etic and behavioral activities by which each society satisfies minimal requirements for subsistence—the *mode of production*—and by which each society regulates population growth—the *mode of reproduction*.

2 *Structure* Consists of the economic and political etic and behavioral activities by which every society organizes itself into groups that allocate, regulate, and exchange goods and labor. Depending on whether the focus of organization is on domestic groups or on the internal and external relationships of the whole society, one may speak of *domestic economies* or *political economies* as universal components on the structural level.

3 *Superstructure* Consists of behavior and thought devoted to artistic, playful, religious, and intellectual endeavors plus all the mental and emic aspects of a culture's infrastructure and structure.

Summary

Anthropology is the study of humankind. Its four major branches are cultural or social anthropology, anthropological linguistics, physical anthropology, and archeology. Its distinctive approach lies in its global, comparative, and multidimensional perspective. Although the majority of anthropologists are employed in academic settings, increasing numbers are engaging in applied anthropology in a variety of human behavior and human relationship fields. The study of anthropology is valuable for anyone contemplating a career in a field affected by the cultural dimension of human existence.

A culture consists of the socially acquired ways of thinking, feeling, and acting of the members of a particular society. Cultures maintain their continuity by means of the process of enculturation. In studying cultural differences, it is important to guard against the habit of mind called ethnocentrism, which arises from a failure to appreciate the far-reaching effects of enculturation on human life. Enculturation, however, cannot explain how and why cultures change. Moreover, not all cultural recurrences in different generations are the result of enculturation. Some are the result of reactions to similar conditions or situations.

Whereas enculturation denotes the process by which culture is transmitted from one generation to the next, diffusion denotes the process by which culture is transmitted from one society to another. Diffusion, like enculturation, is not automatic and cannot stand alone as an explanatory principle. Neighboring societies can have both highly similar as well as highly dissimilar cultures.

Culture, as defined in this book, consists both of events that take place inside people's heads and the behavior that takes place all around them. Human beings can describe their thoughts and behavior from their own point of view. In studying human cultures, therefore, one must make explicit whether it is the native participant's point of view or the observer's point of view that is being expressed. These are the emic and etic points of view, respectively. While the terms emic and etic are borrowed from the linguistic concepts of phonemes and phones, the distinction between the emic and etic viewpoints carries over into nonlinguistic aspects of culture as well. As the distinction between phones and phonemes shows, it is essential to distinguish between emic and etic aspects of cultural phenomena. Both mental and behavioral aspects of culture can be approached from emic or etic points of view. Emic and etic versions of reality often differ markedly, although there is usually some degree of correspondence between them.

In addition to emic, etic, mental, and behavioral aspects, all cultures share a universal pattern. The universal pattern used in this book consists of three main components: infrastructure, structure, and superstructure. These in turn consist, respectively, of the modes of production and reproduction; domestic and political economy; and the creative, expressive, esthetic, and intellectual aspects of human life. The definition of these categories is essential for the organization of research.

2

Genes, Language, and Culture

This chapter discusses the relationship between biological evolutionary processes and the development of a cultural "takeoff" unique to human beings. Culture is shown to be encoded in the brain and not in the genes, the units of biological heredity.

The human capacity for culture is a product of biological evolutionary processes. The most powerful evolutionary process is known as *natural selection*. Natural selection takes place as a result of the potentially infinite reproductive powers of life and the actual finite nature of the space and energy upon which life depends. Natural selection acts upon the units of hereditary instructions, or *genes*, located in the reproductive cells of each organism. It does so by increasing or decreasing the frequency of genetic variants. The main source of genetic variants is *mutations*— "errors" that occur during the process by which genes replicate themselves. Some genetic variants increase the fitness of the individuals possessing them; others decrease the fitness of the individuals possessing them; *Fitness* here means nothing more than the number of offspring in which a particular genetic variant appears in successive generations. Genes that lead to higher fitness are said to be "selected for"; genes that lead to lower fitness are said to be "selected against."

Fitness is associated with many different kinds of factors. It may be related to the organism's ability to resist disease, to gain or hold space more securely, or to obtain energy in larger or more dependable amounts. It may be related to the increased efficiency and dependability of some aspect of the reproductive process itself.

Through differential reproductive success, natural selection can drastically alter the frequency of *genotypes* (i.e., types of genes) after a few tens of generations. An example of the power of natural selection to raise the frequency of a rare gene is the evolution of penicillin-resistant strains of bacteria. The genes conferring resistance are present in normal populations of bacteria, but in only a small percentage of individuals. As a result of the differential reproductive success of such individuals, however, the resistant strain of bacteria soon becomes the most common genotype.

Natural selection versus the struggle for survival

During the nineteenth century, Social Darwinists envisioned Malthus's "struggle for survival" as the mainspring of both biological and cultural evolution (see Appendix, p. 326). Natural selection was thus pictured incorrectly as the direct struggle between individuals for scarce resources and sexual partners, and even more erroneously as the preying upon and destruction of one another by organisms of the same species. Although within-species killing and competition sometimes do play a role in biological evolution, the factors promoting differential reproductive success are in the main not related to an organism's ability to destroy other members of its own population or to prevent them from obtaining nutrients, space, and mates.

Today, biologists recognize that natural selection favors cooperation and altruism within species as often as it favors competition. In social species the perpetuation of an individual's genes often depends as much on the reproductive success of its close relatives as on its own survival and reproduction. Many social insects even have sterile "castes" that assure their own genetic success by rearing the progeny of their fertile siblings.

Natural selection and behavior

Natural selection not only shapes the anatomy and physiology of organisms, it can also shape their behavioral characteristics. Specific genes determine, for example, whether species of fruit flies will fly upward or downward when threatened by a predator; the laying of eggs by a wasp in a particular kind of caterpillar; the mating rituals of fish; the web building of spiders; the specialized behavior of insect castes; and countless other drives and instincts characteristic of animal species.

It is important to understand how such behavior gets established. Organisms make "errors" in their behavior that express "errors" in their genes. In the Galapagos Islands, for example, there are species of iguana which swim and dive in the surf for food. These lizards are descended from species genetically "programmed" to hunt on land. But "errors" developed in the program, which allowed some individuals to venture closer to the sea. The deviant genes were selected for probably because they increased the food resources the sea-venturing iguanas could eat. By being selected for over the course of many generations, the sea-venturing iguanas became programmed for swimming and diving rather than for hunting on land. The sequence here may be described schematically as:

Old genotype → genetic "error"
　　　　　　→ behavioral deviation
　　　　　　→ selection
　　　　　　→ new genotype

The evolution of learning

While it is very useful for organisms to be equipped with a species-specific program of behavioral responses encoded in their genes, there is another type of behavior that has certain advantages over genetic programming. This is behavior that is programmed as a result of learning. Learning permits organisms to adjust to and to take more effective advantage of a wider variety of opportunities for achieving reproductive success than is possible through genetic programming. For example, a seagull that had poor learning ability and was rigidly programmed to search for food only along the shoreline would miss out on many other sources of meals. By learning to recognize fishing boats and by following them and learning the location of fast-food restaurants, town dumps, and other sources of garbage, seagulls greatly improve their fit-

ness *without changing their genotype*, as schematized in the following sequence:

Old genotype → learned responses
　　　　　　→ selection
　　　　　　→ old genotype

In fact, one might say it is essential for seagull fitness that the acquisition of these new behavioral responses *not* be linked to variation in the genotype. A seagull genetically programmed to stay on the shoreline would not be able to take advantage of the opportunities presented by following fishing boats out to sea.

The ability to learn has been selected for in many higher animal species precisely because learning is a more flexible and rapid method of achieving reproductive success than genetic evolution. Learning permits a population to adjust to or take advantage of novel opportunities in a single generation without having to wait for the appearance and spread of genetic mutations.

Nonhuman culture

Selection for increased learning capacity set the stage for the emergence of culture as an important source of *learned behavioral repertories* (i.e., routine patterns of behavior that can be activated on appropriate occasions). This capacity has a neurological base; it depends on the evolution of larger and more complex brains and of more "intelligent" species.

Many nonhuman species are intelligent enough to possess rudimentary traditions. Songbirds, for example, have traditional songs that vary from one population to another within a given species; many animals follow paths to waterholes or feeding grounds laid down over generations; others migrate to traditional nesting sites.

The most elaborate example of nonhu-

2.1 JAPANESE MONKEY CULTURE
A female monkey of Koshima troop washing a sweet potato. [Masao Kawai]

man culture have been found, not unexpectedly, among our species' closest relatives, the monkeys and great apes.

Primatologists of the Primate Research Institute of Kyoto University have found a wide variety of traditions among local troops of monkeys. The males of certain troops, for example, take turns looking after the infants while the infants' mothers are feeding. Such babysitting is characteristic only of the troops at Takasaki-yama and Takahashi. Other cultural differences have been noted too. When the monkeys of Takasaki-yama eat the fruit of the *muku* tree, they throw away the hard stone inside or swallow it and excrete it in their feces. But the monkeys of Arishi-yama break the stone with their teeth and eat the pulpy interior. Some troops eat shellfish; others do not. Cultural differences have also been noted with respect to the characteristic distance the monkeys maintain among themselves during feeding and with respect to the

2.2 JAPANESE MONKEYS WASHING WHEAT (facing page)
Members of Koshima troop separating wheat from sand by placing mixture in water. Central figure in lower photograph is carrying the mixture in its left hand. Two monkeys in foreground are floating the wheat and picking it up. [Masao Kawai—top; Mitsuo Iwamoto—bottom]

CHAPTER 2
Genes, language, and culture

order of males, females, and juveniles in line of march when certain troops move through the forest.

The scientists at the Primate Research Institute have been able to observe the actual process by which behavioral innovations spread from individual to individual and become part of a troop's culture independently of genetic transmission. To attract monkeys near the shore for easier observation, sweet potatoes were set on the beach. One day a young female began to wash the sand from the sweet potatoes by plunging them in a small brook that ran through the beach. This washing behavior spread throughout the group and gradually replaced the former rubbing habit. Nine years later, 80 to 90 percent of the animals were washing their sweet potatoes, some in the brook, others in the sea (Fig. 2.1). When wheat was spread on the beach, the monkeys of Koshima at first had a hard time separating the kernels from the sand. Soon, however, the same young female invented a process for desanding the wheat, and this behavior was also taken over by others. The process was to plunge the wheat into the water (Fig. 2.2): the wheat floats and the sand drops to the bottom (Itani, 1961; Miyadi, 1967; Itani and Nishimura, 1973).

Rudimentary cultures among the great apes

Over a period of many years, Jane Van Lawick-Goodall and her associates have studied the behavior of a single population of free-ranging chimpanzees in the Gombe National Park in Tanzania (Fig. 2.3). One of their most remarkable discoveries is that the chimpanzees "fish" for ants and termites (Fig. 2.4). "Termiting" involves first breaking off a twig or a vine, stripping it of leaves and side branches, and then locating a suitable termite nest. Such a nest is as hard as concrete and impenetrable except for certain thinly

covered tunnel entrances. The chimpanzee scratches away the thin covering and inserts the twig. The termites inside bite the end of the twig, and the chimpanzee pulls it out and licks off the termites clinging to it. Especially impressive is the fact that the chimpanzees will prepare the twig first and then carry it in their mouths from nest to nest while looking for a suitable tunnel entrance (Van Lawick-Goodall, 1968). Anting provides an interesting variation to this theme. The Gombe chimps "fish" for a species of aggressive nomadic driver ant that can inflict a painful bite. Upon finding the tempory subterranean nest of these ants, the chimps make a tool out of a green twig and insert it into the nest entrance. Hundreds of fierce ants swarm up the twig to repel the invader:

The chimpanzee watches their progress and when the ants have almost reached its hand, the tool is quickly withdrawn. In a split second the opposite hand rapidly sweeps the length of the tool . . . catching the ants in a jumbled mass between thumb and forefinger. These are then popped into the open, waiting mouth in one bite and chewed furiously. (McGrew, 1977, p. 278)

Chimpanzees also manufacture "sponges" for sopping up water from a hollow in a tree. They strip a handful of leaves from a twig, put the leaves in their mouths, chew briefly, put the mass of leaves in the water, let them soak, put the leaves to their mouths, and suck the water off. A similar sponge is employed to dry their fur, to wipe off sticky substances, and to clean the bottoms of chimpanzee babies. Gombe chimpanzees also use sticks as levers and digging tools to pry ant nests off trees and to widen the entrance of subterranean beehives.

Elsewhere other observers have watched chimpanzees in their native habitats pound or hammer tough-skinned fruits, seeds, and nuts with sticks and stones. One chimp in the Budongo Forest, Uganda, used a leaf on a twig to fan away flies (Sugiyama, 1969).

2.3 JANE VAN LAWICK-GOODALL
**Making friends with a young chimpanzee in
Gombe National Park, Tanzania. [Baron
Hugo Van Lawick, © National Geographic
Society]**

Chimpanzees appear to go further than
other primates in using weapons and projec-
tiles. They hurl stones, feces, and sticks with
considerable accuracy. Under semicontrolled
conditions they have been observed to wield
long clubs with deadly aim. One investigator
(Kortlant, 1967) built a stuffed leopard whose
head and tail could be moved mechanically.

2.4 CHIMPANZEE TERMITING
**A stick carefully stripped of leaves is in-
serted into the nest. The chimpanzee licks
off the termites that cling to the stick when
it is withdrawn. [Baron Hugo Van Lawick,
© National Geographic Society]**

Rudimentary cultures among the   **25**
great apes

He set the leopard down in open country inhabited by chimpanzees and when the chimpanzees came into view, he animated the leopard's parts. The chimpanzees attacked the leopard with heavy sticks, tore it apart, and dragged the remnants off into the bush.

There appear to be no specific genes that are responsible for chimpanzee termiting, anting, and the other behaviors noted above. True, in order for such behavior to occur, genetically determined capacities for learning, for manipulating objects, and for omnivorous eating must be present in the young chimpanzee. But these general biological capacities and predispositions cannot explain termiting and anting. Given nothing but groups of young chimpanzees, twigs, and termite nests, termiting and anting would be unlikely to occur. The missing ingredient would be the information about termiting and anting stored in the brains of adult chimpanzees.

Among the Gombe Stream chimpanzees, the young do not begin termiting until they are 18 to 22 months old. At first their behavior is clumsy and inefficient, and they do not become proficient until they are about 3 years old. Van Lawick-Goodall witnessed many instances of infants watching intently as the adults termited. Novices often retrieved discarded termiting sticks and attempted to use them on their own. Anting, with its risk of being bitten, takes longer to learn. The youngest chimp to achieve proficiency was about 4 years old (McGrew, 1977, p. 282). The conclusion that anting is a cultural trait is strengthened by the fact that chimps at other sites do not exploit driver ants even though the species is widely distributed throughout Africa. At the same time, other groups of chimps do exploit other species of ants and in ways that differ from the Gombe tradition. For example, chimps in the Mahali mountains 170 kilometers south of Gombe insert twigs and bark into the nests of tree-dwelling ants, which are ignored by the Gombe chimps (Nishida, 1973).

Why is culture so rudimentary among nonhumans?

The development of traditions of tool manufacture and tool use would be of great value to any intelligent species. Why then have such traditions remained so rudimentary among all species except those immediately ancestral to our own? The answer has to do with the need for combining advanced intelligence with an appropriate configuration of limbs, fingers, and thumbs.

Although primates are "brainy" enough to make and use tools, their anatomy and normal mode of existence disincline them to develop extensive tool-using traditions. Among monkeys and apes, the use of the hand for tool use is inhibited by the use of forelimbs in walking and climbing. That is probably why the most common tool-using behavior among many different species of monkeys and apes is the repelling of intruders with a barrage of nuts, pine cones, branches, fruits, feces, or stones. Throwing such objects requires only a

2.5 EARLIEST HOMINID FOOTPRINT
Discovered at Laeotolil, Tanzania, by Mary Leakey, a series of these footprints demonstrate the existence of bipedal hominids over 3 million years ago. [UPI]

momentary loss of the ability to run away or climb if danger threatens.

In the beginning was the foot

The separation of the ancestral line leading to human beings from the line leading to the contemporary great apes probably occurred between 8 and 14 million years ago (Kay, 1981, p. 150). By 3 million years ago there were at least two kinds of *hominids* (members of the human family), one called the *Australopithecines* which became extinct, and the other called *Homo habilis* which was a remote ancestor of our species. The remarkable thing about both kinds of early hominids is that they had brains no larger than a chimpanzee's. We know they were hominids because their limbs and bodies were already completely adapted to walking upright—there are even 3-million-year-old footprints to prove it (Fig. 2.5)! Hominids were not initially selected for their braininess, but for their peculiar upright gait. Why this gait, called *bipedalism*, was selected for is still a matter of debate; but it is clear that once hands were no longer needed for walking or running, tool use could expand far beyond the level characteristic of monkeys and apes. Now tools such as clubs, digging sticks, and stone hammers and knives could be carried in the hands without endangering the ability to explore, move about, and flee from danger. The making and using of these tools could then benefit from the shared experiences of many individuals.

As tool using became more important, natural selection favored brainier individuals who were better able to encode and transmit behavioral traditions. This in turn led to more and better tools and an ever-greater reliance on enculturation as a source of appropriate behavior; this in turn led to still brainier varieties of hominids.

Thus, for several million years the evolution of culture and the evolution of the human

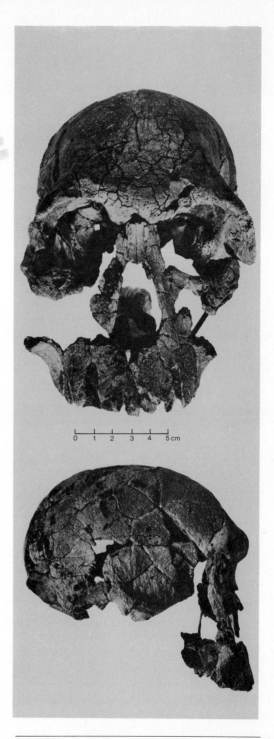

2.6 *HOMO HABILIS*

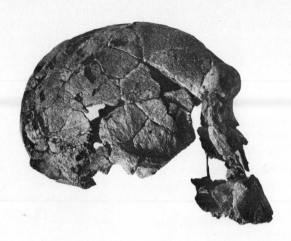

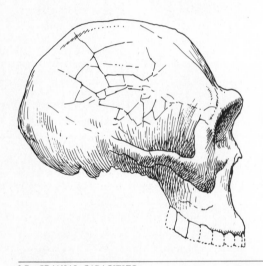

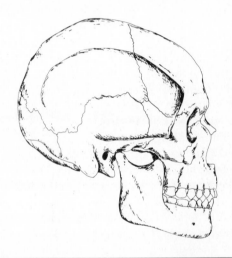

2.7 *CRANIAL CAPACITIES*
Rounding and swelling of brain case marks evolution of hominids from *Homo habilis* **(top), to** *Homo erectus* **(lower left), to** *Homo sapiens* **(lower right).**

brain and body into an increasingly efficient learning machine were part of a single evolutionary process. The stone tools associated with the ape-sized brain cases of the earliest hominids became more complex, more skillfully made, and more specialized for particular cutting, digging, and throwing tasks as *Homo habilis* (Fig. 2.6) was succeeded by *Homo erectus* about 2 million years ago and as *Homo erectus* was succeeded by *Homo sapiens* (Fig. 2.7) about 100,000 years ago.

Cultural takeoff

With the appearance of *Homo sapiens*, the relationship between cultural and biological evolution underwent a profound change. For the last 100,000 years the average size of the human brain has not increased (in fact, it has decreased somewhat!). Yet the complexity and rate of change of human sociocultural systems have increased by many orders of magnitude. This fact makes it clear that to understand the last 100,000 years of the evolution of culture, primary emphasis must be given to processes that are distinctive to culture. Natural selection and organic evolution lie at the base of culture; but once the capacity for culture became fully developed, a vast number of cultural differences and similarities could arise and disappear entirely independent of changes in genotypes.

Language and cultural takeoff

Closely linked with cultural takeoff is the uniquely human capacity for language and for language-assisted systems of thought. While other primates use complex signal systems to facilitate social life, human languages are qualitatively different from all other animal communication systems. The unique features of human languages undoubtedly arose from genetic changes related to the increasing dependence of the earliest hominids on traditions of tool use and other social activities that are facilitated by exchanging and pooling information.

One way to sum up the special characteristics of human language is to say that we have achieved "semantic universality" (Greenberg, 1968). A communication system that has *semantic universality* can convey information about aspects, domains, properties, places, or events in the past, present, or future, whether actual or possible, real or imaginary, near or far.

Another way to express the same thing is to say that human language is infinitely *productive* semantically (Hockett and Ascher, 1964). This means that to every message we send, we can always add another whose meaning

cannot be predicted from the information in previous messages, and that we can continue to expand such messages without any loss in the efficiency with which such information is encoded (although the "decoding"—the understanding of the message—may get progressively more difficult, as in this sentence).

Another component in the concept of semantic universality is the feature known as *displacement* (Hockett and Ascher, 1964). A message is displaced when either sender or receiver has no immediate direct sensory contact with the conditions or events to which the message refers. We have no difficulty, for example, in telling each other about events like football games after they are over or about events like meetings and appointments before they take place. Human language is capable of communicating an infinity of details about an infinity of displaced domains. This contrasts with nonhuman communication systems. Among monkeys and apes, for example, usually only the listener exhibits some degree of displacement, as when a "danger" message is understood at a distance. But the sender must be in sensory contact with the source of danger in order to give an appropriate warning. A chimpanzee does not say "Danger! There may be a leopard on the other side of this hill." On the other hand, in human communication both sender and receiver are frequently displaced: we talk routinely about people, places, and things seen, heard, or felt in the past or future; or that others have told us about; or that enjoy a completely imaginary existence.

In recent years, a revolutionary series of experiments has shown that the gap between human and ape language capacities is not as great as had previously been supposed. Yet these same experiments have shown that innate species-specific factors prevent this gap from being closed. Many futile attempts had been made to teach chimpanzees to speak in human fashion. But after six years of intensive training, the chimpanzee Viki learned to say only "mama," "papa," and "cup." It was found that the vocal tract of apes renders it anatomically impossible for them to produce sounds necessary for human speech. Attention then shifted toward attempting to teach apes to use sign languages and to read and write. Washoe, a female chimpanzee, learned 160 different standard signs of Ameslan (American Sign Language). Washoe used these signs productively. She first learned the sign for "open" with a particular door and later spontaneously extended its use beyond the initial training context to all closed doors, then to closed containers such as the refrigerator, cupboards, drawers, briefcases, boxes, and jars. When Susan, a research assistant, stepped on Washoe's doll, Washoe had many ways to tell her what was on her mind: "Up Susan; Susan up; mine please up; gimme baby; please shoe; more mine; up please; please up; more up; baby down; shoe up; baby up; please move up" (Gardner and Gardner, 1971, 1975).

David Premack (1971, 1976) used a set of plastic chips to teach a chimpanzee named Sarah the meaning of a set of 130 symbols with which they could communicate with each other. Premack could ask Sarah rather abstract questions, such as "What is an apple the same as?" Sarah could respond by selecting the chips that stood for "red," "round," "stem," and "less desirable than grapes." Premack made a special effort to incorporate certain rudimentary grammatical rules into his human-chimp language. Sarah could respond appropriately to the plastic-chip command: "Sarah put the banana in the pail and the apple in the dish." Sarah herself, however, did not make such complex demands of Premack.

Another approach with a 3½-year-old chimpanzee named Lana utilized a keyboard controlled by a computer and a written language known as Yerkish (Fig. 2.8). Lana could read and write such sentences as "Please machine make the window open," correctly distinguishing between sentences that begin appropriately and inappropriately and that

have permitted and prohibited combinations of Yerkish words in permitted and prohibited sequence (Rambaugh, 1977).

Both Washoe and Lucy, a chimpanzee raised by Roger Fouts, learned to generalize the sign for "dirty" from the sign for "feces." Lucy applied it to Fouts when he refused her requests! Lucy also invented the combinations "cry hurt food" to name radishes and "candy fruit" for watermelon. Koko, a female gorilla trained by Francis Patterson, holds the record thus far of 300 Ameslan words (Fig. 2.9). Koko signed "finger bracelet" for ring; "white tiger" for zebra; "eye hat" for mask. Koko has also begun to talk about her inner

---

2.8 *LANA USING YERKISH TO COMMUNICATE WITH A COMPUTER*
She can read and "write" 71 cards. [Yerkes Regional Primate Research Center of Emory University]

2.9 KOKO
Koko is giving the sign "Pour-Drink" to her teacher Francine Patterson. [© Dr. Ronald H. Cohn, The Gorilla Foundation]

feelings, signaling happiness, sadness, fear, and shame (Hill, 1978, pp. 98–99).

It is clear, however, that a vast gap still remains between the language performance of humans and apes. Despite all the effort being expended on teaching apes to communicate, none has acquired the linguistic skills we take for granted in 3-year-old children (Terrace, 1979). What all these experiments have shown is that it is entirely plausible to conceive of natural selection giving rise to the human capacity for semantic universality by selecting for intellectual skills already present in rudimentary form among our apelike hominid ancestors.

Scientific raciology

The position adopted in this book is that the causes of sociocultural similarities and differences are primarily cultural rather than biological. We will see that plausible and testable cultural theories can be constructed to account for many recurrent and variable aspects of human social life.

In the nineteenth century almost all educated Westerners were firm adherents of the doctrines of *scientific raciology*. They believed that Asians, Africans, and native Americans could achieve industrial civilization only slowly and imperfectly. Nineteenth-century scientists insisted that they had scientific proof whites were intellectually superior and that an unbridgeable biological gulf separated them from the rest of humanity (Haller, 1971). They conceded the possibility of an occasional native American, Asian, or African "genius." But they insisted that the average hereditary capabilities of the races were drastically different. These raciological theories were based on the fact that in the nineteenth century Europeans had fought, tricked, and traded their way to control over almost the entire human species. The apparent inability of Asians, Africans, and native Americans to resist the encroachment of European armies, businesspeople, missionaries, and administrators was interpreted as living proof that the Europeans were biologically superior.

The racial explanation of European political domination was a convenient excuse for colonialism and for the exploitation and enslavement of people unable to defend themselves against technologically advanced European armaments. Today few informed scientists would wish to attribute the temporary technological superiority of Europe and North America to genetic factors. Europe has not always had the most advanced technology. At various stages in the evolution of culture, non-Europeans in Asia or Africa have temporarily held the lead. Moreover, with the breakup of the great colonial empires, it would be extremely foolhardy for the advanced industrial nations to imagine that their genetic heritage will protect them from the rising political and economic power of the Third World.

Today the emergence of Japan as the Asian economic match of Great Britain and Germany discourages anyone from believing the achievement of advanced technology can be attributed to genes that are more common in one race than in another (Fig. 2.10). The problem with genetic interpretations of history and of cultural evolution is that they cannot account for the ups and downs of different regions and races except by adding or subtracting hypothetical genes for this or hypothetical genes for that.

To take another example, in the nineteenth century the British believed the Irish were an inferior "race." To account for the economic success of the Irish in the New World, a racist would have to assume that the genes had suddenly changed or that there was something special about the genes of those who emigrated. Such explanations are scientifically undesirable because they depend on the ap-

pearance and disappearance of genes for economic success that no one has ever identified and that may not exist. Cultural explanations of the ups and downs of different human populations are scientifically preferable to racial explanations because they depend on factors such as rainfall, soil conditions, and population density, which are far more concrete and visible than hypothetical genes for technological ingenuity and economic success. The explanation for the rise of Japan as a great industrial power would become *unnecessarily* complicated, and hence scientifically undesirable, if in addition to cultural and ecological factors one were to posit the sudden appearance of Japanese genes for transistors and steel mills.

Similar objections are to be made concerning the attempt to give genetic expla-

2.10 *JAPANESE ASSEMBLY LINE*
Japan has taken the lead in automation.
[J.P. Laffont, Sygma]

nations for traits such as matrilineality, patrilineality, and cognatic descent groups; nuclear and polygamous families; kinship terminologies; reciprocity; redistribution; feudalism; capitalism; and all the other cultural variations to be discussed in this book. To suppose that there are genes for each of these traits is contradicted by established facts concerning the processes of enculturation and diffusion. We know that adopted children who are brought up in cultures different from their parents' cultures acquire the culture of their foster parents. And we know that traits which originate in one culture can spread around the world to all cultures far too fast for any genetic change to have taken place. Infants reared apart from their parents always acquire the cultures of the people among whom they are reared. Children of English-speaking American whites reared by Chinese parents grow up speaking perfect Chinese. They handle their chopsticks with precision and have no urge to eat at McDonald's. Children of Chinese reared in white American households speak the standard English dialect of their foster parents, are inept at using chopsticks, and do not yearn for bird's nest soup or Peking duck. Moreover, a variety of populations has repeatedly demonstrated ability to acquire every conceivable aspect of the world cultural inventory. Native Americans brought up in Brazil incorporate complex African rhythms into their religious performances; American blacks who attend the proper schools become stars in classical European opera. Jews brought up in Germany prefer German cooking; Jews brought up in Yemen prefer Middle Eastern dishes. Under the influence of fundamentalist Christian missionaries, the sexually uninhibited people of Polynesia began to dress their women in long skirts and to follow rules of strict premarital chastity. Native Australians reared in Sydney show no inclination to hunt kangaroo or mutilate their genitals; they do not experience uncontrollable urges to sing about witchetty-grubs and the Emu ancestors (see p. 200). The Mohawk Indians of New York State specialized in construction trades and helped to erect the steel frames of skyscrapers. Walking across narrow beams 80 stories above street level, they were not troubled by an urge to build wigwams rather than office buildings.

The evidence of enculturation and diffusion on every continent and among every major race and microbreeding population proves that the overwhelming bulk of the response repertory of any human population can be acquired by any other human population through learning processes and without the slightest exchange or mutation of genes.

Sociobiology

Sociobiology is a research strategy that attempts to explain some sociocultural differences and similarities in terms of natural selection. It is based on a refinement of natural selection known as the principle of *inclusive fitness*. This principle states that natural selection favors traits which spread an individual's genes not only by increasing the number of an individual's offspring, but by increasing the number of offspring of close relatives such as brothers and sisters, who carry many of the same genes. What controls biological evolution, therefore, is whether a trait increases the inclusive total of an individual's genes in succeeding generations and not merely the number of one's own progeny.

Inclusive fitness has been used to account for certain infrahuman social traits that traditional versions of natural selection found mysterious. For example, it accounts for the evolution of sterile castes among social insects such as bees and ants. By not having progeny of its own and by feeding and caring for its fertile brothers and sisters, it can be shown that each sterile individual's inclusive fitness is increased. Other "altruistic" traits of social species can also be explained in this manner (Barash, 1977; Wilson, 1975). Although sociobiology is a strategy that emphasizes the basic importance of genetic factors as determinants of human social life, its advocates do not necessarily accept the theories of scientists who believe that races and classes differ in intellectual capacity and in other important behavioral traits because they have different genotypes. Most sociobiologists, in fact, stress the unity of the human *biogram*—the basic genetic heritage that defines human nature. They have shown little interest in studying the possibility that each race has its own biogram. One must be careful, therefore, not to lump sociobiologists indiscriminately with scientific raciologists and political racists.

Sociobiologists do not deny that the bulk of human social responses is socially learned and therefore not directly under genetic control. Sociobiologist E. O. Wilson (1977, p. 133) writes: "The evidence is strong that almost but probably not quite all differences among cultures are based on learning and socialization rather than on genes." Sociobiologist Richard Alexander (1976, p. 6) also states: "I hypothesize that the vast bulk of cultural variations among peoples alive today will eventually be shown to have virtually nothing to do with their genetic differences." Few, if any, sociobiologists are interested in linking variations in human social behavior to the variable frequencies with which genes occur in different human populations.

It must be granted that the sociobiologists' interest in identifying the constants of human nature can lead to an understanding of the outer "envelope," to use a metaphor proposed by E. O. Wilson (Harris and Wilson, 1978), within which cultural evolution has thus far been constrained. Virtually all anthropologists agree that there is a human nature which corresponds to the genetic heritage of *Homo sapiens*. But most anthropologists differ from sociobiologists in attributing few cultural practices, such as warfare or male supremacy, directly to the expression of human nature. Moreover, it is clear that human nature can only account for the universals of culture, not for the enormous range of variations at any particular moment in history.

When our species achieved semantic universality and crossed the threshold of cultural takeoff, it completed a transition to a level of existence as momentous as the creation of matter out of energy, or of life out of matter. *Homo sapiens* is not just another animal to be studied like ants or beavers; we are the only animal on earth (and for at least a dozen light years around in the heavens as well) whose primary mode of evolving new ways of coping with the problems of survival and reproduction depends overwhelmingly on cultural selection rather than natural selection. Culture is encoded not in the genes, but in the mind. Therefore, cultural differences and similarities cannot be explained by the principle of inclusive fitness.

Summary

The human capacity for culture is a product of natural selection. Natural selection alters genotypes through differential reproductive success. Natural selection is not synonymous with a struggle for survival between individuals. Fitness may result as often from cooperation and altruism. Both anatomical and behavioral traits can be shaped by natural selection and encoded in the genes. Behavior gets encoded through the sequence:

Old genotype → genetic error
    →behavioral deviation
    →selection
    →new genotype

Learning is a process of behavioral change that is entirely different from the behavioral change induced by natural selection. Learning permits organisms to adjust to or take advantage of novel contingencies and opportunities independently of genetic changes:

Old genotype → new behavior
→selection
→old genotype

Learning is the basis of cultural traditions. Although the capacity for acquiring traditions was shaped by natural selection and awaited the evolution of brainier species, culture is encoded in the brain, not in the genes. Cultural behavior such as tool making and tool use occurs in many infrahuman species, especially monkeys and great apes. Yet even among monkeys and great apes, tool using traditions remain rudimentary. The reason for this is that monkeys and apes use their forelimbs for climbing and walking and hence cannot readily carry tools. Early hominids such as *Homo habilis* and the Australopithecines had ape-size brains but upright posture. The evolution of the human foot thus set the pattern for further evolution of the human brain and the unique degree of human dependence on culture. The increasing braininess of *Homo erectus* and *Homo sapiens* resulted in an increasing reliance on culture; and the increasing reliance on culture resulted in increasing braininess. This process was drastically altered about 100,000 years ago when culture "took off," evolving vast numbers of traditions at a rapid rate without any further significant changes in the size of the brain.

A vital ingredient in this takeoff was the development of the human capacity for semantic universality. As shown by numerous experiments, chimpanzees and gorillas can be taught to use several hundred signs. Compared to 3-year-old human infants, however, apes have only rudimentary capacities for productivity and displacement.

In the nineteenth century the dominant political position of the European powers was interpreted as proof of the superiority of the white race. The main problems with such genetic interpretations of history and of cultural evolution is that they cannot account for the shifting locus of technological and political change except by postulating changes in the frequencies of genes. But the existence of these genes remains purely hypothetical.

The basic independence of cultural differences and similarities from genetic determination is shown by the ability of individuals and whole populations to change their cultural repertories through enculturation and diffusion in one generation.

Sociobiology is a hereditarian research strategy that stands somewhat apart from scientific raciology. It is concerned with the effects of human nature on culture and it seeks to explain cultural similarities and some cultural differences by means of the principle of inclusive fitness. This principle stresses measurement of the reproductive success of closely related individuals as the key to natural selection in social species.

In the known world, cultural takeoff has occurred only among human beings. This takeoff was as momentous as the appearance of matter out of energy or of life out of matter. The great bulk of cultural variations, as even leading sociobiologists admit, cannot be explained by natural selection acting on human genes. Culture is encoded in our brains, not in our genes.

3

Ecology, Energy, and Population

As the people of the Western world have recently come to realize, the amounts and kinds of energy used in daily life affect every aspect of human existence. In this chapter we will examine the interrelationships among energy production, the natural environment, and technology, and their joint effect on everyday patterns of work and leisure in different societies. We will also consider how the problem of controlling human population growth generates pressure to intensify and change modes of production.

Ecology and ecosystems

Ecology is essentially the study of how the energy in sunlight is captured and stored by plants in different natural environments and how various "communities" of plants and animals make use of that energy, aided and abetted by one another and by inorganic factors such as soils, rainfall, and other environmental conditions. Systems by which communities of organisms capture, exchange, and use energy are known as *ecosystems*.

Because of the enormous versatility of culture, human beings are an important although not necessarily dominant feature in most ecosystems. The study of ecosystems that concentrates on the ecological relationships among human beings and their cultures and the rest of the organic and inorganic environment is known as *human ecology* (or cultural ecology). The production and exchange of energy provides the key to understanding the relations between human populations and the other living and nonliving components of ecosystems. This in turn furnishes the key to understanding many basic features of the infrastructural, structural, and superstructural aspects of sociocultural life.

Evolution of energy production

During the time of the earliest hominids, all the energy utilized for the conduct of social life stemmed from food. *Homo erectus* does not appear to have mastered the use of fire until sometime between 500,000 and 1 million years ago, judging from charcoal fragments discovered at fossil sites in Hungary and China. Fire was used at first for cooking, for warmth, for hardening the tips of spears, and for driving game animals over cliffs or into ambushes, and possibly to favor the growth of desired plant species. By 10,000

years ago, animals began to provide energy in the form of muscle power harnessed to plows, sleds, and wheeled vehicles. At about the same time, considerable wood and charcoal fuel energy was expended to produce pottery. With the rise of incipient states (see p. 146), there was the beginning of the use of wind energy for sailing ships and wood energy for melting and casting metals. The energy in falling water was not tapped extensively until the medieval period in Europe. It is only in the last 200 or 300 years that the fossil fuels—coal, oil, and gas—began to dominate human ecosystems.

New sources of energy have followed each other in a logical progression, with mastery of later forms dependent on the mastery of the earlier ones. For example, in both the Old World and the New World the sequence of inventions that led to metallurgy depended upon the prior achievement of high-temperature wood-fire ovens and furnaces for baking ceramics, and this depended on learning how to make and control wood fires in cooking. Low-temperature metallurgical experience with copper and tin almost of necessity had to precede the use of iron and steel. Mastery of iron and steel in turn had to precede the development of the mining machines that made the use of coal, oil, and gas possible. Finally, the use of these fossil fuels spawned the Industrial Revolution, from which the technology for today's nuclear energy derives.

These technological advances have steadily increased the average amount of energy available per human being from Paleolithic times to the present. This increase in energy does not necessarily mean that humankind's ability to control nature has steadily increased. The lesson of today's energy and ecology crisis is that the increased use of energy per capita does not necessarily bring a higher standard of living or less work per capita. Also, a distinction must be made between total amount of energy available and the efficiency with which that energy is produced and put to use.

Modes of food production

Throughout most of humankind's presence on earth, food production was universally based on hunting and fishing and the collection or gathering of wild plants. Anthropologists call this *hunting and gathering* (or sometimes *hunting and collecting*). Hunting and gathering was the only mode of food production during the vast span of time designated by archeologists as the *Paleolithic* and known popularly as the Old Stone Age.

Hunter-gatherers are typically organized into small groups called *bands,* numbering from about twenty to fifty people. Bands consist of individual families who make camp together for periods ranging from a few days to several years before moving on to other campsites. Band life is opposed to village life, which is typically associated with agricultural modes of production. Band life is essentially migratory; shelters are temporary and possessions are few. One must be careful, however, not to overgeneralize, since hunter-gatherers inhabit a wide range of environments. The Eskimo—hunter-gatherers of the Artic—necessarily have ecologies and cultures somewhat different from those of desert-dwelling groups. Moreover, some hunter-gatherers who inhabit environments rich in wild plants and animals live in permanent villages such as those found among the people of the northwest Pacific coast.

About 15,000 to 10,000 years ago food production based on the cultivation of domesticated plants and the rearing of domesticated animals began to supplement or replace hunting and gathering. Archeologists call this time of transition to modes of production based on the raising of crops and the rearing of animals

the *Neolithic* (which literally means "new stone age"). Typically, agricultural peoples live in more permanent settlements than hunter-gatherers. But again, not all agricultural societies are alike. There are many varieties of agriculture, each with its ecological and cultural implications. *Rainfall agriculture* utilizes naturally occurring showers as a source of moisture; *irrigation agriculture* depends on artificially constructed dams and ditches to bring water to the fields. Several varieties of rainfall and irrigation agriculture, each with its own ecological and cultural implications, must also be distinguished.

To practice rainfall agriculture, the problem of replenishing the nutrients taken from the soil by successive crops must be solved. One of the most ancient methods for solving this problem, still widely practiced to this day, is known as *slash-and-burn*. A patch of forest is cut down and left to dry. Then the slash is set on fire and later the ashes, which contain a rich supply of nutrients, are spread over the area to be planted (Fig. 3.1). In re-

3.1 PLANTING IN A SWIDDEN (right)
This Amahuaca woman is using a digging stick to plant corn in a recently burned garden. [Robert Carneiro and American Museum of Natural History]

gions of heavy rainfall, a slash-and-burn garden cannot be replanted for more than two or three seasons before the nutrients in the ashes become depleted. A new patch of forest is then cleared and burned. Slash-and-burn thus requires large amounts of land in fallow awaiting the regrowth of vegetation suitable for burning.

A totally different solution to the problem of maintaining soil fertility is to raise animals as well as crops and to use animal manure as fertilizer. This is known as *mixed farming*, and was once characteristic of the European and American small family farm. With the advent of the industrial era, soil fertility has come to depend primarily on chemical fertilizers, eliminating the need for raising animals and crops on the same farm.

In irrigation agriculture soil fertility is less of a problem, since the irrigation water often

3.2 PHILLIPINE MOUNTAINSIDE TERRACES
These terraces, built by the Ifugao people, are among the engineering wonders of the preindustrial world. [Harold C. Conklin, Yale University]

contains silt and nutrients that are automatically deposited on the fields. But irrigation agriculture varies greatly in type and in scale. Some irrigation systems are confined to terraces on the walls of mountain valleys, as in the Philippeans (Fig. 3.2). Others embrace the flood plains of great rivers such as the Nile and the Yellow River. One form of irrigation involves mounding: mud is scooped from shallow lakes and piled up to form ridges in which crops are planted, as in the famous *chinampas* of Mexico (Fig. 3.3). In the Middle East huge underground aqueducts called *qats* conduct water from mountain streams to distant desert farmlands. Throughout much of India, irrigation water is pulled up by oxpower from deep brick-lined wells or more recently pumped up electrically through drilled pipes.

The influence of the environment

Any item of technology must interact with factors present in a particular environment. Similar kinds of technologies in different environments may lead to different energy outputs. For example, the productivity of irrigation farming varies according to the size and dependability of the water supply, the availability of flat terrain, and the amount of minerals in the water. Similarly, the productivity of slash-and-burn agriculture varies in relation to how much forest is available for burning and how quickly the forest can regenerate itself. It is thus really not possible to speak of technology in the abstract; rather, we must always refer to the interaction between technology and the conditions characteristic of a specific natural environment.

3.3 *CHINAMPAS OF XOCHIMILCO* (below)
The gardens obviously do not float, as can be seen from the trees growing on them. Note corn growing in fields. [Greene, Frederic Lewis]

In industrial societies the influence of environment often appears to be subordinate to the influence exerted by technology. But it is incorrect to believe that industrial societies have liberated themselves from the influence of the environment or that our species now dominates or controls the environment. It is true that replicas of American suburbs have been built in the deserts of Saudi Arabia and the snowfields of Alaska and that they can also be constructed on the moon. But the energy and material involved in such achievements derive from the interactions between technology and environment carried out in mines, factories, and farms in various parts of the world which are depleting irreplaceable reserves of oil, water, soil, forests, and metallic ores. Similarly, at all sites where modern technology extracts or processes natural resources or where any form of industrial construction or production takes place, the problem of disposing of industrial wastes, pollutants, and other biologically significant by-products arises. Efforts are now underway in many industrial nations to reduce air and water pollution and to prevent the depletion and poisoning of the environment. The costs of these efforts testify to the continuing importance of the interaction between technology and environment. These costs will continue to mount, for this is only the very beginning of the industrial era. In the centuries to come, the inhabitants of specific regions may pay for industrialization in ways as yet uncalculated.

Carrying capacity and the law of diminishing returns

Factors such as abundance of game, quality of soils, amounts of rainfall, and extent of forests available for energy production set an upper limit on the amount of energy that can be extracted from a given environment by means of a given technology of energy production. The upper limit on energy production in turn sets an upper limit on the number of human beings who can live in that environment. This upper limit on population is called the environment's *carrying capacity*.

Extreme caution must be exercised before concluding that a particular culture can "easily" raise production by increasing the size of its labor force or by increasing the amount of time devoted to work. Carrying capacity is difficult to measure (Glassow, 1978; Street, 1969). Allegations of untapped environmental potential are often not based upon long enough periods of observation. Many puzzling features of human ecosystems result from adjustments that are made to recurrent but infrequent ecological crises, such as droughts, floods, frosts, hurricanes, and recurrent epidemics of animal and plant diseases that require long periods of observation. Moreover, a basic principle of ecological analysis states that communities of organisms adjust to the minimum life-sustaining conditions in their habitats rather than to the average conditions. One formulation of this principle is known as *Liebig's law of the minimum*. This law states that growth is limited

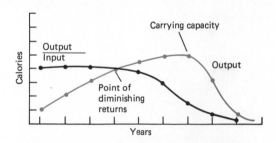

3.4 GRAPH SHOWING RELATIONSHIP BETWEEN CARRYING CAPACITY AND POINT OF DIMINISHING RETURNS
Production continues to increase even after point of diminishing returns is passed. But production cannot increase after carrying capacity is reached.

by the minimum availability of any one necessary factor rather than by the abundance of all necessary factors. The short-time observer of human ecosystems is likely to see the average condition, not the extremes, and is likely to overlook the limiting factor.

Nonetheless, there is now much evidence that food production among preindustrial peoples is often only about one-third of what it might be if full advantage were taken of the environment's carrying capacity by means of the existing technology (Sahlins, 1972). In order to understand why this "underproduction" occurs, we must distinguish between the effect of exceeding carrying capacity and the effect of exceeding the *point of diminishing returns* (Fig. 3.4). When carrying capacity is exceeded, production will begin to decline as a result of irreversible damage to the ecosystem. The depletion of soils is an example of the consequence of exceeding carrying capacity. When the point of diminishing returns is exceeded, however, production may hold steady or may even continue to increase, even though there is less produced per unit of effort as a result of the growing scarcity or impoverishment of one or more environmental factors. The present condition of the ocean fisheries of the world is an example of exceeding the point of diminishing returns. Since 1970 the rate of return per unit of effort has declined by almost half, yet the total catch of fish has held steady (L. Brown, 1978). A similar situation exists with respect to world agriculture and in the production of oil and gas (see below).

Except when they are under certain kinds of political pressures, people will attempt to keep the ratio of output to input below the point of diminishing returns by limiting the expansion of their production efforts; no one willingly wants to work more for less. Thus people may feel the need to change their routines and to institute cultural innovations long before carrying capacity is reached.

Expansion, intensification, and technological change

To understand the way human ecosystems operate, one must also distinguish between expansion and intensification. If technology is held constant, production can be increased by putting more people to work or by having them work longer or faster. If this increase in input occurs without increasing the area in which food production is taking place, *intensification* has occurred. If, however, there is a proportionate increase in the area throughout which food production takes place so that the input per hectare or square kilometer remains the same, then the system is *expanding* or growing but not being intensified.

Since all modes of production (indeed, all modes of activity of any sort) depend on finite resources, expansion cannot continue forever. Sooner or later any further increase in production will have to depend on intensification. And intensification, more or less rapidly, must lead to the point of diminishing returns caused by the depletion of nonrenewable resources, and a drop in efficiency. If the intensification is sustained, sooner or later production will collapse and fall to zero.

The all-important condition in this scenario, however, is that the technology is held constant. In human ecosystems, a common response to diminishing returns is to change the technology. Thus, as suggested in the work of Ester Boserup (1965), when hunters and gatherers deplete their environments and pass the point of diminishing returns, they are likely to begin to adopt an agricultural mode of production; when slash-and-burn peoples pass the point of diminishing returns, they may shift to the cultivation of permanent fields using animal fertilizer; and when rainfall agriculturalists using permanent fields deplete their soils, they may shift to irrigation agriculture. The shift from preindustrial to industrial and petrochemical forms of agriculture can also be seen as a response to depletion and declining yield per unit of effort (Harris, 1977).

Hunter-gatherer ecology

The !Kung San[1] are a hunting and gathering people who live in the Kalahari Desert on both sides of the border between Botswana and Namibia in southern Africa (Lee, 1979). Like most hunter-gatherers, the !Kung San move about a great deal from one camp to another in search of water, game, and wild plant foods. They build only temporary shelters and have a minimum of possessions, yet they are well-nourished and moderately long-lived. As

[1] The ! designates a sound which is not used in English, called a click.

among most hunter-gatherers, the !Kung San men specialize in hunting while !Kung San women specialize in gathering, although on occasion women will bring a small animal back to camp and men will help in carrying heavy loads of nuts (Fig. 3.5).

The number of people in a !Kung camp varies from 23 to 40, with an average camp size of 31 (20 adults and 11 children). During a four-week study period, Richard Lee calculated that 20 adults put in an average 2.4 days per week on hunting and gathering. On any particular day, the number of people hunting or gathering varied from zero to 16.

About 60 percent of the calories consumed by a !Kung camp are provided by women's gathering activities. Women range widely throughout the countryside, walking about 2 to 12 miles a day round trip for a total of about 1500 miles a year each. On an average trip each women brings back a load of from

3.5 !KUNG WOMEN RETURNING TO CAMP
They have been out gathering wild vegetables and are carrying digging sticks. [Richard B. Lee]

15 to 33 pounds of nuts, berries, fruits, leafy greens, and roots whose proportions vary from season to season.

Men hunt on the average only every three or four days and are successful only about 23 percent of the time they hunt. Hunting is therefore not an efficient source of energy for the !Kung. For every calorie (above basal metabolism) expended on hunting, only about 3 calories worth of meat were produced. Of the average total of about 2355 calories consumed per person per day, meat provides about 19 percent, nuts and vegetables the rest. One nut, in particular, the mongongo, alone accounts for about 70 percent of the !Kung caloric intake and a large share of their protein as well.

Studies of the !Kung and other hunter-gatherers who have survived into modern times have dispelled the notion that the hunting-gathering way of life necessarily condemns people to a miserable hand-to-mouth existence, with starvation avoided only by dint of unremitting daily effort. About 10 percent of the !Kung are over 60 years of age (as compared with 5 percent in agricultural countries such as Brazil and India) and medical examination shows them to be in good health.

Judged by the large quantity of meat and other sources of protein in their diet, their sound physical condition, and their abundant leisure, the !Kung San have a high standard of living. The key to this situation is that their population is low in relation to the resources they exploit. There is less than one person per square mile in their land and their production effort remains far below carrying capacity, with no appreciable intensification (except in recent years due to the appearance of neighboring peoples who possess livestock). If the !Kung San were to double their effort at hunting from two days a week to four, they would not only find it progressively more difficult to capture their prey, but they would run the risk of depleting the animal population below the point of recovery. In a sense, the !Kung San benefit from being at the mercy of the natural rates of increase of the plants and animals in their habitat; their mode of production obliges them to work less than agriculturalists or modern factory workers.

A slash-and-burn food energy system

Roy Rappaport (1968) has made a careful study of the food energy system of the Tsembaga Maring, a clan living in semipermanent villages on the northern slopes of the central highlands of New Guinea. The Tsembaga, who number about 204, plant taro, yams, sweet potatoes, manioc, sugarcane, and several other crops in small gardens cleared and fertilized by the slash-and-burn method (Fig. 3.6). Slash-and-burn is a more efficient

3.6 "COOKING" THE GARDEN
Tsembaga Maring woman during the burning phase of swidden cycle. [Roy Rappaport]

method of meeting calorie needs than hunting, yielding 18 calories output for every 1 calorie of input. Thus the Tsembaga are able to satisfy their caloric needs with a remarkably small investment of working time—only 380 hours per year per food-producer spent on raising crops. And at the same time the Tsembaga manage to feed almost ten times as many people as the !Kung and to live in permanent houses (except for routs caused by warfare).

Two environmental limits are especially pertinent to the Tsembaga and to other tropical slash-and-burn ecosystems. First, there is the problem of forest regeneration. Because of leaching by heavy rains and because of the invasion of insects and weeds, the productivity of slash-and-burn gardens drops rapidly after two or three years of use, and additional land must be cleared to avoid a sharp reduction in labor efficiency and output (Clarke, 1976; Janzen, 1973). Optimum productivity is achieved when gardens are cleared from a substantial secondary growth of large trees. If gardens are cleared when the secondary growth is very immature, only a small amount of wood-ash fertilizer will be produced by burning. On the other hand, if the trees revert to climax-forest size, they will be very difficult to cut down. Optimum regeneration may take anywhere from ten to twenty years or more, depending on local soils and climates.

Thus in the long run slash-and-burn ecosystems use up a considerable amount of forest per capita, but in any particular year only 5 percent of the total territory may actually be in production (Boserup, 1965, p. 31). The Tsembaga, for example, plant only 42 acres in a given year. Nonetheless, about 864 acres in their territory have been gardened. This is about the amount of forest that the Tsembaga would need if their population remains at about 200 people and if they burned secondary-growth garden sites every twenty years. Rappaport estimates that the Tsembaga had

at their disposal an amount of forest land sufficient to support another 84 people without permanently damaging the regenerative capacities of the forest. However, the bulk of this land lies above or below the optimum altitude levels for their major crops and thus would probably somewhat diminish efficiency if put into use. All slash-and-burn peoples confront the ultimate specter of "eating up their forest" (Condominas, 1957) by shortening the fallow period to a point where grasses and weeds replace trees. At least this is what has happened to other New Guinea peoples not too far from the Tsembaga (Sorenson, 1972; Sorenson and Kenmore, 1974). Nonetheless, there are situations, such as in the Amazon jungle, where vast untapped reserves of trees remain and where population densities are so low that the supply of burnable trees cannot be the factor limiting carrying capacity or determining the point of diminishing returns.

Many tropical slash-and-burn peoples, however, confront another problem that sets limits to the expansion of their population and work effort. This problem is especially acute where the main staples are protein-deficient crops such as sweet potatoes, plantains, yams, manioc, and taro. Natural tropical forest ecosystems produce a vast amount of *plant* biomass per acre, but they are very poor producers of *animal* biomass as compared, for example, with grasslands and marine ecosystems (Richards, 1973). The animals that inhabit tropical forests tend to be small, furtive, and arboreal. As human population density rises, these animals quickly become very scarce and hard to find. The total animal biomass—the weight of all the spiders, insects, worms, snakes, mammals, and so on—in a hectare of central Amazon rain forest is 45 kilograms. This compares with 304 kilograms in a dry East African thorn forest. In East African savannah grasslands, 627 kilograms of large herbivores are found per hectare, far

3.7 *DISPATCHING A PIG*
Pigs have great ritual significance
throughout New Guinea and Melanesia. The
people in this scene are Fungai Maring,
neighbors of the Tsembaga Maring. [Cherry
Lowman]

outweighing all the large and small animals
found per hectare in the Amazon (Fittkau and
Klinge, 1973, p. 8). Although plant foods can
provide nutritionally adequate amounts of
proteins if eaten in variety and abundance,
meat is the most effective source of all the
amino acids necessary for nutrition. Hence
one of the most important limiting factors in
the growth of slash-and-burn energy systems
is thought to be the availability of animal
protein (Gross, 1975, 1981). This issue, however, is the center of considerable controversy, and we will return to a discussion of
the ecological and nutritional importance of
meat and other forms of animal protein later
on (p. 137).

The high cost of pigs

Whatever etic ecological and nutritional reason there may be for it, there is no doubt that
the Tsembaga, like virtually every other
human group, highly prize animal protein
and fat, especially in the form of fatty meat
(vegetarians who abstain from meat usually
prize animal protein and fat in the form of
milk and yogurt). The Tsembaga, whose population density has risen to 67 persons per
square mile, compared with less than 1 per
square mile among the !Kung San, have depleted the wild animals in their territory. But
they have compensated for this by stocking

their land with a domestic animal—the pig. The Tsembaga's pigs root for themselves during the day but come home to a meal of sweet potatoes and food scraps in the evening. An average Tsembaga pig weighs as much as an average Tsembaga human, and Rappaport estimates that each pig consumes almost as much garden produce as each person. The pigs gain about 50 pounds per year. There were 160 pigs at the pig maximum. Rappaport indicates that 66 Tsembaga women spend 758 hours engaged in pig raising. When the Tsembaga pig herd is at its maximum, almost as much time and energy are devoted to feeding pigs as to feeding people. Like many New Guinea cultures, the Tsembaga allow their pig population to increase over a number of years, slaughtering pigs only on ceremonial occasions (Watson, 1977). When the effort needed to care for the pigs becomes excessive, a pig feast is held, resulting in a sharp decline in the pig population (Fig. 3.7). This feast may be related to the cycle of reforestation in the Tsembaga's gardens and the regulation of war and peace between the Tsembaga and their neighbors.

Irrigation agriculture

Under favorable conditions, irrigation agriculture yields more calories per calorie of ef-

3.8 CHINESE WATERWORKS
Importance of reservoirs like this, and of canals and aqueducts, has led Karl Wittfogel to classify China as an "hydraulic civilization." [China Photo Service]

fort than any other preindustrial mode of food production. And among irrigation farmers, the Chinese have excelled for thousands of years (Fig. 3.8). A detailed study of the labor inputs and weight yield of agricultural production in pre-communist times was carried out by the anthropologists Fei Hsiao-t'ung and Chang chih-I (1947) in the village of Luts'un, Yunnan Province. Over 50 calories were obtained for each calorie of effort in the fields. The principal crops were rice, which accounted for 75 percent of the total, soybeans, corn, manioc, and potatoes. Because of the high productivity of their agriculture, the 700 people of Luts'un produced five times more food than they consumed. What hap-

pened to this *surplus?* It was diverted from the village to towns and cities; it was exchanged via markets and money for nonfarm goods and services; it was taxed away by the local, provincial, and central governments; it went into rent as payment for use of land; and it was used to raise large numbers of children and to sustain a high rate of population increase.

One of the most interesting features of Luts'un's energy system is that despite the high ratio of output to input, the average Luts'un farmer put in 1129 hours of work per year, far more than the average !Kung San hunter-gatherer.

The high population density of parts of China and of other societies that practice irrigation agriculture results from the fact that by expanding the amount of water fed to the fields, increasing amounts of labor can be invested in production without substantial losses in the output-input ratio. Thus, instead of using the labor-saving potential of their technology to work less, irrigation agriculturalists opt for intensifying their effort and increasing their output. (Why this happens will be discussed later on p. 57.)

Energy and pastoral nomadism

Grains convert about 0.4 percent of photosynthetically active sunlight into human edible matter. If one feeds this grain to animals rather than to people and then eats the meat, 90 percent, on the average, of the energy available in the grains will be lost (National Research Council, 1974). The loss in efficiency associated with the processing of plant food through domesticated animals accounts for the relatively infrequent occurrence of cultures whose mode of food production is that called *pastoral nomadism* (Fig. 3.9). Full pastoral nomads are peoples who raise domesticated animals and who do not depend upon

3.9 *PASTORAL NOMADS*
Tuareg family and their most valuable possession. [George Rodger, Magnum]

hunting, gathering, or the planting of their own crops for a significant portion of their diet. Pastoral nomads typically occupy arid grasslands and steppes in which precipitation is too sparse or irregular to support rainfall agriculture and which cannot be irrigated because they are too high or too far from major river valleys. By specializing in animal husbandry, pastoral nomads can move their herds about over long distances and take advantage of the best pasture.

However, pastoral peoples must obtain grain supplements to their diet of milk, cheese, blood, and meat (the last always being a relatively small part of the daily fare). The productivity of herding alone is not adequate to support dense populations. Grains are usually obtained through trade with agricultural neighbors who are eager to obtain hides, cheese, milk, and other animal products that are in short supply wherever preindustrial agricultural systems support dense popula-

tions. Pastoralists frequently attempt to improve their bargaining position by raiding the sedentary villagers and carrying off the grain harvest without paying for it. They can often do this with impunity, since their possession of animals such as camels and horses makes them highly mobile and militarily effective. Continued success in raiding may force the farming population to acknowledge the pastoralists as their overlords. Repeatedly in the history of the Old World, relatively small groups of pastoral nomads—the Mongols and the Arabs being the two most famous examples—have succeeded in gaining control of huge civilizations based on irrigation agriculture. The inevitable outcome of these conquests, however, was that the conquerors were absorbed by the agricultural system as they attempted to feed the huge populations that had fallen under their control (Lattimore, 1962; Lees and Bates, 1974; Salzman, 1971).

3.10 INDUSTRIAL AGRICULTURE
Pea bean combines harvesting baby lima beans in the state of Washington. Are the men in the picture farmers? [Chester, DeWys]

Industrial food energy systems

It is difficult to estimate the output-input ratio of industrial agriculture because the amount of indirect labor put into food production exceeds the amount of direct labor (Fig. 3.10). An Iowa corn farmer, for example, puts in 9 hours of work per acre, which yield 81 bushels of corn with an energy equivalent of 8,164,800 calories (Pimentel et al., 1973). This gives a nominal ratio of 5,000 calories output for every calorie of input! But this is a misleading figure. First of all, three-quarters of all the croplands in the United States are devoted to the production of animal feeds, with a consequent 90 to 95 percent reduction in human consumable calories. Indeed, the livestock population of the United States consumes enough food calories to feed 1.3 billion people (Cloud, 1973). Second, enormous amounts of human labor are embodied in the tractors, trucks, combines, oil and gas, pesticides, herbicides, and fertilizers used by the Iowa corn farmer.

A deceptive aspect of industrial food production is the apparent reduction in the percentage of farm workers in the work force. It is said that less than 3 percent of the United States labor force is employed in agriculture and that one farmer can now feed 50 people. But there is another way to view this ratio. If farmers are dependent on the labor input of workers who manufacture, mine, and transport the fuels, chemicals, and machines employed in food production, these workers must also be considered food producers. In other words, industrial agriculture does not so much reduce the agricultural work force as disperse it away from the farm. The individuals who remain on the land to operate the high-powered machinery resemble (etically speaking) workers in an automobile factory more than they do farmers. Farmers in the United States consume more than 12 percent of the total industrial energy flow. For each person who actually works on the farm, at least two support workers are needed off the farm. In a broader sense, almost all industrial and service workers make some contribution to the support of agroindustrial production: "Yesterday's farmer is today's canner, tractor mechanic, and fast-food carhop" (Steinhart and Steinhart, 1974). Like everyone else, farmers now get their own food at the supermarket. If all this be granted, then perhaps it is more accurate to say that it takes 50 people to feed one agroindustrial farmer than to say that one modern farmer feeds 50 people.

A misunderstood aspect of industrial food energy systems is the difference between higher yields per acre and the ratio of energy input to output. As a result of more and more intensive modes of production involving genetically improved crops, and higher dosages of chemical fertilizers and pesticides, yields per acre have steadily improved (N. Jensen, 1978). But this improvement has been made possible only as a result of a steady increase in the amount of fuel energy invested for each calorie of food energy produced. In the United States 15 tons of machinery, 22 gallons of gasoline, 203 pounds of fertilizer, and 2 pounds of chemical insecticides and pesticides are invested per acre per year. This represents a cost of 2,890,000 calories of nonfood energy per acre per year (Pimentel et al., 1975). This cost has increased steadily since the beginning of the century. Before 1910 more calories were obtained from agriculture than were invested in it. By 1970 it took 8 calories in the form of fossil fuels to produce 1 calorie of food. If the people of India were to emulate the U.S. system of food production, their entire energy budget would have to be devoted to nothing but agriculture (Steinhart and Steinhart, 1974).

The myth of increased leisure

Another common misconception concerning industrial and preindustrial mode of produc-

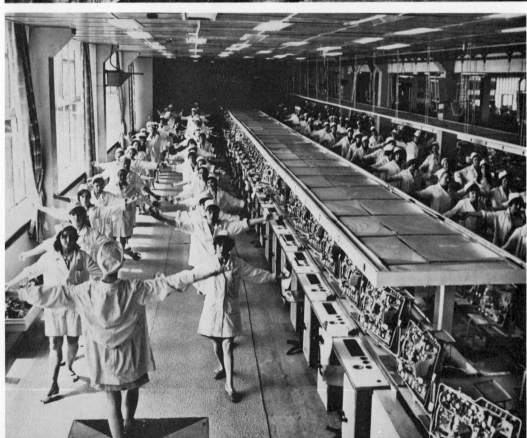

3.12 MACHIGUENGA AT WORK
As in most slash and burn economies, Machiguenga men do the heavy work of felling trees and clearing the forest for new plantings. [Allen and Orna Johnson]

TABLE 3.1 TIME DEVOTED TO VARIOUS ACTIVITIES PER DAY BY MACHIGUENGA MARRIED MEN AND WOMEN

	Married men	Married women
Food production	4.4 hours	1.8 hours
Food preparation	0.2	2.4
Manufacture	1.4	2.1
Child care	0.0	1.1
Hygiene	0.3	0.6
Visiting	1.0	0.8
Idle	2.3	2.5
	9.6	11.3

Source: Johnson, 1975, 1978.

3.11 LABOR-SAVING DEVICES THAT DON'T SAVE WORK *(facing page)*
The first assembly line (top). Ford's Highland Park, Michigan, magneto assembly line saved 15 minutes per unit and initiated the era of mass production in 1913. But the workers worked harder than ever. All work and no play in a Russian television factory (bottom). [Wide World—top; UPI—bottom]

tion is that industrial workers have more leisure than their preindustrial ancestors. The reverse seems to be true, however. With a 40-hour week and a 3-week vacation, the typical modern factory worker puts in close to 2,000 hours per year under conditions hunters and gatherers would probably regard as "inhuman" (Fig. 3.11). When labor leaders boast about how much progress has been made in obtaining leisure for the working class, they have in mind the standard established in "civilized" nineteenth-century Europe, when factory workers put in 12 hours a day or more, rather than the standards observed by the !Kung.

Of course, these data fail to take into consideration other activities which might etically be classified as work. Preindustrial peoples are not merely idle when they are not sleeping or processing or producing food. In every culture much time and energy are devoted to additional tasks and activities, some of which are essential to subsistence. Unfortunately, anthropologists have seldom collected the appropriate data, and hence it is very difficult to generalize about how time is allocated to various tasks and activities in different cultures. A broader definition of "work," however, does not give the middle-class industrial wage earner or office worker an advantage over those peoples whose activity patterns have been studied with more care.

One of the best attempts to quantify daily activity patterns for a whole population has been carried out by Allen Johnson (1974) among the Machiguenga (Fig. 3.12), a slash-and-burn village people who live on the Upper Urubamba River on the eastern slopes of the Andes in Peru. Johnson randomly sampled what the members of 13 households were doing between the hours of 6 A.M. and 7 P.M. throughout an entire year. His results, given in Table 3.1, show that food production plus food preparation plus the manufacture of essential items such as clothing, tools, and shelter consume only 6.0 hours per day for married men and 6.3 hours per day for married women.

If we add hours of commuting time and hours devoted to shopping, cleaning, cooking, and household maintenance to the 8 hours spent by U.S. urban wage workers at their places of work, the Machiguenga clearly come out ahead.

This leads to the question of why the great labor-saving potential of technology has been devoted to the ever-greater expansion of energy systems rather than to the achievement of an ever-greater amount of leisure based on a constant population and a constant level of production and consumption.

Cultural checks on population growth

Most contemporary hunter-gatherer peoples have populations whose densities are considerably less than one person per square mile. If these groups are at all representative of prehistoric times, *Homo sapiens* must have been a very rare creature during the Paleolithic. Perhaps there were only 6 million people in the entire world in those times (Hassan, 1978, p. 78; Dumond, 1975), certainly no more than 15 million (Mark Cohen, 1977, p. 54), compared with almost 4 billion today. Whether one takes the upper or lower estimate, there is no doubt that for tens of thousands of years, the rate of growth of the human population

was very slow (see Table 3.2). Potentially, human populations can easily double every 28 years, which is equivalent to an annual rate of growth rate of about 2.5 percent. This was actually the observed rate of growth of the !Kung during the period 1963 to 1969 (Howell, 1976a, p. 141); and rates of 3.0 percent or more are common today among less developed countries. Yet for most of prehistory, population grew at only a fraction of this potential rate.

Another way to pose this problem is to consider the childbearing capacity of the human female. Among the Hutterites, a religious agrarian sect who live in Canada, each woman averages 10.7 live births during her reproductive career. Yet in order to maintain the 0.0015 rate of increase of the Paleolithic, women would have had to average less than 2.1 children born and surviving to reproductive age. How and why did world population increase so slowly for so long?

Contraception techniques

Population-regulating mechanisms may operate prior to conception or after conception. Contrary to romantic beliefs about folk contraceptives, preindustrial people cannot prevent conception by anything resembling the "pill." Their chief means of preventing women from getting pregnant is abstention from heterosexual genital intercourse. A common form of abstention involves a taboo on such intercourse after a woman has given birth. Encouragement of homosexual relations also occurs, but its effect on birth rates is problematical (see p. 311). The practice of the operation known as clitorodectomy—the removal of part or all of the clitoris—occurs

TABLE 3.2 RATE OF GROWTH OF THE HUMAN POPULATION

Period	World population at end of period	Percentage annual rate of growth during period
Paleolithic	5,000,000	0.0015
Mesolithic	8,500,000	0.0330
Neolithic	75,000,000	0.1000
Ancient empires	225,000,000	0.5000

Source: Hassan, 1978; Spengler, 1974.

3.13 BREAST FEEDING OLDER CHILDREN (facing page)
San women breast feed their children for 4 or 5 years per child. [Konner, Anthro-Photo]

among a number of high-density agriculturalists in Africa and may influence pregnancy rates by diminishing a woman's desire. Some groups also practice *infibulation*, in which the lips of the vagina are sewed together. Like male castration, however, these operations are seldom reported among hunter-gatherers.

An effective means of lowering the number of conceptions per woman is to prolong breast feeding of children (Fig. 3.13). There are currently two theories that account for the contraceptive effects of prolonged breast feeding. One stresses the release of certain hormones that suppress ovulation. The other attributes the failure to resume ovulation to the difficulty in gaining weight while breast feeding. It is possible that a critical minimum percentage of body weight must be fat before a woman's body is prepared to embark upon another pregnancy (or the first one). The calorie drain imposed by breast feeding makes it difficult to pass this limit (Frisch and MacArthur, 1974; Frisch, 1978; see Huffman et al., 1978, 1979; Tyson and Perez, 1978). Regardless of how breast feeding produces its contraceptive effect, there is growing accord that it does work and that it can lengthen the interval between birth and conception by as much as three or four years beyond the three months typical of healthy, sexually active non-nursing mothers (Howell, 1976b; Lee, 1979).

Postconception techniques

The most effective barriers against rapid population growth are events that influence the life span of the newborn after conception or birth has taken place. Most of these events are to some degree subject to human control. For example, almost all known cultures have a variety of methods for terminating unwanted pregnancies. The most common are those that traumatize or poison both mother and fetus. Tying tight bands, delivering blows to the ab-

domen, and jumping on boards laid across the abdomen are some of the physical traumas that produce abortion. Drinking of poisonous concoctions such as violent purgatives is a common form of chemical trauma. All these methods place the mother at as much risk as the fetus. For this reason, induced abortions are probably not a principal factor in population control among hunter-gatherers and other prestate and preindustrial peoples (Devereux, 1967; Nurge, 1975).

Many preindustrial peoples shorten the life of unwanted children after birth. Shortening the lives of unwanted infants and children takes many forms. Fully conscious and deliberate acts of infanticide are reported from many cultures. Still others deny that they practice infanticide, yet have very high rates of infant mortality. When the rate of infant and child mortality is consistently higher for one sex than for the other, there is reason to believe that unwanted children are being fed more poorly or are being less well cared for, even if there is no conscious attempt to shorten their lives. The etic effect of neglect is probably more powerful than outright infanticide in slowing down the rate of population growth. Among measures affecting infant mortality, Susan Scrimshaw (1978) lists premature withdrawal of breast feeding without proper weaning foods; withdrawal of food from children who are sick; withholding of protein-rich foods from weak children; and careless treatment of the umbilical cord.

Considerable controversy surrounds the demographic importance assigned to infanticide and neglect. Some anthropologists hold that during the Paleolithic, between 25 to 50 percent of all infants who did not die from natural diseases had their lives shortened through some form of infanticide or neglect (Birdsell, 1968, 1972; Hassan, 1973). Others hold that prolonged breast feeding did away with the need for relying on infanticide and neglect. Among the !Kung San there appears to be very little overt or covert infanticide (although infant mortality is high). As emphasized by Richard Lee (1979) and Nancy Howell (1976b), prolonged breast feeding is the main method for slowing down population growth. However, the long-term growth rate of the !Kung population is 0.5 percent (Howell, 1976a, p. 150). This amounts to a doubling every 139 years. Had this rate been sustained for only the last 10,000 years of the Upper Paleolithic, the population of the earth would have reached 604,463,000,000,000,000,000,000 at the beginning of the Neolithic instead of the estimated 6 million mentioned above. Moreover, there is some evidence that prolonged dependence on mother's milk might lead to poor health in children whose diets do not contain mineral supplements. There is no iron or copper in mother's milk, for example. Too much breast feeding may be as dangerous to the child as too little, and as a matter of fact, the !Kung do have a high rate of infant mortality (Wilmsen, 1979).

The influence of disease

Anthropologists who assign an important role to infanticide and neglect tend to minimize the effect of disease on Paleolithic rates of growth. Most of the great lethal epidemic diseases—smallpox, typhoid fever, flu, bubonic plague, and cholera—are primarily associated with dense urbanized populations rather than with dispersed hunter-gatherers or small village cultures. Even diseases like malaria and yellow fever were probably less important among low-density populations who could avoid swampy mosquito breeding grounds. (Knowledge of the association between swamps and disease is very ancient, even though mosquitoes were not recognized as disease carriers.) Other diseases such as dysentery, measles, tuberculosis, whooping cough, scarlet fever, and the common cold were also probably less significant among hunter-gatherers and early farmers (Arme-

lagos and McArdle, 1975; Black, 1975; Cockburn, 1971; Wood, 1975). The ability to recuperate from these infections is closely related to the general level of bodily health, which in turn is heavily influence by diet, especially by balanced protein levels (N. Scrimshaw, 1977). The role of disease as a long-term regulator of human population is thus to some extent a consequence of the success or failure of other population-regulating mechanisms. Only if these alternatives are ineffective and population density rises, productive efficiency drops, and diet deteriorates will disease figure as an important check on population growth.

There is some evidence to indicate that Paleolithic and early Neolithic peoples were relatively healthy and that therefore "artificial" population controls rather than severe sickness were relied on for limiting population growth. Based on an examination of the stature and number of missing teeth in prehistoric and historic skeletons, Lawrence Angel (1975) concludes that Paleolithic and early Neolithic peoples were in better physical condition than the commoners of early state-level societies.

Population pressure

All these natural and cultural mechanisms for regulating population have something in common. They all involve psychological, physiological, and behavioral "costs" that most people would prefer to avoid. Even the practice of prolonged breast feeding imposes restrictions or demands on the nursing mother which she presumably would prefer to be rid of. Abstinence from heterosexual genital intercourse constitutes a severe penalty for most adults, and traumatic abortion, infanticide, and premature deaths brought on by neglect, malnutrition, or disease are also clearly burdensome and unwanted. Hence to some degree, all preindustrial societies experience some form of *population pressure*—that is, physiological and psychological costs incurred on behalf of restraining population growth below the level that would result if there were no restraints on the birth rate and resources were infinite. Population pressure in this sense exists even if a preindustrial population is not growing or even if it is getting smaller. In general, population pressure increases at the point of diminishing returns (see p. 42) and is still greater when carrying capacity is reached.

Population pressure and cultural evolution

Many anthropologists regard population pressure (in the sense of the high cost of artificially lowering population growth rates under preindustrial conditions) as an important "engine" of sociocultural evolution. Population pressure predisposes individuals, families, and whole societies to *intensify* the productive effort in order to lessen the need to use physically and psychologically costly means of limiting births and in order to provide better living conditions for infants and children suffering from malnutrition and neglect. Intensification, as we have seen, often leads to depletions that destroy the ecosystem and compel people to adopt new modes of production.

Population pressure thus introduces an element of instability into all human ecosystems. This instability often interacts with purely natural sources of instability (sometimes called "perturbations"), such as changes in ocean currents and advances and retreats of continental glaciers, to bring about large-scale shifts in modes of production.

3.14 WOOLY MAMMOTHS
Artist's rendering of one of the species of big-game animals that became extinct in Europe at the end of the last glaciation. [American Museum of Natural History]

It is this combination of natural and cultural pressures that may account for the transition from Paleolithic to Neolithic modes of production. During late Paleolithic times, hunter-gatherers had become dependent on hunting large game animals such as the horse, reindeer, mammoth, bison, and wild cattle (Fig. 3.14). About 12,000 years ago major climatic shifts marked the end of the last continental glaciation. As a result, forests began to replace the grassy plains on which these animals grazed. As the herds of large animals thinned out, the human hunters responded to population pressure by intensifying their hunting efforts. Through a combination of "overkill" and climate change, many genera of big game animals became extinct in the Old and New Worlds. These depletions and extinctions then set the stage for the adoption of new modes of production involving the cultivation of plants and the rearing of animals (Mark Cohen, 1975, 1977). As we will (see p. 136), population pressure also probably played an important role in the development of warfare, the evolution of the state (p. 146), and the emergence of industrial society.

Summary

The comparative study of infrastructures involves consideration of ecology and ecosystem variables, and these in turn require examination of the quantitative and qualitative aspects of energy production and consumption. Most of the energy flowing through preindustrial energy systems consists of food energy. The technology of energy production cannot be altered at whim. It has evolved through successive stages of technical competence in which the mastery of one set of tools and machines has been built on the mastery of an earlier set. Through technological advance, the energy available per capita has steadily increased. However, technology never exists in the abstract, but only in the particular instances where it interacts with a particular environment; there is no such thing as technology dominating or controlling the natural environment. Even in the most advanced industrial ecosystems, depletion and pollution of habitats add unavoidable costs to energy production and consumption. Technology interacting with environment determines carrying capacity, which is the upper limit of production, and hence of the human population density possible without depletion and permanent damage.

When carrying capacity is exceeded, production will decline precipitously. However, the fact that a food energy system is operating as much as two-thirds below carrying capacity does not mean that ecological restraints are absent. Culture energy systems tend to stop growing before reaching the point of diminishing returns, which is defined as the point at which the ratio of output to input begins to fall, holding technology constant. A distinction must also be made between the effects of growth and the effects of intensification. Growth may continue for a long time without leading to a decline in the ratio of output to input. Intensification, however, which is defined as increased input in a fixed area, may lead to critical depletions, diminishing returns, and irreversible damage to the habitat's carrying capacity. All the factors in ecosystems must be approached from the perspective of Liebig's law, which states that extremes, not averages, set the limits for carrying capacity.

A common human cultural response to declining efficiency brought about by intensification is to alter technology and thereby adopt new modes of production.

Hunting-gathering was the universal mode of food production throughout the Paleolithic age, which represents over 90 percent of humankind's existence. As in the example of the !Kung San, while hunter-gatherers output/input efficiency is low, especially for the male-dominated activity of hunting, by maintaining low population densities and avoiding intensification, hunter-gatherers can enjoy high standards of living. Slash-and-burn agriculturalists such as the Tsembaga Maring produce their caloric needs with greater efficiency than the !Kung San, but they have depleted the game animals in their habitat and must rely on costly domesticated pigs for their animal proteins and fats. By using irrigation agriculture, the people of Luts'un produce a large surplus. Despite their high output/input ratio, they work longer at food production than either the !Kung San or the Tsembaga.

Pastoralism is another but rare preindustrial mode of food production, which is practiced only in areas unsuitable for agriculture. The reason for this is that feeding plant food to domesticated animals rather than consuming crops directly results in a 90 percent reduction in the efficiency of conversion of sunlight to human food.

Industrial agriculture has achieved very high outputs at the cost of very high chemical and energy inputs. When input/output ratios include fuel costs, the efficiency of industrial agricultural systems has been falling, not rising. Finally, it is clear that many industrial peoples work harder for their basic subsistence than hunters and gatherers.

The reproductive capacity of human beings was held in check by cultural mechanisms for most of human history and prehistory. It was kept well below the potential rate of growth, which may be equal to a doubling every 28 years. The chief means of contraception involved prolonged breast feeding and abstention from genital heterosexual intercourse. Prolonged breast feeding may retard the onset of ovulation through the effect of nipple sucking on the hormonal system, or through the effect of the calorie cost of mother's milk on the ability of nursing mothers to increase the percentage of body fat above a critical threshold.

Postconception controls among band and village peoples include abortions, infanticide, and neglect of unwanted children. Nonmedical abortions depend on whole-body traumas produced by mechanical or chemical abuse and threaten the life of the mother. Infanticide, especially female infanticide, is widespread, but it is often not given conscious recognition. Infanticide grades imperceptibly into various forms of neglect in which unwanted infants and children are underprotected from disease and malnutrition.

By using these techniques, band and village peoples can readily keep their populations well below carrying capacity and the point of diminishing returns. By doing so, they can maintain relatively high standards of health among those individuals who survive to adulthood. It seems unlikely that disease per se exercised a significant restraint on population growth as long as population density among band and village peoples remained low, settlements were dispersed over considerable distances, and calorie and protein consumption per capita remained high.

However, the most effective preindustrial modes of controlling reproduction involved considerable waste of human life and severe psychological or physical penalties. One can speak, therefore, of some degree of population pressure being present even when a population is steady or declining, in the sense that a price must always be paid to keep reproduction in balance with production.

Population pressure predisposes human groups to intensify production. In combination with natural perturbations, population pressure is therefore an important factor in shifts from one mode of production to another.

Economy, Exchange, Control

This chapter initiates the comparative study of the structural or organizational aspects of the economic sectors of sociocultural systems. We focus on the distribution of goods and services by means of different modes of exchange and on alternative modes of controlling who gets what. Our focus of inquiry will thus be moving from the infrastructural to the structural components of sociocultural systems. This chapter is intended to form a link between the discussion of modes of production and later chapters devoted to the origin of the state and the maintenance of law and order in egalitarian and stratified societies.

Definition of economy

In a narrow sense, *economy* refers to the allocation of scarce means to competing ends. Most professional economists hold that human beings in general tend to "economize"—that is, to allocate scarce means in such a way as to maximize the achievement of ends while minimizing the expenditure of means. Many anthropologists, however, see economy as the activities responsible for provisioning a society with its goods and services:

An economy is a set of institutionalized activities which combine natural resources, human labor, and technology to acquire, produce, and distribute material goods and specialist services in a structured, repetitive fashion. (Dalton, 1969, p. 97)

The two definitions of economy are not necessarily incompatible. Anthropologists stress the fact that motivations for producing, exchanging, and consuming goods and services are shaped by cultural traditions. Different cultures value different goods and services and tolerate or prohibit different kinds of relationships among the people who produce, exchange, and consume. For example, as we will see in a moment, some cultures emphasize cooperative acquisition and sharing of wealth, whereas others emphasize competitive acquisition and retention of wealth. Some cultures emphasize communal property; others emphasize private property. It is obvious, therefore, that "economizing" has different premises and different consequences in different cultural contexts. Yet it may be possible that underlying apparently diverse cultural specifications of means and ends, there is a common human calculus of minimizing costs and maximizing benefits that accounts for the origin and perpetuation of different economic systems. The viewpoint adopted in this book is that the existence of *minmax* (minimum cost-maximum benefit)

relationships is an empirical question that can be solved by empirical research.

Exchange

Most of what is produced by human labor is distributed by means of exchange. (The exceptions consist of instances of direct consumption by the producers themselves). *Exchange* refers to the panhuman pattern of giving and receiving valuable objects and services. The joint provisioning of children by adult men and women is a form of giving and receiving virtually confined to the hominids and important for the definition of what it means to be human. Human beings can not live without exchanging their labor or the products of their labor with one another (Robinson Crusoe was a taker if not a giver even before Friday arrived; hermits and religious recluses also inevitably depend on goods they take with them into the wilderness, and they usually render some kind of service in return.) However, the patterns of exchange differ markedly from one culture to another. Following the work of the economist Karl Polanyi, anthropologists have come to distinguish three main types of exchange: *reciprocal*, *redistributive*, and *market*. As we will see, these different types of exchange are related to other differences on the infrastructural and structural levels of the universal pattern.

Reciprocal exchanges

One of the most striking features of the economic life of band and prestate village societies is the prominence of exchanges that are conducted according to the principle known as *reciprocity*. In reciprocal exchanges the flow of labor products and services is not contingent upon any definite counterflow. The partners in the exchange take according to need and give back according to no set rules of time or quantity.

Richard Lee has written a succint description of reciprocity as it occurs among the !Kung. In the morning, anywhere from 1 to 16 of the 20 adults in the !Kung band leave camp to spend the day collecting or hunting. They return in the evening with whatever food they have managed to find. Everything brought back to camp is shared equally, regardless of whether the recipients have spent the day sleeping or hunting (Fig. 4.1).

Not only do families pool the day's production, but the entire camp–residents and visitors alike–shares equally in the total quantity of food available. The evening meal of any one family is made up of portions of food from each of the other families resident. Foodstuffs are distributed raw or are prepared by the collectors and then distributed. There is a constant flow of nuts, berries, roots and melons from one family fireplace to another until each person resident has received an equitable portion. The following morning a different combination of foragers moves out of camp and when they return late in the day, the distribution of foodstuffs is repeated. (Lee, 1969, p. 58)

Eventually all the adults will have gathered or hunted and given as well as received food. But wide discrepancies in the balance of giving and receiving may exist between individuals over a long period without becoming the subject of any special talk or action.

Some form of reciprocal exchange occurs in all cultures, especially among relatives and friends. In the United States and Canada, for

4.1 SAN RECIPROCITY
Men awaiting the distribution of meat from a small wart hog. [Richard B. Lee]

example, husbands and wives, friends, and brothers, sisters, and other kin regulate and adjust their economic lives to a minor degree according to informal, uncalculated, give-and-take transactions. Teenagers do not pay cash for their meals at home or rent for their parents' car. Wives do not bill their husbands for cooking a meal. Friends give each other birthday gifts and Christmas presents. These exchanges, however, constitute only a small portion of the total acts of exchange among North Americans. The great majority of exchanges in modern cultures involve rigidly defined counterflows that must take place by a certain time.

The problem of the freeloader

As we know from our own experience with taking from parents and with birthday and Christmas gifts, failure to reciprocate in some degree will eventually lead to bad feelings even between close relatives and friends and husbands and wives. No one likes a "freeloader." Among band and village cultures, a grossly asymmetrical exchange also does not go unnoticed. Some individuals will come to enjoy reputations as diligent gatherers or outstanding hunters, whereas others acquire reputations as shirkers or malingerers. No specific mechanisms exist for obliging the debtors to even up the score. Yet there are subtle sanctions against becoming a complete freeloader. Such behavior generates a steady undercurrent of disapproval. Freeloaders are eventually subject to collective punishment. They may meet with violence because they are suspected of being bewitched or of bewitching others through the practice of sorcery (see p. 126).

What is distinctive about reciprocal exchange, therefore, is not that products and services are simply given away without any thought or expectation of return, but rather that there is (1) no immediate return, (2) no systematic calculation of the value of the services and products exchanged, and (3) an overt denial that a balance is being calculated or that the balance must come out even.

Is there no exchange, then, corresponding to what Bronislaw Malinowski called "pure gift"? Are we always to look for hidden self-seeking, material motives whenever labor products are moved from one individual or group to another? Nothing of the sort is implied. The bestowal of gifts without any tangible reciprocity in services or products is a universal phenomenon. Indeed, this relationship is becoming increasingly common throughout the industrial world. In preindustrial contexts, parents generally expect and receive material reciprocity for their child-rearing efforts. Children begin to reciprocate by working at agricultural and household tasks at an early age, and this relationship continues into the old age of parents, who frequently end their lives with a net favorable balance of labor and products. But all contemporary industrial states display a trend toward a lifetime exchange balance between parents and children that is favorable to the younger generation (see p. 305). Parents must rely increasingly on their own savings and state aid in the form of insurance, pensions, old-age social security, and other public welfare schemes to maintain themselves during periods of sickness and senility (Minge-Kalman, 1977).

There is, then, no question that some human beings will voluntarily give away their most valued possessions and expect nothing material in return. But there is also no question that some human beings in every population will tend to become freeloaders if they get the chance. While every mode of production can tolerate a certain number of freeloaders, the line must be drawn somewhere. Hence no culture can rely exclusively on purely altruistic sentiments to get its goods and services produced and distributed. What does occur, especially on the level of small band and prestate village societies, is that goods and services are produced and reciprocally exchanged in such a way as to keep the notion of material balance, debt, or obligation in an emically subordinate position. As in the case of modern Euramerican intrahousehold exchanges, this is accomplished by expressing the necessity for reciprocal exchanges as kinship obligations. These kinship obligations establish reciprocal expectations with respect to food, clothing, shelter, and other economic goods.

Kinship-embedded transactions constitute only a meager portion of modern exchange systems, whereas among band and village peoples almost all exchanges take place between kin, or at least intimate associates, for whom the giving, taking, and using of goods has sentimental and personal meaning.

Reciprocity and trade

Reciprocity is thus the dominant form of exchange within band and prestate village societies. Even hunters and gatherers, however, want valuables such as salt, flint, obsidian, red ochre, reeds, and honey that are produced or controlled by groups with whom they have no kinship ties. Among band and village peoples, economic dealings between nonkin are based on the assumption that every individual will try to get the best of an exchange through chicanery and theft. As a result, trading expeditions are likely to be hazardous in the extreme and to bear a resemblance to war parties.

One interesting mechanism for facilitating trade between distant groups is known as *silent trade.* The objects to be exchanged are set out in a clearing, and the first group retreats out of sight. The other group comes out of hiding, inspects the wares, and lays down what it regards as a fair exchange of its own products. The first group returns and, if satisfied, removes the traded objects. If not, it leaves the wares untouched as a signal that the balance is not yet even. In this fashion the Mbuti of the Ituri Forest trade meat for bananas with the Bantu agriculturalists, and the Vedda of Sri Lanka trade honey for iron tools with the Sinhalese.

More developed trade relations are found among prestate agricultural villages. Conditions for the occurrence of trade markets seem to have been especially favorable in Melanesia. In Malaita in the Solomon Islands, women regularly trade fish for pigs and vegetables under the armed guard of their menfolk (Fig. 4.2). Among the Kapauku of western New Guinea (Fig. 4.3), full-fledged price markets involving shell and bead money (see below) may have existed before the advent of European control. Generally speaking, however, marketing and money as a regular mode of trade is associated with the evolution of the state and with the enforcement of order by means of police and soldiers.

Perhaps the most common solution to the problem of trading without kinship ties or state-supervised markets is the establishment of special *trade partnerships*. In this arrangement, members of different bands or villages regard one another as metaphorical kin. The members of trading expeditions deal exclusively with their trade partners, who greet them as "brothers" and give them food and shelter. Trade partners attempt to deal with one another in conformity with the principle of reciprocity, deny an interest in getting the best of the bargain, and offer their wares as if they were gifts (Heider, 1969).

The Kula

The classic example of trade partnerships is described in Bronislaw Malinowski's *Argonauts of the Western Pacific*. The argonauts in question are the Trobriand Islanders who trade with the neighboring island of Dobu by means of daring canoe voyages across the open sea (Fig. 4.4). The entire complex associated with this trade is known as the *Kula*. According to the men who take these risky

4.2 NEW GUINEA MARKET
Man at left is giving yams in exchange for fish at right. [United Nations]

4.3 KAPAUKU OF WESTERN NEW GUINEA
The men (wearing penis sheaths) are counting shell money. [Leopold Pospisil]

voyages, the purpose of the Kula trade is to exchange shell ornaments with their trade partners. The ornaments, known to the Trobrianders as *vaygu'a*, consist of armbands and necklaces. In trading with the Dobuans, who live to the southeast, the Trobrianders give armbands and receive necklaces. In trading with the people who live to the southwest, the Trobrianders give necklaces and receive armbands. The armbands and necklaces are traded in opposite directions from island to island and finally pass through their points of origin from the direction opposite to the one in which they were first traded.

Participation in the Kula trade is a major ambition of youth and a consuming passion of senior men. The *vaygu'a* have been compared with heirlooms or crown jewels. The older they are and the more complex their history, the more valuable they become in the eyes of the Trobrianders. Nothing is done

4.4 KULA CANOE
These large canoes are used by the Trobrianders for long-distance voyages. [Wide World]

with them except that on ceremonial occasions they are worn as ornaments; otherwise they remain in the house, where they are occasionally inspected and admired in private. Although regarded as a man's most valuable possessions, they can be used only to obtain other armbands or necklaces.

Each Kula expedition requires extensive social and ritual preparation. Minor gifts as well as *vaygu'a* are brought along to please the trade partners. These partnerships are usually handed down from one kinsman to another, and young men are given a start in the Kula trade by inheriting or receiving an armband or a necklace from a relative. When the expedition reaches shore, the trade partners greet one another and exchange preliminary gifts. Later the Trobrianders deliver the precious armbands, accompanied by ritual speeches and formal acts concerned with establishing the honorable, giftlike character of

the exchange. As in the case of reciprocal transactions within the family, the trade partner may not be immediately able to provide a necklace whose value is equivalent to the armband just received. Although the voyager may have to return home empty-handed except for some preliminary gifts, he does not complain. He knows that his trade partner will work hard to make up for the delay by presenting him with an even more valuable necklace at their next meeting.

Why all this effort in order to obtain a few baubles of sentimental or esthetic value? As is often the case, the etic aspects of the Kula are different from the emic aspects. The boats that take part in the Kula expedition carry trade items of great practical value in the life of the various island peoples who participate in the Kula ring. While the trade partners fondle and admire their priceless heirlooms, other members of the expedition trade for

4.5 SEMAI HUNTER
Among the Semai, reciprocity prevails.
[American Museum of Natural History]

practical items. As long as everyone agrees that the expedition is not really concerned with such mundane necessities as coconuts, sago palm flour, fish, yams, baskets, mats, wooden swords and clubs, green stone for tools, mussel shells for knives, creepers and lianas for lashings, these items can be bargained over with impunity. Although no Trobriander would admit it, or even conceive how it could be true, the *vaygu'a* are valuable not for their qualities as heirlooms, but for their truly priceless gift of trade (see Uberoi, 1962).

Redistributive exchange

The evolution of economic and political systems from bands and villages to states is in large degree a consequence of the develop-

ment of coercive forms of exchange that supplement or almost entirely replace reciprocal exchange. Coercive forms of exchange did not appear in sudden full-blown opposition to reciprocal forms. Rather, they probably first arose through what seemed to be merely an extension of familiar reciprocal forms.

The exchange system known as *redistribution* can best be understood as such an extension. In redistributive exchange, the labor products of several different individuals are brought to a central place, sorted by type, counted, and then given away to producers and nonproducers alike. Considerable organizational effort is requird if large quantities of goods are to be brought to the same place at the same time and given away in definite shares. This coordination is usually achieved by individuals who act as *redistributors*. Typically, the redistributor consciously attempts to increase and intensify production, for which he gains prestige in the eyes of his fellows. As we will see (p. 145), this attempt is closely related to increased population density, depletions, increased warfare, and the emergence of classes and the state.

Egalitarian and stratified forms of redistribution must be distinguished. As an *egalitarian* system of exchange, redistribution is carried out by a redistributor who has worked harder than anyone else producing the items to be given away, who takes the smallest portion or none at all, and who, after it is all over, is left with fewer material possessions than anyone else. In its egalitarian form, therefore, redistribution appears to be merely an extreme example of reciprocity; the generous provider gives everything away and for the moment gets nothing in return, except the admiration of those who benefit from his efforts.

In the *stratified* form, however, the redistributor withholds his or her own labor from the production process, retains the largest share, and ends up with more material possessions than anyone else.

Redistributive exchange, like reciprocal exchange, is usually embedded in a complex set of kinship relations and rituals that may obscure the etic significance of the exchange behavior. Redistribution often takes the form of a feast held to celebrate some important event such as a harvest, the end of a ritual taboo, the construction of a house, a death, a birth, or a marriage. A common feature of Melanesian redistributive feasts is that the guests gorge themselves with food, stagger off into the bush, stick their fingers down their throats, vomit, and then return to eating with renewed zest. Another common feature of redistributive feasting is the boastful and competitive attitude of the redistributors and their kin with respect to other individuals or groups who have given feasts. This contrasts markedly with reciprocal exchange. Let us take a closer look at this contrast.

Reciprocity versus redistribution

Boastfulness and acknowledgment of generosity is incompatible with the basic etiquette of reciprocal exchanges. Among the Semai of Central Malaya, no one even says "thank you" for the meat received from another hunter (Fig. 4.5). Having struggled all day to lug the carcass of a pig home through the jungle heat, the hunter allows his prize to be cut up into exactly equal portions, which are then given away to the entire group. As Robert Dentan explains, to express gratitude for the portion received indicates that you are the kind of person who calculates how much you are giving and taking.

In this context saying thank you is very rude, for it suggests first that one has calculated the amount of a gift and second, that one did not expect the donor to be so generous. (1968, p. 49)

To call attention to one's generosity is to indicate that others are in debt to you and that you expect them to repay you. It is repugnant to egalitarian peoples even to suggest that they have been treated generously. Richard

Lee tells how he learned about this aspect of reciprocity through a revealing incident. To please the !Kung with whom he was staying, he decided to buy a large ox and have it slaughtered as a Christmas present. He spent days searching the neighboring Bantu agricultural villages looking for the largest and fattest ox in the region. Finally, he bought what appeared to be a perfect specimen. But one !Kung after another took him aside and assured him that he had been duped into buying an absolutely worthless animal. "Of course, we will eat it," they said, "but it won't fill us up—we will eat and go home to bed with stomachs rumbling." Yet when Lee's ox was slaughtered, it turned out to be covered with a thick layer of fat. Lee eventually succeeded in getting his informants to explain why they had claimed that his gift was valueless, even though they certainly knew better than he what lay under the animal's skin: *Yes, when a young man kills much meat he comes to think of himself as a chief or a big man, and he thinks of the rest of us as his servants or inferiors. We can't accept this, we refuse one who boasts, for someday his pride will make him kill somebody. So we always speak of his meat as worthless. This way we cool his heart and make him gentle. (1968, p. 62)*

In flagrant violation of these precriptions for modesty in reciprocal exchanges, redistributive exchange systems involve public proclamations that the host is a generous person and a great provider. This boasting is one of the most conspicuous features of the *potlatches* engaged in by the native Americans who inhabit the Northwest Coast of the United States and Canada (Fig. 4.6). In descriptions made famous by Ruth Benedict in *Patterns of Culture*, the Kwakiutl redistributor emerges as a virtual megalomaniac. Here is what the Kawkiutl chiefs had to say about themselves (1934, p. 190):

I am the great chief who makes people ashamed.
I am the great chief who makes people ashamed.

4.6 *KWAKIUTL OF THE NORTHWEST CA. 1900* (above)
The signs over the doors read: "Boston. He is the Head chief of Arweete. He is true Indian. Honest. He don't owe no trouble to white man" and "Cheap. He is one of the head chief of all tribes in this country. White man can get information." [American Museum of Natural History]

Our chief brings shame to the faces.
Our chief brings jealousy to the faces.
Our chief makes people cover their faces by
*   what he is continually doing in this world,*
Giving again and again oil feasts[1] to all the
*   tribes.*

I am the only great tree, I the chief!
I am the only great tree, I the chief!
You are my subordinates, tribes.
You sit in the middle of the rear of the house,
*   tribes.*
I am the first to give you property, tribes.
I am your Eagle, tribes!

Bring your counter of property, tribes, that he
*   may try in vain to count the property that is*
*   to be given away by the great copper maker,*
*   the chief.*

[1] Fish oil, not petroleum.

In the potlatch the guests continue to behave somewhat like Lee's !Kung. They grumble and complain and are careful never to appear satisfied or impressed. Nonetheless, there has been a careful public counting of all the gifts displayed and distributed (Fig. 4.7). Both hosts and guests believe that the only way to throw off the obligations incurred in accepting these gifts is to hold a counter potlatch in which the tables are reversed.

4.7 *POTLATCH* (facing page)
Spokesman for Kwakiutl chief making speech next to blankets about to be given away. [American Museum of Natural History]

The cultural ecology of redistribution and reciprocity

Why do the !Kung esteem a hunter who never draws attention to his generosity, whereas the Kwakiutl and other redistributor peoples esteem a man who can boast about how much he has given away? One theory compatible with min-max principles is that reciprocity reflects an adjustment to technological and environmental conditions in which an increase in production would rapidly lead to diminishing returns and environmental depletions. Hunters and gatherers seldom have an opportunity to intensify production without rapidly reaching the point of diminishing returns. Intensification poses a grave threat to such peoples in the form of faunal overkills. To encourage the !Kung hunter to be boastful is to endanger the group's survival. On the other hand, agricultural villages generally have greater leeway for increasing production by investing more labor. They can raise their standards of consumption if they work harder, and yet not immediately jeopardize their energy efficiency by depleting their habitats. The Kwakiutl are not agriculturalists, but they depended on the annual upriver runs of salmon and candlefish. Using aboriginal dip nets, it was impossible for the Kwakiutl and their neighbors to affect the overall rate of reproduction of these species. Hence they depended on a highly intensifiable mode of production. Moreover, there were periodic fluctuations in the size of the annual migrations of these fish from one year to the next (Langdon, 1979). Hence it was ecologically feasible for the Kwakiutl to try to maximize production and to reward those who played a role in getting everybody to work harder with prestige and the privilege of boasting.

The origin of destructive potlatches

Potlatching came under scientific scrutiny long after the people of the Pacific Northwest had entered into trade and wage-labor relations with Russian, English, Canadian, and American nationals. Declining populations and a sudden influx of wealth had combined

to make the potlatches increasingly competitive and destructive by the time Franz Boas began to study them in the 1880s (Rohner, 1969). At this period the entire tribe was in residence at the Fort Rupert trading station of the Hudson's Bay Company, and the attempt on the part of one potlatch-giver to outdo another had become an all-consuming passion. Blankets, boxes of fish oil, and other valuables were deliberately being destroyed by burning or by throwing them into the sea. On one occasion, made famous by Ruth Benedict in *Patterns of Culture,* an entire house burned to the ground when too much fish oil was poured on the fire. Potlatches that ended in this fashion were regarded as great victories for the potlatch-givers.

It seems likely that before the coming of the Europeans, Kwakiutl potlatch feasts were less destructive and more like Melanesian feasts. Although rivalrous feasts are wasteful, the net increment in total production may exceed the loss due to gorging and spoilage. Moreover, after the visitors have eaten to their satisfaction, there still remains much food, which they carry back home with them.

The fact that guests come from distant villages leads to additional important ecological and economic advantages. It has been suggested that feasting rivalry between groups raises productivity throughout a region more than if each village feasts only its own producers. Second, as has been suggested for the Northwest Coast region by Wayne Suttles (1960) and Stuart Piddocke (1965), rivalrous intervillage redistributions may overcome the effects of localized, naturally induced production failures. Failure of the salmon runs at a particular stream could threaten the survival of certain villages while neighbors on other streams continue to catch their usual quotas. Under such circumstances, the impoverished villagers would want to attend as many potlatches as they could and carry back as many vital supplies as they could get their hosts to part with by reminding them of how

big their own potlatches had been in previous years. Intervillage potlatches thus may have been a form of savings in which the prestige acquired at one's own feast served as a tally. The tally was redeemed when the guests turned hosts. If a village was unable year after year to give potlatches of its own, its prestige credit would disappear.

In this connection, Thomas Hazard (1960) suggests a third ecological function for rivalrous distributions—namely, the shifting of population from less productive to more productive villages. When an impoverished and unprestigious group could no longer hold its own potlatches, the people abandoned their defeated redistributor-chief and took up residence among relatives in more productive villages. In this interpretation the boasting and the giving away and displaying of wealth were advertisements that helped to recruit additional labor power into the work force gathered about a particularly effective redistributor. Incidentally, if this hypothesis is correct, it is easier to understand why the Northwest Coast peoples lavished so much effort on the production of their world-famous totem poles. These poles bore the redistributor-chief's "crests" in the guise of carved mythic figures; title to the crests was claimed on the basis of outstanding potlatch achievements. The larger the pole, the greater the potlatch power, the more the members of poor villages would be tempted to change their residence and gather around another chief.

With the coming of the Europeans, however, there was a shift toward more destructive forms of redistribution. The impact of European diseases had reduced the population of the Kwakiutl from about 10,000 in 1836 to about 2,000 by the end of the century. At the same time the trading companies, canneries, lumber mills, and gold-mining camps pumped an unprecedented amount of wealth into the aboriginal economy. The percentage of people prepared to claim the crests of achievement rose, while the number of people available to celebrate the glory of the potlatcher dropped. Many villages were abandoned; hence rivalry intensified for the allegiance of the survivors.

A final and perhaps the most important factor in the development of destructive potlatches was the change in the technology and intensity of warfare. As suggested by Brian Ferguson (1979), the earliest contacts in the late eighteenth century between the Europeans and the native Americans of the Northwest Pacific Coast centered on the fur trade. In return for sea-otter skins, the Europeans gave guns to the Kwakiutl and their traditional enemies. This had a double effect. On the one hand, warfare became more deadly; and on the other, it forced local groups to fight one another for control of trade in order to get the ammunition on which success in warfare now depended. Small wonder, therefore, that as population declined, the potlatch chiefs were willing to throw away or destroy wealth that was militarily unimportant in order to attract manpower for warfare and the fur trade.

Stratified redistribution

A subtle line separates egalitarian from stratified forms of redistribution. In the egalitarian form, contributions to the central pool are voluntary and the workers get back all or most of what they put into it or items of comparable value. In the stratified form, the workers must contribute to the central pool or suffer penalties, and they may not get back anything. Again, in the egalitarian form, the redistributor lacks the power to coerce followers into intensifying production and must depend on their goodwill; in the stratified form, the redistributor has that power and the workers must depend on his or her goodwill. The processes responsible for the evolution of one form of redistribution into another

will be discussed in Chapter 8. Here we will only note that fully developed forms of stratified redistribution imply the existence of a class of rulers who have the power to compel others to do their bidding. The expression of this power in the realm of production and exchange results in the economic subordination of the labor force and its partial or total loss of control over production and exchange. Specifically, the labor force loses control over:

1 Access to land and raw materials
2 The technology of production
3 Work time and work schedules
4 Place and mode of production activity
5 Disposition of the products of labor

Forms of production and exchange that depend upon the coercive effects of power can be understood only within the framework of a combined political and economic analysis. All the concepts appropriate to the analysis of contemporary economic systems, such as wages, rent, interest, property, and capital, have a political dimension. Just as production and exchange in egalitarian societies are embedded in kinship institutions, the processes of production and exchange in state-level societies are embedded in institutions of political control.

Price-market exchange: buying and selling

Marketplaces occur in rudimentary form wherever groups of nonkin and strangers assemble and trade one item for another. Among band and village peoples, marketplace trading usually involves the barter of one valuable consumable item for another: fish for yams, coconuts for axes, and so forth. In this type of market, before the development of all-purpose money, only a limited range of goods or services is exchanged. The great bulk of exchange transactions takes place outside the marketplace and continues

4.8 *HUNTING AND GATHERING, USA*
[Greenberg, DPI]

to involve various forms of reciprocity and re-distribution. With the development of all-pur-pose money (see next section), however, price-market exchanges come to dominate all other forms of exchange. In a price market, the price of the goods and services exchanged is determined by buyers competing with buyers and sellers competing with sellers. Virtually everything that is produced or consumed comes to have a price, and buying and selling becomes a major cultural preoccupation or even obsession (Fig. 4.8).

It is possible to engage in reciprocal ex-change using money, as when a friend gives a loan and does not specify when it must be re-paid. Redistributive exchange can be carried out via money, as in the collection of taxes and the disbursement of welfare payments. Buying and selling on a price market, how-ever, is a distinctive mode of exchange since it involves the specification of the precise time,

quantity, and type of payment. Furthermore, unlike either reciprocity or redistribution, once the money payment is concluded, no fur-ther obligation or responsibility exists be-tween buyer and seller. They can walk away from each other and never see each other again. Price-market exchanges, therefore, are note-worthy for the anonymity and impersonal-ity of the exchange process and stand in contrast to the personal and kin-based ex-changes of band and village economies. Now let us take a closer look at the nature of that strange entity we call money.

Money

The idea and practice of endowing a material object with the capacity of measuring the so-cial value of other material objects, animals, people, and labor occurs almost universally.

4.9 SHELL AND DOG TEETH MONEY
**Manus dance and display their ceremonial
money prior to exchange with trade
partners. [American Museum of Natural
History]**

Such standard-of-value "stuffs" are widely
exchanged for goods and services. Throughout much of Africa, for example, a young man
gives cattle to his father-in-law and gets a
wife in return (see p. 96). In many parts of
Melanesia, shells are exchanged for stone implements, pottery, and other valuable artifacts. Elsewhere beads, feathers, shark teeth,
dog teeth, or pig tusks are exchanged for other
valuable items and are given as compensation
for death or injury and for personal services
rendered by magicians, canoe-builders, and
other specialists (Fig. 4.9). With rare and
still controversial exceptions, however, these
"money stuffs" lack some of the major characteristics of the money stuffs found in price-
market economies. In price-market economies money is commercial or market money,
an all-purpose medium of exchange. It has the
following features:

1 *Portability* It comes in sizes and shapes
   convenient for being carried about from
   one transaction to the next.
2 *Divisibility* Its various forms and values
   are explicit and multiples of each other.

3 *Convertibility* A transaction completed by
   a higher-valued unit can be made as well
   by its lower-valued multiples.
4 *Generality* Virtually all goods and services have a money value.
5 *Anonymity* For most purchases, anyone
   with the market price can conclude a
   transaction.
6 *Legality* The nature and quantity of
   money in circulation is controlled by a
   government.

Although some of these traits may be associated with money in band and village economies, collectively the traits depend upon an
economy in which selling and buying in a
price market is a daily, lifelong occurrence.
Where reciprocity, egalitarian redistribution,
and trade-partner relations are the dominant
modes of exchange, money in the modern dol-
lar sense does not and cannot exist.

For example, cattle that are exchanged for
wives are not the kind of currency you would
want to take to the supermarket checkout
counter, being neither very portable nor readily divisible. As employed in *bride-price* (see p.
96), cattle are frequently not convertible;
that is, a large, beautiful, fat bull with a local
reputation cannot readily be substituted for
by two small but undistinguished animals.
Furthermore, cattle lack generality since only
wives can be "purchased" with them, and
they lack anonymity because any stranger
who shows up with the right amount of cattle
will find that he cannot simply take the
woman and leave the cattle. Cattle are exchanged for women only between kinship
groups who have an interest in establishing or
reinforcing preexisting social relationships.
Finally, cattle are put into circulation by each
individual household as a result of productive
effort that is unregulated by any central authority.

In other instances, noncommercial money
stuff bears a greater resemblance to commercial money. For example, among the inhabitants of Rossel Island, which lies off the east
coast of New Guinea, a type of shell money

stuff occurs that has sometimes been confused with commercial money. The shells have portability, and they occur in 22 named units of value, that is, 1 to 22. These units, however, fall into three classes: numbers 1 to 10, numbers 11 to 17, and numbers 18 to 22. A person who borrows a number 1 shell must return a number 2. A person who borrows a number 2 must repay with a number 3. This continues through to a number 9. But a person who borrows a number 10 cannot be obliged to return a number 11. Thus the series 1 to 10 is divisible. Moreover, the series 1 to 10 has a considerable amount of generality, being used to buy such items as baskets and pots. But the two series 1 to 10 and 11 to 17 are neither divisible nor convertible with respect to each other. Similarly, the series 18 to 22 stands apart. There are only 60 shells in this series in circulation, and they are non-convertible with respect to each other and to the other series. For example, a number 18 is the only shell that can be used for wife-purchase or for sponsorship of a pig feast. A number 20 is the only shell that can be used as indemnity for ritual murder. As George Dalton (1965) observes: "It is about as useful to describe a pig feast on Rossel as buying a pig with a no. 18 *ndap* as it is to describe marriage in America as buying a wife with a wedding ring."

Capitalism

Price-market exchange reaches its highest development when it is embedded in the form of political economy known as capitalism. In capitalist societies, buying and selling by means of all-purpose money extends to land, resources, and housing. Labor has a price called wages; and money itself has a price called interest. Of course, there is no such thing as a completely free market in which price is set wholly by supply and demand and in which everything can be sold. By comparison with other forms of political economy, however, capitalism is aptly described as a political economy in which money can buy anything. This being so, everyone tries to acquire as much money as possible, and the object of production itself is not merely to provide valuable goods and services, but to increase one's possession of money—that is, to make a profit and accumulate capital (Fig. 4.10). The rate of capitalist production depends upon the rate at which profits can be made, and this in turn depends on the rate at which people purchase, use, wear out, and destroy goods and services. Hence an enormous effort is expended on extolling the virtues and benefits of products in order to convince consumers that they should make additional purchases. Prestige is awarded not to the person who works hardest or gives away the greatest amount of wealth, but rather to the person who has the most possessions and who consumes at the highest rate. For example, the most prestigious profession in the United States—medical doctor—is also the one whose members make the most money (*The New York Times*, 1978).

In theory, Socialist and Communist political economies are supposed to replace price-market consumerism and the capitalist money obsession with egalitarian forms of redistribution and reciprocal exchanges. All contemporary Socialist societies, however, operate with price-market money economies, and many of them are as possession-oriented as capitalist societies. It is also questionable whether any of them has achieved the classlessness that is the prerequisite for truly egalitarian forms of redistribution (see Ch. 9).

Capitalism inevitably leads to marked inequalities in wealth based on differential

4.10 *TOKYO STOCK EXCHANGE (facing page)*
The public sale and purchase of shares in companies and corporations is a fundamental feature of capitalist economies. [UPI]

ownership or access to resources and to the infrastructure of production. As in all stratified economies, political control is necessary to keep the poor from confiscating the wealth and privileges of the rich. Some anthropologists, however, see many of the features of capitalism present in societies that lack state-administered laws and police-military means of control. Let us turn, therefore, to the question of the extent to which capitalism is foreshadowed in band and village societies.

"Primitive capitalism?" The Kapauku case

There is no doubt that, in general, band and village societies lack the essential features of capitalism because, as we have seen, their exchange systems are based on reciprocal and redistributive exchanges rather than on price-market exchanges. In some cases, however, egalitarian reciprocal and redistributive systems may have certain features strongly reminiscent of contemporary capitalist arrangements. Upon closer inspection, as in the case of the Rossel Island "money," such resemblances usually can be shown to be superficial. Nonetheless, these cases are of special interest precisely because they reveal the abiding limitations imposed upon production, exchange, and consumption when there is no central political authority and hence where differential access to resources and technology cannot be sustained.

The Kapauku Papuans of West New Guinea (today, West Irian, Indonesia) are a case in point (see Fig. 4.3). According to Leopold Pospisil (1963), the Kapauku have an economy that is best described as "primitive capitalism." All Kapauku agricultural land is said to be owned individually; money sales are the regular means of exchange; money, in the form of shells and glass beads, can be used to buy food, domesticated animals, crops, and land; money can also be used as payment for labor. Rent for leased land and interest on loans are also said to occur.

A closer look at the land tenure situation, however, reveals fundamental differences between the political economy of Kapauku and capitalist peasant societies (see below). To begin with, there is no landowning class. Instead, access to land is controlled by kinship groups known as *sublineages* (see p. 109). No individual is without membership in such a group. These sublineages control communal tracts of land, which Pospisil calls "territories."

It is only within sublineage territories that one may speak of private titles, and the economic significance of these titles is minimal on several counts. (1) The price of land is so cheap that all the gardens under production have a market value in shell money less than the value of ten female pigs. (2) Prohibition against trespass does not apply to sublineage kin. (3) Although even brothers will ask each other for land payments, credit is freely extended among all sublineage members. The most common form of credit with respect to land consists merely of giving land on a loan, and in expectation that the favor will shortly be returned. (4) Each sublineage is under the leadership of a *headman* (see Ch. 7) whose authority depends on his generosity, especially toward the members of his own sublineage. A rich headman does not refuse to lend his kinsmen whatever they need to gain access to the environment, since "a selfish individual who hoards money and fails to be generous, never sees the time when his word is taken seriously and his advice and decisions followed, no matter how rich he may become" (Pospisil, 1963, p. 49).

Obviously, therefore, the wealth of the headman does not bestow the power associated with capitalist ownership. In Brazil or India tenants or sharecroppers can be barred from access to land and water regardless of their landlord's reputation. Under the rules of capitalist landownership, it is of no significance to the sheriff and the police officers when they evict tenants that the landlord is being "selfish."

Pospisil states that differences in wealth are correlated with striking differences in consumption of food and that Kapauku children from poor homes are undernourished while neighbors are well fed. However, the neighbors are not members of the same sublineage: As Pospisil notes, sublineage kinsmen "exhibit mutual affection and a strong sense of belonging and unity" and "any kind of friction within the group is regarded as deplorable" (1963, p. 39). It is true that certain sublineages are poorer than others. Sickness and misfortune of various sorts frequently lead to inequalities in physical well-being among the kinship units that are the building blocks of band and village societies. But such misfortunes do not lead to the formation of a poverty class as they do under true capitalism. Without central political controls, marked economic inequalities cannot be perpetuated for long, because the rich cannot defend themselves against the demand of the poor that they be given credit, money, land, or whatever is necessary to end their poverty. Under aboriginal conditions some Kapauku villagers might have starved while neighbors ate well; but it is extremely unlikely that those who starved did so because they lacked access to land, money, or credit.

A stingy redistributor in a band or village society is a contradiction in terms, for the simple reason that there are no police to protect such people from the murderous intentions of those whom they refuse to help. As Pospisil tells it:

Selfish and greedy individuals, who have amassed huge personal properties, but who have failed to comply with the Kapauku requirement of "generosity" toward their less fortunate tribesmen may be, and actually frequently are, put to death. . . . Even in regions such as the Kamu Valley, where such an execution is not a penalty for greediness, a nongenerous wealthy man is ostracized, repri-

manded, and thereby finally induced to change his ways. (1963, p. 49)

Landownership

Ownership of land and resources is one of the most important aspects of political control. It is as much political as economic because unequal access to the environment implies some form of coercion applied by political superiors against political inferiors.

As we have just seen, certain forms of land and resource ownership do occur in band and village societies. Ownership of garden lands, for example, is often claimed by kin groups in village communities, but everybody belongs to such kin groups, and hence adults cannot be prevented from using the resources they need to make a living. Landownership by landlords, rulers, or the government, however, means that individuals who lack title or tenure may be barred from using land even if it leads to death through starvation.

As we will see in Chapter 8, ownership of land and resources results from systemic processes that select for more dense and more productive populations. Landownership is a great stimulus to production because it forces food producers to work longer and harder than they would if they had free access to resources. Landownership raises production mainly through the extraction of rent from the food producers. *Rent* is a payment in kind or in money for the opportunity to live or work on the owner's land. This payment automatically compels tenants to increase their work input. By raising or lowering rents, the landlord exercises a fairly direct measure of control over work input and production.

Because the extraction of rent is evolutionarily associated with an increase in food production, some anthropologists regard the payment of rent as indicative of the existence of *surplus* food—an amount greater than what is needed for immediate consumption by the producers. But it is important to note that the "surplus" food the landowner takes away as rent need not be a *superfluous* quantity from the producers' standpoint. The producers usually can very well use the full amount of their output to ease the costs of rearing children or to raise their own standard of living. If they surrender their produce, it is usually because they lack the power to withhold it. In this sense all rent is an aspect of politics, because without the power to enforce property titles, rent would seldom be paid. Thus there is a close resemblance between rent and taxation. Both depend on the existence of coercive power in the form of police and weapons that can be called into action if the taxpayer or tenant refuses to pay.

In certain highly centralized societies, such as in the ancient Inca Empire (see p. 148), there is no distinction between rent and taxes since there is no landlord class. Instead, the government bureaucracy has a monopoly over the means of extracting wealth from commoner food producers. States and empires also exercise direct control over production by setting regional or community quotas for particular crops and by conscripting armies of commoners to work on construction projects. Compulsory labor conscription, known as *corvee*, is merely another form of taxation. As we will see in Chapter 9, all these coercive forms of extracting wealth from commoner food producers probably have their roots in egalitarian forms of redistribution and labor intensification.

Summary

All cultures have an economy, a set of institutions that combine technology, labor, and natural resources to produce and distribute goods and services. To the extent that economizing takes place—that is, minimizing costs and maximizing benefits—it always takes place in a definite cultural context, and it is always embedded in institutional relationships such as kinship or political control. The question whether economies always conform to min-max principles must be investigated empirically, but the possibility that apparently wasteful and "uneconomic" behavior such as gluttonous feasts conforms to min-max at a broader level of analysis should be kept in mind.

Modern-day price markets represent only one of several alternative modes of exchange. Buying and selling is not a universal trait. The idea that money can buy everything (or almost everything) has been alien to most of the human beings who have ever lived. Two other modes of exchange, reciprocity and redistribution, have played a more important economic role than price markets.

In reciprocal exchange the time and quantity of the counterflow is not specified. This kind of exchange can be effective only when it is embedded in kinship or close personal relationships. Daily food distribution among the !Kung San is an example of reciprocal exchange. Control over the counterflow in reciprocal exchange is achieved by communal pressure against freeloaders and shirkers. Reciprocity lingers on in price-market societies within kinship groups and is familiar to many of us as gift-giving to relatives and friends.

In the absence of price markets and police-military supervision, trade poses a special problem to people accustomed to reciprocal exchange. Silent barter is one solution. Another is to create trading partners who treat each other as kin. The Kula is a classic example of how barter for practical necessities is carried out under the cloak of reciprocal exchanges.

Redistributive exchange involves the collection of goods in a central place and its disbursement by a redistributor to the producers. In the transition from egalitarian to stratified forms of redistribution, production and exchange cross the line separating voluntary from coerced forms of economic behavior. In its egalitarian form, the redistributor depends on the goodwill of the producers; in the stratified form, the producers depend on the goodwill of the redistributor.

Redistribution is characterized by the counting of shares contributed and shares disbursed. Unlike reciprocity, redistribution leads to boasting and overt competition for the prestigeful status of great provider. The Kwakiutl potlatch is a classic example of the relationship between redistribution and bragging behavior. The predominance of redistribution over reciprocity may be related to the intensifiability of various modes of production. Where production can be intensified without depletions, rivalrous redistributions may serve adaptive ecological functions, such as providing an extra margin of safety in lean years and equalizing regional production. The development of destructive potlatches among the Kwakiutl may have been caused by factors involved in the European contact situation, such as the intensification of warfare, trade for guns and ammunition, and depopulation.

Price-market exchange depends on the development of all-purpose money as defined by the criteria of portability, divisibility, convertibility, generality, anonymity, and legality. Although some of these features are possessed by limited-purpose standards of value in pre-state societies, price markets imply the existence of state forms of control.

The highest development of the price-market mode of exchange is associated with the political economy of capitalism, in which virtually all goods and services can be bought and sold. Since capitalist production depends on consumerism, prestige is awarded to those who own or consume the greatest amount of goods and services. Price-market exchanges are embedded in a political economy of control made necessary by the inequalities in access to resources and the conflict between the poor and the wealthy. The Kapauku illustrate the reasons why price-market institutions and capitalism cannot exist in the absence of such controls.

The relationship between political forms of control and modes of production and exchange focuses in many societies on the question of landownership. Rent, corvee labor, and taxation all reflect differential access to nature and technology. Thus we see why the comparative study of economics must involve the study of the institutions in which economizing is embedded.

5

The Organization of Domestic Life

In this chapter we continue the comparative study of the structural level of sociocultural systems and examine the major varieties of domestic organizations. We will inquire whether all domestic groups are built up from a single form of family and whether there is a genetic basis for the exchanges of personnel that link domestic groups together. This chapter is primarily descriptive, but some theoretical explanations that are more fully elaborated in later chapters are discussed in a preliminary way. We must have some knowledge of the extent of variation in human affairs before we can tackle the problem of explaining why some varieties occur in one culture and not in another.

The domestic sphere of culture

All cultures have activities and thoughts that can usefully be lumped under the category of the domestic sphere of life. The basic ingredient in the etic notion of domestic life is a dwelling space, shelter, residence, or domicile, which serves as the place in which certain universally recurrent activities take place. But it is not possible to give a rigid checklist of what these activities are. In many cultures, domestic activities include preparation and consumption of food; cleaning, grooming, and disciplining of the young; sleeping; and adult sexual intercourse. However, there is no culture in which these activities are carried out exclusively within domestic settings. For example, sexual intercourse among band and village peoples more often takes place in the bush or forest than in the house where sleeping occurs. In other instances, sleeping itself takes place primarily away from the setting in which eating occurs, and in still other instances domiciles may lack resident children, as when childless adults live alone or when children are sent off to school. The variety of combinations of activities characteristic of human domestic life is so great that it is difficult to find any single underlying common denominator for all of them. (One might insist that there must be at least mothers and very young children, but what about childless households?) This in itself, however, is an important fact, since no other species exhibits such an enormous range of different behaviors associated with patterns of eating, shelter, sleep, sex, and rearing of infants and children.

The nuclear family

Can a particular kind of group be found in all domestic settings? Many anthropologists believe there is such a group and refer to it as the *nuclear family:* husband, wife, and children (Fig. 5.1). According to Ralph Linton, father, mother, child is the "bedrock underlying all other family structures," and he predicted that "the last man will spend his last hours searching for his wife and child" (1959, p. 52). George Peter Murdock found the nuclear family in each of 250 societies. He concluded that it was universal. According to Murdock (1949), the nuclear family fulfills vital functions that cannot be carried out as efficiently by other groups. The functions identified by Murdock are these: (1) sex, (2) reproduction, (3) education, and (4) subsistence.

1 The nuclear family satisfies sexual needs and diminishes the disruptive force of sexual competition.
2 The nuclear family guarantees the protection of the female during her long pregnancy and during the months and years of lactation.
3 The nuclear family is essential for enculturation. Only the coresident adult man and woman possess knowledge adequate for the enculturation of children of both sexes.
4 Given the behavioral specialties imposed upon the human female by her reproductive role, and given the anatomical and physiological differences between men and women, the sexual division of labor makes subsistence more efficient.

The nuclear family thus provides for heterosexual sex, reproduction, enculturation, and economic support more effectively than any other institution, according to this view.

It is important to investigate the validity of these claims at some length. The idea that the nuclear family is universal or nearly universal lends support to the view that nonnuclear family domestic units are inferior, pathological, or contrary to human nature. In actuality, however, no one knows the limits within which human domestic arrangements must be confined in order to satisfy human nature and effectively carry out none, some, or all of the four functions listed above.

5.1 *JAPANESE NUCLEAR FAMILY*
Industrialization in Japan has produced convergence toward a pattern of nuclear family life in the United States. [Consulate General of Japan]

Alternatives to the nuclear family

Even though nuclear families can be found in the overwhelming majority of human cultures, it has long been obvious that every culture has alternative forms of domestic organization and that these frequently are more important—involve a higher proportion of the population—than the nuclear family. Moreover, the four functions listed above, as was already suggested, can readily be carried out in the context of alternative institutions that may lie entirely outside the domestic sphere.

In the case of the nuclear family in modern industrial cultures this is evident with respect to enculturation and education. Encultura-

tion and education in contemporary life are increasingly a nondomestic affair carried out in special buildings—schools—under the auspices of specialist nonkinspeople—teachers.

Many village and band societies also separate their children and adolescents from the nuclear family and the entire domestic scene in order to teach them the lore and ritual of the ancestors, sexual competence, or the military arts. Among the Nyakyusa of southern Tanzania, for example, 6- or 7-year-old boys begin to put up reed shelters or playhouses on the outskirts of their village. These playhouses are gradually improved upon and enlarged, eventually leading to the construction of a whole new village. Between the ages of 5 and 11, Nyakyusa boys sleep in their parents' house; but during adolescence they are permitted to visit only during daylight hours. Sleeping now takes place in the new village, although the mother still does the cooking. The founding of a new village is complete when the young men take wives who cook for them and begin to give birth to the next generation (M. Wilson, 1963).

Another famous variation on this pattern is found among the Masai of East Africa, where unmarried men of the same *age-set*, or ritually defined generation, establish special villages or camps from which they launch war parties and cattle-stealing raids. It is the mothers and sisters of these men who cook and keep house for them.

The common English upper-class practice of sending sons 6 years of age or older to boarding schools should also be noted. Like the Masai, the English aristocracy refused to let the burden of maintaining the continuity of their society rest upon the educational resources of the nuclear household.

In many societies, married men spend a good deal of time in special *men's houses*. Food is handed in to them by wives and children who are themselves forbidden to enter. Men also sleep and work in these "clubhouses," although they may on occasion bed down with their wives and children.

Among the Fur of the Sudan, husbands usually sleep apart from their wives in houses of their own and take their meals at an exclusive men's mess. One of the most interesting cases of the separation of cooking and eating occurs among the Ashanti of West Africa. Ashanti men eat their meals with their sisters, mothers, and maternal nephews and nieces, not with their wives and children. But it is the wives who do the cooking. Every evening in Ashanti land there is a steady traffic of children taking their mother's cooking to their father's sister's house (see Barnes, 1960; Bender, 1967).

Finally, there is at least one famous case— the Nayar of Kerala—in which "husband" and "wife" do not live together at all. Many Nayar women "married" ritual husbands and then stayed with their brothers and sisters. Their mates were men who visited overnight. Children born of these matings were brought up in households dominated by their mother's brother and never knew their father. We will return for a closer look at the Nayar in a moment.

Polygamy and the nuclear family

Next we must consider whether the combination father-mother-child has the same functional significance where either father or mother is married to and is living with more than one spouse at a time. This is an important question because plural marriage—*polygamy*—occurs to some extent in at least 90 percent of all cultures.

In one form, called *polygyny* (Fig. 5.2), a husband is shared by several wives; in another much less common form called *polyandry* (Fig. 5.3), a wife is shared by several husbands (we discuss the reason for the occurrence of polygyny and polyandry in Ch. 6). Is there a nuclear family when there are plural husbands or wives? G. P. Murdock suggested that nuclear families do exist in such situations. The man or woman simply belongs to more than one nuclear family at a time. But this overlooks the fact that plural marriages create domestic situations behaviorally and mentally very different from those created by *monogamous* (one husband, one wife) marriages.

Polygamous sexual arrangements, for example, are obviously quite different from those characteristic of monogamous marriages. The mode of reproduction is also different, especially with polygyny, because the spacing of births is easier to control when husbands have several wives. Also, distinctive

5.2 *POLYGYNY*

Above, polygynous household, Senegal. Islamic law permits this man to take one more wife to fill his quota of four, providing he can take good care of her. Below, Sitting Bull. This famous Sioux chief is shown with two of his wives and three of his children. Polygyny was widespread among native American peoples. The photo was taken in 1882 at Fort Randall, South Dakota. [United Nations—above; Museum of the American Indian, Heye Foundation —below]

5.3 *POLYANDRY*
**This Tibetan woman (wearing the veil) is being married to the
two men on the left who are brothers. [Schuler, Anthro-Photo]**

patterns of nursing and infant care arise when the mother sleeps alone with her children while the father sleeps with a different wife each night (see p. 256). From the point of view of childrearing, there are special psychological effects associated with a father who divides his time among several mothers and who relates to his children through a hierarchy of wives. The monogamous U.S. or Canadian nuclear family places the focus of adult attention on a small group of full siblings. In a polygynous household, a dozen or more half-siblings must share the affection of the same man. Furthermore, the presence of co-wives or co-husbands changes the burden of childcare a particular parent must bear. For example, U.S. and Canadian parents are troubled by the question of what to do with children when both parents are preoccupied with adult-centered activities. Polygynous families, however, have a built-in solution to the babysitting problem in the form of co-wives.

Turning finally to economic functions, the minimal polygamous economic unit often consists of the entire coresident production team and not each separate husband-wife pair. Under polygyny, for example, domestic tasks—nursing, grooming, cleaning, fetching water, cooking, and so on—frequently cannot be satisfactorily performed by a single wife. In polygynous societies, one of the main motivations for marrying a second wife is to spread the workload and increase domestic output. It seems inappropriate, therefore, to equate nuclear families in monogamous domestic contexts with husband-wife-child units embedded in polygamous domestic contexts.

The extended family

In a significant proportion of the societies studied by anthropologists, domestic life is dominated by groupings larger than simple nuclear or polygamous families. Probably the majority of existing cultures still carry on their domestic routines in the context of some form of *extended family*—that is, a domestic group consisting of siblings, their spouses and their children, and/or parents and married children (Fig. 5.4). Extended families may also be polygynous. A common form of extended family in Africa, for example, consists of two or more brothers, each with two or three wives, living with their adult sons, each of whom has one or two wives. Among the Bathonga of southern Mozambique, domestic life fell under the control of the senior males of the polygynous extended family's senior generation. These prestigious and powerful men in effect formed a board of directors of a family-style corporation. They were responsible for making decisions about the domestic group's holdings in land, cattle, and build-ings; they organized the subsistence effort of the coresident labor force, especially of the women and children, by assigning fields, crops, and seasonal work tasks. They tried to increase the size of their cattle herds and supplies of food and beer, obtain more wives, and increase the size and strength of the entire unit. The younger brothers, sons, and grandsons in the Bathonga extended families could reach adulthood, marry, build a hut, carry out subsistence tasks, and have children only as members of the larger group, subject to the policies and priorities established by the senior males. Within the Bathonga extended family households there really was no unit equivalent to a nuclear family, and this is true of extended families in many other cultures, whether they are monogamous or polygamous.

5.4 EXTENDED FAMILY, USA
The demand for labor was high on this Minnesota farm, 1895. [The Bettman Archive]

In traditional Chinese extended families, for example, marriage is usually monogamous (Fig. 5.5). A senior couple manages the domestic labor force and arranges marriages. Women brought into the household as wives for the senior couple's sons are placed under the direct control of their mother-in-law. She supervises their cleaning, cooking, and raising of children. Where there are several daughters-in-law, cooking chores are often rotated so that on any given day a maximum contingent of the domestic labor force can be sent to work in the family's fields (Myron Cohen, 1976). The degree to which the nuclear family is submerged and effaced by these arrangements is brought out by a custom formerly found in certain Taiwanese households: "adopt a daughter-in-law; marry a sister." In order to obtain control over their son's wife, the senior couple adopts a daughter. They bring this girl into the household at a very early age and train her to be hardworking and obedient. Later they oblige their son to marry this stepsister, thereby preventing the formation of an economically independent nuclear family within their midst, while at the same time conforming to the socially imposed incest prohibitions (A. Wolf, 1968).

Among the Rajputs of northern India, extended families take similar stern measures to maintain the subordination of each married pair. A young man and his wife are even forbidden to talk to each other in the presence of senior persons, meaning in effect that they

---

5.5 *TAIWAN MARRIAGE*
Groom's extended family assembled for wedding ceremony. [Myron L. Cohen]

"may converse only surreptitiously at night" (Minturn and Hitchcock, 1963, p. 241). Here the husband is not supposed to show an open concern for his wife's welfare; if she is ill, that is a matter for her mother-in-law or father-in-law to take care of: "The mother feeds her son even after he is married . . . she runs the family as long as she wishes to assume the responsibility."

As a final brief example of how extended families modify the nuclear constellation, there is Max Gluckman's (1955, p. 60) wry comment on the Barotse of Zambia: "If a man becomes too devoted to his wife he is assumed to be the victim of witchcraft."

Why do so many societies have extended families? Probably because nuclear families frequently lack sufficient manpower and womanpower to carry out both domestic and subsistence tasks effectively. Extended families provide a larger labor pool and can carry out a greater variety of simultaneous activities (Pasternak, Ember, and Ember, 1976).

One-parent domestic groups

Millions of children throughout the world are reared in domestic groups in which only one parent is present. This may result from divorce or death of one of the parents. But it also may result from inability or unwillingness to marry. The most common form of nonnuclear one-parent domestic arrangements is for the mother to be present and father to be absent. These are called *matrifocal* households. Mother more or less rapidly accepts a series of men as mates, usually one at a time, but sometimes polyandrously. The man and woman are usually coresident for brief periods, but over the years there may be long intervals during which mother does not have a resident mate.

At one extreme, associated with very rich or very poor women, mother and children may live alone. At the other extreme, mother and

her children may live together with her sisters and her mother and constitute a large extended family in which adult males play only temporary roles as visitors or lovers.

Matrifocal households are best known from studies carried out in the West Indies (Blake, 1961; M. G. Smith, 1966; R. T. Smith, 1973) and Latin America (Adams, 1968; Lewis, 1961, 1964), and among U.S. inner-city blacks (Furstenberg et al., 1975; Stack, 1974; Gonzalez, 1970; N. Tanner, 1974). However, the worldwide incidence of matrifocality has been obscured by the tendency to regard such domestic units as aberrant or pathological (Moynihan, 1965). In describing domestic groups, social scientists frequently concentrate on the emically preferred or ideal form and neglect the etic and behavioral actualities. Mother-child domestic groups are often the result of poverty and hence are associated with many social ills and regarded as undesirable. But there is no evidence that such domestic arrangements are inherently any more pathological, unstable, or contrary to "human nature" than the nuclear family (see p. 309).

Matrifocal extended family households shade imperceptibly into matrilocal (see Table 6.1) extended family households. Among the matrilocal Nayar, for example, mother's mates never resided with mother and children. Moreover, unlike matrifocal households, Nayar households contained several generations of males related through females. It was one of the senior males—that is, a mother's brother—who was the head of the household, not a grandmother, as in the case of the extended matrifocal family.

What is marriage?

One of the problems with the proposition that the nuclear family is the basic building block of all domestic groups is that it rests on the assumption that widely different forms of matings can all be called "marriage." Yet in order to cover the extraordinary diversity of mating behavior characteristic of the human species, the definition of marriage has to be made so broad as to be confusing. Among the many ingenious attempts to define marriage as a universally occurring relationship, the definition proposed by Kathleen Gough, who has studied among the Nayar, merits special attention. But it must be read more than once!

Marriage is a relationship established between a woman and one or more persons, which provides that a child born to the woman under circumstances not prohibited by the rules of the relationship, is accorded full birth-status rights common to normal members of his [or her] society or social stratum. (1968, p. 68)

According to Gough, for most if not all societies, this definition identifies a relationship "distinguished by the people themselves from all other kinds of relationships." Yet Gough's definition seems oddly at variance with English dictionary and native Western notions of marriage. First of all, there is no reference to rights and duties of sexual access, nor to simple sexual performance. Moreover, if Gough's definition is accepted, marriage need not involve a relationship between men and women. Gough merely specifies that there must be a woman and "one or more other persons" of undefined sex!

The main reason Gough does not mention sexual rights and duties is the case of the Nayar. In order to bear children in a socially acceptable manner, pubescent Nayar girls had to go through a four-day ceremony that linked them with a "ritual husband." Completion of this ceremony was a necessary prerequisite for the beginning of a Nayar woman's sexual and reproductive career. Ideally, the Nayar strove to find a ritual husband among the men of the higher-ranking Nambodri Brahman caste. The members of this caste were interested in having sex with Nayar

women, but they refused to regard the children of Nayar women as their heirs. So after the ritual marriage, Nayar women stayed home with their sisters and brothers and were visited by both Nambodri Brahmin and Nayar men. Gough regards the existence of the ritual husbands as proof of the universality of marriage (although not of the nuclear family), since only children born to ritually married Nayar women were "legitimate," even though the identity of their fathers was uncertain.

But what can be the reason for defining marriage as a relationship between a woman and "persons" rather than between "women and men"? There are several instances among African peoples—the Dahomey case is best known—in which women "marry" female "husbands." This is accomplished by having a woman, who herself is already usually married to a man, pay bride-price for a bride. The female bride-price payer becomes a "female husband." She founds a family of her own by letting her "wives" become pregnant through relationships with designated males. The offspring of these unions fall under the control of the "female father" rather than of the biological *genitors* (see p. 104).

Wide as it is, Gough's definition ignores mating relationships that have no women at all. Some anthropologists also include such man-man relationships in their definition of marriage. For example, among the Kwakiutl, a man who desires to acquire the privileges associated with a particular chief can "marry" the chief's male heir. If the chief has no heirs, a man may "marry" the chief's right or left side, or a leg or an arm.

In Euramerican culture, enduring mating relationships between coresident homosexual men are also often spoken of as marriage. It has thus been suggested that all reference to the sex of the people involved in the relationship should be omitted in the definition of marriage in order to accommodate such cases (Dillingham and Isaac, 1975). Yet the task of understanding varieties of domestic organization is made more difficult when all these different forms of mating are crammed into the single concept of marriage. Part of the problem is that when matings in Western culture are refused the designation "marriage," there is an unjust tendency to regard them as less honorable or less authentic relationships. And so anthropologists are reluctant to stigmatize woman-woman or man-man matings or Nayar or matrifocal visiting mate arrangements by saying they are not marriages. But whatever we call them, it is clear that they cover an enormous behavioral and mental range. There is no scientific evidence that any one of them is less desirable or less human, provided that they do not involve the coercion, abuse, and exploitation of one of the partners (a provision that applies, of course, to Western man-woman monogamy as well).

Since the term *marriage* is too useful to drop altogether, a more narrow definition seems appropriate: *Marriage* denotes the behavior, sentiments, and rules concerned with coresident heterosexual mating and reproduction in domestic contexts.

To accommodate sensitivities that may be injured by using marriage exclusively for coresident heterosexual domestic mates, a simple expedient is available. Let such other relationships be designated as "noncoresident marriages," "man-man marriages," "woman-woman marriages," or by any other appropriate specific nomenclature. It is clear that these matings have different ecological, demographic, economic, and ideological implications, so nothing is to be gained by arguing about whether they are "real" marriages.

Legitimacy

The essence of the marital relationship, according to some anthropologists, is embodied in that portion of Gough's definition dealing with the assignment of "birth-status rights" to children. Children born to a married woman "under circumstances not prohibited by the rules of the relationship" (e.g., adultery) are legal or legitimate children. Children born to unmarried women are illegitimate. As Bronislaw Malinowski put it: "Marriage is the licensing of parenthood."

The case for the universality of marriage rests on the claim that every society draws an emic distinction between legitimate or legal childrearing and illegitimate or illegal childrearing. It is true that in all societies women are discouraged from attempting to rear children or dispose of their newborn infants according to their own whim and capacities. But the concept of legal or legitimate childbirth is not universal. Behind this concept lies the assumption that every society has a single, well-defined set of rules that identify legitimate and illegitimate births. There is the further assumption that those who violate these rules will be subject to punishment or disapproval. Both assumptions lack firm empirical support. Many societies have several different sets of rules defining permissible modes of conception and childrearing. Frequently enough some of these alternatives may be esteemed more highly than others, but the less esteemed modes do not necessarily place children in a status analogous to that of Western illegitimacy (Scheffler, 1973, pp. 754–755). For example, among Brazilians living in small towns there are four kinds of relationships between a man and a woman, all of which provide children with full birth rights: church marriage, civil marriage, simultaneous church and civil marriage, and consensual marriage. For a Brazilian woman the most esteemed way to have children is through simultaneous church and civil marriage. This mode legally entitles her to a portion of her husband's property upon his death. It also provides the added security of knowing that her husband cannot desert her and enter into a civil or religious mariage elsewhere. The least desirable mode is the consensual marriage, because the woman can make no property claims against her consort, nor can she readily prevent him from deserting her. Yet the children of a consensual arrangement can make property claims against both father and mother while suffering no deprivation of birth rights in the form of legal disadvantages or social disapproval as long as the father acknowledges paternity.

Among the Dahomey, Herskovits (1938) reported thirteen different kinds of marriage determined largely by bride-price arrangements. Children enjoyed different birth rights depending on the type of marriage. In some marriages the child was placed under the control of the father's domestic group and in others under the control of a domestic group headed by a female "father" (see above). The point is not that a child is legitimate or illegitimate, but rather that there are specific types of rights, obligations, and groupings that emanate from different modes of sexual and reproductive relations. Most of the world's peoples are not concerned with the question of whether a child is legitimate, but with the question of who will have the right of controlling the child's destiny. Thus failure to follow the preferred mode of conception and childrearing rarely results in the child's economic deprivation or social ostracism. Western society has been an exception in this regard.

Various degrees of punishment and disapproval are administered to the woman who fails to fulfill the preferred conditions for motherhood. Even in this respect, however, it is false to assume that women are everywhere subject to some form of disapproval if they depart from the preferred course of childrearing. Everything depends on the larger domestic and social context in which the woman has become pregnant. No society grants women complete "freedom of conception," but the restrictions placed on motherhood and the occasions for punishment and disapproval vary enormously.

Where the domestic scene is dominated by large extended families and where there are no strong restrictions on premarital sex, the pregnancy of a young married woman is rarely the occasion for much concern. Under certain circumstances, an "unwed mother" may even be congratulated rather than condemned. Among the Kadar of northern Nigeria, as reported by M. G. Smith (1968), most marriages result from infant betrothals. These matches are arranged by the fathers of the bride and groom when the girl is 3 to 6 years old. Ten years or more may elapse before the bride goes to live with her betrothed. During this time, a Kadar girl is not unlikely to become pregnant. This will disturb no one, even if the biological father is a man other than her future husband:

Kadar set no value on premarital chastity. It is fairly common for unmarried girls to be impregnated or to give birth to children by youths other than their betrothed. Offspring of such premarital pregnancies are members of the patrilineage . . . of the girl's betrothed and are welcomed as proof of the bride's fertility. (1968, p. 113)

Analogous situations are quite common among other societies whose domestic groups value children above chastity.

Functions of marriage

Every society regulates the reproductive activities of its sexually mature adults. One way of achieving this regulation is to set forth rules that define the conditions under which sexual relations, pregnancy, birth, and childrearing may take place and that allocate privileges and duties in connection with these conditions. Each society has its own sometimes unique combination of rules and rules for breaking rules in this domain. It would be a rather futile exercise to attempt to define marriage by any one ingredient in these rules —such as legitimation of children—even if such an ingredient could be shown to be universal. This point can be illustrated by enumerating some of the variable regulatory functions associated with institutions commonly identified as "marriage." The following list incorporates suggestions made by Edmund Leach (1968). Marriage *sometimes*

1 Establishes the legal father of a woman's children
2 Establishes the legal mother of a man's children
3 Gives the husband or his extended family control over the wife's sexual services
4 Gives the wife or her extended family control over the husband's sexual services
5 Gives the husband or his extended family control over the wife's labor power
6 Gives the wife or her extended family control over the husband's labor power
7 Gives the husband or his extended family control over the wife's property
8 Gives the wife or her extended family control over the husband's property.
9 Establishes a joint fund of property for the benefit of children
10 Establishes a socially significant relationship between the husband's and the wife's domestic groups.

As Leach remarks, this list could be greatly extended, but the point is "that in no single society can marriage serve to establish all these types of rights simultaneously, nor is there any one of these rights which is invariably established by marriage in every known society" (1968, p. 76).

Marriage in extended families

In extended families, marriage must be seen primarily in the context of group interests. Individuals serve the interests of the extended family: The larger domestic group never loses interest in or totally surrenders its rights to

the productive, the reproductive, and the sexual functions of spouses and children. Marriage under these circumstances is aptly described as an "alliance" between groups. This alliance influences present and future matings involving other members of both groups.

Among many societies, the corporate nature of marriage is revealed by the exchange of personnel or of valuable goods between the respective domestic groups in which bride and groom were born. The simplest form of such transactions is called *sister exchange* and involves the reciprocal "giving away" of the groom's sisters in compensation for the loss of a woman from each group.

Among many peoples around the world, corporate interests are expressed in the insti-

5.6 *BRIDE-PRICE*
Among the Kapauku, the bride-price consists of shell money. [Leopold Pospisil]

tution known as *bride-price* (Fig. 5.6). The wife-receiver gives valuable items to the wife-giver. Of course, bride-price is not equivalent to the selling and buying of automobiles or refrigerators in modern industrial price-market societies. The wife-receivers do not "own" their woman in any total sense; they must take good care of her or her brothers and "fathers" (i.e., her father and father's brothers) will demand that she be returned to them. The amount of bride-price is not fixed; it fluctuates from one marriage to another. (In Africa the traditional measure of "bride wealth" was cattle, although other valuables such as iron tools were also used. Nowadays, cash payments are the rule.) Among the Bathonga, a family that had many daughter-sisters was in a favorable position. By exchanging women for cattle, they could exchange cattle back for women. The more cattle, the more mother-wives; the more mother-wives, the larger the reproductive and productive labor force and the greater the corporate material welfare and influence of the extended family.

Sometimes the transfer of wealth from one group to another is carried out in instalments: so much on initial agreement, more when the woman goes to live with her husband, and another, usually final, payment when she has her first child. Failure to have a child often voids the marriage; the woman goes home to her brothers and fathers, and the husband gets his bride-price back.

A common alternative to bride-price is known as *bride-service* (sometimes called *suitor-service*). The groom or husband compensates his in-laws by working for them for several months or years before taking his bride away to live and work with him and his extended family. Bride-service may be involved in the conditions under which matrilocal residence tends to occur, as we will see in Chapter 6. If the suitor lingers on and never takes his bride home, he may be participating in an etic shift from patrilocal to matrilocal residence.

Bride-price and suitor-service tend to occur where production is being increased, land is plentiful, and the labor of additional women and children is seen as scarce and as being in the best interests of the corporate group (Goody, 1976). Where the corporate group is not interested in or not capable of expanding production or in increasing its numbers, wives may be regarded as a burden. Instead of paying bride-price to the family of the bride, the groom's family may demand a reverse payment, called *dowry* (Fig. 5.7). When this payment consists of money or movable property instead of land, it is usually associated with a low or oppressed status for women.

The opposite of bride-price is not dowry but *groom-price*, in which the groom goes to work

for the bride's family and the bride's family compensates the groom's family for the loss of his productive and reproductive powers. This form of marriage compensation is extremely rare—only one well-documented case is known (Nash, 1974)—probably for reasons having to do with the prevalence of male supremacist institutions (see p. 247).

Domestic groups and the avoidance of incest

All these exchanges point to the existence of a profound paradox in the way human beings find mates. Marriage between members of the same domestic group is widely prohibited. Husband and wife must come from separate domestic groups. The members of the domestic group must "marry out"—that is, marry *exogamously;* they cannot "marry in"—that is, marry *endogamously.*

Certain forms of endogamy are universally prohibited. No culture tolerates father-daughter and mother-son marriages. Sister-brother marriage is also widely prohibited, but not among the ruling class of highly stratified societies such as the Inca, native Hawaii, and ancient Egypt. In the emics of Western civilization, sister-brother, father-daughter, and mother-son marriages are called *incest.* Why are these marriages so widely prohibited?

Explanations of nuclear family incest prohibition fall into two major types: (1) those that stress an instinctual component and (2) those that emphasize the social and cultural advantages of exogamy.

1. Instinct There is some evidence that unrelated children of opposite sex who live together during childhood lose interest in each other as sexual partners. Boys and girls brought up together in "children's houses" on Israeli kibbutzim (communal farms) seldom have sexual affairs and rarely marry each other (Shepher, 1971; Spiro, 1954). It has also been found that Taiwanese marriages of

the adopt-a-daughter—marry-a-sister variety (see p. 90) in which husband and wife grow up together lead to fewer children, greater adultery, and higher divorce rates than marriages in which husband and wife remain in different households until the marriage night (A. Wolf, 1974).

These cases have been interpreted as proof of the existence of genetically based mechanisms that produce sexual aversions among people who grow up together. The existence of this aversion has been attributed to natural selection. It is held that individuals who lacked such an aversion and who mated incestuously tended to have decreased fitness (E. Wilson, 1978, pp. 38–39).

Against this line of theories there are the following arguments: Marriage of kibbutz members takes place after a long period of compulsory military service during which young men and women are exposed to a larger range of potential mates. Moreover, on return from military service, kibbutz members are sent out individually to colonize new settlements (Y. Cohen, 1978). As for Wolf's data, the Taiwanese explicitly recognize that the adopt-a-daughter—marry-a-sister marriage is an inferior form of union. The preferred form of marriage, which involves the largest dowries and bride-price exchanges, and hence the greatest degree of support from both the bride's and groom's extended families, is the one in which bride and groom remain separated until the marriage night. It is to be expected, therefore, quite apart from instinctual aversions, that live-together-as-children marriages will not be as successful as the more typical live-apart-as-children marriages.

Further difficulties with the instinct theory arise when one considers the evidence for the harmful effects of homozygosity in small populations. It is true that in large modern populations incest leads to a high proportion of stillbirths and congenitally diseased and impaired children. But there is considerable doubt whether the same applies to small populations in band and village societies. As Frank Livingstone (1969) has pointed out, inbreeding leads to the gradual elimination of harmful recessive genes. If a small inbreeding group is able to overcome the higher rate at which impaired homozygotes initially occur, it will eventually reach a genetic equilibrium involving a lowered percentage of harmful alleles. The effect of close inbreeding depends upon the original frequency of harmful alleles. Theoretically, a succession of nuclear families could practice inbreeding for several generations without adverse effects. Cleopatra (Fig. 5.8), queen of Egypt, was the product of eleven generations of brother-sister marriage within the Ptolemaic dynasty. This should not be passed on as a recommendation to friends and relatives since the odds (in modern populations) appear to be very much against such favorable results (Adams and Neil, 1967; Stern, 1973, p. 497).

Modern populations carry a much greater "load" of harmful genes than small, demographically stable bands and villages. According to Livingstone, the chances of genetic catastrophes arising among groups that are already highly inbred is much less than in a modern outbred population. Small inbred village groups, such as the Kaingang of central Brazil, have remarkably low frequencies of harmful recessives. Most band and village peoples show little tolerance for infants and children who are congenitally handicapped and impaired. Such children are likely to become the victims of infanticide or systematic neglect and unlikely to pass on their harmful genes.

The proposal that there is an instinctual sexual aversion within the nuclear family is also contradicted by evidence of strong sexual attraction between father and daughter and mother and son. Freudian psychoanalysis indicates that children and parents of the opposite sex have a strong desire to have sexual encounters with each other. Indeed, in the case of the father-daughter relationship, at least,

5.8 *CLEOPATRA*
Product of 11 generations of brother-sister marriage. [Granger]

these wishes are acted upon more frequently than is popularly believed. Social workers, for example, estimate that tens of thousands of cases of incest occur in the United States annually, of which the great majority are of the father-daughter variety (Armstrong, 1978). Finally, the instinct theory of incest avoidance is hard to reconcile with the widespread occurrence of endogamous practices that are carried out simultaneously and in support of exogamic arrangements. Members of exogamous extended families, for example, frequently are involved in marriage systems that encourage them to mate with one kind of first cousin (*cross cousin*) but not another (*parallel cousin*, see p. 107). The difference between these two forms of inbreeding cannot be explained satisfactorily by natural selection (but see Alexander, 1977). Furthermore, the widespread preference for some form of cousin marriage itself weighs against the conclusion that exogamy expresses an instinct established by the harmful effects of inbreeding.

2. Social and cultural advantages of exogamy Nuclear family incest avoidance and other forms of exogamy among domestic groups can be explained quite effectively in terms of demographic, economic, and ecological advantages. These advantages are not necessarily the same for all societies. It is known, for example, that band societies rely on marriage exchanges to establish long-distance networks of kinspeople. Bands that formed a completely closed breeding unit would be denied the mobility and territorial flexibility essential to their subsistence strategy. Territorially restricted, endogamous bands of twenty to thirty people would also run a high risk of extinction as a result of sexual imbalances caused by an unlucky run of male births and adult female deaths, which would place the burden for the group's reproduction on one or two aging females. Exogamy is thus essential for the effective utilization of a small population's productive and reproductive potential. Once a band begins to obtain mates from other bands, the prevalence of reciprocal economic relations leads to the expectation that the receivers will reciprocate. The taboos on mother-son, father-daughter, and brother-sister marriages can therefore be interpreted as a defense of these reciprocal exchange relationships against the ever-present temptation for parents to keep their children

for themselves, or for brothers and sisters to keep each other for themselves.

In this connection it is frequently overlooked that sexual encounters between father-daughter and mother-son constitute a form of adultery. Mother-son incest is an especially threatening variety of adultery in societies that have strong male supremacist institutions. Not only is the wife "double-dealing" against her husband, but the son is "double-dealing" against his father. This may explain why the least common and emically most feared and abhorred form of incest is that between mother and son. It follows that father-daughter incest will be somewhat more common, since husbands enjoy double standards of sexual behavior more often than wives and are less vulnerable to punishment for adultery. Finally, the same consideration suggests an explanation for the relatively high frequency of brother-sister matings and their legitimizations as marriages in elite classes—they do not conflict with father-mother adultery rules.

Exogamy increases the total productive and reproductive strength of the intermarried groups. It permits the exploitation of resources over a larger area than the nuclear or extended families could manage on an individual basis; it facilitates trade; and it raises the upper limit of the size of groups that can be formed to carry out seasonal activities (e.g., communal game drives, harvests, and so on) that require large labor inputs. Furthermore, where intergroup warfare poses a threat to group survival, the ability to mobilize large numbers of warriors is decisive. Hence, in militaristic, highly male-centered village cultures, sisters and daughters are frequently used as pawns in the establishment of alliances.

Among elite classes and castes, marriage alliances are often used to maintain wealth and power within the ruling stratum (see p. 150). But as already noted, even the nuclear family may become endogamous when there is an extreme concentration of political, economic, and military power. With the evolution of price-market forms of exchange, the extended family tends to be replaced by nuclear family domestic units. Domestic group alliances lose some of their previous adaptive importance, and the traditional functions of the incest avoidance must be reinterpreted. Yehudi Cohen (1978) suggests that incest taboo may be largely obsolete in the context of modern state societies and that the present laws against incest may soon be repealed. Yet given the scientific knowledge that nuclear family incest is genetically risky in populations carrying a heavy load of harmful recessives, the repeal of anti-incest legislation seems unlikely and unwise.

The possibility that incest avoidance is genetically programmed in *Homo sapiens* has received some support from field studies of monkey and ape mating behavior. As among humans, father-daughter, mother-son, and brother-sister matings are uncommon among our nearest animal relatives. However, to some extent the avoidance of sex by these pairs can be explained in terms of male dominance and sexual rivalry. There is no experimental evidence suggesting an aversion to incest per se among monkeys and apes. Moreover, even if such an instinctual aversion did exist, its significance for human nature would remain in doubt (see Demarest, 1977).

Preferential marriages

The widespread occurrence of exogamy implies that the corporate interests of domestic groups must be protected by rules that stipulate who is to marry whom. Having given a woman away in marriage, most groups expect either material wealth or women in exchange. Consider two domestic groups, A and B, each with a core of resident brothers. If A gives a woman to B, B may immediately reciprocate by giving a woman to A. This reci-

procity is often achieved by a direct exchange of the groom's sister. But the reciprocity may take a more indirect form. B may return a daughter of the union between the B man and the A woman. The bride in such a marriage will be her husband's father's sister's daughter, and the groom will be his wife's mother's brother's son. (The same result would be achieved by a marriage between a man and his mother's brother's daughter.) Bride and groom are each other's cross cousins (see p. 107). If A and B have a rule that such marriages are to occur whenever possible, then they are said to have *preferential cross-cousin marriage*.

Reciprocity in marriage is sometimes achieved by several intermarrying domestic groups that exchange women in cycles. For example, $A \rightarrow B \rightarrow C \rightarrow A$; or $A \rightarrow B$ and $C \rightarrow D$ in one generation and $A \rightarrow D$ and $B \rightarrow C$ in the next, and then back to $A \rightarrow B$ and $C \rightarrow D$. These exchanges are enforced by preferential marriage with appropriate kinds of cousins, nephews, nieces, and other kin.

Another common manifestation of corporate domestic interest in marriage is the practice of supplying replacements for inmarrying women who die prematurely. To maintain reciprocity or to fulfill a marriage contract for which bride-price has been paid, the brother of a deceased woman may permit the widower to marry one or more of the deceased wife's sisters. This custom is known as the *sororate*. Closely related to this practice is the preferential marriage known as the *levirate*, in which the services of a man's widows are retained within the domestic unit by having them marry one of his brothers. If the widows are old, these services may be minimal, and the levirate then functions to provide security for women who would otherwise not be able to remarry.

Thus the organization of domestic life everywhere reflects the fact that husbands and wives usually originate in different domestic groups that continue to maintain a sentimental and practical interest in the marriage partners and their children.

Summary

The structural level of sociocultural systems is made up in part by interrelated domestic groups. Such groups can usually be identified by their attachment to a living space or domicile in which activities such as eating, sleeping, marital sex, and nurturance and the discipline of the very young take place. However, there is no single or minimal pattern of domestic activities. Similarly, the nuclear family cannot be regarded as the minimal building block of all domestic groups. While nuclear families occur in almost every society, they are not always the dominant domestic group, and their sexual, reproductive, and productive functions can readily be satisfied by alternative domestic and nondomestic institutions. In polygamous and extended families, the father-mother-child subset may not enjoy any practical existence apart from the set of other relatives and their multiple spouses. And there are many instances of domestic groups that lack a coresident husband-father. Although children need to be nurtured and protected, no one knows the limits within which human domestic arrangements must be confined in order to satisfy human nature. One of the most important facts about human domestic arrangements is that no single pattern can be shown to be more "natural" than any other.

Human mating patterns also exhibit an enormous degree of variation. While something similar to what is called marriage occurs all over the world, it is difficult to specify the mental and behavioral essence of the marital relationship. Man-man, woman-woman, female father, and childless marriages make it difficult to give a minimal definition of marriage without hurting someone's feelings. Even coresidence may not be essential, as the Nayar and other single-parent households demonstrate. Even when we restrict the definition of marriage to coresident heterosexual matings that result in reproduction, there is a staggering variety of rights and duties associated with the productive sexual and reproductive functions of the marriage partners and their offspring.

In order to understand coresident heterosexual reproductive marriage in extended families, marriage must be seen as a relationship between corporate groups as much as between cohabiting mates. The divergent interests of these corporate groups are reconciled by means of reciprocal exchanges which take the form of sister exchange, bride-price, suitor service, dowry, and groom-price. The common principle underlying these exchanges, except for dowry, is that in giving a man or woman away to another extended family, the domestic corporation does not renounce its interest in the offspring of the mated pair and expects compensation for the loss of a valuable worker.

Most domestic groups are exogamous. This can be seen as a result of instinctual programming or social and cultural adaptation. The discussion of exogamy necessarily centers on the incest prohibitions within the nuclear family. Father-daughter, sister-brother, and mother-son matings and marriages are almost universally forbidden. The chief exception is brother-sister marriages, which occur in several highly stratified societies among the ruling elites. The instinct theory of incest avoidance stresses evidence from Taiwan and Israel, which suggests that children reared together develop a sexual aversion to each other. This aversion is seen as genetically determined, since it reduces the risk of harmful genes. Other interpretations of the Taiwan and Israel studies can be made. A purely cultural theory of incest avoidance can be built out of the need for bands and domestic groups to defend their capacity to engage in reciprocal marriage exchanges by preventing parents from keeping their children for themselves. In the future, the perpetuation of the incest taboos may be related exclusively to the increasing genetic dangers associated with close inbreeding in populations carrying a large load of harmful genes.

Exogamy and incest avoidance form only a small part of the spectrum of preferred and prohibited marriages that reflect the pervasive corporate interests of domestic groups. Marriage exchange between domestic groups may be direct or indirect. Marriage preferences may be expressed as a rule requiring marriage with a particular kind of cousin. Preferential marriage rules such as the levirate and sororate also exemplify the corporate nature of the marriage bond.

Kinship, Locality, and Descent

This chapter continues the discussion of domestic organization. It examines the principal mental and emic components of domestic groups and relates them to the etic and behavioral aspects of those groups. It also sets forth some of the theories that relate the mental and behavioral variations in domestic organization to infrastructural conditions.

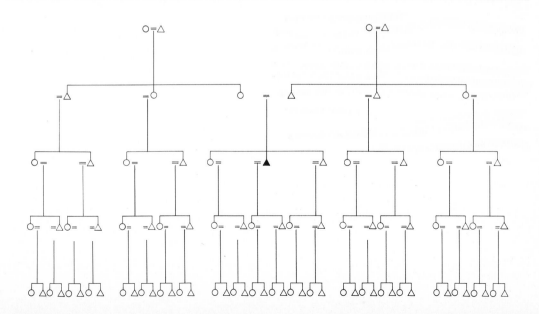

Kinship

The study of domestic life in hundreds of cultures all over the world has led anthropologists to conclude that two ideas or mental principles are involved in the organization of domestic life everywhere. The first of these is the idea of *affinity*, or of relationships through marriage. The second is the idea of *descent*, or parentage. People who are related to each other through descent or a combination of affinity and descent are relatives, or *kin*. The domain of ideas constituted by the beliefs and expectations kin share about one another is called *kinship*. The study of kinship, therefore, must begin with the mental and emic components of domestic life.

Descent[1]

Kinship relations are often confused with biological relations. But the emic meaning of descent is not the biological meaning of descent. As we have seen (p. 92), marriage may explicitly establish "parentage" with respect to children who are biologically unrelated to their culturally defined "father." Even where a culture insists that descent must be based on actual biological fatherhood, domestic arrangements may make it difficult to identify the biological father. For these reasons, anthropologists distinguish between the culturally defined "father" and the *genitor*, the actual biological father. A similar distinction is necessary in the case of "mother." Although the culturally defined mother is usually the *genetrix*, the widespread practice of adoption also creates many discrepancies between emic and etic motherhood.

[1] British social anthropologists restrict the term "descent" to relationships extending over more than two generations and use "filiation" to denote descent relationships within the nuclear family (Fortes, 1969).

Theories of reproduction and heredity vary from culture to culture, "but so far as we know, no human society is without such a theory" (Scheffler, 1973, p. 749). Descent, then, is the belief that certain persons play an important role in the creation, birth, and nurturance of certain children. As Daniel Craig (1979) has suggested, descent implies the preservation of some aspect of the substances or spirit of people in future generations and thus is a symbolic form of immortality. Perhaps that is why parentage and descent are universally believed in.

In Western folk traditions, married pairs are linked to children on the basis of the belief that male and female make equally important contributions to the child's being. The male's semen is regarded as analogous to seed, and the woman's womb is analogous to the field in which the seed is planted. Blood, the most important life-sustaining and life-defining fluid, supposedly varies according to parentage. Each child's body is thought of as being filled with blood obtained from mother and father. As a result of this imagery, "blood relatives" are distinguished from relatives who are linked only through marriage. This led nineteenth-century anthropologists to use the ethnocentric term *consanguine* (of the same blood) to denote relations of descent.

Descent need not depend upon the idea of blood inheritance, nor need it involve equal contributions from both father and mother. The Ashanti, for example, believe that blood is contributed only by the mother and that it determines only a child's physical characteristics. The Ashanti believe that a child's spiritual disposition and temperament is the product of the father's semen. The Alorese of Indonesia believe that the child is formed by a mixture of seminal and menstrual fluids, which accumulate for two months before beginning to solidify. Many other cultures share this idea of a slow growth of fetus as a result of repeated additions of semen during pregnancy. For the polyandrous Tamil of the Malabar Coast of India, the semen of several different males is believed to contribute to the growth of the same fetus. The Eskimo believe that pregnancy results when a spirit child climbs up a woman's bootstraps and is nourished by semen. The Trobrianders profess a famous dogma denying any procreative role to the semen. Here also, a woman becomes pregnant when a spirit child climbs into her vagina. The only physical function of the Trobriand male is to widen the passageway into the womb. The Trobriand "father," nonetheless, has an essential social role, since no self-respecting spirit child would climb into a Trobriand girl who was not married.

A similar denial of the male's procreative role occurs throughout Australia; among the Murngin, for example, there was the belief that the spirit children live deep below the surface of certain sacred waterholes. For conception to take place, one of these spirits appears in the future father's dreams. In the dream the spirit child introduces itself and asks its father to point out the woman who is to become its mother. Later, when this women passes near the sacred waterhole, the spirit child swims out in the form of a fish and enters her womb.

Despite the many different kinds of theories about the nature of procreative roles, there is worldwide acknowledgment of some special contributory action linking both husband and wife to the reproductive process, although they may be linked quite unevenly and with vastly different expectations concerning rights and obligations.

Descent rules

By reckoning descent relationships, individuals are apportioned different duties, rights, and privileges with respect to other people and with regard to many different aspects of social life. A person's name, family, residence, rank, property, and basic ethnic and national status may all depend on such *ascriptions* through descent independent of any *achievements* other than getting born and staying alive. (Ascribed statuses and achieved statuses are found in all cultures.)

Anthropologists distinguish two great classes of descent rules: the *cognatic* and the *unilineal. Cognatic descent rules* are those in which both male and female parentage are used to establish any of the above-mentioned duties, rights, and privileges. Unilineal descent rules restrict parental links exclusively to males or exclusively to females (Fig. 6.1). The most common form of cognatic rule is *bilateral descent*, the reckoning of kinship evenly and symmetrically along maternal and paternal lines in ascending and descending generations through individuals of both sexes (Fig. 6.2).

The second main variety of cognatic rule is called *ambilineal* descent (Fig. 6.3). Here the descent lines traced by *ego*[2] ignore the sex of the parental links, but the lines do not lead in all directions evenly. As in bilateral descent, ego traces descent through males and females, but the line twists back and forth, including some female ancestors or descendants but excluding others and including some male ancestors or descendants and excluding others. In other words, ego does not reckon descent simultaneously and equally through mothers, fathers, and grandparents.

There are also two main varieties of unilineal descent: *patrilineality* and *matrilineality*. When descent is reckoned patrilineally, ego follows the ascending and descending genealogical lines through males only (Fig. 6.4). Note that this does not mean that the descent-related individuals are only males; in each generation there are relatives of both sexes. However, in the passage from one generation

[2] Anthropologists employ the word *ego* to denote the "I" from whose point of view kinship relations are being reckoned. It is sometimes necessary to state whether the reference person is a male ego or a female ego.

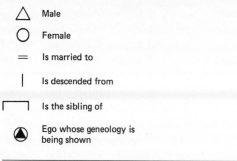

△ Male

○ Female

= Is married to

| Is descended from

⌐⌐ Is the sibling of

◉ Ego whose geneology is being shown

6.1 HOW TO READ KINSHIP DIAGRAMS (*above*)

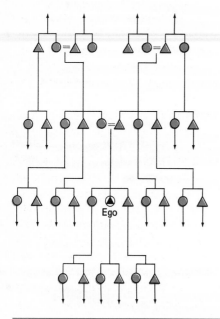

6.2 BILATERAL DESCENT (*above*)
Everyone on the diagram has a descent relationship with Ego.

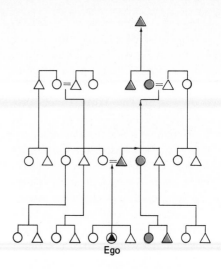

Ego

6.3 AMBILINEAL DESCENT (*above*)
Ego traces descent through both males and females, but not equally and not simultaneously.

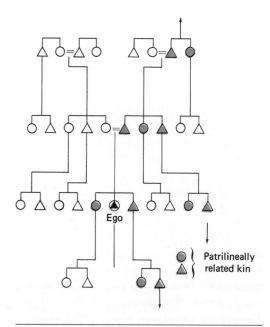

○ ⎱ Patrilineally
△ ⎰ related kin

6.4 PATRILINEAL DESCENT (*above*)
Descent is traced exclusively through males.

to another only the male links are relevant; children of females are dropped from the descent reckoning.

When descent is reckoned matrilineally, ego follows the ascending and descending lines through females only (Fig. 6.5). Once again, it should be noted that males as well as females can be related matrilineally; it is only in the passage from one generation to another

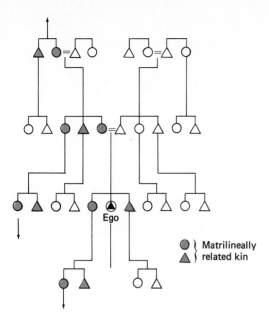

6.5 MATRILINEAL DESCENT
Descent is traced exclusively
through females.

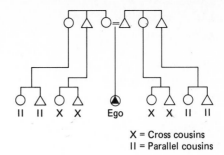

X = Cross cousins
II = Parallel cousins

6.6 CROSS COUSINS AND PARALLEL COUSINS

that the children of males are dropped from
the descent reckoning.

One of the important logical consequences of unilineal descent is that it segre-
gates the children of siblings of the opposite
sex into distinct categories. This effect is especially important in the case of cousins. Note
that with patrilineal descent, ego's father's
sister's son and daughter do not share common descent with ego, whereas ego's father's
brother's son and daughter do share common
descent with ego. In the case of matrilineal
descent, the same kind of distinction results
with respect to ego's "cousins" on the
mother's side. Children whose parents are related to each other as brother and sister are
known as *cross cousins;* children whose parents are related to each other as brother and
brother or sister and sister are known as
parallel cousins (Fig. 6.6).

Anthropologists distinguish an additional
variety of descent rule, called *double descent,*

in which ego simultaneously reckons descent
matrilineally through mother and patrilineally through father. This differs from unilineal descent, in which descent is reckoned only
through males or only through females but
not both together.

Many other combinations of these descent
rules may also occur. In all cultures, for example, there is some degree of bilateral descent in the reckoning of rights and obligations. If a society observes patrilineal descent
in the grouping of people into landowning domestic groups, this does not mean that ego
and mother's brother's daughter do not regard each other as having special rights and
obligations. Modern Euramerican culture
is strongly bilateral in kin group composition
and inheritance of wealth and property; yet
family names are *patronymic*—that is, they
follow patrilineal descent lines. The point is
that several varieties of descent may occur
simultaneously within a given society if the
descent rules are pertinent to different
spheres of thought and behavior.

Each of the above descent rules provides
the logical basis for mentally aligning people
into emic kinship groups. These groups exert
great influence on the way people think and
behave in both domestic and extradomestic
situations. An important point to bear in
mind about kinship groups is that they need
not consist of coresident relatives; that is,
they need not be domestic groups. We pro-

ceed now to a description of the principal varieties of such groups.

Cognatic descent groups: bilateral variety

Bilateral descent applied to an indefinitely wide span of kin and to an indefinite number of generations leads to the concept of groups known as *kindreds* (Fig. 6.7). When modern-day Americans and Europeans use the word "family" and have in mind more than just their nuclear families, they are referring to their kindreds. The main characteristic of the kindred is that the span and depth of bilateral reckoning is open-ended. Relatives within ego's kindred can be judged as "near" or "far" depending on the number of genealogical

6.7 *KINDREDS*
Children have kindreds that are different from either parent's kindred.

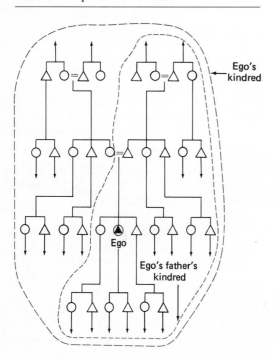

links that separate them, but there is no definite or uniform principle for making such judgments or for terminating the extension of the kinship circle. An important consequence of this feature, as shown in Figure 6.7, is that egos and their siblings are identified with a kindred whose membership cannot be the same for any other persons (except for ego's *double cousins*—cousins whose parents are two brothers who have exchanged sisters). This means that it is impossible for coresident domestic groups to consist of kindreds and very difficult for kindreds to maintain corporate interests in land and people.

Cognatic descent groups: ambilineal variety

The open-ended, ego-centered characteristics of the bilateral kindred can be overcome by specifying one or more ancestors from whom descent is traced either through males and/or females. The resultant group logically has a membership that is the same regardless of which ego carries out the reckoning. This is the *cognatic lineage* (the terms *ramage* and *sept* are also used) (Fig. 6.8).

The cognatic lineage is based on the assumption that all members of the descent group are capable of specifying the precise genealogical links relating them to the lineage founder. A common alternative, as in the ambilineal "clans" of Scotland, is for the descent from the lineage founder to be *stipulated* rather than *demonstrated*. This can be done easily enough if the name of the founder gets passed on ambilineally over many generations. After a while many of the persons who carry the name will belong to the group simply by virtue of the name rather than because they can trace their genealogical relationship all the way back to the founding ancestor. An appropriate designation for such groups is *cognatic clan.* (In recent times, some members of Scots clans have different surnames as a re-

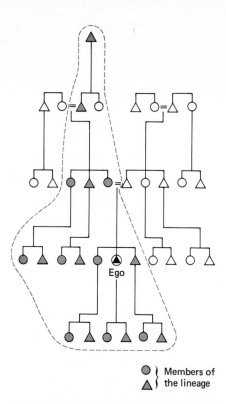

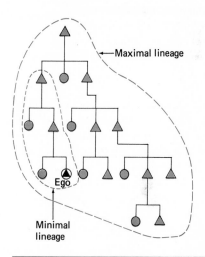

hood. Some lineages include all the generations and collateral descendants of the first ancestor. These are *maximal* lineages. Lineages that contain only three generations are *minimal* lineages (Fig. 6.9).

When unilineal descent from a specific ancestor is stipulated rather than demonstrated, the group that results is known as either a *patriclan* or a *matriclan* (the terms *patrisib* and *matrisib* are also in use). There are many borderline cases, however, in which it is difficult to decide whether one is dealing with a lineage or a clan. Just as lineages may contain lineages, clans may contain clans, which are usually called subclans. Finally, it should be noted that clans may also contain lineages.

Postmarital locality patterns

In order to understand the processes responsible for different varieties of domestic groups and different ideologies of descent, one additional aspect of domestic organization must be discussed. There is considerable agreement among anthropologists that an impor-

○ } Members of
△ } the lineage

6.8 COGNATIC LINEAGE
Descent is traced to an apical ancestor through males and/or females.

sult of patronymy and must demonstrate descent. Neville, 1979.)

Unilineal descent groups

When unilineal descent is systematically demonstrated with respect to a particular ancestor, the resultant kin group is called a *patrilineage* (Fig. 6.9) or a *matrilineage*. All lineages contain the same set of people regardless of the genealogical perspective from which they are viewed. This makes them ideally suited to be coresident domestic groups and to hold joint interests in persons and property. Because of exogamy, however, both sexes cannot remain coresident beyond child-

← Maximal lineage

Minimal lineage

6.9 PATRILINEAGES
Everyone on the diagram belongs to the same maximal lineage.

TABLE 6.1 PRINCIPAL VARIETIES OF POSTMARITAL RESIDENCE

Name of pattern	Place where married couple resides
Neolocality	Apart from either husband's or wife's kin
Bilocality	Alternately shifting from husband's kin to wife's kin
Ambilocality	Some couples with husband's kin, others with wife's kin
Patrilocality	With husband's father
Matrilocality	With wife's mother
Avunculocality	With husband's mother's brother
Amitalocality	With wife's father's sister (this pattern exists only as a theoretical possibility)
Uxorilocality	With the wife's kin (several of the above may be combined with uxorilocality)
Virilocality	With the husband's kin (several of the above may be combined with virilocality)

tant determinant of descent rules is the pattern of residence after marriage. The principal postmarital locality practices are described in Table 6.1.

Postmarital residence practices influence descent rules because they determine who will enter, leave, or stay in a domestic group (Murdock, 1949; Naroll, 1973). They thus provide domestic groups with distinctive cores of relatives that correspond to the inclusions and exclusions produced by the movements of married couples. These movements themselves are influenced by the demographic, technological, economic, and ecological conditions in which people find themselves. Thus in many societies descent rules and other kinship principles can be seen as organizing and justifying domestic group structures in relation to particular infrastructural conditions.

Causes of bilateral descent

Bilateral descent is associated with various combinations of neolocality, ambilocality, and bilocality. These locality practices in turn

usually reflect a high degree of mobility and flexibility among nuclear families. Mobility and flexibility, as we have seen (Ch. 3), are useful for hunters and gatherers and are an intrinsic feature of band organization. The !Kung San, for example, are primarily bilateral, and this reflects in turn a predominant bilocal postmarital residence pattern. !Kung San camps contain a core of siblings of both sexes, plus their spouses and children and an assortment of more distant bilateral and affinal kin. Each year, in addition to much short-time visiting, about 13 percent of the population makes a more or less permanent residential shift from one camp to another, and about 35 percent divide their time equally among two or three different camps (Lee, 1979, p. 54). This mobility and flexibility is advantageous for people who must rely on hunting and gathering for their livelihood.

North American bilaterality is associated with a similar flexibility and mobility of nuclear families. Bilaterality in this case reflects a neolocal pattern that is advantageous with respect to wage-labor opportunities and the substitution of price-market money exchanges for kinship-mediated forms of exchange. Whereas the !Kung San always live with relatives and depend on kindreds and extended families for their subsistence, North American nuclear families live apart from their kindreds. North American domestic groups consist predominantly of nuclear families that are geographically and socially isolated from both husband's and wife's relatives, except for life-cycle rituals (see Ch. 14) and Christmas or Thanksgiving feasts.

Determinants of cognatic lineages and clans

Cognatic lineages and cognatic clans are associated with *ambilocality*. This is a form of postmarital residence in which the married couple elects to stay on a relatively permanent basis with the wife's or the husband's domestic group. Ambilocality differs from the neolocality of the North American family, since residence is established with a definite group of kin. Ambilocality also differs from the bilocality of hunting and gathering bands in that the shifting from one domestic group to another occurs less frequently. This implies a relatively more sedentary form of village life and also a somewhat greater potential for developing exclusive "corporate" interests in people and property. Yet all cognatic descent groups, whether bilateral or ambilineal, have less potential for corporate unity than unilineal descent groups, a point to which we return in a moment.

One example of how cognatic lineages work has already been discussed. Such lineages occurred among the Pacific Northwest Coast potlatchers (see Ch. 4). The Kwakiutl potlatch chiefs sought to attract and to hold as large a labor force as they possibly could. The more people a village put to work during a salmon run, the more fish they would catch.

The core of each village consisted of a chieftain and his followers, usually demonstrably related to him through ambilineal descent and constituting a cognatic lineage known as a *numaym*. The chieftain claimed hereditary privileges and noble rank on the basis of ambilineal reckoning from his noble forebears. Validation of this status depended upon his ability to recruit and hold an adequate following in the face of competition from like-minded neighbor chieftains. The importance placed upon individual choice and the uncertainty surrounding the group's corporate estate is typical of cognatic lineages in other cultures as well.

Determinants of unilineal lineages and clans

Although there is no basis for reviving nineteenth-century notions of universal stages in the evolution of kinship (see p. 320), certain well-substantiated general evolutionary

trends do exist. Hunting and gathering band societies tend to have cognatic descent groups and/or bilocal residence because their basic ecological adjustment demands that local groups remain open, flexible, and nonterritorial. With the development of horticulture and more settled village life, the identification between domestic groups or villages and definite territories increased and became more exclusive. Population density increased and warfare became more intense, for reasons to be discussed (Ch. 7), contributing to the need for emphasizing exclusive group unity and solidarity (Ember, Ember, and Pasternak, 1974). Under these conditions, unilineal descent groups with well-defined localized membership cores, a heightened sense of solidarity, and an ideology of exclusive rights over resources and people became the predominant form of kinship group. Using a sample of 797 agricultural societies, Michael Harner (1970) has shown that a very powerful statistical association exists between an increased reliance on agriculture as opposed to hunting and gathering and the replacement of cognatic descent groups by unilineal descent groups.

This is not a one-way process, however. Reversion of cognatic forms can be expected if warfare is eliminated and/or population declines precipitously. Kwakiutl cognatic descent groups probably represent such reversions from formerly unilineal organizations. As will be recalled, the Kwakiutl population was decimated as a result of contagious diseases introduced by Euramerican and Russian traders. And the Canadian government suppressed the warfare characteristic of the early days of contact. Horticultural village societies that are organized unilineally outnumber those that are organized cognatically, 380 to 111 in Harner's sample. Moreover, almost all the unilineal societies display signs of increased population pressure, as indicated by the depletion of wild plant and food resources.

Unilineal descent groups are closely asso-

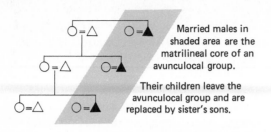

Married males in shaded area are the matrilineal core of an avunculocal group.

Their children leave the avunculocal group and are replaced by sister's sons.

6.10 AVUNCULOCALITY

ciated with one or the other variety of unilocal residence: that is, patrilineality with patrilocality and matrilineality with matrilocality. In addition, there is a close correlation between avunculocality and matrilineality. With patrilineality, fathers, brothers, and sons form the core of the domestic group; and with matrilocality, mothers, sisters, and daughters form the core of the domestic group. The connections between these locality practices and descent rules should be clear, although the reason for the connection between avunculocality and matrilineality is more complex. With avunculocality, mother's brothers and sister's sons form the core of the domestic unit. Sister's son is born in her husband's mother's brother's household, but as a juvenile or adult, sister's son leaves this household and takes up residence with his own mother's brother (Fig. 6.10). The way in which avunculocality works and the reason for its association with matrilineality will become clearer in a moment as we examine the infrastructural causes of matrilocality and patrilocality.

Causes of patrilocality

The overwhelming majority of known societies has male-centered residence and descent patterns. Seventy-one percent of 1179 societies classified by George Murdock (1967) are either patrilocal or virilocal; and in the same sample, societies that have patrilineal kin groups outnumber societies that have matrilineal kin groups 558 to 164. Patrilocality and patrilineality are the statistically "normal" mode of domestic organization. They have been predominant not only, as was once thought, in societies that have plows and draft animals or that practice pastoral nomadism, but in simple horticultural and slash-and-burn societies as well (Divale, 1974).

It is difficult to escape the conclusion that the underlying reason for the prevalence of patrilocality among village societies is that cooperation among males is more crucial than cooperation among females. Men are more effective in hand-to-hand combat than women, and women are less mobile than men during pregnancy and when nursing infants. As a consequence, men generally monopolize the weapons of war and the hunt, leading to male control over trade and politics. The practice of intense small-scale warfare between neighboring villages may be a crucial factor in promoting a widespread complex of male-centered and male-dominated institutions (see Ch. 7). By structuring domestic groups around a core of fathers, brothers, and sons, patrilocality facilitates military cooperation among males who have grown up together. It also avoids pitting fathers, sons, and brothers against each other in combat when one village attacks another (Divale and Harris, 1976).

Causes of matrilocality

It is generally agreed that matrilineal descent groups will not form independently—that is, in the absence of matrilineal neighbors—unless matrilocality is the postmarital residence practice. But why matrilocality? One theory holds that when women's role in food production became more important, as in horticultural societies, domestic groups would tend to be structured around a core of females. This theory, however, must be rejected, because there is no greater association between horticulture and matrilocality than between horticulture and patrilocality (Ember and Ember, 1971; Divale, 1974). Moreover, it is difficult to see why field labor would require a degree of cooperation so high that only women from the same domestic groups could carry it out efficiently, nor why it would require all brothers and sons to be expelled from the natal domestic group (see Burton et al., 1977; Sanday, 1973; White et al., 1977).

The question that must be asked concerning the origin of matrilocality is this: What kinds of modifications in the male specialties of warfare, hunting, and trade would benefit from a shift to matrilocality? The most likely answer is that when warfare, hunting, and trade change from quick short-distance forays to long-distance expeditions lasting several months, matrilocality is more advantageous than patrilocality. When patrilocal males leave a village for extended periods, they leave behind their patrilineal kin group's corporate interests in property and people to be looked after solely by their wives. The allegiance of their wives, however, is to another patrilineal kin group. The local group's women are drawn from different kin groups and have little basis for cooperative activity when they are unsupervised by the male managers of the corporate domestic units into which they have married. There is no one home, so to speak, "to mind the store." Matrilocality solves this problem because it structures the domestic unit around a permanent core of resident mothers, daughters, and sisters who are trained in cooperative labor patterns from birth and who identify the "minding of the store" with their own material and sentimental interests. Thus males reared in matrilocal domestic groups are less constrained to return to their villages and can remain on the trail or at sea for long periods.

The ability to launch and successfully complete long-distance expeditions implies that neighboring villages will not attack each other when the men are away. This is best assured by forming the expeditions around a core of males drawn from several neighboring villages or different households within a given village. Among patrilocal, patrilineal villages, the belligerent territorial teams consist of patrilineally related kin who constitute competitive "fraternal interest groups." These groups make shifting alliances with neighboring villages, exchange sisters, and raid each other. Most combat takes place between villages that are about a day's walk from each other. Matrilocal, matrilineal cultures, on the other hand, are bonded not by the exchange of women, but by the inmarrying of males from different domestic groups, and this prevents the formation of competitive and disruptive fraternal interest groups by scattering fathers and brothers into several different households in different villages.

Thus matrilocal, matrilineal societies like the Iroquois of New York and the Huron of Ontario enjoy a high degree of internal peace. But most matrilineal societies, like the Iroquois and the Huron, have a history of intense warfare directed outward against powerful enemies (Gramby, 1977; Trigger, 1978). The Nayar, for example, were a soldier caste in the service of the kings of Malabar. Among the matrilocal Mundurucu of the Amazon, conflict between villages was unheard of and interpersonal aggression was suppressed. But the Mundurucu launched raids against enemies hundreds of miles away, and unrelenting hostility and violence characterized their relations with the "outside world" (Murphy, 1956).

An additional reason for the suppression of internal hostility among matrilocal groups is that matrilocality is incompatible with polygyny. The males who are in charge of the matrilineal estate are not interested in marrying several of their sisters to one male, and they themselves will not benefit from having many wives and children. Conflict over women, one of the major causes of war between neighboring villages, is thus reduced.

There remains the further question of why long-distance raiding-hunting-trading expeditions come to be important for some village societies and not others. The answer probably resides in increased population pressure brought about by intensification of production and depletion of local resources. Matrilineal, matrilocal societies tend to have larger villages and better-developed political institutions than patrilocal villages. We will return to this subject in Chapter 8.

Causes of avunculocality

In matrilocal, matrilineal societies males are reluctant to relinquish control over their own sons to the members of their wives' kin groups, and they are not easily reconciled to the fact that it is their sons rather than their daughters who must move away from them at marriage. Because of this contradiction, matrilocal, matrilineal systems tend to revert to patrilocal, patrilineal systems as soon as the forces responsible for keeping males away from their natal village and domestic groups are removed or moderated.

One way to solve this contradiction is to loosen the male's marital obligations (already weak in matrilocal societies) to the point where he need not live with his wife at all. This is the path followed by the Nayar. As we have seen, Nayar men had no home other than their natal domestic unit; they were untroubled by what happened to their children —whom they were scarcely able to identify —and they had no difficulty keeping their sisters and their nephews and nieces under proper fraternal and avuncular control.

But the most common solution to the tension between male interests and matrilineality is the development of avunculocal patterns of residence. It is a remarkable fact that there are more matrilineal descent groups that are avunculocal than matrilineal descent groups that are matrilocal (see Table 6.2).

Under avunculocality a male eventually goes to live with his mother's brothers in their matrilineal domestic unit. His wife will join him there. Upon maturity, a male ego's son will in turn depart for ego's wife's brother's domestic unit (ego's daughter, however, may remain resident if she marries her father's sister's son). Thus the core of an avunculocal domestic unit consists of a group of brothers and their sister's sons. The function of this arrangement seems to be to reinsert a male fraternal interest group as the residential core of the matrilineal descent group.

Avunculocality probably occurs so often because males continue to dominate the affairs of matrilineal groups when warfare has not been suppressed. This interpretation accords well with another remarkable fact: The logical opposite of avunculocality never occurs. The logical opposite of avunculocality is *amitalocality* (aunt-locality). Amitalocality would exist if brother's daughters and father's sisters constituted the core of a patrilineal do-

TABLE 6.2 RELATIONSHIP BETWEEN RESIDENCE AND DESCENT IN THE ETHNOGRAPHIC ATLAS

	Postmarital residence				
Kin groups	Matrilocal or uxorilocal	Avunculocal	Patrilocal or virilocal	Other	Total
Patrilineal	1	0	563	25	588
Matrilineal	53	62	30	19	164

Source: Murdock, 1967; Divale and Harris, 1976.

mestic unit. Women, however, have never been able to control patrilineal kin groups in the same way men have been able to control matrilineal kin groups. Hence males, not females, constitute the resident core of virtually all patrilineal kin groups as well as most of the known cases of matrilineal kin groups.

A rather thin line separates avunculocality from patrilocality. If the resident group of brothers decides to permit one or more of its sons to remain with them after marriage, the residential core will begin to resemble an ambilocal domestic group. If more sons than nephews are retained in residence, the locality basis for a reassertion of patrilineal descent will be present.

After a society has adopted matrilocality and developed matrilineal descent groups, changes in the original conditions may lead to a restoration of the patrilocal, patrilineal pattern. At any given moment many societies are probably in a transitional state between one form of residence and another and one form of kinship ideology and another. Since the changes in residence and descent may not proceed in perfect tandem at any given moment—that is, descent changes may lag behind residence changes—one should expect to encounter combinations of residence with the "wrong" descent rule. For example, a few patrilocal societies and quite a large number of virilocal societies have matrilineal descent, and one or two uxorilocal societies have patrilineal descent (Table 6.2). But there is evidence for a very powerful strain toward consistency in the alignment between domestic groups, their ecological, military and economic adaptations, and their ideologies of descent.

Kinship terminologies

Another aspect of domestic ideology that participates in the same strain toward functional consistency is kinship terminology. Every culture has a special set of terms for designating types of kin. The terms plus the rules for using them constitute a culture's *kin terminological system.*

Lewis Henry Morgan was the first anthropologist to realize that despite the thousands of different languages over the face of the globe and despite the immense number of different kinship terms in these languages, there is only a handful of basic types of kin terminological systems. These systems can best be defined by the way in which terms are applied to an abbreviated genealogical grid consisting of two generations, including ego's siblings of the same and opposite sex and ego's cross and parallel cousins. Here we will examine only three of the best-known systems in order to illustrate the nature of the causal and functional relationships that link alternative kinship terminologies to the other aspects of domestic organizations. (It should be emphasized that these are basic terminological *types*. Actual instances often vary in details.)

Eskimo terminology

The kind of kin terminological systems with which North Americans are most familiar is known as Eskimo, shown in Figure 6.11. Two important features of this system are these: First, none of the terms applied to ego's nuclear relatives—1, 2, 6, 5—is applied outside the nuclear family; and second, there is no distinction between maternal and paternal sides. This means that there is no distinction between cross and parallel cousins or between cross and parallel aunts or uncles. These features reflect the fact that societies using Eskimo terminology generally lack corporate descent groups. In the absence of such groups, the nuclear family tends to stand out as a separate and functionally dominant productive and reproductive unit. For this reason, its members are given a terminological

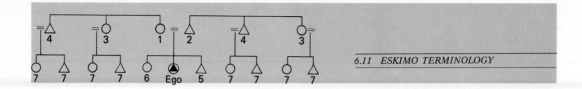

identity separate from all other kin types. On the other hand, the lumping of all cousins under a single term (7) reflects the strength of bilateral as opposed to unilineal descent. The influence of bilateral descent is also reflected in the failure to distinguish terminologically between aunts and uncles on the mother's side as compared with aunts and uncles on the father's side. The theoretical predictions concerning Eskimo terminology are strongly confirmed by the tabulations of Murdock's *Ethnographic Atlas* (1967). Of the 71 societies having Eskimo terminology, only 4 have large extended families and only 13 have unilineal descent groups. In 54 of the 71 Eskimo terminology societies, descent groups are entirely absent or are represented only by kindreds.

Eskimo is the terminological system of modern North America. But as the name "Eskimo" implies, the same pattern is frequently found among hunters and gatherers. The reason is that any factors which isolate the nuclear family increase the probability that an Eskimo terminology will occur. As we have seen, among hunting and gathering groups, the determining factors are low population densities and the need for maximum geographical mobility in relationship to fluctuations in the availability of game and other resources. In the USA and Canada the same terminological pattern reflects the intrusion of price-market institutions into the domestic routine and the high level of wage-induced social and geographic mobility.

Hawaiian terminology

Another common kin terminological system is known as Hawaiian. This is the easiest system to portray, since it has the least number of terms (Fig. 6.12). In some versions even the distinction between the sexes is dropped, leaving one term for the members of ego's generation and another for the members of ego's parents' generation. The most remarkable feature of Hawaiian terminology, as compared with Eskimo, is the application of the same terms to people inside and outside the nuclear family. Hawaiian is thus compatible with situations where the nuclear family is submerged within a domestic context dominated by extended families and other corporate descent groups. In Murdock's *Ethnographic Atlas*, 21 percent of the Hawaiian terminology societies do indeed have large extended families. In addition, well over 50 percent of Hawaiian terminology societies have some form of corporate descent group other than extended families.

Theoretically, most of these descent groups should be cognatic rather than unilineal. The

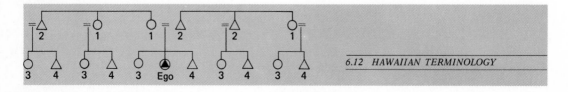

reason for this prediction is that the merging of relatives on the maternal side with those on the paternal side indicates an indifference toward unilineality, and an indifference toward unilineality is logically consistent with ambilineal or bilateral descent.

Data from Murdock's ethnographic sample only partially support this prediction: There are, indeed, many more Hawaiian terminology societies that have cognatic as opposed to unilineal descent. But there are many exceptions for which as yet no generally accepted explanation is available.

Iroquois terminology

In the presence of unilineal kin groups, there is a worldwide tendency to distinguish parallel from cross cousins, as previously noted. This pattern is widely associated with a similar distinction in the first ascending generation, whereby father's brothers are distinguished from mother's brothers and father's sisters are distinguished from mother's sisters.

An Iroquois terminology exists where—in addition to these distinctions between cross and parallel cousins and cross and parallel aunts and uncles—mother's sister is terminologically merged with mother, father's brother is terminologically merged with father, and parallel cousins are terminologically merged with ego's brothers and sisters (Fig. 6.13).

This pattern of merging occurs in large part as a result of the shared membership of siblings in corporate unilineal descent groups

and of the marriage alliances based on cross-cousin marriage between such groups. In Murdock's ethnographic sample there are 166 societies having Iroquois terminology. Of these, 119 have some form of unilineal descent group (70 percent).

We have only skimmed the surface of a few of the many fascinating and important problems in the field of kinship terminology (Fig. 6.14). But perhaps enough has been said to establish at least one point: Kin terminological systems possess a remarkable logical coherence. Yet like so many other aspects of culture, kin terminological systems are never the planned product of any inventive genius. Most people are unaware that such systems even exist. Clearly, the major features of these systems represent recurrent unconscious adjustments to the prevailing conditions of domestic life. Yet there are many details of kin terminologies, as well as of other kinship phenomena, that are as yet not well understood.

Summary

To study kinship is to study the ideologies that justify and normalize the corporate structure of domestic groups. The basis of kinship is the tracing of relationships through marriage and descent. Descent is the belief that certain persons play a special role in the conception, birth, or nurturance of certain children. Many different folk theories of descent exist, none of which corresponds precisely to modern-day scientific understandings of procreation and reproduction.

The principal varieties of cognatic descent

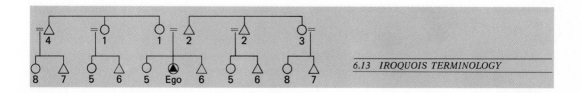

6.13 IROQUOIS TERMINOLOGY

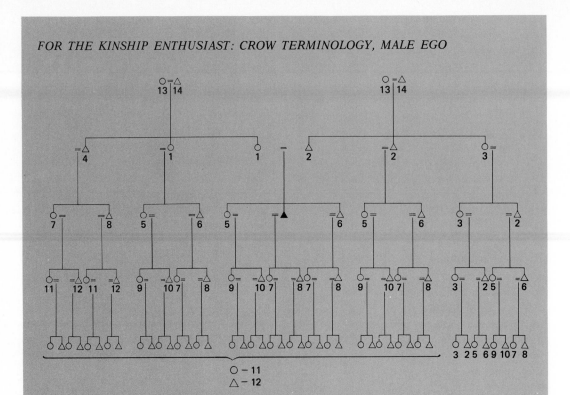

Many cultures have terminological systems in which the influence of lineality overwhelms generation criteria. These systems occur in both matrilineal and patrilineal versions. The matrilineal variety is known as Crow. These Crow systems involve the distinction between patrilateral and matrilateral cross cousins. These "cousins" are not only distinguished from each other, but the patrilateral cross cousins are equated with father's sister, and father. There is also the curious fact that the matrilateral cross cousins are equated with ego's daughter and son.

rules are the bilateral and the ambilineal; these are associated, respectively, with kindreds on the one hand, and with cognatic lineages and clans on the other. The principal varieties of unilineal descent are matrilineality and patrilineality. These are associated, respectively, with patri- and matrilineages or patri- and matriclans.

An important key to the understanding of alternative modes of descent and domestic organization is the pattern of postmarital resi-dence. Bilateral descent and bilateral descent groups are associated with neolocality, bilocality, and ambilocality. More specifically, the flexible and mobile forms of band organization are facilitated by bilocality, whereas the greater isolation of nuclear families in price-market economies gives rise to neolocality. Cognatic lineages and clans, on the other hand, give functional expression to ambilocality.

Unilineal domestic groups reflect unilocal

patterns of residence. These in turn imply well-defined membership cores and an emphasis upon exclusive rights over resources and people. There is a strong correlation between patrilocality and patrilineality on the one hand, and among matrilineality, matrilocality, and avunculocality on the other. Patrilocal and patrilineal groups are far more common than matrilineal or avunculocal groups. A reason for this is that warfare, hunting, and trading activities among village societies are monopolized by males. These activities, in turn, are facilitated by stressing the coresidence of fathers, brothers, and sons and the formation of fraternal interest groups. Under conditions of increasing population density and pressure on resources, local groups may find it adaptive to engage in long-distance war-trade-hunting expeditions. Such expeditions are facilitated by breaking up the fraternal interest groups and structuring domestic life around a core of mothers, sisters, and daughters or, in other words, by developing a matrilocal, matrilineal organization. Since males in matrilineal, matrilocal societies continue to dominate military and political institutions, they are inclined to reinject the patrilineal principle into domestic life and to moderate the effects of matrilocality on their control over their sons and daughters. This accounts for the fact that as many matrilineal societies are avunculocal as are matrilocal. Thus the principal function of alternative rules of descent may be described as the establishment and maintenance of networks of cooperative and interdependent kinspeople aggregated into ecologically effective and militarily secure domestic production and reproduction units. In order for such units to act effectively and reliably, they must share an organizational ideology that interprets and validates the structure of the group and the behavior of its members. This interpretation of kinship rules can also be applied to the principal varieties of kin terminological systems. Such systems tend to aggregate relatives in conformity with the major features of domestic organization, locality practices, and descent rules. Eskimo terminology, for example, is functionally associated with domestic organizations in which nuclear families tend to be mobile and isolated; Hawaiian terminology is functionally associated with cognatic lineages and cognatic clans; and Iroquois terminology, with its emphasis on the distinction between cross and parallel cousins, is functionally associated with unilinear descent groups.

7

Law, Order, and War in Egalitarian Societies

In this chapter we continue our discussion of the structural level of sociocultural systems. The focus now shifts from the structure of domestic groups to the regulation of interpersonal relationships and the maintenance of political cohesion and law and order within and between band and village societies. Conflict resolution through warfare will be shown to be present in both band and village societies, and theories of why this should be the case will be presented.

Law and order in band and village societies

People in every society have conflicting interests (Fig. 7.1). Even in band-level societies, old and young, sick and healthy, men and women do not want the same thing at the same time. Moreover, in every society people want something that others possess and are reluctant to give away. Every culture, therefore, must have structural provisions for resolving conflicts of interest in an orderly

7.1 YANOMAMO CLUB FIGHT

7.1 YANOMAMO CLUB FIGHT
Egalitarian peoples are not without problems of law and order. [Napoleon Chagnon]

fashion and for preventing conflicts from escalating into disruptive confrontations. There are marked qualitative and quantitative differences, however, between the kinds of conflicting interests found in band and village societies and those found in more complex societies. There are also marked differences in the methods employed to prevent disruptive confrontations.

The enormous apparatus of "law and order" associated with modern life is absent among village- and band-level cultures. Yet there is no "war of all against all." The Eskimo, the !Kung San of the Kalahari, the native Australians, and many other peoples enjoy a high degree of personal security without having any rulers or law and order specialists. They have no kings, queens, dictators, presidents, governors, or mayors; police forces, soldiers, sailors, or marines; CIA, FBI, treasury agents, or federal marshals. They have no written law codes and no formal law courts; no lawyers, bailiffs, judges, district attorneys, juries, or court clerks; and no patrol cars, paddy wagons, jails, or penitentiaries. How do band and village peoples get along without these law enforcement specialists and facilities, and why are modern societies so dependent on them?

The basic reasons for these differences are to be found in (1) the small size of band and village societies; (2) the central importance of domestic groups and kinship in their social organization; and (3) the absence of marked inequalities in access to technology and resources. Small size means that everyone knows everyone else personally. Therefore, stingy, aggressive, and disruptive individuals can be identified by the group and exposed to the pressure of public opinion. The centrality of domestic group and kinship relations means that reciprocity can be the chief mode of exchange and that the collective interests of the domestic unit can be recognized by all its members. Finally, equality of access to technology and natural resources means that

food and other forms of wealth cannot be withheld by a wealthy few while others endure shortages and hardships.

"Primitive communism"

Among band-level societies, all adults usually have open access to the rivers, lakes, beaches, oceans; all the plants and animals; and the soil and the subsoil. Insofar as these are basic to the extraction of life-sustaining energy and materials, they are communal "property."

Anthropologists have reported the existence of nuclear families and even individual ownership of hunting and gathering territories among native American band-level societies in Canada. But subsequent research has shown that these ownership patterns were associated with the fur trade and that such patterns did not exist aboriginally (Speck, 1915; Knight, 1974; Leacock, 1973). In other cases, reports of family territories fail to distinguish between ideological claims and actual behavior. The fact that a nuclear family regards a particular area as its "own" must be weighed against the conditions under which others can use the area and the consequences of trespass. If permission to use the area is always freely granted and if use without permission results merely in some muttering or name-calling, the modern concept of "ownership" may be the wrong concept to use.

Among the !Kung San, waterholes and hunting and gathering territories are emically "owned" by the core groups of particular bands. But since neighboring bands contain many intermarried kin, there is a great deal of sharing of access to resources as a result of mutual visiting. Neighbors who ask for permission to visit and exploit the resources of a particular camp are seldom refused. Even people who come from distant bands and who lack close kin ties with the hosts are usually given permission to stay, especially for short periods, since it is understood that the hosts may return the visit at some future date (Lee, 1979, p. 337).

The prevalence of communal ownership of land, however, does not mean that hunter-gatherer bands lack private property altogether. There is little support for the theory of "primitive communism," which holds that there was a universal stage in the development of culture marked by the complete absence of private property (see Epstein, 1968). Many material objects of band-level societies are effectively controlled ("owned") by specific individuals, especially items the user has produced. The members of even the most egalitarian societies usually believe that weapons, clothing, containers, ornaments, tools, and other "personal effects" ought not to be taken away or used without the consent of the "owner." However, the chance is remote that theft or misappropriation of such objects will lead to serious conflict.

First of all, the accumulation of material possessions is rigidly limited by the recurrent need to break camp and travel long distances on foot. In addition, most utilitarian items may be borrowed without difficulty when the owner is not using them. If there are not enough such items to go around (arrows, projectile points, nets, bark, or gourd containers), easy access to the raw materials and mastery of the requisite skills provide the have-nots with the chance of making their own. Moreover, among societies having no more than a few hundred people, thieves cannot be anonymous. If stealing becomes habitual, a coalition of the injured parties will eventually take action. If you want something, better to ask for it openly. Most such requests are readily obliged, since reciprocity is the prevailing mode of exchange. Finally, it should be pointed out that, contrary to the experience of the successful modern bank robber, no one can make a living from stealing bows and arrows or feather headresses, since there is no regular market at which such items can be exchanged for food (see Ch. 4).

Mobilizing public opinion: song duels

The most important requirement for the control of disputes in band and village societies is the temporary insulation of the disputants from the corporate response of their respective kin. As long as the disputants feel they have the backing of their kin, they will continue to press their claims and counterclaims. The members of kin groups, however, never react mechanically. They are eager not to be caught in a situation in which they are opposed by a majority of people in the band or village. Public opinion, in other words, influences the support disputants can expect from their kin. Because of the importance of aligning potential kin group supporters with the drift of public opinion, band and village concepts of justice seem peculiar to Westerners. What matters is not so much who is morally right or wrong, or who is lying or telling the truth; the important thing is to mobilize public opinin on one side or the other decisively enough to prevent the outbreak of large-scale feuding.

A classic example of how such mobilization can be achieved independently of abstract principles of justice is the song contest of the central and eastern Eskimo (Fig. 7.2). Here it frequently happens that one man claims another man has stolen his wife. The counterclaim is that she was not stolen but left voluntarily because her husband "was not man enough" to take good care of her. The issue is settled at a large public meeting that might be likened to a court. But no testimony is taken in support of either of the two versions of why the wife has left her husband. Instead, the "disputants" take turns singing insulting

7.2 SONG CONTEST
**Eskimo "disputants" in "court" in eastern
Greenland. [Courtesy of Royal Danish
Ministry of Foreign Affairs]**

songs at each other. The "court" responds to
each performance with differential degrees of
laughter. Eventually one of the singers gets
flustered, and the hooting and hollering
raised against him becomes total—even his
relatives have a hard time not laughing.

Something was whispered
Of a man and wife
Who could not agree
And what was it all about?
A wife who in rightful anger
Tore her husband's furs,
Took their boat
And rowed away with her son.
Ay-ay, all who listen,
What do you think of him
Who is great in his anger
But faint in strength,
Blubbering helplessly?

He got what he deserved
Though it was he who proudly
Started this quarrel with stupid words
(Adapted from Rasmussen, 1929, pp. 231–232)

The Eskimo have no police-military specialists to see to it that the "decision" is enforced. Yet chances are that the man who has
lost the song duel will give in, since he can no
longer count on anyone to back him up if he
chooses to escalate the dispute. Nonetheless,
the defeated man may choose to go it alone.

Wife stealing does occasionally lead to
murder. When this happens, the man who has
lost public support may survive on the
strength of his own vigilance and fighting
skill. He will probably have to kill again,
however, and with each transgression the co-

alition against him becomes larger and more determined, until finally he falls victim to an ambush.

Mobilizing public opinion: witchcraft accusations

Among egalitarian band and village societies, part-time magico-religious specialists known as *shamans* frequently play an important role in mobilizing public opinion and in eliminating persistent sources of conflict. Most cultures reject the idea that misfortune can result from natural causes. If animals suddenly become scarce or if several people fall sick, it is assumed that somebody is practicing witchcraft. It is the shaman's job to identify the culprit. Normally this is done through the art of *divination* or clairvoyance. Putting themselves into trances with the aid of drugs, tobacco smoke, or monotonous drumming, shamans discover the name of the culprit. The people demand vengeance, and the culprit is ambushed and murdered.

It might be thought that this sequence of events would lead to more rather than less internal conflict. Even if the accused had actually been practicing witchcraft, the consequences of this form of symbolic aggression would seem to be considerably less disruptive than those resulting from actual murder. But the chances are that the murdered individuals never even attempted to carry out the witchcraft of which they were accused, or indeed any witchcraft at all! In other words, the witches are probably wholly "innocent" of the crime with which they have been charged. Nonetheless, the shaman's witchcraft accusations usually conserve rather than destroy the group's feeling of unity.

Consider the case reported by Gertrude Dole (1966) for the Kuikuru—an egalitarian, village-dwelling group of Brazilian Indians. Lightning had set fire to two houses. The shaman went into a trance and discovered that the lightning had been sent by a man who had left the village some years previously and had never returned. This man had only one male relative, who was also no longer living in the village. Before the accused witch had left the village, he had become engaged to a young girl. The shaman's brother had persuaded the girl's mother to break the betrothal and to permit him to marry the girl.

During the course of the divining ceremony, the shaman carried on dialogues with various interested members of the community. When he finally disclosed the identity of the culprit, it created considerable anxiety. One after another, several individuals stood apart in the plaza and spoke in long monologues. . . . In the heat of the excitement, the shaman's brother left with a few companions to kill the man suspected of witchcraft. (1966, p. 76)

The ethnographer points out that among the Kuikuru a change of residence from one village to another usually indicates that there is trouble brewing and that, in effect, the individual has been ostracized. (The Kuikuru suspected Dole and her anthropologist husband of having been "kicked out" of their own society.) Thus the man accused of sorcery was not a randomly chosen figure but one who fulfilled several well-defined criteria: (1) a history of disputes and quarrels within the village; (2) a motivation for continuing to do harm (the broken engagement); and (3) a weak kinship backing.

Thus the shaman's accusation was not based on a spur-of-the-moment decision; there had been a long incubation period during which the shaman in or out of trance sounded out his fellow villagers on their attitude toward the accused. As Dole indicates, the supernatural authority of the shaman allows him to make public indictments. But shamans are not in control, as in late-night movie versions of the sinister medicine man turning the "natives" against the friendly European explorers. Rather, they are largely constrained by public opinion. Although the act of divination appears to put the onus of the judicial process on the shaman, clearly the shaman actually "deduces, formulates, and expresses the will of the people" (Dole, 1966, p. 76). Shamans abuse their supernatural gifts if they accuse people who are well liked and who enjoy strong kin group support. If they persist in making such mistakes, they themselves will be ostracized and eventually murdered.

The peculiar thing about witchcraft as a means of social control is that its practitioners, if they exist at all, can seldom be detected. The number of persons falsely accused of witchcraft probably far exceeds the number who are justly accused. It is clear, therefore, that nonpractice of witchcraft is no safeguard against an accusation of witchcraft. How then do you protect yourself from such false accusations? By acting in an amiable, open, generous manner; by avoiding quarrels; by doing everything possible not to lose the support of your kin groups. Thus the occasional killing of a supposed sorcerer results in much more than the mere elimination of a few actual or potential antisocial individuals. These violent incidents convince everyone of the importance of not being mistaken for an evildoer. As a result, as among the Kuikuru, people are made more amiable, cordial, generous, and willing to cooperate:

The norm of being amiable deters individuals from accusing one another of delicts, hence in the absence of effective political or kin-group control, interpersonal relations have become a kind of game, in which almost the only restrictive rule is not to show hostility to one another for fear of being suspected of witchcraft. (Dole, 1966, p. 74)

This system is not "fail-safe." Many cases are known of witchcraft systems that seem to have broken down, involving the community in a series of destructive retaliatory accusations and murders. These cases, however (especially in situations of intensive colonial contact, as in Africa and Melanesia), must be carefully related to the underlying conditions of communal life. In general, the incidence of witchcraft accusations varies with the amount of community dissension and frustration (Mair, 1969; Nadel, 1952). When a traditional culture is upset by exposure to new diseases, increased competition for land, and recruitment for wage labor, an epoch of increased dissension and frustration can be expected. This period will also be characterized by frenzied activity among those who are skilled in tracking down and exposing the malevolent effects of witches, as in the case of the breakup of feudal society in Europe and the great witch craze of the fifteenth to seventeenth centuries.

Headmanship

To the extent that political leadership can be said to exist at all among band and village societies, it is exercised by headmen (or far less commonly, headwomen). The headman, unlike such specialists as king, president, or dictator, is a relatively powerless figure incapable of compelling obedience. He lacks sufficient force to do so. When he gives a command, he is never certain of being able to punish physically those who disobey. (Hence if he wants to stay in "office," he gives few direct commands.) In contrast, the political power of rulers depends on their ability to expel or exterminate any readily foreseeable combination of nonconforming individuals and groups. Genuine rulers control access to basic resources and to the tools and weapons for hurting or killing people.

Among the Eskimo, leadership is especially diffuse, being closely related to success in hunting. A group will follow an outstanding hunter and defer to his opinion with respect to choice of hunting spots. But in all other matters, the "leader's" opinion carries no more weight than any other man's.

Similarly, among the !Kung San, each band has its recognized "leaders," most of whom are males. Such leaders may speak out more than others and are listened to with a bit more deference than is usual, but they "have no formal authority" and "can only persuade, but never enforce their will on others" (Lee, 1979, pp. 333–334). When Richard Lee asked the !Kung San if they had "headmen" in the sense of a powerful chief, he was told: "Of course we have headmen! In fact we are all headmen . . . each one of us is headman over himself" (p. 348).

A similar pattern of leadership is reported for the Semai of Malaya. Despite recent attempts by outsiders to bolster up the power of Semai leaders, the headman is merely the most prestigious figure among a group of peers. In the words of Robert Dentan, who carried out fieldwork among these egalitarian shifting horticulturalists in 1962–1963:

[The headman] keeps the peace by conciliation rather than coercion. He must be personally respected. . . . Otherwise people will drift away from him or gradually stop paying attention to him. Moreover, the Semai recognize only two or three occasions on which he can assert his authority: dealing as a representative of his people with non-Semai; mediating a quarrel, if invited by the quarreling parties to do so but not otherwise; and . . . selecting and apportioning land for fields. Furthermore, most of the time a good headman gauges his general feeling about an issue and bases his decision on that, so that he is more a spokesman for public opinion than a molder of it. (1968, p. 68)

Somewhat confusingly, the term "chief" is often used to designate the kind of leadership embodied in the concept of headman. But the context usually clarifies the kind of leadership involved. For example, Claude Lévi-Strauss refers to the Nambikwara Indians of Brazil as having "chiefs." Yet he states firmly:

It should be said at once that the chief cannot seek support either in clearly defined powers or in publicly recognized authority. . . . One or two malcontents may throw the chief's whole programme out of joint. Should this happen, the chief has no powers of coercion. He can disembarrass himself of undesirable elements only in so far as all the others are of the same mind as himself. (1963b, p. 303)

Headmanship is likely to be a frustrating and irksome position. The cumulative impression given by descriptions of leadership among Brazilian Indian groups is that of an overzealous scoutmaster on an overnight cookout. The first one up in the morning, the headman tries to rouse his companions by standing in the middle of the village plaza and shouting. The headman seems to cajole, harangue, and plead from morning to night. If a task needs to be done, it is the headman who starts doing it; and it is the headman who works at it harder than anyone else. Moreover, not only must the headman set an example for hard work, but he must also set an example for generosity. After a fishing or hunting expedition, he is expected to give away more of the catch than anyone else; if trade goods are obtained, he must be careful not to keep the best pieces for himself.

Thomas Gregor, who studied the Mehinacu Indians of Brazil's Xingu National Park in 1967 (Fig. 7.3), describes the Mehinacu "chief" (i.e., headman) as follows:

The most significant qualifications for Mehinacu chieftainship are learned skills and personal attributes. The chief, for example, is expected to excel at public speaking. Each evening he should stand in the center of the plaza and exhort his fellow tribesmen to be good citizens. He must call upon them to work hard in their gardens, to take frequent baths, not to sleep during the day, not to be angry with each other, and not to have sexual relations too frequently. . . . In addition to being a skilled orator, the chief is expected to be a generous man. This means that when he returns from a successful fishing trip, he will bring most of his catch out to the men's houses where it is cooked and shared by the men of the tribe. His wife must be generous, bringing manioc cakes and pepper to the men whenever they call for it. Further, the chief must be willing to part with possessions. When one of the men catches a harpy eagle,

CHAPTER 7
Law, order, and war in
egalitarian societies

7.3 MEHINACU CHIEFTAINSHIP

In front of the men's house the chief is redistributing presents given to him by the ethnographer. [Thomas Gregor]

for example, the chief must buy it from him with a valuable shell belt in the name of the entire tribe. . . . A chief should also be a man who never becomes angry in public. . . . In his public speeches he should never criticize any of his fellow tribesmen, no matter how badly they may have affronted the chief or the tribe as a whole. (Gregor, 1969, pp. 88–89)

It is pertinent at this point to recall the plight of the ungenerous Kapauku headman (Ch. 4). Even the most generous headman in good standing cannot force obedience to his decisions.

If the principals are not willing to comply, the authority becomes emotional and starts to shout reproaches; he makes long speeches in which evidence, rules, decisions, and threats form inducements. Indeed, the authority may go as far as to start wainai *(the mad dance), or change his tactics suddenly and weep bitterly about the misconduct of the defendant and the fact that he refuses to obey. Some native authorities are so skilled in the art of persuasion that they can produce genuine tears which almost always break the resistance of the unwilling party. (Pospisil, 1968, p. 221)*

One wonders if the Kapauku headman does not shed tears more because he is frustrated than because he is skilled.

Complementary opposition: the Nuer

Beyond a certain point it is technically impossible for headmen to intuit public opinion and act on behalf of a firm consensus. Yet it has been found that for limited purposes, especially for warfare, large numbers of people can join together in temporary alliances without centralized political leadership.

The prime ethnographic case is that of the Nuer, a pastoral and farming people who live astride the marshy grasslands of the Upper Nile in the Sudan. There is no doubt about the absence of centralized political leadership throughout Nuerland:

The lack of governmental organs among the Nuer, the absence of legal institutions of developed leadership, and generally, of organized political life is remarkable. . . . The ordered anarchy in which they live accords well with their character, for it is impossible to live among Nuer and conceive of rulers ruling over them. . . . The Nuer is a product of a hard and egalitarian upbringing, is deeply democratic, and is easily roused to violence. This turbulent spirit finds any restraint irksome and no man recognizes a superior. Wealth makes no difference. A man with many cattle is envied but not treated differently from a man with few cattle. Birth makes no difference. . . . There is no master or servant in their society but only equals who regard themselves as God's noblest creation. . . . Among themselves even the suspicion of an order riles a man . . . he will not submit to any authority which clashes with his own interest and he does not consider himself bound to anyone. (Evans-Pritchard, 1940, pp. 181–182)

The Nuer are organized according to kinship principles. The largest political unit is a huge patriclan divided into numerous lineages. Generally speaking, genealogical distance increases with geographical distance, so that adjacent villages usually have lineage cores belonging to the same major lineage. What is distinctive about the Nuer organization is that varying depths and spans of lineage kin can be brought into military alliance, ranging all the way from the members of a single minimal lineage to all the maximal lineages. The extent of the activation of these segments depends entirely upon the size and nature of the opposing forces. Sometimes the opposition arises among the Nuer themselves; each segment then calls upon kin up to the level and span of the opposition, or until a common ancestor is reached. When the threat originates among the non-Nuer, the call for assistance spreads up and out through wider and wider segments until all Nuer have the opportunity to be involved. Indeed, the very existence of the segments can be said to depend on the opposition they confront. To give the phenomenon its technical name, the segments exist by virtue of their *complementary opposition;* that is, they join together only to the extent that they confront a common enemy.

Complementary opposition seems to be related to the Nuer's expansion into their present habitat at the expense of groups that had previously occupied the region. The habitat itself is distinguished by a regular alternation of floods and severe droughts. Large, permanent, year-round settlements are impossible. During the rainy season the low-lying areas are completely under water, isolating the various territorial segments. During the droughts the cattle must be dispersed in search of waterholes. There is no infrastructural basis, therefore, for the centralization of power and leadership. Yet by the "massing effect" of complementary opposition, the Nuer have been able to drive out and displace neighboring peoples, especially the Dinka, against whose remaining territory they continue to press with unrelenting zeal (Sahlins, 1961; Salzman, 1978).

Blood feud

The ever-present danger confronting band and village societies is that their kinship groups tend to react as units to real or alleged aggression against one of their members. In this way disputes involving individuals may escalate to include whole villages or groups of villages. The worst danger, of course, arises from disputes that lead to homicide. Among kinship-organized band and village peoples, there is intense adherence to the conviction that the only proper reaction to a murder is to kill the murderer or any convenient member of the murderer's kin group.

All Nuer dread the danger of an escalating feud. The main reason for this is the principle of complementary opposition: Wider and wider lineage segments are activated by virtue of their opposition under conditions of stress. But at each escalation more and more people who are interested in a peaceful settlement are brought into the quarrel. In Evans-Pritchard's words: "Fear of incurring a blood-feud is, in fact, the most important legal sanction within a tribe and the main guarantee of an individual's life and property" (1940, p. 150).

Among many decentralized societies, the formal mechanisms for preventing homicide from flaring into a protracted feud include the transference of substantial amounts of prized possessions from the slayer's kin group to the victim's kin group. This practice is especially common and effective among pastoral peoples whose animals are a concentrated form of material wealth and for whom bride-price is a regular aspect of kin group exogamy. The Nuer settle their feuds (or at least deescalate them) by transferring forty or more head of cattle to the victim's lineage. If a man has been killed, these animals will be used to "buy" a wife whose sons will fill the void left by his death. The dead man's kin are obliged to resist the offer of cattle, demanding instead a life for a life. However, members of the lineage segments standing next in line to become involved are under no such compulsion. They do their best to convince the injured kin group to accept the compensation. In this effort they are aided by certain semi-sacred arbitration specialists. The latter, known as leopard skin chiefs (Fig. 7.4), are usually men whose lineages are not represented locally and hence who can more readily act as neutral intermediaries.

The leopard skin chief is the only one who can ritually cleanse a murderer. If a homicide takes place, the killer flees at once to the leopard skin chief's house, which is a sanctuary respected by all Nuer. Nonetheless, the leopard skin chief lacks even the rudiments of political power; the most that he can do to the reluctant members of the slain man's lineage is to threaten them with various supernatural curses. Yet the determination to prevent a feud is so great that the injured lineage eventually accepts the cattle as compensation.

Nonkin associations: sodalities

Although relations of affinity and descent dominate the political life of band and village peoples, nonkin forms of political organization also occur to a limited extent. Such groups are called *sodalities*. A common form of sodality is the exclusive men's or women's association or "club." These usually involve men and women drawn from different domestic groups who cooperate in secret ritual or craft performances. We will discuss these organizations in the chapter devoted to sex roles (Ch. 12). Age-grade associations are another common form of sodality, already mentioned with respect to the Masai warrior camps (p. 86). Among the Samburu, another group of East African pastoralists, all men initiated into manhood over a span of about twelve to fourteen years comprised an age set whose members had a special feeling of solidarity that cut across domestic and lineage kin groups. The age-set members advanced as a group from junior to senior status. As juniors they were responsible for military combat and as seniors they were responsible for initiating and training the upcoming age sets (P. Spencer, 1965; see Kertzer, 1978).

A classic case of a sodality is the native North American military associations which developed on the Great Plains after the introduction of the horse. Among the Crow and the Cheyenne, these associations tried to outdo

7.4 *LEOPARD SKIN CHIEF*
[E. E. Evans-Pritchard and Claredon Press]

Law, order, and war in
egalitarian societies

one another in acts of daring during combat and in horse-stealing expeditions. Although the members of each club did not fight as a unit, they met in their respective tepees to reminisce and sing about their exploits, and they wore distinctive insignia and clothing. Gretel and Perttie Pelto (1976, p. 324) have aptly compared them to organizations like the Veterans of Foreign Wars and the American Legion because their main function was to celebrate military exploits and to uphold the honor and prestige of the "tribe." However, on the occasion of a long march to a new territory or large-scale collective hunts, the military clubs took turns supervising and policing the general population. For example, they prevented overeager hunters from stampeding the buffalo herds, and they suppressed rowdy behavior at ceremonials by fining or banishing disruptive individuals. But these were only seasonal functions, since it was only during the spring and summer that large numbers of unrelated people could congregate together at the same camp.

Warfare among hunters and gatherers

War is defined as armed combat between groups of people who constitute separate territorial teams or political communities (Otterbein, 1973). Some anthropologists believe warfare was universally practiced, even among Paleolithic hunters and gatherers (Lizot, 1979, p. 151). Others hold that warfare was uncommon until the advent of state societies. It has been said that warfare was absent among the following hunter-gatherers: the Andaman Islanders, the Shoshoni, the Yahgan, the Mission Indians of California, and the Tasaday of the Philippines (Lesser, 1968; MacLeish, 1972). Even these groups, however, may have practiced warfare at some time in the past. On the other hand, William Divale (1972) lists thirty-seven hunting-and-

gathering cultures in which warfare is known to have been practiced. Some anthropologists attribute these cases to the shocks of contact with state-level colonial systems. Warfare was probably practiced by Paleolithic hunters and gatherers, but on a small scale and infrequently. Warfare probably increased in intensity during the Neolithic among village-organized farming cultures.

The archeological evidence for warfare in the Paleolithic is inconclusive. Mutilated skulls found in Paleolithic caves have sometimes been interpreted as indicating prehistoric head-hunting and cannibalism. But no one really knows how the individuals died. Even if cannibalism was practiced, the cannibalized individuals were not necessarily enemies. Eating the brains of deceased kin is a common form of mortuary ritual (see p. 281). The earliest definite archeological evidence for warfare is found in Neolithic Jericho in the form of defensive walls, towers, and ditches (Roper, 1969, 1975; Bigelow, 1975).

After the development of permanent villages with large investments in crops, animals, and stored foods, the form of warfare changed. Among nonsedentary hunters and gatherers, warfare involved a higher degree of individualized combat directed toward the adjustment of real or imagined personal injuries and deprivations. Although the combat teams may have had a temporary territorial base, the organization of battle and the consequences of victory or defeat reflected the loose association between people and territory. The victors did not gain territory by routing their enemies. Warfare among village-dwelling cultivators, however, frequently involves a total team effort in which definite territories are fought over and in which defeat may result in the rout of a whole community from its fields, dwellings, and natural resources.

The slippery line between warfare and personal retribution among hunters and gatherers is well illustrated in the example of armed conflict among the Tiwi of Bathurst and Melville Islands, northern Australia (Fig. 7.5). As recounted by C. W. Hart and Arnold Pilling (1960), a number of men from the Tiklauila and Rangwila bands developed personal grievances against a number of men who were residing with the Mandiimbula band. The aggrieved individuals, together with their relatives, put on the white paint of war, armed themselves, and set off, some thirty strong, to do battle with the Mandiimbula:

On arrival at the place where the latter, duly warned of its approach, had gathered, the war party announced its presence. Both sides then exchanged a few insults and agreed to meet formally in an open space where there was plenty of room. (1960, p. 84)

7.5 *TIWI WARRIOR*
Tiwi man dressed in traditional dance body paint and feathers. [Australian Information Service]

During the night, individuals from both groups visited each other, renewing acquaintances. In the morning the two armies lined up at the opposite sides of the battlefield. Hostilities were begun by elders shouting insults and accusations at particular individuals in the "enemy" ranks. Although some of the old men urged that a general attack be launched, their grievances turned out to be directed not at the Mandiimbula band, but at one or at most two or three individuals: "Hence when spears began to be thrown, they were thrown by individuals for reasons based on individual disputes" (Hart and Pilling, 1960, p. 84). Marksmanship was poor because it was the old men who did most of the spear-throwing.

Not infrequently the person hit was some innocent noncombatant or one of the screaming old women who weaved through the fighting men, yelling obscenities at everybody, and whose reflexes for dodging spears were not as fast as those of the men. . . . As soon as somebody was wounded . . . fighting stopped immediately until the implications of this new incident could be assessed by both sides. (p. 84)

Although hunters and gatherers seldom try to annihilate each other and often retire from the field after one or two casualties have occurred, the cumulative effect may be quite considerable. Remember that the average !Kung San band has only about thirty people in it. If such a band engages in war only twice per generation, and each time with the loss of only one adult male, casualties due to warfare would account for more than 10 percent of all adult male deaths. This is an extremely high figure when one realizes that less than 1 percent of all male deaths in Europe and the United States during the twentieth century have been battlefield casualties. In contrast, Lloyd Warner estimated that 28 percent of the adult male deaths among the Murngin, a hunting and gathering culture of northern Australia, were due to battlefield casualties (Livingstone, 1968).

CHAPTER 7
Law, order, and war in
egalitarian societies

Warfare among village agriculturalists

Although village peoples were not the first to practice warfare, they did expand the scale and ferocity of military engagements. Village houses, food-processing equipment, crops in the field, domestic animals, secondary-growth forests, and prime garden lands represent capital investments closely identified with the arduous labor inputs by specific groups of individuals. The defense of this investment laid the basis for the development of stable, exclusive territorial identities. Villages often oppose each other as traditional enemies, repeatedly attack and plunder each other, and often expropriate each other's territories. Archeologically, the onset of territoriality is suggested by the practice of burying deceased villagers beneath the houses they occupied during life (Flannery, 1972). Ethnologically, the intensification of local identities is suggested by the development of unilineal systems of reckoning descent. The develop-ment of the concern with descent and inheritance, as Michael Harner (1970) has shown, is closely related to the degree to which agricultural populations cease to depend on hunting and gathering for their food supply.

Warfare among village cultivators is likely to be more costly in terms of battle casualties than among seminomadic hunters and gatherers. Among the Dani of West Irian, New Guinea, warfare has an open-field, ritualistic phase (which resembles the encounters described for the Tiwi) in which casualties are light. But there are also sneak attacks resulting in a hundred fatalities at a time and in the destruction and expulsion of whole villages. Karl G. Heider (1972) estimates that the Dani lost about 5 percent of their population per year to warfare and that 29 percent of the men and 3 percent of the women died as a result of battle injuries incurred primarily in raids and ambushes. Among the Yanomamo (Fig. 7.6) of Brazil and Venezuela, who are reputed to have one of the world's "fiercest" and most warlike cultures, sneak raids and ambushes account for about 33 percent of adult

7.6 YANOMAMO WARRIORS
Preparations for battle include body painting and "line-ups." [Kenneth R. Good]

male deaths from all causes and about 7 percent of adult female deaths from all causes (Chagnon, 1974, pp. 160–161).

Warfare and the regulation of population growth

It may seem obvious that since people kill each other in warfare, warfare restrains population growth. But the matter is not so simple. War makers like the Yanomamo and Tsembaga Maring cannot control the growth of their population merely by killing each other at the rates reported above. The problem is that the individuals who are killed in battle are mostly males. Male deaths due to warfare among the Yanomamo have no long-run effect on the size of the population because, like most war-making preindustrial societies, the Yanomamo are polygynous. This means that any woman whose husband is killed is immediately remarried to another man. The reported female death rates from battle casualties is almost everywhere below 10 percent (see Polgar, 1972, p. 206), not enough to produce by itself a substantial lowering of population growth. Similar conclusions about the ineffectuality of combat deaths as a population control device have been reached with respect to warfare in industrial contexts. Catastrophes like World War II "have no effect on the population growth or size" (Livingstone, 1968, p. 5). This can be seen vividly in the case of Vietnam, where population continued to increase at a phenomenal 3 percent per year during the decade 1960 to 1970.

Among band and village peoples, however, warfare may achieve its major effect as a regulator of population growth through an indirect consequence. William Divale has shown that there is a strong correlation between the practice of warfare and high levels of female mortality in the age group from birth through 14 years (Divale and Harris, 1976; see Hirschfeld et al., 1978; Divale et al., 1978). This is revealed by the ratio of males to females in the 0–14 age bracket among societies actively engaged in warfare when they were first censused (see Table 7.1).

It is generally accepted that slightly more boys than girls are born on a worldwide basis and that the average sex ratio at birth is about 105 males to 100 females. This imbalance, however, is much smaller than that found in the war-making societies. The discrepancy may be accounted for by a higher rate of death among female infants, children, and juveniles than among their male counterparts. This higher rate of female mortality probably reflects the practice of more female infanticide than male infanticide and the practice of various forms of neglect more often against young girls than against young boys. There is a strong correlation between societies which admit that they practice infanticide and those which were actively engaged in warfare when they were first censused; in these societies, at least, it is clear that female infanticide was more common than male infanticide.

Perhaps the reason for the killing and neglect of female children is that success in preindustrial warfare depends on the size of the male combat teams. When weapons are muscle-powered clubs, spears, and bows and arrows, victory will fall to the group that has the biggest and most aggressive males. Since there are ecological limits to the number of people who can be reared by band and village

---

TABLE 7.1 *SEX RATIOS AND WARFARE*

	Young males per 100 females
Warfare present	128
Stopped 5–25 years before census	113
Stopped over 25 years before census	109

Source: Divale and Harris, 1976. Reproduced by permission of the American Anthropological Association from the *American Anthropologist* 78:527, 1976.

societies, war-making band and village societies tend to rear more males than females. This favoring of male over female children reduces the rate of growth of regional populations and, whether or not intended, may help to explain why warfare is so widely practiced by preindustrial peoples. According to this theory, slowing of regional population growth could not be achieved without warfare, since without the war-induced motivation to prefer male children to female children, each group would tend to reduce its postconception penalties, rear all its female children, and expand its population at its neighbor's expense. Warfare tends to equalize these costs or at least to spread them among all the bands and villages in the region in the form of both high rates of female mortality produced by infanticide and neglect and high rates of male mortality produced by combat. Although this system seems cruel and wasteful, the preindustrial alternatives for keeping population below the point of diminishing returns were equally if not more cruel and wasteful—abortion, malnutrition, and disease. The reader is warned that this theory remains highly controversial.

Animal protein and warfare: the Yanomamo

The Yanomamo derive their main source of food calories with little effort from the plantains and banana trees that grow in their forest gardens. Like the Maring, they burn the forest to get these gardens started, but bananas and plantains are perennials that provide high yields per unit of labor input for many consecutive years. Since the Yanomamo live in the midst of the world's greatest tropical forest, the little burning they do scarcely threatens to "eat up the trees." A typical Yanomamo village has less than 100 people in it, a population that could easily grow enough bananas or plantains in nearby garden sites without ever having to move (Fig. 7.7). Yet the Yanomamo villages constantly break up into factions that move off into new territories.

It has been suggested that despite the apparent abundance of resources, the high level of Yanomamo warfare is caused by resource depletion and population pressure. The resource in question is animal protein. The Yanomamo lack domesticated sources of animal protein and must obtain their animal protein from hunting and collecting. Moreover, unlike many other inhabitants of the Amazon Basin, the Yanomamo traditionally did not have access to big river fish and other aquatic animals which elsewhere provided high-quality animal protein sufficient to supply villages that contained over 1000 people. The theory relating animal protein to warfare among the Yanomamo is this: As Yanomamo villages grow, intensive hunting diminishes the availability of game nearby. Meat from large animals grows scarce and people eat more small animals, insects, and larva. The point of diminishing returns is reached. Tensions within and between villages increases and this leads to villages breaking apart before they permanently deplete the animal resources. It also leads to the escalation of raiding, which disperses the Yanomamo villages over a wide territory, and this also protects vital resources by creating no-man's-lands, which function as game preserves (Harris, 1977).

Some anthropologists with firsthand knowledge of the Yanomamo have rejected this theory. They point to the fact that there are no clinical signs of protein deficiencies among the Yanomamo—no *kwashiorkor*, a disease that results from acute protein deficiency. Also they have shown that in at least one village whose population is thirty-five, daily per capita overall protein intake was 75 grams per day per adult, which is far higher than the minimum 35 grams for all forms of protein recommended by the Food and Agricultural Organization. They have also shown that Yanomamo villages that have low levels of protein intake (36 grams) seem to engage in

7.7 *YANOMANO VILLAGE*
**This scene is more representative of everyday
life among the Yanomamo, despite their
warlike reputation. Note the plantains, the
staple food of the Yanomamo, hanging from
the rafters. [Kenneth R. Good]**

warfare just as frequently as those that have
high protein intake (75 grams) per adult. Finally, they point out that other groups in the
Amazon such as the Achuara enjoy as much as
107 grams of animal protein per capita and
still go to war frequently (Chagnon and
Hames, 1979; Lizot, 1977, 1979). Kenneth
Good (n.d.), however, has shown that obtaining adequate supplies of meat is a constant
preoccupation among the Yanomamo, and
that meat is actually consumed only once or
twice a week on the average. Good also points
out that the efficiency of hunting declines in
areas close to villages, necessitating frequent
long distance hunts, some of which take the
whole village on protracted treks.

Eric Ross (1979) also points out that the average daily amount of animal protein consumed is a misleading figure. Because of fluctuations in the number and size of animals
captured there are actually many days during
which there is little or no meat available. On
days when a large animal such as a tapir is
caught, the consumption rate may rise to 250
or more grams per adult; but for weeks at a
time, the consumption rate may not rise
above 30 grams per adult per day.

The absence of clinical signs of protein deficiency is not an argument against the theory,
but rather supports the general point that
band and village peoples can enjoy high standards of health as long as they control population growth and that warfare protects the
Yanomamo from diminishing returns and the
effects of depletions. The fact that villages
that have both high and low protein intake
have the same level of warfare also does not
test the theory because, as among the Maring
and Mae Enga, warfare necessarily pits villages at different stages of growth against

each other. Hence Yanomamo groups with little immediate ecological motivation to go to war may have no choice but to engage in counterraids against large groups that are depleting their game reserves and raiding their less populous neighbors in order to expand their hunting territory. The theory in question stresses that warfare is a regional phenomenon involving regional adjustments of population and resources.

How then can the ecological explanation of Yanomamo warfare be tested? What we need to know is this: First, whether the quantity and quality of animal protein declines and/or the labor cost of obtaining it increases as villages grow from 35 to 100 or more people; and second, whether the frequency of warfare in the region in general increases as the average size of villages increases and the per capita quantity and quality of animal protein falls. These data are not yet available and are difficult to obtain.

Summary

Orderly relationships between individuals and domestic groups in band and village societies are maintained without governments and law enforcement specialists. This is possible because of small size, predominance of kinship and reciprocity, and egalitarian access to vital resources. Public opinion is the chief source of law and order in these societies.

There is an absence of individual or nuclear family ownership of land among hunting and gathering bands and most village peoples. However, even in the most egalitarian societies there is private ownership of some items. The prevalence of the reciprocal mode of exchange and the absence of anonymous price markets renders theft unnecessary and impractical.

The major threat to law and order among band and village societies stems from the tendency of domestic and kinship groups to escalate conflicts in support of real or imagined injuries to one of their members. Such support is not dependent upon abstract principles of right and wrong, but upon the probable outcome of a particular course of action in the face of public opinion. The Eskimo song duel is an illustration of how public opinion can be tested and used to end conflicts between individuals who belong to different domestic and kinship groups.

Witchcraft accusations are another means of giving public opinion an opportunity to identify and punish persistent violators of the rules of reciprocity and other troublemakers. Shamans act as the mouthpiece of the community, but their position is precarious and they themselves are frequently identified as the source of misfortune and conflict. As among the Kuikuru, the fear of being accused of witchcraft encourages people to be amiable and generous. However, under stressful conditions witchcraft accusations may build to epidemic proportions and become a threat to the maintenance of law and order.

Headmanship reflects the pervasive egalitarian nature of the institutions of law and order in band and village societies. Headmen can do little more than harangue and plead with people for support. They lack physical or material means of enforcing their decisions. Their success rests on their ability to intuit public opinion.

As exemplified by the Nuer, large numbers of people can be mobilized for warfare without the concentration of the political power in law and order specialists by means of the principle of complementary opposition. In the presence of complementary opposition, the avoidance of blood feud becomes a paramount concern of all the higher-order lineages. Among the Nuer, this concern is expressed in the institution of the leopard skin chief, whose ritual authority has no basis whatsoever in political and economic power or in kinship relationships.

Other instances of nonkin political organization take the form of voluntary associations or sodalities such as men's and women's clubs, secret societies, and age-grade sets. However, all these nonkin modes of political organization remain rather rudimentary and are overshadowed by the pervasive networks of kinship alliances based on marriage and descent, which constitute the "glue" of band and village societies.

Although both hunter-gatherers and village farmers engage in warfare, there is reason to believe that warfare was less frequent in the Paleolithic than in the Neolithic and that village farmers are more likely to attempt to rout each other. It seems likely that warfare in some preindustrial contexts helped to restrain population growth and to protect resources from depletion. Warfare could have this effect through combat deaths, the encouragement of female infanticide, and the creation of no-man's-land game preserves. Evidence for this ecological interpretation of warfare consists of cross-cultural studies that correlate unbalanced sex ratios with active warfare.

The theory that warfare regulates population growth or prevents depletions is not accepted by many anthropologists. Others even deny that warfare is caused by population pressure and insist that the causes are mainly psychological. In the case of the Yanomamo, considerable controversy surrounds the role of protein as a limiting factor in regional carrying capacities. It cannot be said that the Yanomamo suffer from a shortage of protein. Yet it seems likely that as their villages grow in size, the quality and quantity of animal protein resources decline and the costs of obtaining high-quality diets increase. It is useful to strive to maintain animal protein production and consumption at levels far higher than those minimally necessary to avoid malnutrition. More research encompassing long-range regional trends in population density, frequency of warfare, and changes in quantity and quality of protein consumption is needed to resolve these controversies.

The Political Economy of the State

In this chapter we contrast the egalitarian forms of political life characteristic of band and village societies with the political life of chiefdoms and states. We will examine a plausible theory of how the great transformations from bands and villages to chiefdoms and states took place. We will also discuss the role of coercive physical force and of more subtle forms of thought control in the maintenance of inequality and the status quo in ancient and modern states.

Bigmanship

As we have seen (p. 71), headmen often function as intensifiers of production and as redistributors. They get their relatives to work harder, and they collect and then give away the extra product. A village may have several headmen. Where technological and ecological conditions encourage intensification, a considerable degree of rivalry may develop among headmen living in the same village. They vie with each other to hold the most lavish feasts and to redistribute the greatest amount of valuables. Often, the most successful redistributors earn the reputation of being "big men."

Anthropologist Douglas Oliver (1955) carried out a classic study of "bigmanship" during his fieldwork among the Siuai on Bougainville in the Solomon Islands. Among the Siuai a "big man" is called a *mumi*, and to achieve *mumi* status is every youth's highest ambition. A young man proves himself capable of becoming a *mumi* by working hard and by carefully restricting his consumption of meat and coconuts. Eventually, he impresses his wife, children, and near relatives with the seriousness of his intentions, and they vow to help him prepare for his first feast. If the feast is a success, his circle of supporters widens and he sets to work readying an even greater display of generosity. He aims next at the construction of a men's clubhouse in which his male followers can lounge about and in which guests can be entertained and fed. Another feast is held at the consecration of the clubhouse, and if this is also a success, the circle of people willing to work for him grows still larger and he will begin to be spoken of as a *mumi*. Larger and larger feasts mean that the *mumi's* demands on his supporters become more irksome. Although they grumble about how hard they have to work, they remain loyal as long as their *mumi* continues to maintain or increase his renown as a "great provider."

Finally, the time comes for the new *mumi* to challenge the others who have risen before him. This is done at a *muminai* feast, where a tally is kept of all the pigs, coconut pies, and sago-almond puddings given away by the host *mumi* and his followers to the guest *mumi* and his followers. If the guest *mumi* cannot reciprocate in a year or so with a feast at least as lavish as that of his challengers, he suffers a great social humiliation and his fall from *mumi*hood is immediate. In deciding on whom to challenge, a *mumi* must be very careful. He tries to choose a guest whose downfall will increase his own reputation, but he must avoid one whose capacity to retaliate exceeds his own.

At the end of a successful feast, the greatest of *mumis* still faces a lifetime of personal toil and dependence on the moods and inclinations of his followers. *Mumi*hood does not confer the power to coerce others into doing one's bidding, nor does it elevate one's standard of living above anyone else's. In fact, since giving things away is the essence of *mumi*hood, great *mumis* may even consume less meat and other delicacies than an ordinary, undistinguished Siuai. Among the Kaoka, another Solomon Island group reported on by H. Ian Hogbin (1964, p. 66), there is the saying: "The giver of the feast takes the bones and the stale cakes; the meat and the fat go to the others." At one great feast attended by 1100 people, the host *mumi*, whose name was Soni, gave away 32 pigs plus a large quantity of sago-almond puddings. Soni and his closest followers, however, went hungry. "We shall eat Soni's renown," his followers said.

Big men and warfare

Formerly, the *mumis* were as famous for their ability to get men to fight for them as they were for their ability to get men to work for them. Warfare had been suppressed by the co-

142   CHAPTER 8
The political economy
of the state

lonial authorities long before Oliver carried out his study, but the memory of *mumi* war leaders was still vivid among the Siuai. As one old man put it:

In the olden times there were greater mumi *than there are today. Then they were fierce and relentless war leaders. They laid waste to the countryside and their clubhouses were lined with the skulls of people they had slain.* (Oliver, 1955, p. 411)

In singing praises of their *mumis*, the generation of pacified Siuai call them "warriors" and "killers of men and pigs" (Oliver, 1955, p. 399):

Thunderer, Earth-shaker
Maker of many feasts,
How empty of gong sounds will all the places
*   be when you leave us!*
Warrior, Handsome Flower,
Killer of men and pigs,
Who will bring renown to our places
When you leave us.

Oliver's informants told him that *mumis* had more authority in the days when warfare was still being practiced. Some *mumi* war leaders even kept one or two prisoners who were treated like slaves and forced to work in the *mumi*'s family gardens. And people could not talk "loud and slanderously against their *mumis* without fear of punishment." This fits theoretical expectations, since the ability to redistribute meat and other valuables goes hand in hand with the ability to attract a following of warriors, equip them for combat, and reward them with spoils of battle. Rivalry between Bougainville's war-making *mumis* appeared to have been leading toward an islandwide political organization when the first European voyagers arrived. According to Oliver (1955, p. 420): "For certain periods of time many neighboring villages fought together so consistently that there emerged a pattern of war-making regions, each more or less internally peaceful and each containing one outstanding mumi whose war activities provided internal "social cohesion." These *mumis* enjoyed regional fame, but their pre-

rogatives remained rudimentary. This is shown by the fact that the *mumis* had to provide their warriors with prostitutes brought into the clubhouses and with gifts of pork and other delicacies. Said one old warrior:

If the mumi *didn't furnish us with women, we were angry. . . . All night long we would copulate and still want more. It was the same with eating. The clubhouse used to be filled with food, and we ate and ate and never had enough. Those were wonderful times.* (Oliver, 1955, p. 415)

Furthermore, the *mumi* who wanted to lead a war party had to be prepared personally to pay an indemnity for any of his men who were killed in battle and to furnish a pig for each man's funeral feast.

Chiefs, war, and redistribution: Trobrianders and Cherokee

Only a thin line separates a successful big man from a chief. Whereas big men must achieve and constantly validate their status by recurrent feasts, chiefs inherit their office and hold it even if they are temporarily unable to provide their followers with generous redistributions. Chiefs tend to live better than commoners; unlike big men, they do not always keep only the "bones and stale cakes for themselves." Yet in the long run, chiefs too must validate their title by waging successful war, obtaining trade goods, and giving away food and other valuables to their followers.

The Trobriand Islanders

The difference between big men and chiefs can be illustrated with the case of the Trobriand Islanders. Trobriander society was divided into several matrilineal clans and subclans of unequal rank and privilege through which access to garden lands was inherited.

Bronislaw Malinowski (1920) reported that the Trobrianders were keen on fighting and that they conducted systematic and relentless wars, venturing across the open ocean in their canoes to trade—or, if need be, to fight—with the people of islands over 100 miles away. Unlike the Siuai *mumis*, the Trobriand chiefs occupied hereditary offices and could be deposed only through defeat in war. One of these, whom Malinowski considered to be the "paramount chief" of all the Trobrianders, held sway over more than a dozen villages, containing several thousand people all told. Chieftainships were hereditary within the wealthiest and largest subclans, and the Trobrianders attributed these inequalities to wars of conquest carried out long ago. Only the chiefs could wear certain shell ornaments as the insignia of high rank, and it was forbidden for any commoner to stand or sit in a position that put a chief's head at a lower elevation than anyone else's. Malinowski (1922) tells of seeing all the people present in the village of Bwoytalu drop from their verandas as if blown down by a hurricane at the sound of a drawn-out cry announcing the arrival of an important chief.

The Trobriand chief's power rested ultimately upon his ability to play the role of "great provider," which depended on customary and sentimental ties of kinship and marriage rather than on the control of weapons and resources. Residence among the Trobriand commoners was normally avunculocal (see Ch. 6). Adolescent boys lived in bachelor huts until they got married. They then took their brides to live in their mother's brother's household, where they jointly worked the garden lands of the husband's matrilineage. In recognition of the existence of matrilineal descent, at harvest time brothers acknowledged that a portion of the produce of the matrilineal lands was owed to their sisters and sent them presents of baskets filled with yams, their staple crop. The Trobriand chief relied on this custom to validate his

title. He married the sisters of the headmen of a large number of sublineages. Some chiefs acquired several dozen wives, each of whom was entitled to an obligatory gift of yams from her brothers. These yams were delivered to the chief's village and displayed on special yam racks. Some of the yams were then distributed in elaborate feasts at which the chief validated his position as a "great provider," while the remainder were used to feed canoe-building specialists, artisans, magicians, and family servants who thereby became partially dependent on the chief's power. In former times the yam stores also furnished the base for launching long-distance Kula trading expeditions (see p. 65) among friendly groups and raids against enemies (Malinowski, 1935; Brunton, 1975).

The Cherokee

The political organization of the Cherokee of Tennessee (and of other southeastern woodland native Americans) bears striking resemblances to the Trobrianders' redistribution-warfare-trade-chief complex. The Cherokee, like the Trobrianders, were matrilineal, and they waged external warfare over long distances. At the center of the principal settlements was a large, circular "council house" where the council of chiefs discussed issues involving several villages and where redistributive feasts were held. The council of chiefs had a supreme chief who was the central figure in the Cherokee redistributive network. At harvest time a large crib, identified as the "chief's granary," was erected in each field. "To this each family carries and deposits a certain quantity according to his ability or inclination, or none at all if he so chooses." The chief's granaries functioned as "a public treasury . . . to fly to for succor" in the case of crop failure, as a source of food "to accommodate strangers, or travellers," and as a military store "when they go forth on hostile ex-

144 CHAPTER 8
The political economy
of the state

peditions." Although every citizen enjoyed "the right of free and public access," commoners had to acknowledge that the store really belonged to the supreme chief who had "an exclusive right and ability . . . to distribute comfort and blessings to the necessitous" (Bartram in Renfrew, 1973, p. 234).

Limitations of chiefly power: the Tikopia

Even though the Trobrianders feared and respected their "great provider" war chiefs, they were still a long way from a state society. Living on islands, the Trobrianders were not free to spread out, and their population density had risen in Malinowski's time to sixty persons per square mile. Nonetheless, the chiefs could not control enough of the production system to acquire great power. Perhaps one reason for this is that Trobriand agriculture lacked cereal grains. Since yams rot after three or four months (unlike rice or maize), the Trobriand "great provider" could not manipulate people through dispensing food year-round, nor could he support a permanent police-military garrison out of his stores. Another important factor was the open resources of the lagoons and ocean from which the Trobrianders derived their protein supply. The Trobriand chief could not cut off access to these resources and hence could not exercise permanent coercive political control over subordinates. Only with more intense forms of agriculture and large harvests of grains could the power of the "great provider" evolve beyond that of the Trobriand chiefs.

Another classic illustration of the limited nature of chiefly power is that of the chiefs of Tikopia, one of the smallest of the Solomon Islands. Here the chiefs' pretensions were even greater than those of the Trobriand chief, but their actual power was considerably less. The Tikopian chiefs claimed that they "owned" all the land and sea resources, yet the size of the redistributive network and of the harvests under their control made such claims unenforceable. Tikopian chiefs enjoyed few privileges. Nominally they claimed control of their cognatic kin group's gardens; but in practice they could not restrict their kin from any unused sites. Labor for their own gardens was in scarce supply, and they themselves worked like any "commoner" in the fields. To validate their positions, they were obliged to give large feasts, which in turn rested upon the voluntary labor and food contributions of their kin. Ties of kinship tended to efface the abstract prerequisites and etiquette of higher rank. Raymond Firth describes how a man from a commoner family, who in the kin terminology of the Tikopians was classified as a "brother," could exchange bawdy insults with the island's highest ranking chief:

On one occasion I was walking with the Ariki (chief) Kafika . . . when we passed the orchard of Pae Sao . . . all the principals present were "brothers" through various ties, and with one accord they fell upon each other with obscene chaff. Epithets of "Big testicles!" "You are the enormous testicles!" flew back and forth to the accompaniment of hilarious laughter. I was somewhat surprised at the vigor of the badinage for the Ariki Kafika, as the most respected chief of the island, has a great deal of sanctity attached to him. . . . However, this did not save him and he took it in good part. (1957, pp. 176–177)

Similar remarks pertain to the Cherokee chief. Outside the council, "He associates with the people as a common man, converses with them, and they with him in perfect ease and familiarity" (Bartram in Renfrew, 1973, p. 233).

From chiefdom to state

The larger and denser the population, the larger the redistributive network and the more powerful the redistributor war chief. Under certain circumstances, to be specified in a moment, the exercise of power by chiefs on the one hand and by ordinary food producers on the other becomes highly unbalanced. Contributions to the central store cease to be voluntary contributions. They become taxes. Access to the farmlands and natural resources cease to be rights. They become dispensations. Food producers cease being the chief's followers. They become peasants. Redistributors cease being chiefs. They become kings. And chiefdoms cease being chiefdoms. They become states.

The *state*, then, is a form of politically centralized society whose governing elites have the power to compel subordinates into paying taxes, rendering services, and obeying the law.

Mature states have several levels of *government;* that is, administrative bureaucracies that coordinate the military, economic, legal, and ritual activities of a network of villages (Wright, 1977). Archeologically, the state can often be identified by *site stratification:* large villages with public buildings surrounded by smaller villages and hamlets (McEwan and Dickson, 1978; Price, 1977).

One of the conditions that probably contributed to the development of the first states was the concentration of population in restricted habitats such as narrow river valleys surrounded by deserts or mountain valleys surrounded by precipitous slopes. These are said to be *circumscribed* habitats, because if people attempt to migrate away from them in order to escape from the burden of paying taxes, they will not be able to use the same mode of production and will have to endure hardships or accept a lower standard of living (Carneiro, 1970). In large chiefdoms located in circumscribed environments, some people or even whole villages would be inclined to accept a permanently subordinate political status rather than migrate to an unfavorable habitat where they would have to change their whole way of life.

Archeological evidence suggests that the first states arose in river valleys, seacoasts, mountain valleys, and other circumscribed habitats (Renfrew, 1973). In circumscribed habitats, little direct physical coercion would be needed to keep the subordinate peasantry in line. Kinship would be used to justify the legitimacy of differential access to resources on the part of junior and senior lineages or of wife-giving, wife-taking alliance groups (those who gave wives would expect tribute and labor services in return). Access to stored crops might be made contingent upon rendering craft or military services. Warfare would increase, and defeated villages would be incorporated into the tax and tribute network. A growing corps of military, religious, and craft specialists would be fed out of the central food stores, supporting the image of the rulers as beneficent "great providers." And the social distance between the police-military-priestly-managerial elite and the class of food-producing peasants would widen still more as food production increased, as trade networks expanded, as population grew, and as production was intensified through taxation and labor conscription (see Fried, 1978; Service, 1975).

On archeological evidence it seems probable that some of the very earliest states arose in river and mountain valleys and other circumscribed environments of the ancient Middle East and Mesoamerica (Renfrew, 1973). However, there is also considerable archeological evidence that indicates some of the earliest states may have arisen in noncircumscribed environments (MacNeish, 1972). Once the first states came into existence, they themselves constituted barriers against the flight of people who sought to preserve egalitarian systems. Moreover, with states as neighbors, egalitarian peoples found themselves increasingly drawn into warfare and were compelled to increase production and to give their redistributor-chiefs more and more power in order to prevail against the expansionist tendencies of their neighbors. Thus most of the states of

146   CHAPTER 8
The political economy
of the state

the world were produced by a great diversity of specific historical and ecological conditions (Fried, 1967). But once states come into existence, they tend to spread, engulf, and overwhelm nonstate peoples (Carneiro, 1978).

An African kingdom: Bunyoro

The difference between a chiefdom and a state can be illustrated with the case of the Bunyoro, a kingdom located in Uganda and studied by John Beattie (1960). Bunyoro had a population of about 100,000 people and an area of 5000 square miles. Supreme power over the Bunyoro territory and its inhabitants was vested in the Mukama, senior member of a royal lineage that reckoned its descent back to the beginning of time. The use of all natural resources, but especially of farming land, was a dispensation specifically granted by the Mukama to a dozen or more "chiefs" or to commoner peasants under their respective control. In return for these dispensations, quantities of food, handicrafts, and labor services were funneled up through the power hierarchy into the Mukama's headquarters. The Mukama in turn directed the use of these goods and services on behalf of state enterprises. The basic redistributive pattern was still plainly in evidence:

In the traditional system the king was seen both as the supreme receiver of goods and services, and as the supreme giver. . . . The great chiefs, who themselves received tribute from their dependents, were required to hand over to the Mukama a part of the produce of their estates in the form of crops, cattle, beer or women. . . . But everyone must give to the king, not only the chiefs. . . . The Mukama's role as giver was accordingly no less stressed. Many of his special names emphasize his magnanimity and he was traditionally expected to give extensively in the form both of feasts and of gifts to individuals. (Beattie, 1960, p. 34)

However great the Mukama's reputation for generosity, it is clear that he did not give away as much as he received. He certainly did not follow the Solomon Island *mumis* and keep only the stale cakes and bones for himself. Moreover, much of what he gave away did not flow back down to the peasant producers. Instead, it remained in the hands of his genealogically close kin, who constituted a clearly demarcated aristocratic class. Part of what the Mukama took away from the peasants was bestowed on nonkin who performed extraordinary services on behalf of the state, especially in connection with military exploits. Another part was used to support a permanent palace guard and resident staff who attended to the Mukama's personal needs and performed religious rites deemed essential for the welfare of the Mukama and the nation, such as custodian of spears, custodian of royal graves, custodian of the royal drums, custodian of royal crowns, "putters-on" of the royal crowns, custodians of royal thrones (stools) and other regalia, cooks, bath attendants, herdsmen, potters, barkcloth makers, musicians, and others. Many of these officials had several assistants.

In addition, there was a loosely defined category of advisers, diviners, and other retainers who hung around the court, attached to the Mukama's household as dependents, in the hope of being appointed to a chieftainship. To this must be added the Mukama's extensive harem, his many children, and the polygynous households of his brothers and of other royal personages. To keep his power intact, the Mukama and portions of his court made frequent trips throughout Bunyoro land, staying at local places maintained at the expense of his chiefs and commoners.

Feudalism

As Beattie points out, there are many analogies between the Bunyoro state and the "feudal" system existing in England at the time of the Norman invasion (1066). As in early medieval England, Bunyoro stratification involved a pledge of loyalty on the part of the district chiefs (lords) in return for grants of land and of the labor power of the peasants (serfs) who lived on these lands. The English king, like the Mukama, could call upon these chiefs to furnish weapons, supplies, and warriors whenever an internal or external threat to the king's sovereignty arose. The survival of the English feudal royal lineage, as in Bunyoro, was made possible by the ability of the king to muster larger coalitions of lords and their military forces than could be achieved by any combination of disloyal lords. But there are important differences in demographic scale and in the ruler's role as redistributor that must also be noted. While redistribution was continued through a system of royal taxation and tribute, the police-military function of the English king was more important than among the Bunyoro. The English sovereign was not the "great provider." He was, instead, the "great protector." With a population numbering over a million people and with agricultural and handicraft production organized on the basis of self-sustaining independent local estates, redistribution was wholly asymmetrical. It was not necessary for William the Conqueror to cultivate an image of generosity among the mass of peasants throughout his kingdom. Although he was careful to be generous to the lords who supported him, the display of generosity to the peasants was no longer important. A vast gulf had opened between the styles of life of peasants and overlords. And the maintenance of these differences no longer rested mainly on the special contribution the overlords made to production, but largely on their ability to deprive the peasants of subsistence and of life itself. But on the European medieval manorial estates, feudal lords were well advised not to push the exploitation (see p. 163) of their peasants beyond certain limits, lest they destroy the basis of their own existence.

In comparing African with European political development, it must be remembered that there were two periods of feudalism in Western and Northern Europe. The first, about which little is known, preceded the growth of the Roman Empire and was cut off by the Roman conquest. The second followed the collapse of the Roman Empire. Although the latter period provides the standard model of feudalism, the Bunyoro type of polity is actually a much more widely distributed form and probably closely resembles the political systems the Romans encountered and overran in their conquest of Western Europe (see Bloch, 1964; Piggott, 1966; Renfrew, 1973).

Because of the Roman Empire, the feudalism of medieval Europe rested on a technology far in advance of the technology found in even the most populous kingdoms south of the Sahara. The product taxed away by the Bunyoro ruling class was small compared to what was taxed away by the English feudal aristocracy. Architecture, metallurgy, textiles, and armaments were far more advanced in medieval Europe.

A native American empire: the Inca

Alternative evolutionary steps led to state systems that were larger and more centralized than those of medieval Europe. In several regions, there arose state systems in which scores of former small states were incorporated into highly centralized superstates or empires. In the New World, the largest and most powerful of these systems was the Inca Empire.

At its prime the Inca Empire stretched 1500 miles from northern Chile to southern Colombia and contained possibly as many as six million inhabitants. Because of government intervention in the basic mode of production, agriculture was not organized in terms of feudal estates, but rather in terms of villages, districts, and provinces. Each such unit was under the supervision not of a feudal lord who

148 CHAPTER 8
The political economy
of the state

8.1 SACSAHUAMAN
The principal fortress of the Inca Empire, near Cuzco, Peru. [American Museum of Natural History]

had sworn loyalty to another lord slightly his superior and who was free to use his lands and peasants as he saw fit, but of appointed government officials responsible for planning public works and delivering government-established quotas of laborers, food, and other material (Morris, 1976). Village lands were divided into three parts, the largest of which was probably the source of the workers' own subsistence; harvests from the second and third parts were turned over to religious and government agents who stored them in granaries. The distribution of these supplies was entirely under the control of the central administration. Likewise when labor power was needed to build roads, bridges, canals, fortresses, or other public works, government recruiters went directly into the villages. Because of the size of the administrative network and the density of population, huge

numbers of workers could be placed at the disposal of the Inca engineers. In the construction of Cuzco's fortress of Sacsahuaman (Fig. 8.1), probably the greatest masonry structure in the New World, 30,000 people were employed in cutting, quarrying, hauling, and erecting huge monoliths, some weighing as much as 200 tons. Labor contingents of this size were rare in medieval Europe but were common in ancient Egypt, the Middle East, and China.

Control over the entire empire was concentrated in the hands of the Inca. He was the first-born of the first-born, a descendant of the god of the sun and a celestial being of unparalleled holiness. This god-on-earth enjoyed power and luxury undreamed of by the poor Mehinacu chief in his plaintive daily quest for respect and obedience. Ordinary people could not approach the Inca face to

A native American empire: the Inca   **149**

face. His private audiences were conducted from behind a screen, and all who approached him did so with a burden on their back. When traveling he reclined on an ornate palanquin carried by special crews of bearers (Mason, 1957, p. 184). A small army of sweepers, water carriers, woodcutters, cooks, wardrobemen, treasurers, gardeners, and hunters attended the domestic needs of the Inca in his palace in Cuzco, the capital of the empire. If members of this staff offended the Inca, their entire village was destroyed.

The Inca ate his meals from gold and silver dishes in rooms whose walls were covered with precious metals. His clothing was made of the softest vicuna wool, and he gave away each change of clothing to members of the royal family, never wearing the same garment twice. The Inca enjoyed the services of a large number of concubines who were methodically culled from the empire's most beautiful girls. His wife, however, to conserve the holy line of descent from the god of the sun, had to be his own full sister. When the Inca died, his wife, concubines, and many other retainers were strangled during a great drunken dance in order that he suffer no loss of comfort in the afterlife. Each Inca's body was eviscerated, wrapped in cloth, and mummified. Women with fans stood in constant attendance upon these mummies, ready to drive away flies and to take care of the other things mummies need to stay happy.

8.2 STRATIFICATION: THE KING OF MOROCCO
Social inequality cannot endure without the use or threat of force. [UPI]

The state and the control of thought

Large populations, anonymity, use of market money, and vast differences in wealth make the maintenance of law and order in state societies more difficult to achieve than in bands, villages, and chiefdoms. This accounts for the great elaboration of police and paramilitary forces, and the other state-level institutions and specialists concerned with crime and punishment (Fig. 8.2). Although every state ultimately stands prepared to crush criminals and political subversives by imprisoning, maiming, or killing them, most of the daily burdens of maintaining law and order against discontented individuals and groups is borne by institutions that seek to confuse, distract, and demoralize potential troublemakers before they have to be subdued by physical force. Therefore, every state, ancient and modern, has specialists who perform ideological services in support of the status quo. These services are often rendered in a manner

150   CHAPTER 8
The political economy
of the state

and in contexts that seem unrelated to economic or political issues.

The main thought control apparatus of preindustrial states consists of magico-religious institutions. The elaborate religions of the Inca, Aztecs, ancient Egyptians, and other preindustrial civilizations sanctified the privileges and powers of the ruling elite. They upheld the doctrine of the divine descent of the Inca and the pharaoh and taught that the entire balance and continuity of the universe required the subordination of commoners to persons of noble and divine birth. Among the Aztecs, the priests were convinced that the gods must be nourished with human blood; and they personally pulled out the beating hearts of the state's prisoners of war on top of Tenochtitlan's pyramids (see Ch. 10). In many states, religion has been used to condition large masses of people to accept relative deprivation as necessity, to look forward to material rewards in the afterlife rather than in the present one, and to be grateful for small favors from superiors lest ingratitude call down a fiery retribution in this life or in a hell to come.

To deliver messages of this sort and demonstrate the truths they are based on, state societies invest a large portion of national wealth in monumental architecture. From the pyramids of Egypt or Teotihuacan in Mexico to the Gothic cathedrals of medieval Europe, state-subsidized monumentality in religious structures makes the individual feel powerless and insignificant. Great public edifices, whether seeming to float as in the case of the Gothic cathedral of Amiens, or to press down with the infinite heaviness of the pyramids of Khufu (Fig. 8.3), teach the futility of discontent and the invincibility of those who rule as well as the glory of heaven and the gods. (This is not to say that they teach nothing else.)

8.3 *THE GREAT PYRAMID OF KHUFU*
[Henle, Monkmeyer]

Thought control in modern contexts

A considerable amount of conformity is achieved not by frightening or threatening people, but by inviting them to identify with the governing elite and to enjoy vicariously the pomp of state occasions. Public spectacles such as religious processions, coronations, and victory parades work against the alienating effects of poverty and exploitation (Fig. 8.4). During Roman times, the masses were kept under control by letting them watch gladiatorial contests and other circus spectaculars. In the movies, television, radio, organized sports, Sputnik orbitings, and lunar landings, modern state systems possess powerful techniques for distracting and amusing their citizenry. Through modern media the consciousness of millions of listeners, readers, and watchers is often manipulated along rather precisely determined paths by government-subsidized specialists (Efron, 1972; Ellul, 1965; Key, 1976). But "entertainment" delivered through the air or by cable directly into the shantytown house or tenement apartment is perhaps the most effective form of "Roman circus" yet devised. Television and radio not only prevent alienation through the spectator's powers of enjoyment, they also keep people off the streets.

Yet the most powerful modern means of thought control may not lie in the electronic opiates of the entertainment industry, but in state-supported universal education. Teachers and schools obviously serve the instrumental needs of complex industrial civilizations by training each generation to provide the skills and services necessary for survival and well-being. But teachers and schools also devote a great deal of time to civics, history, citizenship, and social studies. These subjects are loaded with implicit or explicit assumptions about culture, people, and nature indicative of the superiority of the political-economic system in which they are taught. In the Soviet Union and other highly centralized Communist countries, no attempt is made to disguise the fact that one of the principal functions of universal education is political indoctrination. Western capitalist democracies are less open in acknowledging that their educational systems are also instruments of political control. Many teachers and students, lacking a comparative perspective, are not conscious of the extent to which their books, curricula, and classroom presentations uphold the status quo. Elsewhere, however, school boards, boards of regents, library committees, and legislative committees openly call for conformity to the status quo (Friere, 1973; Gearing and Tindale, 1973; Ianni and Story, 1973; Kozol, 1967; D. Smith, 1974; Wax et al., 1971).

Modern universal educational systems from kindergarten to graduate school operate with a politically convenient double standard. In the sphere of mathematics and the biophysical sciences, every encouragement is given to students to be creative, persistent, methodical, logical, and independently inquisitive. On the other hand, courses dealing with social and cultural phenomena systematically avoid "controversial subjects" such as concentration of wealth, ownership of multinational corporations, nationalizatin of the oil companies, involvement of banks and real estate interests in urban blight, ethnic and racial minority viewpoints, control of the mass media, military defense budgets, viewpoints of underdeveloped nations, alternatives to capitalism, alternatives to nationalism, atheism, and so on. But schools do not merely avoid controversial subjects. Certain political viewpoints are so essential to the maintenance of law and order that they cannot be entrusted to objective methods of instruction; instead, the viewpoints are implanted in the minds of the young through appeal to fear and hatred. The reaction of North Americans to socialism and communism is as much the result of indoctrination as is the reaction of Russians to capitalism. Flag saluting, oaths of allegiance, patriotic songs, and patriotic rites (assemblies, plays, pageants) are some of the other familiar ritualized political aspects of public school curricula.

Jules Henry, who went from the study of Indians in Brazil to the study of high schools in St. Louis, has contributed to the understanding of some of the ways by which universal education molds the pattern of national conformity. In his *Culture Against Man*, Henry shows how even in the midst of spelling and

---

8.4 *THOUGHT CONTROL IN THREE MODERN STATES* (facing page)
Top left, USA. Top right, Soviet Union. Bottom, China. [Wide World—top left; © Franck, Woodfin Camp—top right; UPI—bottom]

152   CHAPTER 8
The political economy
of the state

Thought control in modern contexts   **153**

singing lessons, there can be basic training in support of the competitive "free enterprise system." Children are taught to fear failure; they are also taught to be competitive. Hence they soon come to look upon each other as the main source of failure, and they become afraid of each other. As Henry (1963, p. 305) observes: "School is indeed a training for later life not because it teaches the 3R's (more or less), but because it instills the essential cultural nightmare—fear of failure, envy of success."

Today in the United States, acceptance of economic inequality depends on thought control more than on the exercise of naked repressive force. Children from economically deprived families are taught to believe that the main obstacle to achievement of wealth and power is their own intellectual merit, physical endurance, and will to compete. The poor are taught to blame themselves for being poor, and their resentment is directed primarily against themselves or against those with whom they must compete and who stand on the same rung of the ladder of upward mobility. In addition, the economically deprived portion of the population is taught to believe that the electoral process guarantees redress against abuse by the rich and powerful through legislation aimed at redistributing wealth. Finally, most of the population is kept ignorant of the actual workings of the political-economic system and of the disproportionate power exercised by lobbies representing corporations and other special interest groups. Henry concludes that U.S. schools, despite their ostensible dedication to creative inquiry, punish the child who has intellectually creative ideas with respect to social and cultural life:

Learning social studies is, to no small extent, whether in elementary school or the university, learning to be stupid. Most of us accomplish this task before we enter high school. But the child with a socially creative imagination will not be encouraged to play among new social systems, values, relationships; nor *is there much likelihood of it, if for no other reason than that the social studies teachers will perceive such a child as a poor student. Furthermore such a child will simply be unable to fathom the absurdities that seem transparent* truth *to the teacher. . . . Learning to be an idiot is part of growing up or, as Camus put it, learning to be absurd. Thus the child who finds it impossible to learn to think the absurd truth . . . usually comes to think himself stupid. (1963, pp. 287–288)*

The state and physical coercion

Law and order in stratified societies depends upon an infinitely variable mixture of physical compulsion through police-military force and thought control based on the kinds of techniques discussed in the previous section. In general, the more marked the social inequalities and the more intense the labor exploitation, the heavier must be the contribution of both forms of control. The regimes relying most heavily on brutal doses of police-military intervention are not necessarily those that display the greatest amount of visible social inequality. Rather, the most brutal systems of police-military control seem to be associated with periods of major transformations, during which the governing classes are insecure and prone to overreact. Periods of dynastic upheaval and of prerevolutionary and postrevolutionary turmoil are especially productive of brutality.

The most enduring of the world's despotisms keep their powers of coercion coiled in readiness. For example, as long as the Chinese emperors felt politically secure, they needed to give only an occasional demonstration of physical destruction in order to repress disloyal factions. Karl Wittfogel (1957) has provided a vivid account of the coiled terrors at the disposal of ancient despotisms. He writes of "total loneliness in the hour of doom" awaiting those who gave the slightest cause

154 CHAPTER 8
The political economy
of the state

for apprehension to the emperor. In the torture rooms and at the execution blocks, the vast power of the state, symbolized so perfectly in colossal public monuments and edifices, routinely obliterated potential troublemakers.

Some of the most brutal episodes in the career of the state occurred in the aftermath of the Russian revolution, when millions of people suspected of "counterrevolutionary" thoughts and attitudes were executed or sent to slower deaths in a vast system of slave labor camps (Solzhenitsyn, 1974). The Chinese revolution was also followed by waves of unrestrained attacks against millions of persons suspected of bourgeois sympathies (Bao and Chelminski, 1973; Bettleheim, 1978; London and London, 1979).

Yet, according to Karl Marx, communism is not only antithetical to despotism, but to any form of the state whatsoever. Marx was convinced that the state had come into existence only to protect the economic interests of the ruling class. He believed that if economic equality could be restored, the state would "wither away." The very notion of a "Communist state" is a contradiction in terms from the point of view of Marxist theory (Marx and Engels, 1948; Lichtheim, 1961). The existence of the Communist state is officially attributed to the need to protect the people who are building a Communist order from the aggression of the capitalist states or the lingering threat of procapitalist citizens (Lenin, 1965 [1917]). An equally plausible interpretation, however, is that the ruling classes in the Soviet Union and China will never voluntarily dissolve the still rapidly growing apparatus of thought control and physical coercion.

Although the ruling classes of Western parliamentary democracies rely more on thought control than on physical coercion to maintain law and order, in the final analysis they too depend on guns and jails to protect their privileges. Strikes by police in cities such as Montreal and blackouts such as occurred in New York City in 1977 (Fig. 8.5) quickly led to extensive looting and widespread disorder, proving that thought control is not enough and that large numbers of ordinary citizens do not believe in the system and are held in check only by the threat of physical punishment (Curvin and Porter, 1978; Weisman, 1978).

The fate of prestate bands and villages

The career of state-level societies has been characterized by continuous expansion into and encroachment upon the lands and freedoms of prestate peoples. For advanced chiefdoms the appearance of state-level soldiers, traders, missionaries, and colonists often resulted in a successful transition to state-level organization. But over the vast regions of the globe inhabited by dispersed bands and villages, the spread of the state has resulted in the annihilation or total distortion of the way of life of thousands of once free and proud peoples. These devastating changes are aptly described as *genocide*—the extinction of whole populations—or as *ethnocide*—the systematic extinction of cultures.

The spread of European states into the Americas had a devastating effect upon the inhabitants of the New World. Many methods were employed to rid the land of its original inhabitants in order to make room for the farms and industries needed to support Europe's overflowing population. Native American peoples were exterminated during unequal military engagements that pitted guns against arrows; others were killed off by new urban diseases brought by the colonists—diseases such as smallpox, measles, and the common cold—against which people who lived in small, dispersed settlements lacked immunity. The colonists were not above deliberately giving away infected clothing to hasten the spread of these diseases as a type of bacte-

8.5 *NEW YORK CITY, JULY 14, 1977*
Looting in the aftermath of a blackout.
[UPI]

156 CHAPTER 8
The political economy
of the state

riological warfare. Against the cultures of the natives there were other weapons. Their modes of production were destroyed by slavery, debt forms of peonage, and wage labor; their political life was destroyed by the creation of chiefs and tribal councils who were puppets and convenient means of control for state administrators (Fried, 1975); and their religious beliefs and rituals were demeaned and suppressed by missionaries who were eager to save their souls but not their lands and freedom (Ribeiro, 1971; Walker, 1972).

These genocidal attacks were not confined to North and South America. They were also carried out in Australia, on the islands of the Pacific, and in Siberia. Nor are they merely events that took place a long time ago and about which nothing can now be done. For they are still going on in the remote vastness of the Amazon Basin and other regions of South America where the last remaining New World free and independent band and village peoples have been cornered by the remorseless spread of colonists, traders, oil companies, teachers, ranchers, and missionaries (Bodley, 1975; Davis, 1977).

The tragic plight of the Aché Indians of eastern Paraguay is a case in point. As documented by Mark Münzel (1973), these independent foragers are being systematically hunted, rounded up, and forced to live on small reservations in order to make room for ranchers and farmers. Aché children are separated from their parents and sold to settlers as servants. The manhunters shoot anyone who shows signs of resistance, rape the women, and sell the children. In March and April of 1972, about 171 "wild" Aché were captured and deliberately taken to the Aché reservation, where it was known that an influenza epidemic was already raging. By July, 55 Achés on the reservation had died. Concludes Münzel (1973, p. 55): "Taking a large number of forest Indians there at this time, without providing for their health requirements, was indirect mass murder."

As Gerald Weiss points out, the last remaining "tribal" cultures are found in the remote regions of developing countries that often regard the survival of such independent peoples as a threat to their national unity.

The last of the tribal cultures are in serious jeopardy. When they are gone, we will not see their like again. The nonindustrialized statal cultures have joined forces with the industrialized states to eliminate them. The reason for this lies in the contrasting natures of statal and tribal cultures: the former are larger, more powerful, and expansionistic. Tribal cultures, representing an earlier cultural form, are denigrated as "savage" and viewed as an anachronism in the "modern world." The statal cultures have exercised their power by dividing all land on this planet among themselves. . . . This is as true for the Third World—where concerted efforts are made to destroy the last vestiges of tribalism as a threat to national unity—as it has been for the Western World. (1977a, p. 890)

Weiss argues it is probable but not inevitable that none of the tribal societies will survive. Yet he insists that anthropologists must not be defeatists and must strive to prevent that from happening:

No biologist would claim that evolution in the organic realm makes either necessary or desirable the disappearance of earlier forms, so no anthropologist should be content to remain a passive observer of the extinction of the Tribal World. (1977a, p. 891)

Summary

Societies with big men, chiefs, and ruling classes represent three different forms of political organization involved in the transformation of egalitarian into stratified state societies. The big man is a rivalrous form of headmanship marked by competitive redistributions that expand and intensify production. As illustrated by the *mumis* of the Solomon Islands, bigmanship is a temporary status requiring constant validation through displays of generosity that leave the big man poor in possessions but rich in prestige and authority. Since they are highly respected, big men are well suited to act as leaders of war parties, long-distance trading expeditions, and other collective activities that require leadership among egalitarian peoples.

Like big men, chiefs also play the role of great provider, expand and intensify production, give feasts, and organize long-distance warfare and trading expeditions. However, as illustrated by the Trobriand, Cherokee, and Tikopian chiefdoms, chiefs enjoy hereditary status, tend to live somewhat better than the average commoner, and can be deposed only through defeat in warfare. Nonetheless, the power of chiefs is distinctly limited because they lack support from a permanent group of police-military specialists and cannot permanently deprive significant numbers of their followers from access to the means of making a living.

In stratified state societies, the power of kings is the power of taxation. Failure of peasants to contribute to the redistributive system may result in their being cut off from the means of subsistence. The military, economic, and ritual activities of a network of villages is coordinated by an administrative bureaucracy, and the settlements themselves exhibit hierarchical differences known as site stratification.

The pristine forms of stratification and statehood were probably often linked to the development of dense populations in circumscribed habitats. Peasantries arose when subordinate villages and lineages could not avoid taxation by fleeing to other habitats without changing their whole way of life. Secondary states, however, arose under a variety of conditions related to the spread of the pristine states.

The difference between chiefdoms and states is illustrated by the case of the Bunyoro. The Mukama was a great provider for himself and his closest supporters but not for the majority of the Bunyoro peasants. The Mukama, unlike the Trobriand chief, maintained a permanent court of personal retainers and a palace guard. There are many resemblances between the Bunyoro and the "feudal" kingdoms of early medieval Europe. But the power of the early English kings was greater and depended less on the image of the great provider than on that of the great protector.

The most developed and highly stratified form of statehood is that of empire. As illustrated by the Inca of Peru, the leaders of ancient empires possessed vast amounts of power and were unapproachable by ordinary citizens. Production was supervised by a whole army of administrators and tax collectors. While the Inca was concerned with the welfare of his people, they viewed him as a god to whom they owed everything rather than as a headman or chief who owed everything to them.

Since all state societies are based on marked inequalities between rich and poor and rulers and ruled, maintenance of law and order presents a critical challenge. In the final analysis it is the police and the military with their control over the means of physical coercion that keep the poor and the exploited in line. However, all states find it more expedient to maintain law and order by controlling people's thoughts. This is done in a variety of ways, ranging from state religions to public rites and spectacles and universal education.

The plight of the remaining prestate band and village societies must not be overlooked. As in the case of the Aché, civilization and modernization lead to slavery, disease, and poverty for such people.

158 CHAPTER 8
The political economy
of the state

9

Stratified Groups: Class, Caste, Minority, Ethnicity

This chapter examines the principal varieties of stratified groups found in state-level societies. We will see that people who live in such societies think and behave in ways that are determined to a great extent by their membership in stratified groups and by their position in a stratification hierarchy. The values and behavior of such groups are in turn often related to a struggle for access to the structural and infrastructural sources of wealth and power.

Class and power

All state-level societies are organized into a hierarchy of groups known as classes (Fig. 9.1). A *class* is a group of people who have a similar relationship to the apparatus of control in state-level societies and who possess similar amounts of power (or lack of power) over the allocation of wealth and privileges and access to resources and technology.

All state societies necessarily have at least two classes arranged hierarchically—rulers and ruled. But where there are more than two classes, they are not necessarily all arranged hierarchically with respect to each other. For example, fishermen and neighboring farmers are usefully regarded as two separate classes because they relate to the ruling class in distinctive ways, have different patterns of ownership, rent, and taxation, and exploit entirely different sectors of the environment. Yet neither has a clear-cut power advantage or disadvantage with respect to the other. Similarly, anthropologists often speak of an urban as opposed to a rural lower class, although the quantitative power differentials between the two may be minimal.

Before proceeding any further, the nature of power involved in class hierarchies should be made as explicit as possible. *Power* in human affairs, as in nature, consists of the ability to control energy. Control over energy is mediated by the tools, machines, and techniques for applying that energy to individual or collective enterprises. To control energy in this sense is to possess the means for making, moving, shaping, and destroying minerals, vegetables, animals, and people. Power is control over people and nature (R. Adams, 1970).

The power of particular human beings cannot be measured simply by adding up the amount of energy they regulate or channel. If that were the case, the most powerful people in the world would be the technicians who

9.1 POVERTY AND POWER
This man is not only poor, but he is relatively powerless. [Charles Gatewood]

turn the switches at nuclear power plants, or the commercial jet pilots who open the throttle on four engines, each of which has the power of 40,000 horses. Military field officers in the armed forces, with their enormous capacity for killing and maiming, are not necessarily powerful people. The crucial question in all such cases is this: Who controls these technicians, civil servants, and generals, and makes them turn their "switches" on or off? Who tells them when, where, or how to fly? Who and when to shoot and kill? Or, equally important, who has the power to determine where and when a nuclear power plant or a space shuttle will be built, or how large a police-military force is to be recruited and with what machinery of destruction it is to be equipped?

One cannot simply add up all the energy in the form of food, chemicals, and kinetic forces that flow through the masses of the Inca commoners as compared with the Inca nobility and arrive at an assessment of their relative power positions. The fact is that much of the energy expended by subordinate classes in stratified societies is expended under conditions and on behalf of tasks that are stipulated or constrained by the ruling class. In other words, the question of whether or not such tasks are carried out depends on whether or not their performance enhances the power and well-being of the ruling class. This does not mean that the subordinate masses will derive no benefit from what they do at the behest of the ruling class, but simply that the performance will probably not take place if the ruling class does not derive some benefit as well.

Sex, age, and class

Sex hierarchies are conventionally distinguished from class hierarchies. We will do the same and postpone the discussion of sex hierarchies to Chapter 12. This distinction rests on the fact that class hierarchies include both sexes, whereas sex hierarchies refer to the domination of one sex by another within and across classes. Moreover, unlike class hierarchies, sex hierarchies occur in bands, villages, and chiefdoms as well as in states. This does not mean that sex hierarchies are less important or less severe, but merely that their analysis is best carried out in the context of a discussion of general sex roles rather than in the context of state forms of stratification.

It should also be noted that age groups within both state and prestate societies are also often associated with unequal distributions of power. Indeed, hierarchical differences between mature adults and juveniles and infants are virtually universal. Moreover, the treatment of children by adults sometimes involves highly exploitative and physically and mentally punitive practices. One might argue that age hierarchies are fundamentally different from class and sex hierarchies because the maltreatment and exploita-

tion of children is always "for their own good." Superordinate groups of all sorts, however, usually say this of the subordinate groups under their control. The fact that some degree of subordination of juveniles and infants is necessary for enculturation and population survival does not mean that such hierarchies are fundamentally different from class and sex hierarchies. Brutal treatment of children can result in death or permanent damage to their health and well-being. The resemblance between age hierarchies and class hierarchies is also strong in the cases in which old people constitute a despised and powerless group. In many societies senior citizens are victims of punitive physical and psychological treatment comparable to that meted out to criminals and enemies of the state. Descriptions of class structure, therefore, must never lose sight of the differences in power and life-style associated with sex and age groups within each class.

Emics, etics, and class consciousness

Class is an aspect of culture in which there are sharp differences between emic and etic points of view. Many social scientists accept class distinction as real and important only when consciously perceived and acted upon by the people involved. They hold that in order for a group to be considered a class, its members must have a consciousness of their own identity, exhibit a common sense of solidarity, and engage in organized attempts to promote and protect collective interests (T. Parsons, 1970; Fallers, 1977). Moreover, some social scientists (see Bendix and Lipset, 1966) believe that classes exist only when persons with similar forms and quantities of social power organize into collective organizations such as political parties or labor unions. Other social scientists believe that the most important features of class hierarchies are the actual concentrations of power in certain groups and the powerlessness of others, regardless of any conscious or even unconscious awareness of these differences on the part of the people concerned and regardless of the existence of collective organizations (Roberts and Brintnall, 1982, pp. 195–217).

From an etic and behavioral viewpoint, a class can exist even when the members of the class deny that they constitute a class, and even when instead of collective organizations they have organizations (such as rival business corporations or rival unions) that compete. The reason for this is that subordinate classes which lack class consciousness are obviously not exempt from the domination of ruling classes. Similarly, ruling classes containing antagonistic and competitive elements nonetheless dominate those who lack social power. Members of ruling classes need not form permanent, hereditary, monolithic, conspiratorial organizations in order to protect and enhance their own interests. A struggle for power within the ruling class does not necessarily result in a fundamentally altered balance of power between the classes. The

9.2 THE SOVIET RULING CLASS
Looking down from the top of Lenin's tomb, these powerful men are watching the celebration of the 64th anniversary of the Russian revolution in 1981. Where once the Czar ruled in the name of God, generals and bureaucrats now rule in the name of the proletariat. [Tass from Sovfoto]

Stratified groups: class, caste, minority, ethnicity

struggle for control of the English crown, the Chinese dynasties, the Soviet Party apparatus (Fig. 9.2), and modern multinational corporations all testify to the fact that the members of a ruling class may fight among themselves at the same time that they dominate or exploit subordinates.

Of course, there is no disputing the importance of a people's belief about the shape and origin of their stratification system. Consciousness of a common plight among the members of a downtrodden and exploited class may very well lead to the outbreak of organized class warfare. Consciousness is thus an element in the struggle between classes, but it is not the cause of class differences.

Economic exploitation

The control over large amounts of power by one class relative to another permits the members of the more powerful class to exploit the members of the weaker class. There is no generally accepted meaning of the term *exploitation,* but the basic conditions responsible for economic exploitation can be identified by reference to the previous discussion of reciprocity and redistribution (Ch. 4). When balanced reciprocity prevails or when the redistributors keep only the "stale cakes and bones" for themselves, there is no economic exploitation. But when there is unbalanced reciprocity or when the redistributors start keeping the "meat and fat" for themselves, exploitation may soon develop.

In the theories of Karl Marx, all wage laborers are exploited because the value of what they produce is always greater than what they are paid. Similarly, some anthropologists take the view that exploitation begins as soon as there is a structured flow of goods and services between two groups (Newcomer, 1977; Ruyle, 1973, 1975). Against this view it can be argued that the activities of employers and of stratified redistributors may result in an improvement in the well-being of the subordinate class and that without entrepreneurial or ruling class leadership everyone would be worse off (Dalton, 1972, 1974). One cannot say, therefore, that every inequality in power and in consumption standards necessarily involves exploitation. If, as a result of the rewards given to or taken by the ruling class, the economic welfare of all classes steadily improves, it would seem inappropriate to speak of the people responsible for that improvement as exploiters.

Exploitation may be said to exist when the following four conditions exist: (1) The subordinate class experiences deprivations with respect to basic necessities such as food, water, air, sunlight, leisure, medical care, housing, and transport; (2) the ruling class enjoys an abundance of luxuries; (3) the luxuries enjoyed by the ruling class depend upon the labor of the subordinate class; and (4) the deprivations experienced by the subordinate class are caused by the failure of the ruling class to apply its power to the production of necessities instead of luxuries and to redistribute these necessities to the subordinate class (Boulding, 1973). These conditions constitute an etic and behavioral definition of exploitation.

Because of the relationship between exploitation and human suffering, the study of exploitation is an important responsibility of social scientists who are concerned with the survival and well-being of our species. We must see to it that the study of exploitation is conducted empirically and with due regard to mental and emic as well as to etic and behavioral components.

Peasant classes

The majority of people alive today are members of one kind or another of peasant class. Peasants are the subordinate food-producing classes of state societies who use preindustrial technologies of food production. Many different types of rent and taxes are extracted from peasants. But "peasants of all times and places are structured inferiors" (Dalton, 1972, p. 406). The kind of rent or taxes extracted from peasants defines the essential features of their structured inferiority.

Each major type of peasant is the subject of a vast research literature. Anthropological studies of peasants have usually taken the form of "community studies." Anthropologists have studied peasant communities more than they have studied village peoples or hunters and gatherers (Pelto and Pelto, 1973). Three major types of peasant classes can be distinguished.

1. Feudal peasants These peasants are subject to the control of a decentralized hereditary ruling class whose members provide military assistance to one·another but do not interfere in one another's territorial domains. Feudal peasants, or "serfs," inherit the opportunity to utilize a particular parcel of land; hence they are said to be "bound" to the land. For the privilege of raising their own food, feudal peasants render unto the lord rent in kind or in money. Rent may also take the form of labor service in the lord's kitchens, stables, or fields.

Some anthropologists, following the lead of historians of European feudalism, describe feudal relationships as a more or less fair exchange of mutual obligations, duties, privileges, and rights between lord and serf. George Dalton (1969, pp. 390–391), for example, lists the following European feudal lord's services and payments to peasants:

1 Granting peasants the right to use land for subsistence and cash crops
2 Military protection (e.g., against invaders)
3 Police protection (e.g., against robbery)
4 Juridical services to settle disputes
5 Feasts to peasants at Christmas, Easter; also harvest gifts
6 Food given to peasants on days when they work the lord's fields

7 Emergency provision of food during disaster

Dalton denies that feudal peasants are exploited because it is not known if "the peasant paid out to the lord much more than he received back." Other anthropologists point out that the reason feudal peasants are "structured inferiors" is that the feudal ruling class deprives them of access to the land and its life-sustaining resources, which is antithetical to the principle of reciprocity and egalitarian redistribution. The counterflow of goods and services listed by Dalton merely perpetuates the peasants' structured inferiority. The one gift which would alter that relationship—the gift of land, free of rent or taxes—is never given.

History suggests that the structured inferiority of feudal peasants is seldom acceptable to the peasants. Over and over again the world has been convulsed by revolutions in which peasants struggled in the hope of restoring free access to land (E. Wolf, 1969).

Many feudal peasantries owe their existence to military conquest, and this further emphasizes the exploitative nature of the landlord-serf relationship. For example, the Spanish crown rewarded Cortès and Pizarro and the other *conquistadores* with lordships over large slices of the territories they had conquered in Mexico and Peru. The heavy tax and labor demands placed on the conquered native Americans thereafter contributed to a precipitous decline in their numbers (Henry Dobyns, 1966; C. Smith, 1970).

2. Agromanagerial state peasantries Where the state is strongly centralized, as in ancient Peru, Egypt, Mesopotamia, and China, peas-

---

9.4 CHINESE PEASANTS (facing page)
Water control is still one of the main functions of the Chinese state. Some of the 25,000 workers employed in construction of Shih Man Tan Reservoir on Huai River are shown with their earth-moving equipment. [Eastfoto]

9.3 ALBANIAN PEASANTS (*above*)
Commune members plowing. [Eastfoto]

9.5 PERUVIAN PEASANTS (*above*)
**Man's wife is planting potatoes as he plows.
[Walter Aguiar]**

ants may be directly subject to state control in addition to, or in the absence of, control by a local landlord class. Unlike the feudal peasants, agromanagerial peasants are subject to frequent conscription for labor brigades drawn from villages throughout the realm to build roads, dams, irrigation canals, palaces, temples, and monuments. In return the state makes an effort to feed its peasants in case of food shortages caused by droughts or other calamities. The pervasive bureaucratic control over production and life-styles in the ancient agromanagerial states has often been compared with the treatment of peasants in modern Socialist and Communist societies such as China, Albania (Fig. 9.3), Vietnam, and Cambodia. The state in these countries is all-powerful—setting production quotas, controlling prices, extracting taxes in kind and in labor. Much depends, of course, on the extent to which the peasants can exchange their lot with Party bosses and bureaucrats, and vice versa. In Communist China (Fig. 9.4), a considerable effort was made under Mao Tse-tung to destroy the class nature of peasant identity and to merge all labor—intellectual, industrial, and agricultural—in a single working class. But some analysts hold that the political economy of China amounts to little more than the restoration of the despotic agromanagerial state socialism that had existed for thousands of years under the Ming, Han, and Chou dynasties (Wittfogel, 1960; 1979).

3. Capitalist peasants In Africa, Latin America (Fig. 9.5), India, and Southeast Asia, feudal and agromanagerial types of peasantries have been replaced by peasants who enjoy increased opportunities to buy and sell land, labor, and food in competitive price markets. Most of the existing peasantries of the world outside of the Communist block belong to this category. The varieties of structured inferiority within this group defy any simple taxonomy. Some capitalist peasants are subordinate to large landowners; others are subordinate to banks that hold mortgages and promissory notes.

When the crops in production enter the international market, holdings are of the large, or *latifundia*, type and the real landowners tend to be the commercial banks. Elsewhere, in more isolated or unproductive regions, holdings may be very small, giving rise to postage-stamp farms known as *minifundia* (Fig. 9.6) and to the phenomenon Sol Tax has aptly called "penny capitalism."

Capitalist peasants correspond to what Dalton calls "early modernized peasants." They display the following features:

1 Marketable land tenure
2 Predominance of production for cash sale
3 Growing sensitivity to national commodity and labor price markets
4 Beginnings of technological modernization

Although many capitalist peasants own their own land, they do not escape payment of rent or its equivalent. Many communities of landowning peasants constitute labor reserves for larger and more heavily capitalized plantations and farmers. Penny capitalists are frequently obliged to work for wages paid by these cash-crop enterprises. Penny capitalist peasants cannot obtain enough income to satisfy subsistence requirements from the sale of their products in the local market.

The image of limited good

A recurrent question concerning the plight of contemporary peasant communities is the extent to which they are victims of their own values. It has often been noted, for example, that peasants are very distrustful of innovations and cling to their old ways of doing things. Based on his study of the village of

9.6 *ECUADORIAN PEASANTS* (*facing page*)
Note the postage stamp minifundia on the steep hillsides. [United Nations]

Stratified groups: class, caste, minority, ethnicity

Tzintzuntzan in the state of Michoacan, Mexico, George Foster (1967) has developed a general theory of peasant life based on the concept of the "image of limited good." According to Foster, the people of Tzintzuntzan, like many peasants throughout the world, believe that life is a dreary struggle, that very few people can achieve "success," and that they can improve themselves only at the expense of other people. If someone tries something new and succeeds at it, the rest of the community resents it, becomes jealous, and snubs the "progressive" individual. So, many peasants are afraid to change their way of life because they do not want to stir up the envy and hostility of friends and relatives.

Although there is no doubt that an image of limited good exists in many peasant villages in Mexico and elsewhere, the role it plays in preventing economic development is not clear. Foster provides much evidence for doubting the importance of the image of limited good in Tzintzuntzan (Fig. 9.7). He tells the story of how a community development project sponsored by the United Nations achieved success initially, only to end in disasters that had little to do with the values held by the villagers. Also, most of the com-

---

9.7 *IMAGE OF LIMITED GOOD*
Peasant women of Tzintzuntzan with their homemade pottery. [United Nations]

CHAPTER 9
Stratified groups: class, caste, minority, ethnicity

BAND
San hunter-gatherers [© Newman, 1980, Woodfin Camp]

VILLAGE
Yanomamo villagers [Kenneth R. Good]

The color photos on these two pages illustrate the four major levels of sociocultural evolution: band, village, chiefdom, state.

CHIEFDOM
Fiji island chief (wearing tie) [Katz, Anthro-Photo]

STATE
The Emir of Kano, a Nigerian kingdom [© Watriss, Woodfin Camp]

munity's cash income was derived by working as *braceros* (migrant laborers) in the United States. To get across the border, the *braceros* must bribe, scheme, and suffer great hardships. Yet 50 percent of them had succeeded in getting through, "many of them ten times or more" (Foster, 1967, p. 277).

As Foster suggests, the "image of limited good" is not a crippling illusion, but rather a realistic appraisal of the facts of life in a society where economic success or failure is capricious and hinged to forces wholly beyond one's control or comprehension (as, for example, when the United States unilaterally terminated the *bracero* program).

For the underlying, fundamental truth is that in an economy like Tzintzuntzan's, hard work and thrift are moral qualities of only the slightest functional value. Because of the limitations on land and technology, additional hard work does not produce a significant increment in income. It is pointless to talk of thrift in a subsistence economy, because usually there is no surplus with which to be thrifty. Foresight, with careful planning for the future, is also a virtue of dubious value in a world in which the best-laid plans must rest on a foundation of chance and capriciousness. (1967, pp. 150–151)

With the passage of time it has become clear that many of the heavily staffed development schemes in Mexico have been less successful than development efforts made by the people themselves with capital accumulated from working as *braceros*. James Acheson (1972), who studied a community near Tzintzuntzan, has argued that without realistic economic opportunities, development will not occur. If opportunities present themselves, some individuals will always take advantage of them, regardless of the image of limited good.

It is one thing to say that Tarascans [the people of the region of Tzintzuntzan] are suspicious, distrustful, and uncooperative; it is another to assume that this lack of cooperation precludes all possibility for positive economic change. (Acheson, 1972, p. 1165; see Foster, 1974; Acheson, 1974)

Class and life-style

Classes differ from one another not only in amount of power per capita, but also in broad areas of patterned thought and behavior called *life-style* (Fig. 9.8). Peasants, urban industrial wage workers, middle-class suburbanites, and upper-class industrialists have different life-styles (Fig. 9.9). Cultural contrasts among class-linked life-styles are as great as contrasts between life in an Eskimo igloo and life in a Mbuti village of the Ituri forest. For example, the former Mrs. Seward Prosser Mellon had a household budget of $750,000 a year, not including a $20,000 budget for the family dog (Koskoff, 1978, p. 467).

Classes, in other words, have their own *subcultures* made up of distinctive work patterns, architecture, home furnishings, diet, dress, domestic routines, sex and mating practices, magico-religious rituals, art, ideology. In many instances, classes even have accents that make it difficult for them to talk to one another. Because of exposure of body parts to sun, wind, and callus-producing friction, working-class people tend to look different from their "superiors." Further distinctions are the result of dietary specialties—the fat and the rich were once synonymous. Throughout almost the entire evolutionary career of stratified societies, class identity has been as explicit and unambiguous as the distinction between male and female. The Chinese Han dynasty peasant, the Inca commoner, or the Russian serf could not expect to survive to maturity without knowing how to recognize members of the "superior" classes. Doubt was removed in many cases by state-enforced standards of dress: Only the Chinese nobility could wear silk clothing; only the European feudal overlords could carry daggers and swords; only the Inca rulers could wear gold ornaments. Violators were put to death. In the presence of their "superiors," commoners still perform definite rituals of subordina-

9.8 *CLASS AND LIFE-STYLE* (above)
South Bronx. [Kroll, Taurus]

9.9 *CLASS AND LIFE-STYLE* (below)
Miami Beach. [Vanderwall, DeWys]

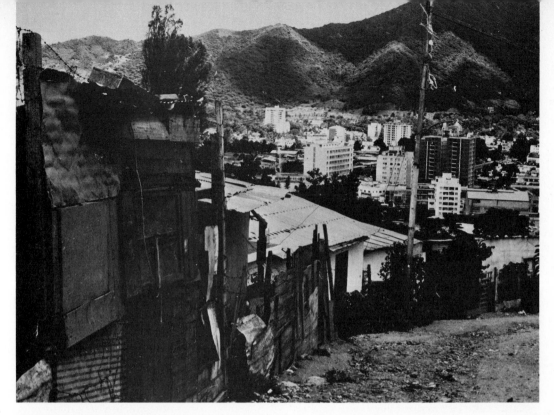

9.10 CARACAS SHANTYTOWN
**Squatters in Latin American cities often enjoy
the best views, since apartment houses were
not built on hilltops due to lack of water.
But this means that the squatters have to carry
their water up the hill in cans. [UPI]**

tion, among which lowering the head, removing the hat, averting the eyes, kneeling, bowing, crawling, and maintaining silence unless spoken to occur almost universally.

Throughout much of the world, class identity continues to be sharp and unambiguous. Among most contemporary nations, differences in class-linked life-styles show little prospect of diminishing or disappearing. Indeed, given the increase in luxury goods and services available to contemporary elites, contrasts in life-styles between the rich and powerful and the people of peasant villages or urban shantytowns (Fig. 9.10) may be reaching an all-time high. During the recent epochs of industrial advance, governing classes throughout the world have gone from palanquins to Cadillacs to private jets, while their subordinates find themselves without even a donkey or a pair of oxen. The elites now have their medical needs taken care of at the world's best medical centers, while vast numbers of less fortunate people have never even heard of the germ theory of disease and will never be treated by modern medical techniques. Elites attend the best universities, while half of the people in the world remain illiterate.

Class mobility

Classes differ greatly in the manner in which membership is established and in the rate at which membership changes. When class membership is established exclusively through hereditary *ascription*—through the inheritance of durable power in the form of money, property, or some other form of wealth—there is necessarily a low rate of *mobility* in or out. Such a class is spoken of as being "closed" (it is also sometimes referred to as being a *caste* or being "castelike"; see below). The ruling classes of despotic states, the nobility of seventeenth-century Europe, and the highest echelons of contemporary billionaire elites in the United States and Canada are examples of superordinate closed classes.

Closed classes tend to be endogamous. Among superordinate groups, endogamy is practiced as a means of preventing the dispersal of power; marriage alliances among families consolidate and concentrate lines of control over the natural and cultural sources of power (see p. 150). For the subordinate classes, endogamy is almost always an imposed condition that prevents men and women of humble birth from changing their class identity and from sharing in the power prerogatives of the superordinate segments.

Will it ever be possible to produce a completely open class structure? What would such a system look like? If there were only two classes, complete mobility could be achieved if each person spent half a lifetime in the upper group and half in the lower group. Aside from the incredible confusion this transfer of wealth, power, and leadership would create, there is another reason intrinsic to the nature of class stratification that makes a completely open system improbable. For a class system to be completely open, the members of the ruling class must voluntarily abdicate their power positions. But in the entire evolutionary career of state-level societies, no ruling class has been known voluntarily to surrender its power simply out of a sense of obligation to ethical or moral principles. Of course individuals may do so, but there will always be a residue who will use their power to stay in power. One interpretation of the recurrent upheavals in China, known as "cultural revolutions," is that they are designed to prevent government bureaucrats from showing favoritism to their own children with respect to educational opportunities and exemptions from labor battalions. These cultural revolutions, however, are obviously not designed to destroy the power of those who command each successive upheaval to start and stop. Perhaps a completely open class system is a contradiction in terms; the best that can be hoped for are relatively high rates of mobility.

In the great world museum of exotic ethnographic forms, at least one society made an ingenious attempt to create a maximally open class system through special rules of marriage and descent. The Natchez of the lower Mississippi were organized into two classes—rulers and commoners. The early French explorers called the latter *stinkards*. The members of the ruling group were obliged to marry commoners (but since there were more commoners than rulers, most commoners married commoners). Children of female members of the ruling class inherited the positions of their mothers, but children of the male members of the ruling class dropped down a grade with each marriage. Thus a male *sun* had a *noble* male child, who in turn had a *stinkard* male child. The female *sun's* children, however, remained *suns;* the female *noble's* children remained *nobles*, and so on. This system might be compared to a custom that would oblige all male millionaires to marry paupers; it would not put an end to the distinction between millionaires and paupers, but it would certainly reduce the social distance between them. The exogamy of the

Natchez ruling class probably indicates a fairly recent emergence from an unstratified form of organization (C. Mason, 1964). Under other circumstances, however, there are no structural reasons for expecting a ruling class to accept power-dispersing, exogamic marriage rules.

The culture of poverty

In studying the problems of people living in urban slums and shantytowns, Oscar Lewis found evidence for a distinct set of values and practices he called the "culture of poverty." Although not exactly comparable point by point, the concepts of the culture of poverty and of the image of limited good resemble each other in many respects and represent similar attempts to explain the perpetuation of poverty by focusing on the traditions and values of the underprivileged groups. Lewis (1966) pictures the poor in cities like Mexico City, New York, and Lima (Fig. 9.11) as tending to be fearful, suspicious, and apathetic toward the major institutions of the larger society, as hating the police and being mistrustful of government, and "inclined to be cynical of the church." They also have "a strong present-time orientation with relatively little disposition to defer gratification and plan for the future." This implies that poor people are less willing to save money and are more interested in "getting mine now" in the form of stereos, color television, the latest style clothing, and gaudy automobiles. It also implies

9.11 SQUATTERS IN LIMA
Life on a garbage heap. [United Nations]

that the poor "blow" their earnings by getting drunk or going on buying sprees. Like George Foster, Lewis recognizes that in some measure the culture of poverty is partly a rational response to the objective conditions of powerlessness and poverty: "an adaptation and a reaction of the poor to their marginal position in a class-stratified society" (Lewis, 1966, p. 21). But he also states that once the culture of poverty comes into existence, it tends to perpetuate itself:

By the time slum children are six or seven they have usually absorbed the basic attitudes and values of their subculture. Thereafter they are psychologically unready to take full advantage of changing conditions or improving opportunities that may develop in their lifetime. (1966, p. 21)

Lewis proposes that only 20 percent of the urban poor actually have the culture of poverty, implying that 80 percent fall into the category of those whose poverty results from infrastructural and structural conditions, rather than from the traditions and values of a culture of poverty. The concept of the culture of poverty has been criticized on the grounds that the poor have many values other than those stressed in the culture of poverty and which they share in common with other classes (Leeds, 1970; Valentine, 1970; see Parker and Kleiner, 1970).

Although the poor may have some values different from those of members of other classes, they cannot be shown to be harmful. Helen Icken Safa (1967) has shown, for example, that developed patterns of neighborly cooperation frequently exist in established slums and shantytowns. And Oscar Lewis himself (1961, 1966) has shown in the tape-recorded words of the people themselves that many individuals who are trapped in poverty nonetheless achieve great nobility of spirit.

Values said to be distinctive of the urban poor are actually shared equally by the middle class. For example, being suspicious of government, politicians, and organized reli-

gion is not an exclusive poverty class trait; nor is the tendency to spend above one's means. There is little evidence that the middle class as a whole lives within its income more effectively than poor people do. But when the poor mismanage their incomes, the consequences are much more serious. If the male head of a poor family yields to the temptation to buy nonessential items, his children may go hungry or his wife may be deprived of medical attention. But these consequences result from being poor, not from any demonstrable difference in the capacity to defer gratification.

The stereotype of the improvident poor masks an implicit belief that the impoverished segments of society ought to be more thrifty and more patient than the members of the middle class. It is conscience-saving to be able to attribute poverty to values for which the poor themselves can be held responsible (Piven and Cloward, 1971).

Now whose fault is that?

The tendency to blame the poor for being poor is not confined to relatively affluent members of the middle class. The poor or near-poor themselves are often the staunchest supporters of the view that people who really want to work can always find work. This attitude forms part of a larger world view in which there is little comprehension of the structural conditions that make poverty for some inevitable. What must be seen as a system is seen purely in terms of individual faults, individual motives, individual choices. Hence the poor turn against the poor and blame one another for their plight.

In a study of a Newfoundland community called Squid Cove, Cato Wadel (1973) has shown how a structural problem of unemployment caused by factors entirely beyond the control of the local community can be interpreted in such a way as to set neighbor against neighbor. The men of Squid Cove earn their living from logging, fishing, and construction (Fig. 9.12). Mechanization in logging, depletion of the fishing grounds, and upgrading of construction skills have left most of the men without a steady, year-round means of making a living. A certain number of men, especially those who have large families and who are past their physical prime, place themselves on the able-bodied welfare rolls. In doing so they must be prepared to wage a desperate struggle to preserve their self-esteem against the tendency of their neighbors to regard them as shirkers who "don't do nothin' for the money they get." What makes the plight of the Squid Cove welfare recipients especially poignant is that Newfoundlanders have long been noted for their intense work ethic. Many welfare recipients formerly worked at extremely arduous unskilled jobs. For example, Wadel's principal informant, George, was a logger for twenty-nine years. George stopped logging because he injured a disk in his spine. The injury was sufficient to prevent him from competing for the better-paying unskilled jobs but insufficient to place him on the welfare roles as a disabled worker. George says he is willing to work, provided it is not too heavy and does not require him to

9.12 NEWFOUNDLAND VILLAGE
Fishermen mending their nets. Hard work is a traditional part of life in this rugged habitat. [Fujihira, Monkmeyer]

leave the house he owns in Squid Cove. "I'm willin' to work but there's no work around." "Now who's fault is that?" he asks. Others disagree. In Squid Cove welfare is thought of as something "we," the taxpayers, give to "them," the unemployed. There is no generally accepted feeling that it is the responsibility of the government or the society to secure appropriate work; the responsibility for finding a job falls upon the individual and no one else:

For a welfare recipient to say outright that if work is not available, it is only proper for the government to provide adequate assistance, is not approved. Recipients thus have to be careful not to talk about their "rights" . . . On the other hand, if a recipient does not complain at all, this might be taken as a sign that he is satisfied with being on welfare, that he, in fact, is unwilling to work. Whatever the recipient does, complain or not, he is likely to be sanctioned. (Wadel, 1973, p. 38)

In explaining why he chose to study the plight of people on welfare, Cato Wadel writes: "From what has been said so far, it should be clear that I am not much in doubt about 'whose fault it is.'"

It is not *the fault of the unemployed individual. If this study were summarized into a simple and clear statement, it would be that it is unemployment itself which produces behavior on the part of the unemployed which makes people blame the unemployment on the individual, and* not *the other way around: that a special attitude or personal defect produces unemployment. (p. 127)*

Minorities and majorities

In addition to classes, most state societies are also stratified into so-called racial, ethnic, and cultural groups (R. Cohen, 1978*a* and *b*). These groups—often called *minorities* or *majorities*—differ from classes in three ways: (1) They have distinctive life-styles that can be traced to the cultural traditions of another so-

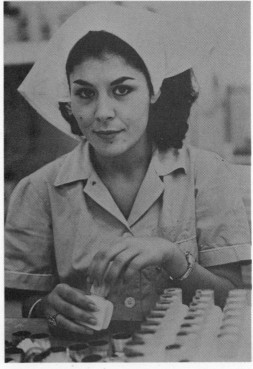

ciety; (2) their members often belong to different classes; (3) their members are conscious of their existence as a group set apart from the rest of the population.

The separation into racial, ethnic, or cultural minorities is based upon whether the criteria of group membership are primarily physical appearance, common origin in another country or region, or possession of a distinctive life-style. In reality, however, all three criteria occur in a bewildering number of combinations. Racial and cultural differences and common ancestry are often claimed by or attributed to groups that lack them, giving rise to sharp discrepancies between emic and etic versions of group identity (Fig. 9.13).

Racial, ethnic, and cultural *minorities* are groups that are subordinate or whose position is vulnerable to subordination. The term *majority* refers to the higher-ranking and more secure racial, ethnic, or cultural segments of the population. Minority and majority are unsatisfactory terms because "majorities" like the whites in South Africa are sometimes vastly outnumbered by the "minorities" whom they oppress and exploit (Fig. 9.14). No satisfactory substitute for these terms has been devised, however (Simpson and Yinger, 1962).

The most important point to bear in mind about minorities and majorities is that they are invariably locked into a more or less open form of political, social, and economic struggle to protect or raise their position in the stratification system (Despres, 1975; Schermerhorn, 1970; Wagley and Harris, 1958). Depending on their respective numbers, their special cultural strengths and weaknesses, and their initial advantages or disadvantages during the formation of the stratification system, their status as a group may rise or fall in the hierarchy. Thus, although many minorities are subject to excruciating forms of discrimination, segregation, and exploitation, others may actually enjoy fairly high although not dominant positions.

9.13 ETHNIC IDENTITY
All of these people identify themselves as Jews. The man (facing page, top) was born in Yemen and the girl (this page, top) in India. The young woman (facing page, bottom) was born in Morocco and both boys (this page, bottom) in Israel. [Israeli Information Service]

Minorities and majorities 177

9.14 APARTHEID
[United Nations]

Assimilation versus pluralism

Like classes, minorities occur in both relatively open and closed versions. Some minorities are almost completely endogamous, and of these many are endogamous by "choice." The Jews, Chinese, and Greeks in the United States, the Hindus in Guyana, the Muslims in India, and the Japanese in Brazil are examples of groups for whom endogamy is a practice valued as much by the minority as by the rest of the population. Other minorities, such as the blacks of the United States and the coloreds of South Africa, have no strong motivation to be endogamous but find intermarriage blocked largely by the hostility of the rest of the population. Still other minorities neither possess internal barriers to exogamy nor encounter external resistance. Such groups (e.g., the Germans or Scots in the United States

and the Italians in Brazil) usually move toward *assimilation*—the loss of separate identity as a minority group.

Where endogamy prevails, either by choice of the minority or by imposition of the "majority," a *pluralistic* condition may endure for centuries or even millennia. Assimilation may also fail to take place even when a certain amount of intermarriage occurs if there is a form of descent rule, as in the United States, that assigns the mixed offspring to the minority or if the rate of intermarriage is not very high relative to the rate of population increase.

What accounts for these variations? The attempt to explain why a minority will develop along pluralistic rather than assimilationist lines requires a broad evolutionary and comparative approach. The most important fact to consider is this: Minorities enter a particular state society under disadvantageous circumstances. They enter as migrants seeking relief from exploitative class systems in their native lands; they enter as defeated people who have been overrun during wars of conquest and expansion; or they enter as defeated peoples transferred from colonial outposts as indentured servants or slaves.

Each minority has a unique *adaptive capacity* to survive and prosper in the particular situation in which it finds itself. This capacity is based on its prior experiences, history, language, and culture. If the class structure of the majority's social system is marked by individualized competition for upward mobility and a corresponding lack of class identity or class solidarity, the minority may derive advantages from the practice of endogamy, settlement in restricted regions or neighborhoods, and pursuit of pluralistic goals.

The reasons for the development of pluralistic goals are as diverse as the adaptive capacities in the world inventory of minorities and the structure of state societies in which they live. Some groups appear to be more likely than others to benefit from the preservation of their traditional culture patterns because these patterns have a high adaptive capacity. Jews, for example, long excluded from land-based means of earning a living in Europe, arrived in the rapidly urbanizing society of the late nineteenth-century United States "pre-adapted" to compete for upward mobility in urban occupations requiring high levels of literacy. Contemporary Japanese migrants to Brazil bring with them special skills related to intensive agriculture and truck farming. Chinese migrants in many parts of the world achieve outstanding success by adhering to traditional family-based patterns of business activity.

The emphasis upon differences in language, religion, and other aspects of life-styles can increase the minority's sense of solidarity and may help its members to compete in impersonalized, class-structured, competitive societies such as that of the United States and Canada. Jewish, Chinese, Japanese, Greek, Syrian, Hindu, or Muslim merchants and businesspeople, for example, frequently enjoy important commercial advantages in highly competitive situations. Based on his study of the relations between Afro-Americans and Hindus in Guyana, Leo Despres (1975) suggests that ethnic, cultural, and racial identities confer competitive advantages with respect to environmental resources. The Hindu segment of Guyana society, for example, has a firmer grip on the land than the black segment.

In many situations, however, strong minority solidarity carries with it the danger of overexposure and reaction. In maintaining and increasing their own solidarity, minorities run the risk of increasing the sense of alienation of the larger population and hence of becoming the scapegoats of genocidal policies. The fate of the Jews in Germany and Poland, the Hindu Indians in east and southern Africa, the Chinese in Indonesia, and the Muslims in India are some of the better-known examples of "successful" minority adaptations that were followed by mass slaughter and/or expulsion.

Moreover, it is well to keep in mind that minorities are themselves stratified and that, therefore, the upper classes and elites within the minority may stand to gain more from the perpetuation of the minority than the average member. One important reason for the perpetuation of pluralist aims and symbols is that the wealthier and more powerful segments of both the minority and majority often derive economic and political strength from the maintenance of a separate identity for their subordinates. Roger Sanjek (1972, 1977) studied the relationship among twenty-three different "tribal" groups who live in the city of Accra, Ghana, and found that in terms of language, behavior, dress, residence, and facial markings there was little to distinguish one group from another. Nonetheless, politicians relied heavily on their "tribal" identities in competing for political office. Similarly, the tragic history of Lebanon cannot be understood apart from the private fortunes that both Christian and Muslim elites have been able to amass as a result of drawn-out communal strife (Joseph, 1978).

Castes in India

Indian castes are closed, endogamous, and stratified descent groups. They bear many resemblances to both endogamous classes and racial, ethnic, and cultural minorities. No sharp line can be drawn between groups such as the Jews or blacks in the United States or the Inca elite and the castes of India. However, some features of the Indian caste hierarchy are unique and deserve special attention.

The unique features of Indian castes have to do with the fact that the caste hierarchy is an integral part of Hinduism, which is the religion of most of the people of India. It is a matter of religious conviction in India that all people are not spiritually equal and that the gods have established a hierarchy of groups. This hierarchy consists of the four major *varnas*, or grades of being. According to the earliest traditions (e.g., the Hymns of Rigveda), the four *varnas* correspond to the physical parts of Purusa, who gave rise to the human race through dismemberment. His mouth became the *Brahmans* (priests), his arms the *Kshatriyas* (warriors), his thighs the *Vaishyas* (merchants and craftsmen), and his feet the *Shudras* (menial workers) (Gould, 1971). According to Hindu scripture, an individual's *varna* is determined by a descent rule; that is, it corresponds to the *varna* of one's parents and is unalterable during one's lifetime.

The basis of all Hindu morality is the idea that each *varna* has its appropriate rules of behavior, or "path of duty" (*dharma*). At the death of the body, the soul meets its fate in the form of a transmigration into a higher or lower being (*karma*). Those who follow the "path of duty" will find themselves at a higher point on Purusa's body during their next life. Deviation from the "path of duty" will result in reincarnation in the body of an outcaste or even an animal.

One of the most important aspects of the "path of duty" is the practice of certain taboos regarding marriage, eating, and physical proximity. Marriage below one's *varna* is generally regarded as a defilement and pollution; acceptance of food cooked or handled by persons below one's *varna* is also a defilement and pollution; any bodily contact between Brahman and Shudra is forbidden (Fig. 9.15). In some parts of India there were not only untouchables but unseeables—people who could come out only at night.

Although the general outlines of this system are agreed upon throughout Hindu India, there are enormous regional and local differences in the finer details of the ideology and practice of caste relationships. The principal source of these complications is the fact that it is not the *varna* but thousands of internally

9.15 UNTOUCHABLES
Caste in India must be seen from the bottom up to be understood. [UPI]

stratified subdivisions known as *jatis* (or subcastes) that constitute the real functional endogamous units. Moreover, even *jatis* of the same name (e.g., "washermen," "shoemakers," "herders," and so on) further divide into local endogamous subgroups and exogamous lineages (Klass, 1979).

Caste from the top down and bottom up

There are two very different views of the Hindu caste system. The view that predominates among Westerners is that which conforms largely to the emics of the top-ranking Brahman caste. According to this view, each caste and subcaste has a hereditary occupation that guarantees its members basic subsistence and job security. The lower castes render vital services to the upper castes. Hence the upper castes know they cannot get along without the lower castes and do not abuse them. And in times of crisis, the upper castes will extend emergency assistance in the form of food or loans. Moreover, since the Hindu religion gives everyone a convincing explanation of why some are inferior and others superior, members of lower castes do not resent being regarded as a source of pollution and defilement and have no interest in changing the status of their caste in the local or regional hierarchy (Dumont, 1970).

The other view—the view from the bottom up—makes the Indian caste system hard to distinguish from the racial, ethnic, and cultural minorities with which Westerners are familiar. Critics of the top-down view point out that whites in the United States once insisted that the Bible justified slavery, that blacks were well treated, contented with their lot in life, and not interested in changing their status. According to Joan Mencher, who has worked and lived among the untouchable castes of southern India, the error in the top-down view is just as great in India as in the United States. Mencher reports that the lowest castes are not satisfied with their station in life and do not believe they are treated fairly by their caste superiors. As for the security allegedly provided by the monopoly over such professions as smiths, washermen, barbers, potters, and so on, such castes taken together never constituted more than 10 to 15 percent of the total Hindu population. And even within such castes, the caste profession never provided basic subsistence for the majority of people. Among the Chamars, for example, who are known as leatherworkers, only a small portion of the caste engages in leatherwork. In the countryside almost all Chamars are a source of cheap agricultural labor. When questioned about their low station in life, many of Mencher's low-caste informants explained that they had to be dependent on the other castes since they had no land of their own. Did landowners in times of extreme need or crisis actually give free food and assistance to their low-caste dependents? ". . . to my informants, both young and old, this sounds like a fairytale" (Mencher, 1974b).

Anthropological studies of actual village life in India have yielded a picture of caste relationships drastically opposed to the ideals posited in Hindu theology (Carrol, 1977). One of the most important discoveries is that local *jatis* recurrently try to raise their ritual status. Such attempts usually take place as part of a general process by which local ritual status is adjusted to actual local economic and political power. There may be low-ranking subcastes that passively accept their lot in life as a result of their *karma* assignment; such groups, however, tend to be wholly lacking in the potential for economic and political mobility. "But let opportunities for political and economic advance appear barely possible and such resignation is likely to vanish more quickly than one might imagine" (Orans, 1968, p. 878).

One of the symptoms of this underlying propensity for *jatis* to redefine their ritual position to conform with their political and economic potential is a widespread lack of agreement over the shape of local ritual hierarchies as seen by inhabitants of the same village, town, or region.

As the sociologist Bernard Barber (1968) has noted, the study of caste "dissensus" is a central concern of village Indian research. Kathleen Gough (1959) indicates that in villages of South India, the middle reaches of the caste hierarchy may have as many as fifteen castes whose relative ritual ranks are ambiguous or in dispute. Different individuals and families even in the same caste give different versions of the rank-order of these groups. Elsewhere, even the claims of Brahman sub-castes to ritual superiority are openly contested (Srinivas, 1955). The conflict among *jatis* concerning their ritual position may involve prolonged litigation in the local courts and if not resolved may, under certain circumstances, lead to much violence and bloodshed (see Berreman, 1975; Cohn, 1955).

Contrary to the view that these features of caste are a response to the recent "modernization" of India, Karen Leonard (1978) has shown that similarly fluid and flexible individual, family, and subcaste strategies date back at least to the eighteenth century. According to Leonard, the internal organization and external relationships of the Kayastks, originally a caste of scribes and record-keepers, shifted continuously to adapt to changing economic, political, and demographic circumstances. Kayastks attempted to better their lot in life as individuals, as families, and as subcastes according to changing opportunities. Marriage patterns and descent rules were constantly modified to provide maximum advantages with respect to government and commercial employment, and even the rule of endogamy was broken when alliances with other subcastes became useful: "Adaptability, rather than conformity to accepted Brahmanical or scholarly notions about caste, has always characterized the Kayastk marriage networks and kin groups" (Leonard, 1978, p. 294).

In comparing Indian castes with minorities in other parts of the world, it should be emphasized that substantial cultural differences are frequently associated with each local *jati*. Subcastes may speak different languages or dialects, have different kinds of descent and locality rules, different forms of marriage, worship different gods, eat different foods, and altogether present a greater contrast in life-style than that which exists between New Yorkers and the Zuni Indians. Moreover, many castes of India are associated with ra-cial differences comparable to the contrast between whites and blacks in the United States. In view of all these resemblances, it might very well be argued that we could dispense either with the term *caste* or the term *minority*.

The stratification system of India is not noteworthy merely for the presence of endogamous descent groups possessing real or imagined racial and cultural specialties. Every state-level society has such groups. It is, rather, the extraordinary profusion of such groups that merits our attention. Nonetheless, the caste system of India is fundamentally similar to that of other countries that have closed classes and numerous ethnic and racial minorities: Like the blacks in the United States or the Catholics in Northern Ireland, low castes in India

resist the status accorded them, with its concomitant disabilities and discrimination, and strive for higher accorded status and its attendant advantages. High castes attempt to prevent such striving and the implied threat to their position. In this conflict of interests lies the explosive potential of all caste societies. (Berreman, 1966, p. 318)

Summary

All state societies are organized into stratified groups such as classes, minorities, and castes. Stratified groups consist of people who relate to the apparatus of control in similar ways and who possess similar amounts of power over the allocation of wealth, privileges, resources, and technology. Power, in this context, means control over energy or the ability to move and shape people and things. All state societies have at least two classes—rulers and ruled. Theoretically, ruling classes may voluntarily act in the best interests of commoners, but only if ruling class power is not thereby diminished.

Sex and age hierarchies are also important forms of stratification, but they are not confined to state societies. Class differences involve both differential access to power and profound differences in life-styles. The understanding of class and all other forms of social stratification is made difficult by the failure to separate emic and etic versions of stratification hierarchies. From an etic and behavioral point of view, classes can exist even if there is no emic recognition of their existence and even if segments of the same class compete. Ruling classes need not form permanent, hereditary, monolithic, conspiratorial organizations. Their membership can change rapidly and they may actively deny that they constitue a ruling class. Similarly, subordinate classes need not be conscious of their identity and may exist only in an etic and behavioral sense.

The understanding of the phenomenon of exploitation also depends on the distinction between emic and etic perspectives. It cannot be maintained that the mere existence of differential power, wealth, and privilege guarantees the existence of exploitation; nor that exploitation exists only when or as soon as people feel exploited. Etic criteria for exploitation focus on the acquisition of luxuries among elites based on the deprivation of necessities among commoners and perpetuation or intensification of misery and poverty.

The majority of the people in the world today are members of peasant classes. Peasants are structured inferiors who farm with preindustrial technologies and pay rent or taxes. Three major varieties of peasants can be distinguished: feudal, agromanagerial, and capitalist. Their structured inferiority depends in the first case on the inability to acquire land; in the second, on the existence of a powerful managerial elite that sets production and labor quotas; and in the third, on the operation of a price market in land and labor controlled by big landlords, corporations, and banks.

Among peasant classes, an "image of limited good" is widespread. However, there are also contradictory values and attitudes that lead to innovations under appropriate structural and infrastructural conditions. In Tzintzuntzan, despite the image of limited good, men struggled for a chance to work as migrant laborers, and both men and women participated in a series of ill-fated development experiments in the hope of bettering their lives.

The counterpart of the image of limited good for urban subordinate classes is the culture of poverty. This concept focuses on the values and the traditions of the urban poor as an explanation for poverty. However, many of the values in the culture of poverty, such as distrust of authority, consumerism, and improvidence, are also found in more affluent classes. The irrelevance of the emphasis people place on the value of work for understanding the genesis of poverty classes can be seen in the case of Squid Cove. Newfoundlanders are known the world over for their work ethic, yet when mechanization and resource depletion left them without year-round jobs, they had no alternative but to accept welfare assistance.

Systems of class stratification differ widely in the amount of upward mobility they permit. If classes were exogamous and if children of the very rich were disinherited, mobility would be much higher. One of the most fluid systems of social stratification known is that of the Natchez.

Racial, ethnic, and cultural minorities and majorities are present in virtually all state societies. These groups differ from classes in having distinctive life-styles derived from another society; internal class differences; and a high degree of group consciousness. Minorities and majorities struggle for access to and control over the sources of wealth and power, aided or hindered by their adaptive strengths and weaknesses in relation to specific arenas of competition. It is the specific nature of this struggle in the history of each minority-majority relationship that determines whether assimilation or pluralism will be emphasized by the minority and/or the majority. Advantages and disadvantages are associated with both options. Neither assimilationist nor pluralist commitments may suffice to overcome the effects of segregation, discrimination, and exploitation. It can be argued that racial and ethnic chauvinism benefits the ruling class more than the ordinary members of either the minority or majority.

Social scientists usually identify a third type of stratified group known as castes. Castes are epitomized by the case of Hindu India. Traditional views of Indian castes have been dominated by top-down idealizations in which the lower castes are represented as voluntarily accepting their subordinate status. Bottom-up studies show that Indian castes struggle for upward mobility in a flexible and adaptive fashion and that they closely resemble cultural, ethnic, and racial minorities in other societies.

10

Religion

This chapter surveys general aspects of culturally patterned ideas that are conventionally known as religion, myth, and magic. It also surveys the patterns of behavior that are called ritual and that are intended to mediate between human beings and natural forces, on the one hand, and supernatural beings and supernatural forces, on the other. It defines basic concepts such as religion and magic and sets forth the basic types of religious organizations and rituals. We shall see that although infrastructural and structural conditions provide a means for understanding the origin of specific beliefs and rituals, religion frequently plays a crucial role in organizing the impulses leading toward major transformations of social life.

Animism

What is religion? The earliest anthropological attempt to define religion was that of E. B. Tylor. For Tylor, the essence of religion was belief in the idea of "god." Most Western peoples would probably still find such a belief an essential ingredient in their own conception of what constitutes religion. The Victorian Age in which Tylor lived, however, tended to regard religion in even narrower terms, often restricting the concept to Christianity. Other people's beliefs in god were relegated to the realm of "superstition" and "paganism." Tylor's principal contribution was to show that the Judeo-Christian concept of god was essentially similar to beliefs about supernatural beings found the world over.

Tylor attempted, with considerable success, to show that the idea of god was an elaboration of the concept of "soul." In his book *Primitive Culture*, Tylor (1971) demonstrated that belief in "the doctrine of souls" occurs to some extent and in one form or another in every society. He gave the name *animism* to the belief that inside ordinary visible, tangible bodies there is a normally invisible, normally intangible being: the soul. Throughout the world souls are believed to appear in dreams, trances, visions, shadows, and reflections, and to be implicated in fainting, loss of consciousness, and birth and death. Tylor reasoned that the basic idea of soul must have been invented in order to explain all these puzzling phenomena. Once established, the basic idea was embroidered upon and ultimately gave rise to a variety of supernatural beings including the souls of animals, plants, and material objects, as well as of gods, demons, spirits, devils, ghosts, saints, fairies, gnomes, elves, angels, and so forth.

Tylor has been criticized by twentieth-century anthropologists for his suggestion that animism arose merely as a result of the attempt to understand puzzling human and natural phenomena. Today we know that religion is much more than an attempt to explain puzzling phenomena. Like other aspects of superstructure, religion serves a multitude of economic, political, and psychological functions.

Another important criticism of Tylor's stress on the puzzle-solving function of religion concerns the role of hallucinations in shaping religious beliefs. During drug-induced trances and other forms of hallucinatory experience, people "see" and "hear" extraordinary things that seem even more "real" than ordinary people and animals. One can argue, therefore, that animistic theories are not intellectual attempts to explain trances and dreams, but direct expressions of extraordinary psychological experiences. Nonetheless, it cannot be denied that religion and the doctrine of souls also have the function of providing people with answers to fundamental questions about the meaning of life and death and the causes of events.

The three souls of the Jívaro

Although certain animistic beliefs are universal, each culture has its own distinctive animistic beings and its own specific elaboration of the soul concept. Some cultures insist that people have two or more souls; and some cultures believe that certain individuals have more souls than others. Among the Jívaro of eastern Ecuador, for example, three kinds of souls are recognized: an ordinary, or "true," soul; an *arutam* soul; and a *musiak* soul (Harner, 1972b).

The Jívaro believe that the true soul is present from birth inside every living Jívaro, male and female. Upon a person's death, this soul leaves the body and undergoes a series of changes. During the first phase of its afterlife, the true soul returns to its body's birthplace and relives its former life in an invisible form. The major difference between the two existences is that after death the true soul cannot eat real food and thus remains perpetually hungry. Needless to say, the Jívaro do not look forward to this experience. After the true soul has relived the entire life of its deceased owner, the second phase begins. It changes into a demon. This demon roams the forest, solitary, hungry, and lonely. The second phase lasts for the equivalent of another lifetime. The true soul then dies again and enters its third phase. It changes into a *wampang*, a species of giant moth that is occasionally seen flitting about. The living try to feed it because it too is perpetually hungry. In its fourth and final phase, the true soul turns to mist:

After a length of time about which the Jívaro are uncertain, the wampang *finally has its wings damaged by raindrops as it flutters through a rainstorm, and falls to die on the ground. The true soul then changes into water vapor amidst the falling rain. All fogs and clouds are believed to be the last form taken by true souls. The true soul undergoes no more transformations and persists eternally in the form of mist. (Harner, 1972b, p. 151)*

No one is born with the second Jívaro soul —the *arutam*. It must be acquired. All men and occasionally some women try to acquire one. The possessor of an *arutam* feels great power and cannot be killed. To obtain an *arutam*, one must fast, bathe in a sacred waterfall, and drink tobacco water or the juice of a plant containing the hallucinogenic substance *datura*. The *arutam* comes out of the depths of the forest in the form of a pair of giant jaguars or a pair of huge snakes rolling over and over toward the soulseeker. When the apparition gets close, the terrified soul seeker must run forward and touch it. If this is done, when the soulseekers go to sleep, the *arutam* will enter the body and lodge in the chest. People who possess an *arutam* soul are different from other men and women. They speak and act with great confidence and they feel an irresistible craving to kill their enemies. Great warriors and other exceptionally

powerful individuals may possess more than one *arutam* soul at a time. Unfortunately, *arutam* souls cannot be kept forever. They leave their temporary abode just before their possessor kills someone. Eventually, wandering in the forest, they will be captured by other soulseekers brave enough to touch them.

The third Jívaro soul is the *musiak*—the avenging soul. The *musiak* comes into existence when people who formerly possessed an *arutam* are killed by their enemies. The *musiak* develops inside the victim's head and tries to get out and attack the killer. To prevent this from happening, the best thing to do is to cut off the victim's head, "shrink" it, and bring it back home. If it is handled properly in various rituals and dances, the *musiak* can make the killer strong and happy. After the *musiak* has been used to the killer's advantage, a ritual is performed to send it back to the village from which it came. To get it to go back, the women sing this song (Harner, 1972b, p. 146):

Now, now, go back to your house where you lived.
Your wife is there calling from your house.
You have come here to make us happy.
Finally we have finished.
So return.

Animatism and mana

As Robert Marett (1914) pointed out, Tylor's definition of religion as animism is too narrow. When people attribute lifelike properties to rocks, pots, storms, and volcanoes, they do not necessarily believe that souls are the cause of the lifelike behavior of these objects. Hence there is a need to distinguish a concept of a supernatural force that does not derive its effect from souls. Marett therefore introduced the term *animatism* to designate the belief in such nonsoul forces. Possession of concentrated animatistic force can give certain objects, animals, and people extraordinary powers independent of power derived from souls and gods. To label this concentrated form of animatistic force, Marett used the Melanesian word *mana*. An adze that makes intricate carvings, a fishhook that catches large fish, a club that kills many enemies, or a rabbit's foot that brings "good luck" have large amounts of *mana*. People, too, may be spoken of as having more or less *mana*. A woodcarver whose work is especially intricate and beautiful possesses *mana*, whereas a warrior captured by the enemy has obviously lost his *mana*.

In its broadest range of meaning, *mana* simply indicates belief in a powerful force. Many vernacular relationships not normally recognized as religious beliefs in Western cultures can be regarded as *mana*. For example, vitamin pills are consumed by many millions of people in expectation that they will exert a powerful effect on health and well-being. Soaps and detergents are said to clean because of "cleaning power"; gasolines provide engines with "starting power" or "go-power"; salespeople are prized for their "selling power"; and politicians are said to have *charisma* or "vote-getting power." Many people fervently believe that they are "lucky" or "unlucky"—which could easily be translated as a belief that they control varying quantities of *mana*.

Natural and supernatural

One way to prevent the definition of religion from getting so broad as to include virtually every belief is to distinguish between natural and supernatural forces. It must be emphasized, however, that few cultures neatly and conveniently divide their beliefs into natural and supernatural categories. In a culture where people believe ghosts are always present, it is not necessarily either natural or supernatural to provide dead ancestors with food and drink. The culture may simply lack emic categories for "natural" and "supernat-

10.1 GURURUMBA MEDICINE
This man is inducing vomiting by swallowing a 3-foot length of cane. After he has pushed it all the way into his stomach he will work it up and down until he vomits. It is thought to be necessary to do this to rid the individual of contaminating influences gotten through contact with women. [American Museum of Natural History]

ural." Similarly, when a shaman blows smoke over a patient and triumphantly removes a sliver of bone allegedly inserted by the patient's enemy, the question of whether the performance is natural or supernatural may have no emic meaning.

Writing of the Gururumba (Fig. 10.1) of the highlands of western New Guinea, Philip Newman notes that they "have a series of beliefs postulating the existence of entities and forces we would call supernatural." Yet the contrast between natural and supernatural is not emically relevant to the Gururumba themselves:

It should be mentioned . . . that our use of the notion "supernatural" does not correspond to any Gururumba concept: they do not divide the world into natural and supernatural parts. Certain entities, forces, and processes must be controlled partially through lusu, *a term denoting rituals relating to growth, curing, or the stimulation of strength, while others need only rarely be controlled in this way. . . . However,* lusu *does not contrast with any term denoting a realm of control where the nature of controls differ from* lusu. *Consequently* lusu *is simply part of all control techniques and what it controls is simply part of all things requiring human control.* (1965, p. 83)

Sacred and profane

Some anthropologists have suggested that the true hallmark of a religious belief or religious practice is the emotional state of the participant. Robert R. Marett, Alexander Goldenweiser, and Robert Lowie were among those who sought the essence of religion in the "religious experience." Lowie (1948, p. 339) characterized this experience as consisting of "amazement and awe," a feeling that one is in the presence of something extraordinary, weird, sacred, holy, divine. Lowie was even willing to rule that beliefs about gods and souls were not religious beliefs if the existence of these beings was taken for granted and if,

in contemplating them, the individual did not experience awe or amazement.

The theoretician who made the greatest contribution to this way of looking at religion was Emile Durkheim. Like many others, Durkheim proposed that the essence of religious belief was that it evoked a mysterious feeling of communion with a sacred realm. Every society has its *sacred* beliefs, symbols and rituals, which stand opposed to ordinary or *profane* events (Fig. 10.2). Durkheim's distinctive contribution was to relate the realm of the sacred to the control exercised by society and culture over each individual's consciousness. When people feel they are in communion with occult and mysterious forces and supernatural beings, what they are really experiencing is the force of social life. For Durkheim, the essence of being human was to be born into and sustained by society and culture. In our awe of the sacred, we express our dependence on society in symbolic form. Thus, according to Durkheim, the idea of "god" is but one form of the worship of society.

It seems likely that every culture does make a distinction between sacred and profane realms and that there is some element of truth in Durkheim's idea that the sacred represents the worship of collective life. As we will see, the ability to appeal to the sacred character of certain beliefs and practices has great practical value in diminishing dissent, compelling conformity, and resolving ambiguities (see Rappaport, 1971a and b).

Magic and religion

Sir James Frazer attempted to define religion in his famous book *The Golden Bough*. For Frazer, the question of whether a particular belief was religious or not centered on the extent to which the participants felt that they could make an entity or force do their bidding. If the attitude of the participants was

10.2 *SACRED AND PROFANE*
**Shoes are left outside the Mosque,
symbolizing the transition from ordinary,
mundane affairs to the realm of the holy
and extraordinary. [UPI]**

one of uncertainty, if they felt humble and were inclined to supplicate and request favors and dispensations, their beliefs and actions were essentially religious. If they thought they were in control of the entities and forces governing events, felt no uncertainty about the outcome, and experienced no need for humble supplication, their beliefs and practices were examples of magic rather than of religion.

Frazer regarded prayer as the essence of religious ritual. But prayers are not always rendered in a mood of supplication. For example, prayers among the Navajo must be letter-perfect to be effective. Yet the Navajo do not expect that letter-perfect prayers will always get results. Thus, the line between prayers and "magical spells" is actually hard to draw. Supplication cannot be taken as characteristic of verbal communication between people and their gods. As Ruth Benedict (1938, p. 640) pointed out, "cajolery and bribery and false pretense are common means of influencing the supernatural." Thus the Kai of New Guinea swindle their ancestral ghosts as they swindle each other; some cultures try to outwit the spirits by lying to them. The Tsimshian of the Canadian Pacific Coast stamp their feet and shake their fists at the heavens and call their gods "slaves" as a term of reproach. The Manus of the Bismarck Archipelago keep the skulls of their ancestors in a corner of the house and try their best to please "Sir Ghost." However, if someone gets sick, the Manus may angrily threaten to throw Sir Ghost out of the house. This is what they tell Sir Ghost:

This man dies and you rest in no house. You will but wander about the edges of the island (used for excretory purposes). (Fortune, 1965, p. 216)

An additional important part of Frazer's scheme was his attempt to distinguish magic from science. The magician's attitude, he claimed, was precisely that of the scientist. Both magician and scientist believe that if A is done under the proper set of conditions, B will follow regardless of who the practitioner is or what the attitude toward the outcome may be. A piece of an intended victim's fingernail tossed into the fire or pins stuck into an effigy doll are believed to accomplish their results with the automatic certainty characteristic of the release of an arrow from a bow or the felling of a tree with an ax. Frazer recognized that if this was going to be the essence of the distinction between magic and religion, then magic differed little from science. Indeed, he called magic "false science" and postulated a universal evolutionary sequence in which magic, with its concern about cause and effect relationships, gave birth to science, whereas religion evolved along completely independent lines.

Frazer's scheme has not withstood the test of fieldwork. The attitudes with which fearful Dobuan magicians dispose of fingernails and confident Zuni priests whip up yucca suds to bring rain do not conform to Frazer's neat compartments. Human religious behavior unfolds as a complex mixture in which awe and wonder, boredom and excitement, power and weakness are all present at the same time.

The degree of anxiety and supplication associated with any sequence of behavior is probably regulated more by the importance of the outcome to the participants than by their philosophy of cause and effect. Not enough is known about the inner psychological state of priests, magicians, shamans, and scientists to make any firm pronouncements in this field.

The organization of religious beliefs and practices

As we have just seen, religious beliefs and rituals involve a great variety of thoughts, feelings, and practices. Yet in this domain, as in all others, there are orderly processes. A good way to begin to understand the diversity of religious phenomena is to inquire if there are beliefs and practices associated with particular levels of political and economic development.

Anthony Wallace (1966) has distinguished four principal varieties of religious "cults"—that is, forms of organization of religious doctrines and activities—that have broad evolutionary implications. The four principal forms are these: (1) *individualistic cults*, (2) *shamanistic cults*, (3) *communal cults*, and (4) *ecclesiastical cults*, defined as follows:

1. Individualistic cults The most basic form of religious life involves individualistic (but culturally patterned) beliefs and rituals. Each person is a specialist; each individual enters into a relationship with animistic and animatistic beings and forces as each personally experiences the need for control and protection. One might call this "do-it-yourself" religion.

2. Shamanistic cults As Wallace points out, no culture known to anthropology has a religion that is completely individualistic, although the Eskimo and other hunters and food gatherers lean heavily in this direction. Every known society also exhibits at least the *shamanistic* level of religious specialization (Fig. 10.3). The term *shaman* derives from the word used by the Tungus-speaking peoples of Siberia to designate the part-time religious specialist consulted in times of stress and anxiety. In cross-cultural applications, however, shaman may refer to individuals who act as diviners, curers, spirit mediums, and magicians for other people in return for gifts, fees, prestige, and power.

3. Communal cults At a more complex level of political economy, communal forms of beliefs and practices become more elaborate. Groups of nonspecialists organized in terms of age grades, men's societies, clans, or lineages assume responsibility for regular or occasional performancees of rituals deemed essential for their own welfare or for the survival of the society. While communal rituals may employ specialists such as shamans, orators, and highly skilled dancers and musicians, once the ritual performance is concluded, the participants revert to a common daily routine. There are no full-time religious specialists.

4. Ecclesiastical cults The ecclesiastical level of religious organization involves a full-time professional clergy or priesthood. These professionals form a bureaucracy that monopolizes the performance of certain rites on behalf of individuals, groups, and the whole society. Ecclesiastical bureaucracies are usually closely associated with state-level political systems. In many instances the leaders of the ecclesiastical hierarchy are members of the ruling class and, in some instances, a state's political and ecclesiastical hierarchies are indistinguishable.

Wallace notes that the individualistic, shamanistic, communal, and ecclesiastical forms of beliefs and rituals constitute a *scale*. That is, each of the more complex levels contains the beliefs and practices of all the less complex levels. Consequently, among societies with ecclesiastical cults, there are also communal cults, shamanistic cults, and strictly individualistic beliefs and rituals (Fig. 10.4). In the following sections, examples of each of these forms of religious organization will be given.

Individualistic beliefs and rituals: the Eskimo

The individualism of much of Eskimo belief and ritual parallels the individualism of the Eskimo mode of production. Hunters alone or in small groups constantly match their wits against the cunning and strength of animal prey and confront the dangers of travel over

10.3 SAN CURING
Shaman in trance. [DeVore, Anthro-Photo]

10.4 LEVEL OF RELIGIOUS ORGANIZATION
**Left, a Guatemalan shaman obtaining personal power at a
shrine. This does not prevent him from participating in the
ecclesiastical cult of the Catholic church, right.
[Eugene Gordon—left; United Nations—right]**

the ice and the threats of storms and month-long nights. The Eskimo hunter was equipped with an ingenious array of technological devices that made life possible in the Arctic. But the outcome of the daily struggle remained in doubt. From the Eskimo's point of view, it was not enough to be well equipped with snow goggles, fur parkas, spring-bone traps, detachable, barbed harpoon points, and powerful compound bows. One also had to be equipped to handle unseen spirits and forces that lurked in all parts of nature and that, if offended or not properly warded off, could reduce the greatest hunter to a starving wretch. Vigilant individual effort was needed to deal with wandering human and animal souls, place spirits, Sedna (the Keeper of the Sea Animals), the Sun, the Moon, and the Spirit of the Air (Wallace, 1966, p. 89). Part of each hunter's equipment was his hunting song—a combination of chant, prayer, and magic formula—which he inherited from his father or father's brothers or purchased from some famous hunter or shaman. This he would sing

Individualistic beliefs and
rituals: the Eskimo

under his breath as he prepared himself for the day's activities. Around his neck he wore a little bag filled with tiny animal carvings, bits of claws and fur, pebbles, insects, and other items, each corresponding to some Spirit Helper with whom he maintained a special relationship. In return for protection and hunting success given by his Spirit Helpers, the hunter had to observe certain taboos, refrain from hunting or eating certain species, or avoid trespassing in a particular locale. A hunter should never sleep out on the ice edge. Every evening he had to return to land or to the old firm ice that lies some distance back from the open sea, because the Sea Spirit does not like her creatures to smell human beings while they are not hunting (Rasmussem, 1929, p. 76). Care also must be taken not to cook land and sea mammals in the same pot; fresh water must be placed in the mouth of recently killed sea mammals, and fat must be placed in the mouth of slain land mammals (Wallace, 1966, p. 90). Note that some of these "superstitions" may have alleviated psychological stress or have had a practical value for hunting or some other aspect of Eskimo life. Not sleeping out on the ice, for example, is a safety precaution.

The patterning of individualistic beliefs and rituals

Individualistic religious "do-it-yourselfers" never invent the major part of their religions. This is true even under the influence of drugs, during trance states, and in dreams and visions. For example, a form of individualistic religion common in North and South America involves the acquisition of a personal *guardian spirit* or supernatural protector. Typically, this spirit protector is acquired by means of a visionary experience induced by fasting, self-inflicted torture, or hallucinogenic drugs. The Jívaro youth's search for an

arutam soul is one variant of this widespread complex. Although each *arutam* vision is slightly different from the next, they all follow a similar pattern.

For many native North Americans the central experience of life was also a hallucinatory vision (Fig. 10.5). Young men needed this hallucinatory experience to be successful in love, warfare, horse stealing, trading, and all other important endeavors. In keeping with their code of personal bravery and endurance, they sought these visions primarily through self-inflicted torture.

Among the Crow, for example, a youth who craved the visionary experience of his elders went alone into the mountains, stripped off his clothes, and abstained from food and drink. If this was not sufficient, he chopped off part of the fourth finger of his left hand. Coached from childhood to expect that a vision would come, most Crow vision seekers were successful. A buffalo, snake, chicken hawk, thunderbird, dwarf, or mysterious stranger would appear; miraculous events would unfold; and then these strange beings would "adopt" the vision seeker and disappear.

Although each Crow's vision had some unique elements, they usually had the following similar elements. (1) There was some revelation of future success in warfare, horse raiding, or other acts of bravery. (2) The visions occurred at the end of the fourth day—four being the sacred number of the native North Americans. (3) There was the acquisition of a sacred song. (4) Friendly spirits adopted the youth. (5) Trees or rocks turned into enemies who vainly shot at the invulnerable spirit being. Lowie concludes:

He sees and hears not merely what any faster, say in British Columbia or South Africa, would see and hear under like conditions of physiological exhaustion and under the urge of generally human desires, but what the social tradition of the Crow tribe imperatively suggests. (1948, p. 14)

10.5 SIOUX VISION

Section of pictographic biography done by Rain in The Face. In a dream (left), the lightning tells him that unless he gives a buffalo feast, the lightning will kill him. He gives the feast, one part of which consists of filling a kettle with red hot buffalo tongues, of which he eats in order to save his life. He dreams (right) of buffalo again. While dancing, he is shot by an arrow which enters the feathers. In removing it, he soon vomits and grabbing a handful of earth, rubs it into the wound, healing it rapidly. [Museum of the American Indian, Heye Foundation]

Shamanistic cults

Shamans are those who are socially recognized as having special abilities for entering into contact with spirit beings and for controlling supernatural forces. The full shamanistic complex includes some form of trance experience during which the shaman's powers are increased. *Possession*, the invasion of the human body by a god or spirit, is the most common form of shamanistic trance. The shaman goes into a trance by smoking tobacco, taking drugs, beating on a drum, dancing monotonously, or simply by closing his eyes and concentrating. The trance begins with rigidity of the body, sweating, and heavy breathing. While in the trance the shaman may act as a *medium*, transmitting messages from the ancestors. With the help of friendly spirits, shamans predict future events, locate lost objects, identify the cause of illness, prescribe cures, and give advice on how clients can protect themselves against the evil intentions of enemies.

There is a close relationship between shamanistic cults and individualistic vision quests. Shamans are usually personalities who are psychologically predisposed toward hallucinatory experiences. In cultures that use hallucinogenic substances freely in order to penetrate the mysteries of the other world, many people may claim shamanistic status. Among the Jívaro, one out of every four men is a shaman, since the use of hallucinogenic vines makes it possible for almost everyone to achieve the trance states essential for the practice of shamanism (Harner, 1972b, p. 154). Elsewhere, becoming a shaman may be restricted to people who are prone to having auditory and visual hallucinations.

An important part of shamanistic performance in many parts of the world consists of simple tricks of ventriloquism, sleight of hand, and illusion. The Siberian shamans, for example, signaled the arrival of the possessing spirit by secretly shaking the walls of a darkened tent. Throughout South America the standard shamanistic curing ceremony involves the removal of slivers of bone, pebbles, bugs, and other foreign objects from the patient's body. The practice of these tricks should not be regarded as evidence that the shaman has a cynical or disbelieving attitude toward the rest of the performance. The human mind is fully capable of blocking out and compartmentalizing contradictory or inconvenient information through suppression into unconsciousness and through rationalization ("it's a trick but it's for their own good"; or "it's a trick but it works").

Although trance is part of the shamanistic repertory in hundreds of cultures, it is not universal. Many cultures have part-time specialists who do not make use of trance but who diagnose and cure disease, find lost objects, foretell the future, and confer immunity in war and success in love. Such persons may be referred to variously as magicians, seers, sorcerers, witch doctors, medicine men, and curers. The full shamanistic complex embodies all these roles.

Tapirapé shamanism

The Tapirapé, who are village people of central Brazil, have a typical shamanistic cult (Wagley, 1977). Tapirapé shamans (Fig. 10.6) derive their powers from dreams in which

10.6 TAPIRAPÉ SHAMAN
**The shaman has fallen into a tobacco-induced trance and cannot walk unaided.
[Charles Wagley]**

they encounter spirits who become the shaman's helpers. Dreams are caused by souls leaving the body and going on journeys. Frequent dreaming is a sign of shamanistic talent. Mature shamans, with the help of the spirit familiars, can turn into birds or launch themselves through the air in gourd "canoes," visit with ghosts and demons, or travel to distant villages forward and backward through time. Here is an account of how the shaman Ikanancowi acquired his powers:

In his dream [Ikanancowi] walked far to the shores of a large lake deep in the jungle. There he heard dogs barking and ran in the direction from which the noise came until he met several forest spirits of the breed called munpi anka. They were tearing a bat out of a tree for food. [The spirits] talked with Ikanancowi and invited him to return to their village, which was situated upon the lake. In the village he saw periquitos [paraqueets] and many soco . . . birds which they kept as pets. [They] had several pots of kaui [porridge] and invited Ikanancowi to eat with them. He refused for he saw that their kaui was made from human blood. Ikanancowi watched one spirit drink of the kaui and saw him vomit blood immediately afterwards; the shaman saw a second spirit drink from another pot and immediately spurt blood from his anus. He saw the munpi anka vomit up their entrails and throw them upon the ground, but he soon saw that this was only a trick; they would not die, for they had more intestines. After this visit the munpi anka called Ikanancowi father and he called them his sons; he visited them in his dreams frequently and he had munpi anka near him always. (Wagley, 1943, pp. 66–67).

Tapirapé shamans are frequently called upon to cure illness. This they do with sleight of hand and the help of their spirit familiars while in a semitrance condition induced by gulping huge quantities of tobacco. Here is Charles Wagley's classic account of cure by vomit:

Unless the illness is serious enough to warrant immediate treatment, shamans always cure in the late evening. A shaman comes to his patient, and squats near the patient's hammock; his first act is always to light his pipe. When the patient has a fever or has fallen unconscious from the sight of a ghost, the principal method of treatment is by massage. The shaman blows smoke over the entire body of the patient; then he blows smoke over his own hands, spits into them, and massages the patient slowly and firmly, always toward the extremities of the body. He shows that he is removing a foreign substance by quick movement of his hands as he reaches the end of an arm or leg.

The more frequent method of curing, however, is by the extraction of a malignant object by sucking. The shaman squats alongside the hammock of his patient and begins to "eat smoke"—swallow large gulps of tobacco smoke from his pipe. He forces the smoke with great intakes of breath deep down into his stomach; soon he becomes intoxicated and nauseated; he vomits violently and smoke spews from his stomach. He groans and clears his throat in the manner of a person gagging with nausea but unable to vomit. By sucking back what he vomits he accumulates saliva in his mouth.

In the midst of this process he stops several times to suck on the body of his patient and finally, with one awful heave, he spews all the accumulated material on the ground. He then searches in this mess for the intrusive object that has been causing the illness. Never once did I see a shaman show the intrusive object to observers. At one treatment a Tapirapé [shaman] usually repeats this process of "eating smoke," sucking, and vomiting several times. Sometimes, when a man of prestige is ill, two or even three shamans will cure side by side in this manner and the noise of violent vomiting resounds throughout the village. (1943, pp. 73–74)

It is interesting to note in conjunction with the widespread use of tobacco in native American rituals that tobacco contains hallucinogenic alkaloids and may have induced visions when consumed in large quantities.

Communal cults

No culture is completely without communally organized religious beliefs and practices. Even the Eskimos have group rites. Frightened and sick Eskimo individuals under the cross-examinations of shamans publicly confess violations of taboos which have made them ill and which have endangered the rest of the community.

Among the native Americans of the Western Plains there were annual public rites of self-torture and vision quest known as the Sun Dance (Fig. 10.7). Under the direction of sha-

10.7 DAKOTA SUN DANCE
Painted by Short-Bull, chief of the Oglala Dakota (Sioux), this painting represents the Sun Dance of 90 years ago. The circle in the center represents a windbreak formed of fresh cottonwood boughs. In the center is the Sun Dance pole and hanging from it the figure of a man and a buffalo. Outside of the Sun Dance enclosure, devotees perform. One of them is dragging four buffalo skulls by cords run through openings in the skin on his back. He will continue to drag these until they tear loose. [American Museum of Natural History]

man leaders, the sun dancers tied themselves to a pole by means of a cord passed through a slit in their skin. Watched by the assembled group, they walked or danced around the pole and tugged at the cord until they fainted or the skin ripped apart. These public displays of endurance and bravery were part of the intense marauding and warfare complex that developed after the coming of the Europeans.

Communal rites fall into two major categories: (1) *rites of solidarity* and (2) *rites of passage*. In the rites of solidarity, participation in dramatic public rituals enhances the sense of group identity, coordinates the actions of the individual members of the group, and prepares the group for immediate or future cooperative action. Rites of passage celebrate the social movement of individuals into and out of groups or into or out of statuses of critical importance to the individual and to the community. Reproduction, the achievement of manhood and womanhood, marriage, and death are the principal worldwide occasions for rites of passage.

Communal rites of solidarity: totemism

Rites of solidarity are common among clans and other descent groups. Such groups usually have names and emblems that identify group members and set one group off from another. Animal names and emblems predominate, but insects, plants, and natural phenomena such as rain and clouds also occur. These group-identifying objects are known as *totems*. Many totems such as bear, breadfruit, or kangaroo are useful or edible species, and often there is a stipulated descent relationship between the members of the group and their totemic ancestor. Sometimes the members of the group must refrain from harming or eating their totem. There are many variations in the specific forms of totemic belief, however, and no single totemic complex can be said to exist. Lévi-Strauss (1963a) has suggested that the unity of the concept of totemism consists not in any specific belief or practice, but in certain general logical relationships between the named groups and their names. No matter what kind of animal or thing serves as a totem, it is the contrast with other totems rather than their specific properties that renders them useful for group identification.

The Arunta of Australia provide one of the classic cases of totemic ritual (Fig. 10.8). Here an individual identifies with the totem of the sacred place near which one's mother passed shortly before becoming pregnant (see p. 105). These places contain the stone objects known as *churinga*, which are the visible manifestations of each person's spirit. The *churinga* are believed to have been left behind by the totemic ancestors as they traveled about the countryside at the beginning of the world. The ancestors later turned into animals, objects, and other phenomena constituting the inventory of totems. The sacred places of each

10.8 TOTEMIC SOLIDARITY
Arunta men preparing themselves for totemic ritual. [American Museum of Natural History]

totem are visited annually during rites known as *Intichiuma*.

Here is a description of the Intichiuma of the witchetty-grub men: They slip away from camp. Under the direction of their headman they retrace the trail taken by Intwailiuka, the dawn-time witchetty-grub leader. All along this trail they come upon the *churinga* and other mementos of Intwailiuka's journey. One sacred place consists of a shallow cave, inside of which is a large rock surrounded by small rounded stones. The headman identifies the large rock as the body of the witchetty-grub and the small stones as the witchetty-grub's eggs. The headman begins to sing, tapping the rocks with a wooden bough while the others join in, tapping with twigs. The song asks the witchetty-grub to lay more eggs. The headman then strikes each man in the stomach with one of the "egg stones" saying, "You have eaten much food."

The party then moves on to the next sacred place underneath a large rock where Intwailiuka used to cook and eat. The men sing, tap with their twigs, and throw egg stones up the cliff, as Intwailiuka did. Then they march on to the next sacred place, which is a hole four or five feet deep. The headman scrapes away the dirt at the bottom of this hole, turning up more witchetty-grub *churinga*. The stones are carefully cleaned, handed about, and then replaced. The party stops at a total of ten such spots before returning to camp. In preparation for their return, the men decorate themselves with strings, nose bones, rat tails, and feathers. They also paint their bodies with the sacred design of the witchetty-grub. While they have been gone, one of the witchetty-grub men has constructed a brush hut in the shape of the witchetty-grub chrysalis. The men enter the hut and sing of the journey they have made. Then the headman comes shuffling and gliding out, followed by all the rest, in imitation of adult witchetty-grubs emerging from their chrysalis. This is repeated several times. During this phase of the ceremony,

10.9 *RELIGION AND LIFE CRISIS*
Above, male puberty initiate in Arnhemland, Australia, being painted with white clay. Below, Dogon funeral dancers.

all nonwitchitty-grub spectators are kept at a distance and obliged to follow the orders of witchetty-grub men and women (Spencer and Gillen, 1968).

These rituals have many meanings and functions. Witchetty-grub people are earnestly concerned with controlling the reproduction of witchetty-grubs, which are considered a great delicacy. But the exclusive membership of the ritual group also indicates that they are acting out the mythological dogma of their common ancestry. The witchetty-grub totem ceremonies reaffirm and intensify the sense of common identity of the members of a regional community. The ceremonies confirm the fact that the witchetty-

The Crow scaffold burial (above) shows a common means of disposing of the dead in sparsely inhabited regions; the Peruvian mummies (below) show another method, which is common in arid climates. [American Museum of Natural History—facing page, above; Eugene Gordon— facing page, below; Museum of the American Indian, Heye Foundation—this page, above; American Museum of Natural History—this page, below]

grub people have "stones" or, in a more familiar metaphor, "roots" in a particular land.

Communal rituals: rites of passage

Rites of passage accompany changes in structural position or statuses that are of general public concern. Why are birth, puberty, marriage, and death so frequently the occasions for rites of passage (Fig. 10.9)? Probably because of their public implications: The individual who is born, who reaches adulthood, who takes a spouse, or who dies is not the only one implicated in these events. Many other people must adjust to these momentous changes. Being born not only defines a new life, but brings into existence or modifies the position of parent, grandparent, sibling, heir, age mate, and many other domestic and political relationships. The main function of rites of passage is to give communal recognition to the entire complex of new or altered relationships and not merely to the changes experienced by the individuals who get born, married, or who die.

Rites of passage conform to a remarkably similar pattern among widely dispersed cultures (Elaide, 1958; see Schlegel and Barry, 1979). First, the principal performers are separated from the routines associated with their earlier life. Second, decisive physical and symbolic steps are taken to extinguish the old statuses. Often these steps include the notion of killing the old personality. To promote "death and transfiguration," old clothing and ornaments are exchanged for new and the body is painted or mutilated. Finally, the participants are ceremoniously returned to normal life.

Circumcision

The pattern of rites of passage can be seen in the male initiation ceremonies of the Ndembu of northern Zambia. Here, as among many African and Middle Eastern peoples, the transition from boyhood to manhood involves the rite of circumcision. Young boys are taken from their separate villages and placed in a special bush "school." They are circumcised by their own kinsmen or neighbors, and after their wounds heal, they are returned to normal life. Among the Ndembu the process of publicly transforming boys to men takes four months and is known as *mukanda* (Turner, 1967). A *mukanda* begins with the storage of food and beer. Then a clearing is made in the bush and a camp established. This camp includes a hearth at which the mothers of the boys undergoing circumcision cook for them. On the day preceding the circumcision the circumcisers dance and sing songs in which they express antagonism to the boys' mothers and make reference to the "killing" that is about to take place. The boys and their families assemble at the campsite, fires are lit, and a night of dancing and sexual license begins. *Suddenly the circumcisers entered in procession, carrying their apparatus. . . . All the rest of the gathering followed them as they danced crouching, holding up different items of apparatus, and chanting hoarsely. In the firelight and moonlight the dance got wilder and wilder. (Turner, 1967, p. 205)*

Meanwhile, "those who were about to die" sit in a line attended by their mothers and fathers. During the night they are repeatedly awakened and carried about by their male relatives. The next morning they are given a "last supper" (i.e., a last breakfast) by their mothers, "each mother feeding her son by hand as though he were an infant." The boys try not to look terrified as, after breakfast, the circumcisers, their brows and foreheads daubed with red clay, dance about brandishing their knives.

The actual circumcision takes place in another clearing some distance away from the cooking camp. The boys remain in seclusion at this site, which is known as the "place of dying." They sleep in a brush lodge watched over and ordered about by a group of male "guardians" (Fig. 10.10). After their "last breakfast" the boys are marched down the trail toward the "place of dying." The guardians come rushing out, seize them, and tear off their clothes. The mothers are chased back to the cooking camp, where they begin to wail as at the announcement of a death. The boys are held by guardians while circumcisers *stretch out the prepuce, make a slight nick on top and another underneath as guides, then cut through the dorsal section with a single movement and follow this by slitting the ventral section, then removing sufficient of the prepuce to leave the glans well exposed.* (Turner, 1967, p. 216)

During the seclusion at the place of dying the boys are subject to the strict discipline of their guardians. They have to maintain a modest demeanor, speak only when spoken to, fetch and carry anything required on the double, and run errands. In former times they were sent on dangerous hunting missions and subjected to severe beating for breaking discipline or displaying cowardice, and terrorized

10.10 NDEMBU CIRCUMCISION CAMP
"The place of dying." [Victor Turner, *The Forest of Symbols*, **Cornell University Press**]

at night by the sound of the *bullroarer*—a flat disk that makes a howling noise as it is whirled about on the end of a string (Fig. 10.11). Masked dancers whom they believe to be "red grave people" appear suddenly and beat them with sticks. These same monsters visit the cooking camp, dance before the

10.11 BULL ROARER
String is tied through hole and used to whirl bull roarer around head. This specimen is from Australia. [American Museum of Natural History]

Circumcision **203**

women, and terrorize the little children (Fig. 10.12). Throughout their seclusion, the boys are taught the rules of manhood, how to be brave and sexually potent. They are lectured to, harangued, and made to answer riddles rich in symbolic meanings.

For their "rebirth" the boys are daubed all over with white clay, signifying their new being. Then they are brought into the cooking camp and shown to their mothers.

At first the mothers wailed, then their mourning turned to songs of rejoicing as each realized that her son was safe and well. It is impossible to describe adequately the ensuing scene of complete, uninhibited jubilation. The guardians ran around in an inner circle, the mothers danced beside them . . . while other female relatives and friends made up an outer ring of joyful chanting and dancers. The men stood outside the whirl, laughing with pure pleasure. Dust rose in clouds. (Turner, 1967, p. 255)

The next morning the seclusion lodge is burned, the boys are washed in the river and given new clothes, and then each performs the dance of war as a sign of manhood.

In many cultures girls are subject to similar rites of separation, seclusion, and return in relationship to their first menses and their eligibility for marriage. Genital mutilation is also common among girls, and there is a widely practiced operation known as *clitoridectomy*. In this operation, the external tip of the clitoris is cut off. Among many Australian groups, both circumcision and clitoridectomy were practiced. In addition, the Australians knocked out the pubescent child's front tooth. Males were subject to the further operation of *subincision*, in which the underside of the penis was slit open to the depth of the urethra.

10.12 NDEMBU MONSTER
Although the women are supposed to be terrified, they are amused and skeptical. [**Victor Turner,** *The Forest of Symbols,* **Cornell University Press**]

Ecclesiastical cults

As stated above, ecclesiastical cults have in common the existence of a professional clergy or priesthood organized into a bureaucracy. This bureaucracy is usually associated with and under the control of a central temple. At secondary or provincial temple centers, the clergy may exercise a considerable amount of independence. In general, the more highly centralized the political system, the more highly centralized the ecclesiastical bureaucracy.

The ecclesiastic specialists are different from both the Tapirapé shamans and the Ndembu circumcisers and guardians. They are formally designated persons who devote themselves to the rituals of their office (Fig. 10.13). These rituals usually include a wide variety of techniques for influencing and controlling animistic beings and animatistic forces. The material support for these full-time specialists is usually closely related to power and privileges of taxation. As among the Inca (p. 149), the state and the priesthood may divide up the rent and tribute exacted from the peasants. Under feudalism (see p. 147), the ecclesiastical hierarchy derives its earnings from its own estates and from the gifts of powerful princes and kings. High officials in feudal ecclesiastical hierarchies are almost always kin or appointees of members of the ruling class.

The presence of ecclesiastical organizations produces a profound split among those who participate in ritual performances. On the one hand, there is an active segment, the priesthood; on the other, the passive "congregation," who are virtual spectators. The members of the priesthood must acquire intricate ritual, historical, calendrical, and astronomical knowledge. Often they are scribes and learned persons. It must be stressed, however, that the "congregation" does not altogether abandon individualistic shamanistic and communal beliefs and rituals. These are all continued, sometimes secretly, in neighborhoods, villages, or households, side by side with the "higher" rituals, despite more or less energetic efforts on the part of the ecclesiastical hierarchy to stamp out what it often calls idolatrous, superstitious, pagan, heathen, or heretical beliefs and performances.

The religion of the Aztecs

Many of the principal characteristics of belief and ritual in stratified contexts can be seen in the ecclesiastical organization of the Aztecs of Mexico. The Aztecs held their priests respon-

10.13 ECCLESIASTICAL CULT
Ordaining the Episcopalian bishop in the Cathedral of St. John the Divine [Charles Gatewood]

sible for the maintenance and renewal of the entire universe. By performing annual rituals, priests could obtain the blessing of the Aztec gods, ensure the well-being of the Aztec people, and guard the world against collapse into chaos and darkness. According to Aztec theology, the world had already passed through four ages, each of which ended in cataclysmic destruction. The first age ended when the reigning god, Tezcatlipoca, transformed himself into the sun and all the people of the earth were devoured by jaguars. The second age, ruled over by the feathered serpent Quetzalcoatl (Fig. 10.14) was destroyed by hurricanes that changed people into monkeys. The third age, ruled over by Tlaloc, god of rain, was brought to a close when the heavens rained fire. Then came the rule of Chalchihuitlicue, goddess of water, whose time ended with a universal flood, during which people turned into fish. The fifth age is in progress, ruled over by the sun god Tonatiuh, and doomed to destruction sooner or later by earthquakes.

The principal function of the 5000 priests living in the Aztec capital was to make sure the end of the world came later rather than sooner. This could be assured only by pleasing the legions of gods reputed to govern the world. The best way to please the gods was to give them gifts, the most precious being fresh human hearts. The hearts of war captives were the most esteemed gifts, since they were won only at great expense and risk.

Aztec ceremonial centers were dominated by large pyramidal platforms topped by temples (Fig. 10.15). These structures were vast stages upon which the drama of human sacrifice was enacted at least once a day throughout the year. On especially critical days there were multiple sacrifices. The set pattern for these performances involved first the victim's ascent of the huge staircase to the top of the pyramid; then, at the summit, the victim was seized by four priests, one for each limb, and bent face up, spread-eagled over the sacrificial stone. A fifth priest cut the victim's chest open with an obsidian knife and wrenched out the beating heart. The heart was smeared over the statue of the god and later burned. Finally, the lifeless body was flung over the edge of the pyramid where it rolled back down the steps.

All aspects of Aztec ritual were regulated by intricate calendrical systems understood only by the priests. By means of their calendars, the priests kept track of the gods who had to be appeased and of the dangerous days, neglect of which might have occasioned the end of the world.

The Aztecs calculated the year as having 365 days. They divided this period into 18 months of 20 days each ($18 \times 20 = 360$), leaving 5 days over as an annual unlucky period. Each of the 20 days had a name, and each was numbered consecutively from 1 to 13. Every $13 \times 20 = 260$ days, the number 1 occurred at the beginning of a month. This period of 260 days was meshed with the 365-day year. Every 52 years the beginning of the 260-day and 365-day cycles coincided. The most holy days were those associated with the end of each 52-year cycle. At this time, the priests struggled mightily to prevent the end of the world. The altar fires, which had burned perpetually for 52 years, were extinguished along with all fires throughout the kingdom. The people destroyed their household furnishings, fasted, and prayed, awaiting the ultimate catastrophe. Pregnant women were hidden away and children were prevented from falling asleep. At sunset on the last day, the priests ascended an extinct volcanic crater at the center of the Valley of Mexico and anxiously watched the skies for signs that the world would continue. When certain stars passed the meridian, they sacrificed a captive and kindled a new fire in the victim's breast. Runners bore torches lit from this sacred fire throughout the kingdom.

It is believed that during a four-day dedication ceremony of the main Aztec temple in

10.14 TEMPLE OF QUETZALCOATL (above)
The plumed Serpent, Mexico City (formerly
Tenochtitlán). [Mexican National Tourist
Council]

10.15 TENOCHTITLAN (below)
A reconstructed view of the Aztec capital
with its numerous temple-topped pyramids.
[American Museum of Natural History]

Tenochtitlan, 20,000 prisoners of war were sacrificed in the manner described above. A yearly toll estimated to have been as high as 15,000 people was sent to death to placate the bloodthirsty gods. Most of these victims were prisoners of war, although local youths, maidens, and children were also sacrificed from time to time (Vaillant, 1966; Coe, 1977; Soustelle, 1970). The bodies of most of those who were sacrificed were rolled down the pyramid steps, dismembered, and probably cooked and eaten (Harner, 1977).

Religion and political economy: high gods

Full-time specialists, monumental temples, dramatic processions, and elaborate rites performed for spectator congregations are incompatible with the infrastructure and political economy of hunters and food gatherers. Similarly, the complex astronomical and mathematical basis of ecclesiastical beliefs and rituals is never found among band and village peoples.

The level of political economy also influences the way in which gods are thought to relate to each other and to human beings. For example, the idea of a single high god who creates the universe is found among cultures at all levels of economic and political development. These high gods, however, play different kinds of roles in running the universe after they have brought it into existence. Among hunter-gatherers and other prestate peoples, the high gods tend to become inactive after their creation task is done. It is to a host of lesser gods, demons, and ancestor souls that one must turn in order to obtain assistance. On the other hand, in stratified societies the high god bosses the lesser gods and tends to be a more active figure to whom priests and commoners address their prayers (Swanson, 1960).

A plausible explanation for this difference is that prestate cultures have no need for the idea of a central or supreme authority. Just as there is an absence of centralized control over people and strategic resources in life, so in religious belief, the inhabitants of the spirit world lack decisive control over each other. They form a more or less egalitarian group. On the other hand, the belief that superordination and subordination characterizes relationships among the gods helps to obtain the cooperation of the commoner classes in stratified societies (Fig. 10.16).

One way to achieve conformity in stratified societies is to convince commoners that the gods demand obedience to the state. Disobedience and nonconformity result not only in

10.16 RELIGION AND STRATIFICATION
Bishops and other high prelates of the Corpus Christi Cathedral in Cuzco, Peru, are an awe-inspiring sight to an Indian peasant. [Sergio Larrain, Magnum]

TABLE 10.1   RELIGION, CLASS, AND MORALITY

| Gods interested in morality | Societies | |
	With social classes	Without social classes
Present	25	2
Absent	8	12

Source: Adapted from Swanson, 1960, p. 166.

retribution administered through the state's police-military apparatus, but also in punishments in present or future life administered by the high gods themselves. In prestate societies, for reasons discussed in Chapter 7, law and order are rooted in common interest. Consequently, there is little need for high gods to administer punishments for those who have been "bad" and rewards for those who have been "good." but as Table 10.1 shows, where there are class differences, the gods are believed to take a lively interest in the degree to which each individual's thoughts and behavior are immoral or ethically subversive.

Revitalization

The relationship between religion and political and economic conditions can also be seen in the process known as *revitalization*. Under the severe stresses associated with colonial conquest and intense class or minority exploitation, religions tend to become movements concerned with achieving a drastic improvement in the immediate conditions of life and/or in the prospects for an afterlife. These movements are sometimes referred to as *nativistic, revivalistic, millennarian,* or *messianic*. The term "revitalization" is intended to embrace all the specific cognitive and ritual variants implied by these terms (see Wallace, 1966).

Revitalization is a process of political and religious interaction between a depressed caste, class, minority, or other subordinate social group and a superordinate group. Some revitalization movements emphasize passive attitudes, the adoption of old rather than new cultural practices, or salvation through rewards after death; others advocate more or less open resistance or aggressive political or military action. These differences largely reflect the extent to which the subordinate groups are prepared to cope with the challenge to their power and authority. Direct challenges to political authority, as, for example, in a Joan of Arc type vision, are not to be expected where there is no possibility of military action. If the revitalization is sufficiently passive, the superordinate group may find it advantageous to encourage, or at least not to suppress, the revitalization movement. Many fundamentalist and revivalist Christian sects are politically conservative revitalizations that throw the onus of sickness, poverty, and psychological distress back onto the individual. Disciples are urged to stop smoking, drinking, lying, cheating, and fornicating in order to achieve a new identity free from sin that will entitle them to eternal life. In some cases, Christian fundamentalist revitalization is explicitly linked with conservation of the political status quo through patriotic sermons and devotion to the struggle against atheism and "godless communism." Many revitalizations, however, lack an overt political theme, whether conservative or revolutionary. This does not mean that the political functions of revitalization can be disregarded, but that the particular circumstances may not be appropriate for a mature phase of political struggle. As Peter Worsley (1968) has shown, revitalizations that take place under conditions of massive suffering and exploitation sooner or later result in political and even military probes or confrontations, even though both sides may overtly desire to avoid conflict.

Native American revitalizations

Widespread revitalizations were provoked by the European invasion of the New World and the conquest and expulsion of the native American peoples and the destruction of their natural resources.

As early as 1680, the Pueblos of New Mexico underwent a violent political-religious conversion led by the prophet Popé. According to Popé's visions, the Christian God had died. Under Popé's direction, the Catholic missionaries were burned at the altars of their churches and all European artifacts were destroyed.

Other parts of the United States experienced armed or passive revitalization organized around visions and prophecies stimulatd by the European expansion. A common theme of these revitalizations concerned the defeat and expulsion of the white invaders. In the Great Lakes region, the chief Pontiac attacked the whites as foretold in a prophetic vision.

Later there arose the Shawnee prophet Tenskwatawa, who foresaw the expulsion of the whites if the native Americans would give up alcohol and depose their chiefs. The prophet's twin brother, Tecumseh, formed a military alliance among tribes as far apart as Florida and the Rocky Mountains. Tenskwatawa himself was killed at Tippecanoe on the Wabash River during an attack against forces led by William Henry Harrison. This battle made Harrison famous. He and John Tyler successfully campaigned for president and vice-president under the slogan "Tippecanoe and Tyler Too" as heroes responsible for the suppression of the rebellious "savages."

As the more openly political and militaristic revitalizations were crushed by disease, starvation, and military defeat, they were replaced by more passive forms. Thus the suc-

cessor to Tenskwatawa was Kanakuk, who prophesied that if the Kickapoo would give up warfare, lying, stealing, and alcohol, they would find vast green lands to replace those stolen from them by the whites. Kanakuk's prophecies were as inaccurate as Tenskwatawa's, since the obedient Kickapoo were forced farther and farther west onto smaller and smaller reservations.

Revitalization in the Northwest Territories was led by the prophet Smohalla, known as the "Dreamer." Conversations with the Great Spirit had convinced Smohalla that the native Americans must resist the white man's attempt to convert them to farmers. His visions and prophecies inspired Chief Joseph of the Nez Percé, who led an unsuccessful rebellion in 1877.

The most famous of the nineteenth-century revitalization movements was the Ghost Dance, also known as the Messiah craze. This movement originated near the California-Nevada border and roughly coincided with the completion of the Union Pacific Railroad. The Paviotso prophet Wodziwob envisioned the return of the dead from the spirit world in a great train whose arrival would be signaled by a huge explosion. Simultaneously the whites would be swept from the land, but their buildings, machines, and other possessions would be left behind. (The resemblance to the neutron bomb is worth noting.) To hasten the arrival of the ancestors, there was to be ceremonial dancing accompanied by the songs revealed to Wodziwob during his visions.

A second version of the Ghost Dance was begun in 1889 under the inspiration of Wovoka (Fig. 10.17). A vision in which all the dead had been brought back to life by the Ghost Dance was again reported. Ostensibly Wovoka's teachings lacked political content, and as the Ghost Dance spread eastward across the Rockies, its political implications remained ambiguous. Yet for the native

10.17 WOVOKA
Leader of the Ghost Dance. [Nevada
Historical Society]

termination of the whites under a huge land-slide. The Sioux warriors put on Ghost Dance shirts, which they believed would make them invulnerable to bullets. Clashes between the U.S. Army and the Sioux became more frequent, and the Sioux leader Sitting Bull was arrested and killed. The second Ghost Dance movement came to an end with the massacre of 200 Sioux at Wounded Knee, South Dakota (Fig. 10.18), on December 29, 1890 (Mooney, 1965).

After all chance of military resistance was crushed, the native American revitalization movement became more introverted and passive. Visions in which all the whites were wiped out cease to be experienced, confirming once again the responsiveness of religion to political reality. The development and spread of beliefs and rituals centering upon peyote, mescal, and other hallucinogenic drugs are characteristic of many twentieth-century native American revitalizations. Peyote ritual involves a night of praying, singing, peyote eating, and ecstatic contemplation followed by a communal breakfast (Fig. 10.19). The peyote eaters are not interested in bringing back the buffalo or making themselves invulnerable to bullets; they seek self-knowledge, personal moral strength, and physical health (La Barre, 1938; Stewart, 1948).
The peyote religion is a syncretistic cult, incorporating ancient Indian and modern Christian elements. The Christian theology of love, charity, and forgiveness has been added to the ancient Indian ritual and aboriginal desire to acquire personal power through individual visions. Peyotism has taught a program of accommodation for over 50 years and the peyote religion has succeeded in giving Indians pride in their native culture while adjusting to the dominant civilization of the whites. (Stewart, 1968, p. 108)

Americans of the Plains, the return of the dead meant that they would outnumber the whites and hence be more powerful.

Among the Sioux, there was a version that included the return of all the bison and the ex-

Peyotism and allied cult movements do not, of course, signal the end of political action on the part of the native Americans. With the emergence of the "Red Power" movement, the

10.18 WOUNDED KNEE
In the first battle (above), 1890, 200 Sioux Indians were killed by the U. S. Army. In the second battle (below), 1973, militant Indians occupied the village of Wounded Knee, South Dakota, and exchanged gunfire with U. S. Marshalls. [Museum of the American Indian, Heye Foundation—above; Wide World Photos—below]

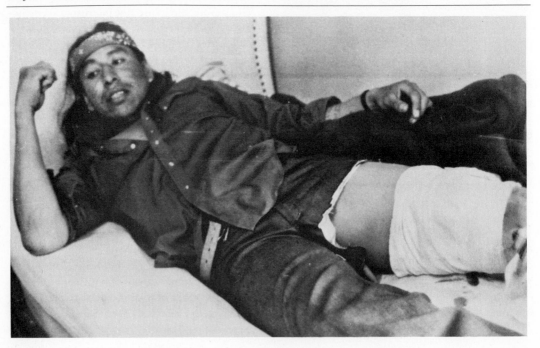

10.19 PEYOTE CEREMONY
**Delaware Indians of Oklahoma spend the night
in prayer and meditation. At right, they emerge
to greet the dawn. [Painting by Ernest Spybuck,
Museum of the American Indian, Heye Foundation]**

native Americans' attempt to hold on to and
regain their stolen lands is now being carried
out through lawyers, politicians, novelists,
Washington lobbyists, sit-ins, and land-ins
(De Loria, 1969; D. Walker, 1972).

Cargo cults

In New Guinea and Melanesia, revitalization
is associated with the concept of *cargo* (Fig.
10.20). The characteristic vision of the Melanesian revitalization prophets is that of a ship
bringing back the ancestors and a cargo of
European goods. In recent times airplane and

spaceships have become the favorite means of
delivering the cargo (see Worsley, 1968).

As a result of the abundance of goods displayed by U.S. military forces during the Pacific island campaigns of World War II, some
revitalizations stressed the return of the
Americans. In Espiritu Santo in 1944, the
prophet Tsek urged his people to destroy all
trade goods and throw away their clothes in
preparation for the return of the mysteriously
departed Americans. Some of the American-
oriented revitalizations have placed specific
American soldiers in the role of cargo deliv-
erers. On the island of Tana in the New He-
brides, the John Frumm cult cherishes an old

10.20 CARGO CULT
[Muller, Woodfin Camp]

GI jacket as the relic of one John Frumm, whose identity is not otherwise known. The prophets of John Frumm build landing strips, bamboo control towers, and grass-thatched cargo sheds. In some cases beacons are kept ablaze at night and radio operators stand ready with tin-can microphones and earphones to guide the cargo planes to a safe landing.

An important theme is that the cargo planes and ships have been successfully loaded by the ancestors at U.S. ports and are on their way, but the local authorities have refused to permit the cargo to be landed. In other versions, the cargo planes are tricked into landing at the wrong airport. In a metaphorical sense these sentiments are applicable to the actual colonial contexts. The peoples of the South Seas have indeed often been tricked out of their lands and resources (Harris, 1974).

In 1964 the island of New Hanover became the scene of the Lyndon Johnson cult. Under the leadership of the prophet Bos Malik, cult members demanded that they be permitted to vote for Johnson in the village elections scheduled for them by the Australian administration. Airplanes passing overhead at night were said to be President Johnson's planes searching for a place to land. Bos Malik advised that in order to get Johnson to be their president, they would have to "buy" him. This was to be done by paying the annual head tax to Malik instead of to the Australian tax collectors. When news reached New Hanover that an armed force had been dispatched to suppress the tax revolt, Malik prophesied that the liner *Queen Mary* would soon arrive bearing cargo and U.S. troops to liberate the islanders from the Australian oppresors. When the ship failed to materialize, Malik accused the Australian officials of stealing the cargo.

The confusion of the Melanesian revitalization prophets is a confusion about the workings of cultural systems. They do not understand how modern industrial wage-labor societies are organized, nor comprehend how law and order are maintained among state-level peoples. To them, the material abundance of the industrial nations and the penury of others constitute an irrational flaw, a massive contradiction in the structure of the world.

The belief system of the cargo cults vividly demonstrates why the assumption that all people distingush between natural and supernatural categories is incorrect (see p. 188). Cargo prophets who have been taken to see modern Australian stores and factories in the hope that they would give up their beliefs return home more convinced than ever that they are following the best prescription for obtaining cargo. With their own eyes they have observed the fantastic abundance the authorities refuse to let them have (Lawrence, 1964).

Taboo, religion, and ecology

As discussed in the previous chapter, religion can be seen as the concentration of the sense of the sacred. In the theories of Emile Durkheim, the sacred is the sense of awe evoked by the power of social life. It follows that an appeal to the sacred nature of a rule governing interpersonal relations or of a rule governing the relationship between a population and its environment will be useful in resolving the uncertainties that people may sometimes experience concerning what they ought to do.

For example, the prohibition on incest within the nuclear family is widely seen as a sacred obligation. The violation of an incest taboo is looked upon as a dirty or antisacred act. One plausible explanation for these powerful sentiments is that people are strongly tempted to commit incest, but that the short-run satisfactions they might receive from such acts would have long-run negative consequences for them and for the continuity of social life because of the reduced ability of individuals and local groups to establish adaptive intergroup relationships (see p. 97). By surrounding incest prohibitions with the aura of sacredness, the long-term individual and collective interest comes to prevail, and the ambiguities and doubts individuals feel about renouncing the prohibited sexual relationships are resolved more decisively than would otherwise be possible. This does not mean that incest ceases to occur or that all psychological doubts are removed, but merely that such doubts are brought under effective social control.

A similar tension between short-run and long-run costs and benefits may explain the origin of certain food taboos that are regarded as sacred obligations. For example, it seems likely that the ancient Israelite prohibition on the consumption of pork reflects the contradiction between the temptation to rear pigs and the negative consequences of raising animals that are useful only for meat. Pigs require shade and moisture to regulate their body temperature. With the progressive deforestation and desertification of the Middle East caused by the spread and intensification of agriculture and stock raising and by population growth, habitat zones suitable for pig rearing became scarce. Hence an animal that was at one time reared and consumed as a relatively inexpensive source of fat and protein could no longer be reared and consumed by large numbers of people without reducing the efficiency of the main system of food production (Harris, 1979a; see Diener and Robkin, 1978). The temptation to continue the practice of pig raising persisted, however; hence the invocation of sacred commandments in the ancient Hebrew religion. Note that the explanation of the ancient origins of this taboo does not account for its perpetuation into the present. Once in existence, the taboo against pork (and other foods) acquired the function of demarcating or bounding Jewish ethnic minorities from other groups and of increasing their sense of identity and solidarity (see p. 179). Outside the Middle East the taboo no longer served an ecological function, but it continued to be useful on the level of structural relationships.

The general ecological adaptiveness of taboos regulating potentially important sources of animal protein in the Amazon Basin has been studied by Eric Ross (1978). Ross holds that certain large animals, such as deer, the tapir, and the white-lipped peccary, are not hunted or eaten by the Achuara who live on the border of Peru and Ecuador because to do so would be to misdirect the hunting effort away from gregarious, abundant, relatively accessible, and less costly species such as monkeys, birds, and fish. The costs of obtaining species such as deer and tapir among the Achuara are prohibitive because the Achuara live in very small dispersed villages and cannot form hunting parties with enough men to pursue, kill, and bring back the bigger animals.

It is interesting to note in this connection the origin of the word *taboo*. This is a Polynesian word that denotes the practice followed by Polynesian chiefs in limiting access to certain depleted agricultural lands or overfished portions of the seacoast. Anyone violating such taboos was subject to both natural and supernatural punishment.

The sacred cow

The case of the sacred cow of India conforms to the general theory that the flesh of certain animals becomes taboo when it becomes very expensive as a result of ecological changes. Like pigs in the Middle East, cattle were sacrificed and eaten quite freely in India during the Neolithic. With the rise of the state and of dense rural and urban populations, however, cattle could no longer be raised in sufficient numbers to be used both as a source of meat and as the principal source of traction power for pulling plows. But as the taboo on cattle use developed, it took a form quite different from the Israelite taboo on the pig. Whereas the pig was valued almost exclusively for its flesh, cattle were also valued for their milk and especially for their traction power. When pigs became too costly to be raised for meat, the whole animal became taboo and an abomination. But as cattle in India became too costly to be raised for meat, their value as a source of traction power increased (the land had to be plowed more intensively as population increased). Therefore, they had to be protected rather than abominated, and so the Hindu religion came to emphasize everyone's sacred duty to refrain from killing cattle or eating beef. Interestingly enough, the Brahmans, who at one time were the caste responsible for ritually slaughtering cattle, later became the caste most concerned with their protection and most op-

posed to the development of a beef slaughter industry in India (Harris, 1977; see Simoons, 1979; Harris, 1979a).

What about the sacred cow today? Is the religious ban on the slaughter of cattle and the consumption of beef a functionally useful feature of modern Hinduism? Everyone agrees that the human population of India needs more calories and proteins. Yet the Hindu religion bans the slaughter of cattle and taboos the eating of beef. These taboos are often held responsible for the creation of large numbers of aged, decrepit, barren, and useless cattle. Such animals are depicted as roaming aimlessly across the Indian countryside, clogging the roads, stopping the trains, stealing food from the marketplace, and blocking city streets (Fig. 10.21). A closer look at some of the details of the ecology and economy of the Indian subcontinent, however, suggests that the taboo in question does not decrease the capacity of the present Indian system of food production to support human life.

The basis of traditional Indian agriculture is the ox-drawn plow. Each peasant farmer needs at least two oxen to plow the fields at the proper time of the year. Despite the impression of surplus cattle, the central fact of Indian rural life is that there is a shortage of oxen, since one-third of the peasant households own less than the minimum pair. It is true that many cows are too old, decrepit, and sick to do a proper job of reproducing. At this point the ban on slaughter and beef consumption is thought to exert its harmful effect. For rather than kill dry, barren, and aged cows, the Hindu farmer is depicted as ritually obsessed with preserving the life of each sacred beast, no matter how useless it may become. From the point of view of the poor farmer, however, these relatively undesirable creatures may be quite essential and useful. The farmer would prefer to have more vigorous cows, but is prevented from achieving this goal not by the taboos against slaughter, but by the shortage of land and pasture.

10.21 SACRED COWS
This resident of Calcutta (left) is not wandering aimlessly. Its owner knows where it is. These cows (right) are "parked," not blocking traffic. Cattle are ecologically more valuable than cars in India. [Moni Nag—left; UPI—right]

Even barren cows, however, are by no means a total loss. Their dung makes an essential contribution to the energy system as fertilizer and as cooking fuel. Millions of tons of artificial fertilizer at prices beyond the reach of the small farmer would be required to make up for the loss of dung if substantial numbers of cattle were sent to slaughter. Since cattle dung is also a major source of cooking fuel, the slaughter of substantial numbers of animals would require the purchase of expensive dung substitutes, such as wood, coal, or kerosene. Cattle dung is relatively cheap because the cattle do not eat foods that can be eaten by people. Instead, they eat the stubble left in the fields and the marginal patches of grass on steep hillsides, roadside ditches, railroad embankments, and other nonarable lands. This constant scavenging gives the impression that cows are roaming around aimlessly devouring everything in sight. But most cows have an owner, and in the cities, after poking about in the market refuse and nibbling on neighbors' lawns, each cow returns to its stall at the end of the day.

In a study of the bioenergetic balances involved in the cattle complex of villages in West Bengal, Stuart Odend'hal (1972) found that "basically, the cattle convert items of little direct human value into products of immediate human utility." Their gross energetic efficiency in supplying useful products was several times greater than that characteristic of agroindustrial beef production. He concludes that "judging the productive value of Indian cattle based on western standards is inappropriate."

Although it might be possible to maintain or exceed the present level of production of oxen and dung with substantially fewer cows of larger and better breeds, the question arises as to how these cows would be distributed among the poor farmers. Are the farmers who have only one or two decrepit animals to be driven from the land?

Aside from the problem of whether present levels of population and productivity could be maintained with fewer cows, there is the theoretically more crucial question of whether it is the taboo on slaughter that accounts for the

The sacred cow   **217**

observed ratio of cattle to people. This seems highly unlikely. Despite the ban on slaughter, Hindu farmers cull their herds and adjust sex ratios to crops, weather, and regional conditions. The cattle are killed by various indirect means equivalent to the forms of benign and malign neglect discussed in Chapter 3 with respect to human population controls. In the Gangetic plain, one of the most religiously orthodox regions of India, there are over 200 oxen for every 100 cows (Vaidyanathan, Nair, and Harris, 1982).

Stepping away from the point of view of the individual farmer, here are a number of additional reasons for concluding that the Hindu taboos have a positive rather than a negative effect upon carrying capacity. The ban on slaughter, whatever its consequences for culling the herds, discourages the development of a meat-packing industry. Such an industry would be ecologically disastrous in a land as densely populated as India. In this connection it should be pointed out that the protein output of the existing system is not unimportant. Although the Indian cows are very poor milkers by Western standards, they nonetheless contribute critical if small quantities of protein to the diets of millions of people. Moreover, a considerable amount of beef does get eaten during the course of the year, since animals that die a natural death are consumed by carrion-eating outcastes. Finally, the critical function of the ban on slaughter during famines should be noted. When hunger stalks the Indian countryside, the slaughter taboo helps the peasants to resist the temptation to eat their cattle. If this temptation were to win out over religious scruples, it would be impossible for them to plant new crops when the rains began. Thus the intense resistance among Hindu saints to the slaughter and consumption of beef takes on a new meaning in the context of the Indian infrastructure. In the words of Mahatma Gandhi:

Why the cow was selected for apotheosis is obvious to me. The cow was in India the best companion. She was the giver of plenty. Not only did she give milk but she also made agriculture possible. (1954, p. 3)

Summary

Edward Tylor defined religion as animism or the doctrine of souls. According to Tylor, from the idea of the soul the idea of all godlike beings arose, while the idea of the soul itself arose as an attempt to explain phenomena such as trances, dreams, shadows, and reflections. Tylor's definition has been criticized for failing to consider the multifunctional nature of religion and for overlooking the compelling reality of direct hallucinatory contact with extraordinary beings.

As the Jívaro belief in three souls demonstrates, each culture uses the basic concepts of animism in its own distinctive fashion.

Tylor's definition of religion was supplemented by Marett's concepts of animatism and mana. Animatism refers to the belief in an impersonal life force in people, animals, and objects. The concentration of this force gives people, animals, and objects *mana*, or the capacity to be extraordinarily powerful and successful.

It should also be noted that the Western distinction between natural and supernatural is of limited utility for defining religion emically. As the case of the Gururumba indicates, the need for rituals to control certain entities, processes, or forces does not mean that other entities, processes, or forces can be controlled by a contrastive set of rituals. In other words, in many cultures there are no supernatural versus natural controls, only controls.

The distinction between sacred and profane realms of human experience may have greater universal validity than that between natural and supernatural. According to Durkheim, the feeling that something is sacred expresses the awe in which the hidden force of social consensus is held. Thus, although the content of the realm of the sacred may vary from one culture to another, the contrast between sacred and profane matters probably occurs universally.

Frazer tried to cope with the enormous variety of religious experience by separating religion from magic. Humility, supplication, and doubt characterize religion; routine cause and effect characterize magic. This distinction is difficult to maintain in view of the routine and coercive fashion in which animistic beings are often manipulated. There is no sharp difference between prayers and magic spells. Religion is a mix of awe and wonder, boredom and excitement, power and weakness.

The principal varieties of beliefs and rituals show broad correlations with levels of political economic organization. Four levels of religious organizations or cults can be distinguished: individualistic, shamanistic, communal, and ecclesiastical.

Eskimo religion illustrates the individualistic or do-it-yourself level. Each individual carries out a series of rituals and observes a series of taboos that are deemed essential for survival and well-being, without the help of any part-time or full-time specialist. Do-it-yourself cults, however, are not to be confused with "anything goes." As the example of Crow vision quests demonstrates, individualistic beliefs and rituals always follow culturally determined patterns.

No culture is devoid of shamanistic cults, defined by the presence of part-time magico-religious experts or shamans who have special talents and knowledge, usually involving sleight of hand, trances, and possession. As the case of Tapirapé shamanism indicates, shamans are frequently employed to cure sick people, as well as to identify and destroy evildoers. Many shamans think they can fly and move backward and forward through time.

Communal cults—involving public rituals deemed essential for the welfare or survival of the entire social group—also occur to some extent at all political-economic levels. Even in cultures such as the Eskimo and the Crow, where individualistic and shamanistic rituals predominate, communal rituals such as confession and the Sun Dance also take place. Two principal types of communal rituals can be distinguished: rites of solidarity and rites of passage. As illustrated by the Arunta totemic rituals, rites of solidarity reaffirm and intensify a group's sense of common identity and express in symbolic form the group's claims to territory and resources. As illustrated in the Ndembu circumcision rituals, rites of passage symbolically and publicly denote the extinction or "death" of an individual's or group's socially significant status and the acquisition or "birth" of a new socially significant status.

Finally, ecclesiastical cults are those that are dominated by a hierarchy of full-time specialists or "priests" whose knowledge and skills are usually commanded by a state-level ruling class. To preseve and enhance the well-being of the state and of the universe, historical, astronomical, and ritual information must be acquired by the ecclesiastical specialists. Ecclesiastical cults are also characterized by huge investments in buildings, monuments, and personnel and by a thoroughgoing split between the specialist performers of ritual and the great mass of more or less passive spectators who constitute the "congregation." The religion of the Aztecs illustrates all these aspects of ecclesiastical cults.

Revitalization is another category of religious phenomena that cannot be understood apart from political-economic conditions. Under political-economic stress, subordinate castes, classes, minorities, and ethnic groups develop beliefs and rituals concerned with achieving a drastic improvement in their immediate well-being and/or their well-being in a life after death. These movements have the latent capacity to attack the superordinate groups directly or indirectly through political or military action; on the other hand, they may turn inward and accommodate by means of passive doctrines and rituals involving individual guilt, drugs, and contemplation.

Native American revitalizations were initially violent protests against genocide and ethnocide. Prophets predicted the expulsion of the whites if native Americans gave up drinking and fighting among themselves. Later, there were visions of the whites being swept back into the sea after the arrival of a great train filled with ancestors brought back to life. The Sioux put on Ghost Dance shirts to protect themselves against bullets. After the suppression of the Ghost Dance movement, revitalization returned to contemplative renewal of native traditions, as in the peyote religion. More recently, the struggle of native Americans has become more secular and legalistic.

Melanesian and New Guinea cargo revitalizations foresaw the ancestors returning in ships laden with European trade goods. Later, airplanes and spaceships were substituted for sailing ships and steamboats. Cargo cults reflected a misunderstanding of industrial state systems by peoples who were living on the village level of political evolution when they were brought into the wage-labor system.

Religious beliefs and rituals also exhibit adaptive relationships in the form of taboos. Taboos often take the form of sacred injunctions that resolve ambiguities and control the temptation to engage in behavior, such as incest, that has short-term benefits but that is socially disruptive in the long run. Many taboos on animals whose exploitation leads to ambiguous ecological and economic consequences can be seen in the same light. The ancient Israelite pig taboo, for example, can be understood as an adaptation to the changing costs and benefits of pig rearing brought about by population increase, deforestation, and desertification. Similar short-term versus long-term cost-benefits among villages of different sizes in the Amazon tropical forest may also account for the pattern of animal use and nonuse and taboos associated with various intensities of sacredness. A final example of the way in which taboos and whole religions adapt to changing political, economic, and ecological contexts is the sacred cow of India.

11

Art

This chapter is concerned with finding the common element that underlies the thought and behavior associated with painting, music, poetry, sculpture, dance, and other media of artistic creation. At the same time, it is concerned with explaining why the specific forms and styles of artistic expression vary from one culture to another. We will see that art is not an isolated sector of human experience; it is intimately connected with and embedded in other aspects of sociocultural systems.

What is art?

Alexander Alland (1977, p. 39) defines *art* as "play with form producing some aesthetically successful transformation-representation." The key ingredients in this definition are "play," "form," "aesthetic," and "transformation." *Play* is an enjoyable, self-rewarding aspect of activity that cannot be accounted for simply by the utilitarian or survival functions of that activity. *Form* designates a set of restrictions on how the art play is to be organized in time and space—the rules of the game of art. *Esthetic* designates the existence of a universal human capacity for an emotionally charged response of appreciation and pleasure when art is successful. *Transformation-representation* refers to the communicative aspect of art. Art always represents something—communicates information—but this something is never represented in its literal shape, sound, color, movement, or feeling. To be art, as distinct from other forms of communication, the representation must be transformed into some metaphoric or symbolic statement, movement, image, or object which stands for that which is being represented. A portrait, for example, no matter how "realistic," can only be a transformation of the individual it depicts.

As Alland points out, play, adherence to form, and an esthetic sense are found in many nonhuman animals. Chimpanzees, for example, like to play with paints (Fig. 11.1). Their adherence to form can be demonstrated by their placement of designs in the center of blank spaces or by their balancing of designs on different parts of a page. (They don't simply paint right off the page.) An esthetic sense can be inferred by their repeated attempts to copy simple designs such as circles and triangles accurately. Moreover, as we have seen in Chapter 2, the capacity to use symbols and to learn rules of symbolic transformation is not entirely confined to human beings. The 3-year-old chimp Moja drew a bird and gave the sign for it. The trainer tried to make sure that it was a bird rather than a berry, so he asked her to draw a berry, which she promptly did (Hill, 1978, p. 98).

Nonetheless, just as grammatical language remains rudimentary among apes in nature, so too does their artistry. Although the rudiments of art can be found in our primate heritage, only *Homo sapiens* can justly be called the artistic animal.

Art as a cultural category

Although it is possible to identify art as an etic category of thought and behavior in all human cultures, an emic distinction between art and nonart is not universal (just as the distinction between natural and supernatural is not universal). What most Westerners mean by art is a particular emic category of modern Euramerican civilization. Euramerican schoolchildren are enculturated to the idea that art is a category of activities and products that stands opposed to the category of nonart. They learn to believe, in other words, that some paintings, carvings, songs, dances, and stories are not art. In Western civilization a particular performance is deemed artistic or not by a distinct group of authorities who make or judge art and who control the museums, conservatories, critical journals, and other organizations and institutions devoted to art as a livelihood and style of life. Most cultures lack any semblance of an art establishment. This does not mean they lack art or artistic standards. A painted design on a pot or a rock, a carved mask or club, or a song or chant in a puberty ordeal are subject to critical evaluation by both performers and spectators. All cultures distinguish between less satisfactory and more satisfactory esthetic experiences in decorative, pictorial, and expressive matters.

Basic to the modern Western idea of art and

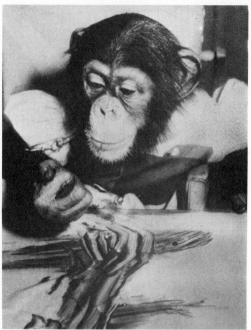

11.1 *CHIMPANZEE ARTISTS*
A 2-year-old chimpanzee (top) finger painting at the Baltimore, Md., Zoo. Note attempt to center painting. A chimpanzee named Candy (bottom) exhibits her artwork at the San Francisco Zoo. [Wide World]

nonart is the exclusion of designs, stories, and artifacts that have a definite use in day-to-day subsistence activities and that are produced primarily for practical purposes or for commercial sale. Carpenters are distinguished from people who make wooden sculptures; bricklayers from architects; house painters from those who apply paint to canvas; and so forth. A similar opposition between art and practicality is seldom found in other cultures. Many works of art are produced and performed in complete harmony with utilitarian objectives. People everywhere, whether specialists or nonspecialists, derive pleasure from playfully embellishing and transforming the contours and surfaces of pots, fabrics, wood, and metal products (Fig. 11.2). All cultures, however, recognize that certain individuals are more skilled than others in making utilitarian objects and in embellishing them with pleasurable designs. Most anthropologists regard the skilled woodcarver, basketmaker, potter, weaver, or sandalmaker as an artist.

11.2 ART HAS MANY MEDIA (facing page)
Native American cultures produced these objects. Gold mummy mask with green stone eyes, Chimu, Peru (top left). Globular basket with coiled weave, Chumash, California (top right). Feathers of blue and yellow form design of Tapirapé mask, Brazil (center left). Painted wooden kero, or beaker, representing ocelot head, Inca, Peru (center right). Ceramic jar, Nazca, Peru (bottom left). Blanket, in blue, black, and white, with stripes and frets, Navajo (bottom right). [Museum of the American Indian, Heye Foundation]

11.3 SOLUTREAN LAUREL LEAF BLADE
An Upper Paleolithic utilitarian art form from prehistoric France.

Art and invention

As Alland (1977, p. 24) suggests, play is a form of exploratory behavior that permits human beings to try out new and possibly useful responses in a controlled and protected context. The playful creative urge that lies behind art, therefore, is probably closely related to the creative urge that lies behind the development of science, technology, and new institutions. Art and technology often interact. For example, throughout the Paleolithic period it is difficult to say where technology ends and art begins, or where art ends and technology begins. A Solutrean laurel leaf blade is as much an esthetic expression as it is a device for cutting flesh (see Fig. 11.3). The beautiful symmetry of nets, baskets, and woven fabrics is essential for their proper functioning. Even in the development of media of musical expression there may be technological benefits. For example, there was probably some kind of feedback between the invention of the bow as a hunting weapon and the twanging of taut strings for musical effect. No one can say

11.4 MASKS
Above, mask within mask. Wearer of this Kwakiutl mask uses strings to pull eagle apart revealing human face. Left, mask within mask within mask. Whale conceals bird, which conceals human face, which conceals face of wearer. Another Kwakiutl masterpiece. [American Museum of Natural History]

which came first, but cultures with bows and arrows invariably have musical strings. Wind instruments, blowguns, pistons, and bellows are all related. Similarly, metallurgy and chemistry relate to experimentation with the ornamental shape, texture, and color of ceramic and textile products. Thus it is practical to encourage craftworkers to experiment with new techniques and materials. Small wonder that many cultures regard technical virtuosity as *mana*. Others regard it as the gift of the gods, as in the classical Greek idea of the Muses—goddesses of orators, dancers, and musicians—whose assistance was needed if worthy artistic performances were to occur.

Art and cultural patterning

Most artwork is deliberately fashioned in the image of preexisting forms. It is the task of the artist to replicate these forms by original combinations of culturally standardized elements—familiar and pleasing sounds, colors, lines, shapes, movements, and so on. Of course, there must always be some playful and creative ingredient, or it will not be art.

On the other hand, if the transformation-representation is to communicate something—and it must communicate something if it is to be a successful work of art—the rules of the game cannot be the artist's own private invention. Complete originality, therefore, is not what most cultures strive after in their art.

It is the repetition of traditional and familiar elements that accounts for the major differences between the artistic products of different cultures. For example, Northwest Coast native American sculpture is well known for its consistent attention to animal and human motifs rendered in such a way as to indicate internal as well as external organs. These organs are symmetrically arranged within bounded geometrical forms (Fig. 11.4). Maori sculpture, on the other hand, requires that wooden surfaces be broken into bold but intricate filigrees and whorls (Fig. 11.5). Among the Mochica of ancient Peru, the sculptural medium was pottery, and the Mochica pots are famous for their representational realism in portraiture and in depictions of domestic and sexual behavior (Fig. 11.6). Hundreds of other easily recognizable and distinctive art styles of different cultures can

11.5 MAORI CANOE PROW
The Maori of New Zealand are among the world's greatest wood carvers. [American Museum of Natural History]

11.6 MOCHICA POT
**A Precolumbian portrait made by the
Mochica of Northern Peru. [American
Museum of Natural History]**

be identified. The continuity and integrity
of these styles provide the basic context for a
people's understanding and liking of art.

Establishment art in modern Western culture is unique in its emphasis upon formal originality. It is taken as normal that art must be interpreted and explained by experts in order to be understood and appreciated. Since the end of the nineteenth century, the greatest artists for the Western art establishment are those who break with tradition, introduce new formal rules, and at least for a time render their work incomprehensible to a large number of people. Joined to this de-emphasis of tradition is the peculiar recent Western notion of artists as lonely people struggling in poverty against limitations set by the preexisting capability of their audience to appreciate and understand true genius.

Thus the creative, playful, and transformational aspects of modern art have gotten the upper hand over the formal and representational aspects (Fig. 11.7). Contemporary Euramerican artists consciously strive to be the originators of entirely new formal rules. They compete to invent new transformations to replace the traditional ones. Modern esthetic standards hold that originality is more important than intelligibility. Indeed, a work of art that is too easily understood may be condemned. Many art critics more or less consciously take it for granted that novelty must result in a certain amount of obscurity. What accounts for this obsession with being original?

One important influence is the reaction to mass production. Mass production leads to a downgrading of technical virtuosity. It also leads to a downgrading of all artwork that closely resembles the objects or performances others have produced. Another factor to be considered is the involvement of the modern artist in a commercial market in which supply perennially exceeds demand. Part-time band- and village-level artists are concerned with being original only to the extent that it enhances the esthetic enjoyment of their

11.7 WHAT DOES IT MEAN?
**Fur-covered cup, saucer, and spoon by
Méret Oppenheim. (Cup, 4⅜" diameter;
saucer 9¾" diameter; spoon 8" long.)
[Museum of Modern Art]**

work. Their livelihood does not depend on obtaining an artistic identity and a personal following. Still another factor to be considered is the high rate of cultural change in modern societies. To some extent, the emphasis upon artistic originality merely reflects this rate of change. Finally, the alienating and isolating tendencies of modern mass society may also play a role. Much modern art reflects the loneliness, puzzlement, and anxiety of the creative individual in a depersonalized and hostile urban, industrial milieu.

Art and religion

The history and ethnography of art are inseparable from the history and ethnography of religion. Art as an aspect of supernatural belief and ritual goes back at least 40,000 years. On the walls and ceilings of deep caves in Spain and France, in hidden galleries far from the light of day, Upper Paleolithic peoples painted and engraved pictures of the animals they hunted. To a lesser extent, similar paintings are found in caves as far across Europe as Russia. An occasional human figure—sometimes wearing a mask—outlines of hands, pictographs, and geometric symbols also occur, but the vast majority of the paintings and engravings depict horses, bison, mam-

moths, reindeer, ibex, wild boar, wild cattle, woolly rhinoceros, and other big-game animals. In spite of the magnificent economy of line and color, so much admired today, Upper Paleolithic cave art must be considered at least as much an expression of cultural established ritual as of individual or cultural esthetic impulses. The animals were often painted one on top of another even though unused surfaces were available, indicating that they were done both as ritual and as art (Fig. 11.8). It is generally assumed that the paintings were some form of hunting magic, but their precise function cannot be reconstructed reliably. All that can safely be asserted is that the hunters were impressed by the power and beauty of the animals whose death made their own lives possible (Leroi-Gourhan, 1968, 1982; Ucko and Rosenfield, 1967). Art is intimately associated with all four organizational levels of religion. For example, at the individualistic level, magical songs are often included among the revelations granted the vision seekers of the Great Plains. Even the preparation of trophy heads among the Jívaro must meet esthetic standards, and singing and chanting are widely used during shamanistic performances. There are many esthetic components in the Tapirapé shaman's description (p. 196) of how he met the *munpi anka* forest spirits.

On the communal level, puberty rituals as

11.8 PALEOLITHIC MASTERPIECES

It is as if Picasso were to paint on a canvas already used by Rembrandt. Cabrerets, France (below left) and Altamira, Spain (below right). In the photo on the right, the bison is shown with the other animals deleted [French Government Tourist Office—below left, American Museum of Natural History—below right]

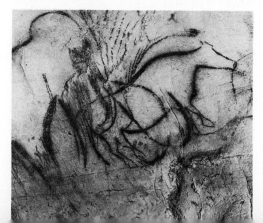

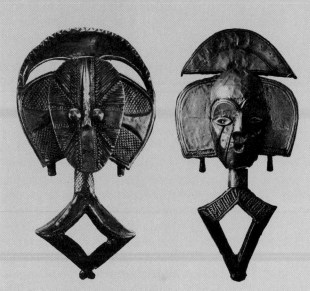

among the Ndembu (p. 203) provide occasions for dancing and myth and storytelling. Body painting is also widely practiced in communal ceremonies, as among the Arunta. Singing, dancing, and the wearing of masks are common at both puberty and funeral rituals. Much artistic effort is expended in the preparation of religiously significant funeral equipment such as coffins and graveposts (Figs. 11.9 and 11.10). Many cultures include ceremonial artifacts like pottery and clubs, points, and other weapons among a deceased person's grave goods. Ancestors and gods are often depicted in statues and masks that are kept in men's houses or in shrines (Fig. 11.11). *Churingas* (p. 199), the Arunta's most sacred objects, are artfully incised with whorls and loops depicting the route followed by the ancestors during the dream time.

Finally, on the ecclesiastical level, art and religion are fused in pyramid, monumental avenues, stone statuary, monolithic calendar carvings, temples, altars, priestly garments, and a nearly infinite variety of ritual ornaments and sacred paraphernalia.

It is clear that art, religion, and magic satisfy many similar psychological needs in human beings. They are media for expressing sentiments and emotions not easily expressed in ordinary life. They impart a sense of mastery over or communion with unpredictable events and mysterious unseen powers. They impose human meanings and values upon an indifferent world—a world that has no humanly intelligible meanings and values of its own. They seek to penetrate behind the façade of ordinary appearance into the true, cosmic significance of things. And they use illusions, dramatic tricks, and sleight of hand to get people to believe in them.

Art and politics

Art is also imtimately related to politics. This is especially clear in the context of state-sponsored art. As we have seen, in stratified societies religion is a means of social control. The skills of the artist are harnessed by the ruling class to implant religious notions of obedience and to sanctify the status quo (Fig. 11.12). Contrary to the popular modern image of the artist as a free spirit disdainful of authority, most state-level art is politically con-

11.10 ASMAT GRAVEPOST
**Around the world much talent has been lavished on commemorating the dead.
But styles and media vary enormously.** [Eugene Gordon]

servative. Ecclesiastical art interprets the
world in conformity with prevailing myths
and ideologies justifying inequities and exploitation. Art makes the gods visible as idols.
Gazing upon massive stone blocks carved as if
by superhuman hands, commoners comprehend the necessity for subservience. They are
awed by the immense size of pyramids and
fascinated and befuddled by processions,
prayers, pomp, and the sacrifices of priests in

Brightly painted faces on a men's house in the Sepik River basin, New Guinea. [UPI]

Another example of the interrelationship of art, religion, and politics. [Metropolitan Museum of Art]

dramatic settings—golden altars, colonnaded temples, great vaulted roofs, huge ramps and stairways, windows through which only the light from heaven passes (Fig. 11.13).

The church and state have been the greatest patrons of the arts in all but the last few hundred years of history. With the rise of capitalism, ecclesiastical and civil institutions in the West became more decentralized, and wealthy individuals to a considerable extent replaced church and state as the patrons of the arts. Individualized sponsorship promoted greater flexibility and freedom of expression. Politically neutral, secular, and

even revolutionary and sacrilegious themes became common. The arts became established as individualistic, secular forms of expression and entertainment. To protect and preserve their new-found autonomy, the art establishment adopted the doctrine of "art for art's sake." But once they were free to express themselves as they saw fit, artists were no longer sure what they wanted to express. They devoted themselves more and more to idiosyncratic and obscure symbols organized into novel and unintelligible patterns, as noted earlier in this chapter. And the patrons of art, concerned less and less with communication, increasingly looked toward the acquisition and sponsorship of art as a prestigious commercial venture that yielded substantial profits, tax deductions, and a hedge against inflation. In contrast, art in the Communist

11.13 ART AND RELIGION
**Notre Dame Cathedral, Paris. No one ever had to ask
what it meant, but how it was built remains a mystery.
[French Government Tourist Office]**

countries has been returned to state sponsorship and is deliberately used as a means of convincing citizens that the postrevolutionary status quo is equitable and inevitable (Fig. 11.14). Thus it has come about that artists in both the East and West, and in the Third World, have found themselves embroiled in political controversy as well as in creative transformation-representations designed to satisfy our human craving for esthetic pleasure. For every artist in the world today who places art before politics, there is at least one other who places politics before art.

The evolution of music and dance

Some anthropologists hold that the influence of structural and infrastructural components upon art extends directly into the formal characteristics and esthetic standards of different cultural styles. According to Allan Lomax (1968; Lomax and Arensberg, 1977) and his associates, for example, certain broad characteristics of song, music, and dance are closely correlated with a culture's level of subsistence. Band and village peoples in gen-

11.14 SOVIET REALISM
**Gavrül Gorelov, "Honored Worker of Art,"
won a Stalin Prize for this painting of a steel
smelter brigade leader and his comrades.
This is art for politic's sake. [Sovfoto]**

eral tend to have a different complex of
music, song, and dance than chiefdoms and
states. Dividing cultures into those that are
low and those that are high on the scale of
subsistence technology leads to the following
correlations:

Musical intervals The less advanced subsistence systems employ musical scales in
   which notes are widely separated—that
   is, have intervals of one-third or more. Advanced subsistence systems employ scales
   that are marked by more and smaller intervals.

Repetition in song text The less advanced
   subsistence cultures employ more repetition in their songs—fewer words over and
   over again.

Complexity and type of orchestra Advanced
   subsistence is correlated with musical performances involving more performers and
   a greater variety of instruments. Less advanced subsistence systems use only one

or two instruments and small numbers of
them.

Dance styles The advanced subsistence systems are correlated with dance styles in
   which many body parts—fingers, wrists,
   arms, torso, legs, feet, toes—have distinctive movements to make or "parts to
   play." Also, the more advanced the sub-
   system, the more the dance style tends to
   emphasize complex curving motions, as
   opposed to simple up and down or side-to-
   side steps like hopping or shuffling.

Lomax sees these correlations between subsistence and art as resulting from direct and
indirect influences of subsistence. Large, complex orchestration, for example, reflects the
structural ability of a society to form large,
coordinated groups. Dance styles, on the
other hand, may simply express the characteristic movements employed in using such
implements of production as digging sticks
versus plows or complex machines. Some
dances can be looked upon as training for
work, warfare, or self-defense.

Lomax's correlations have been criticized
on technical grounds relating to sampling
and coding procedures (see Kaeppler, 1978).
Nonetheless, Lomax's attempt to measure
and compare music and dance styles, and to
relate them to social structure and subsistence, constitutes an important avenue of approach.

The complexity of primitive art:
Campa rhetoric

Westerners must guard against the notion
that art among band and village societies is
necessarily more simple or naive than art in
modern industrial societies. Although, as we
have just seen, many stylistic aspects of art
have undergone an evolution from simple to
more complex forms, other aspects may have
been as complex among Stone Age hunter-

gatherers as they are today. The case of Campa rhetoric illustrates this point.

Rhetoric is the art of persuasive public discourse and is closely related to the theatrical arts. As Gerald Weiss (1977b) has discovered, the preliterate Campa who live in eastern Peru near the headwaters of the Amazon River use most of the important rhetorical devices cultivated by the great philosophers and orators of ancient Greece and Rome. Their object in public discourse is not merely to inform, but to persuade and convince. "Campa narration is 'a separate time,' where a spellbinding relationship between narrator and audience is developed, with powerful rhetorical devices employed to create and enhance the quality of that relationship" (1977b, p. 173).

Here are a few examples of these devices, as translated by Weiss from the Campa language, which belongs to the native American family of languages known as Arawak.

Rhetorical questions The speaker makes the point that the Campa are deficient in their worship of their sky god, the sun, by asking a question which he will answer. *Do we supplicate him, he here, he who lives in the sky, the sun? We do not know how to supplicate him.*

Iterations (effect by repetition) The speaker imparts an emphatic, graphic, movielike quality to the point by repeating some key words. The enemy comes out of the lake: *And so they emerged in great numbers—he saw them emerge, emerge, emerge, emerge, emerge, emerge, emerge, emerge, emerge, all, all.*

Imagery and metaphor Death is alluded to in the phrase: *The earth will eat him.* The body is described as: *The clothing of the soul.*

Appeal to evidence To prove that the oilbird was formerly human in shape: *Yes, he was formerly human—doesn't he have whiskers?*

Appeal to authority They told me long ago, the elders, they who heard these words, long ago, so it was.

Antithesis (effect by contrast) A hummingbird is about to raise the sky rope, which the other larger creatures have failed to do: *They are all big whereas I am small and chubby.*

In addition, the Campa orator uses a wide variety of gestures, exclamations, sudden calls for attention ("watch out, here it comes"); asides ("imagine it, then"; "careful that you don't believe, now"). Altogether, Weiss lists nineteen formal rhetorical devices used by the Campa.

Myth and binary contrasts

Anthropologists have found considerable evidence suggesting that certain kinds of formal structures recur in widely different traditions of oral and written literature, including myths and folktales. These structures are characterized by binary contrasts—that is, by two elements or themes that can be viewed as standing in diametric opposition to each other. Many examples of recurrent binary contrasts can be found in Western religion, literature, and mythology: good versus bad; up versus down; male versus female; cultural versus natural; young versus old; and so forth. According to French anthropologist Lévi-Strauss, the founder of the research strategy known as structuralism (see p. 325), the reason these binary contrasts recur so often is that the human brain is "wired" in such a way as to make binary contrasts especially appealing or "good to think." From the structuralist point of view, the main task of the anthropological study of literature, mythology, and folklore is to identify the common, unconscious binary contrasts that lie beneath the surface of human thought and to show how these binary contrasts undergo unconscious transformation-representations.

Consider the familiar tale of Cinderella: A mother has two daughters and one stepdaughter. The two daughters are older; the stepdaughter is younger; the older ones are ugly and mean while Cinderella is beautiful and kind. The older sisters are aggressive; Cinderella is passive. Through a kind fairy godmother, as opposed to her mean stepmother, Cinderella goes to the ball, dances with the prince, and loses her magical shoe. Her sisters have big feet, she has little feet. Cinderella wins the prince. The unconscious binary oppositions in the deep structure of this story might include:

passive	aggressive
younger	older
small	large
good	evil
beautiful	ugly
culture	nature
(fairy godmother)	(stepmother)

Structuralists contend that the enjoyment people derive from such tales and their durability across space and time derive mainly from the unconscious oppositions and their familiar yet surprising representations.

11.15 TETUM HOUSE
Women's entrance around back on right.
Men's entrance through door, left of center. [**Maxine Hicks**]

Structuralist analyses can be extended from the realm of myth and ritual to the entire fabric of social life. According to David Hicks, who studied the Tetum of Timor in Indonesia, Tetum culture as a whole is structured by the following "binary matrix":

human beings	ghosts
secular	sacred
secular world	sacred world
above	below
men	women
right	left
superior	inferior
wife-givers	wife-takers
aristocrats	commoners
secular authority	sacred authority
elder brother	younger brother

Any single binary contrast can symbolize any other (Hicks, 1976, p. 107); that is, in contrasting men with women, one could just as readily be contrasting elder brothers with younger brothers (among the Tetum, younger brothers must serve elder brothers just as women must serve men). The secular, above-ground, masculine world contrasts with the ghostly, sacred, below-ground, feminine world. Thus Tetum mythology recounts how the first humans emerged from vaginalike holes in the ground and how after leading a secular life on the surface of the earth, humans return to the sacred world below and to the ghostly ancestors. Tetum house architecture also participates in the same set of symbolic oppositions (Fig. 11.15). The house has two entrances; the back entrance for the women leads to the "womb" or women's part of the house, which contains the hearth and a sacred house post. The front entrance is for the men and leads to the male living quarters.

Structural analyses of literature, art, myths, rituals, and religion abound in anthropology. However, they are surrounded by considerable controversy, primarily because it is not clear whether the binary matrices discerned by the anthropologists really exist as unconscious realities in the minds of the people being studied. It is always possible to reduce complex and subtle symbols to less complex and gross symbols and then finally to emerge with such flat oppositions as culture versus nature or male versus female (Harris, 1979b).

Summary

Creative play, formal structure, esthetic feelings, and symbolic transformations are the essential ingredients in art. Although the capacity for art is foreshadowed in the behavior of nonhuman primates, only *Homo sapiens* is capable of art involving "transformation-representations." The distinctive human capacity for art is thus closely related to the distinctive human capacity for the symbolic transformation that underlies the semantic universality of human language.

Western emic definitions of art depend on the existence of art authorities and critics who place many examples of play, structured esthetic, and symbolic transformation into the category of nonart. The distinction between crafts and art is part of this tradition. Anthropologists regard skilled craftspersons as artists.

Art has adaptive functions in relation to creative changes in the other sectors of social life. Art and technology influence each other, as in the case of instruments of music and the hunt, or in the search for new shapes, colors, textures, and materials in ceramics and textiles.

Despite the emphasis upon creative innovation, most cultures have art traditions or styles that maintain formal continuity through time. This makes it possible to identify the styles of cultures such as the Northwest Coast, Maori, or Mochica. The continuity and integrity of such styles provide the basic context for a people's understanding of and liking for the artist's creative transformations. Establishment art in modern Western culture is unique in emphasizing structural or formal creativity as well as creative transformations. This results in the isolation of the artist. Lack of communication may be caused by factors such as the reaction to mass production, commercial art markets, a rapid rate of cultural change, and the depersonalized milieu of urban industrial life.

Art and religion are closely related. This can be seen in the Upper Paleolithic cave paintings, songs of the vision quest, preparation of shrunken heads, singing and chanting in shamanistic performances, Tapirapé shamanistic myths, Ndembu circumcision, storytelling, singing and dancing, Arunta *churingas*, and many other aspects of individual, shamanistic, communal, and ecclesiastical cults. Art and religion satisfy many similar psychological needs, and it is often difficult to tell them apart.

Art and politics are also closely related. This is clear in state-sponsored ecclesiastical art, much of which functions to keep people in awe of their rulers. It is only in recent times, with the rise of decentralized capitalist states, that art has enjoyed any significant degree of freedom from direct political control. Even today, however, many artists in both capitalist and socialist societies regard art as an important medium of political expression, both conservative and revolutionary.

To the extent that bands, villages, chiefdoms, and states represent evolutionary levels, and to the extent that art is functionally related to technology, economy, politics, religion, and other aspects of the universal cultural pattern, it is clear that there has been an evolution of the content of art. There is evidence that styles of song, music, and dance—including musical intervals, repetition in song texts, complexity and type of orchestra, body part involvement, and amount of curvilinear motion—have also undergone evolutionary changes. This finding, however, remains highly controversial. The example of Campa rhetoric shows that extreme caution must be exercised in judging the complexity and sophistication of preliterate art styles.

A currently popular mode of anthropological analysis—structuralism—attempts to interpret the surface content of myths, rituals, and other expressive performances in terms of a series of unconscious universal binary oppositions. Common binary oppositions can be found in the Cinderella myth and in Tetum cosmology, ritual, and house architecture.

12

Personality and Sex

In this chapter we examine the ways in which culture influences personality. We examine the central concepts of Freudian theories of personality, and then go on to more recent theories that attempt to account for the variations and changes in male and female personality types.

Culture and personality

Culture refers to the patterned ways in which the members of a population think, feel, and behave. Personality also refers to patterned ways of thinking, feeling, and behaving, but the focus is on the individual. *Personality*, as defined by Victor Barnouw (1973, p. 10), "is a more or less enduring organization of forces within the individual associated with a complex of fairly consistent attitudes, values, and modes of perception which account, in part, for the individual's consistency of behavior." More simply, "personality is the tendency to behave in certain ways regardless of the specific setting" (Whiting and Whiting, 1978, p. 57).

The concepts employed in describing the thinking, feeling, and behavior of personality types are different from those employed in describing infrastructure, structure, and superstructure. In describing personalities, psychologists use concepts such as aggressive, passive, anxious, obsessive, hysterical, manic, depressed, introverted, extroverted, paranoid, authoritarian, schizoid, masculine, feminine, infantile, repressed, dependent, and so forth. Here is a part of a more extensive list of terms appropriate for the study of personality that appeared in a study of culture and personality in a Mexican village (Fromm and Maccoby, 1970, p. 79).

practical	anxious
economical	orderly
steadfast, tenacious	methodical
composed under stress	loyal
careful	unimaginative
reserved	stingy
patient	stubborn
cautious	indolent
imperturbable	inert
suspicious	pedantic
cold	obsessive
lethargic	possessive

If these concepts are employed to describe an entire population, the result will not add up to a description of modes of production and reproduction, domestic and political economy, systems of war and peace, or magico-religious rites and institutions.

Childhood training and personality

Anthropologists interested in culture and personality have generally accepted Sigmund Freud's fundamental proposal that childhood experiences are the primary source of differences in adult personality. But anthropologists take account of the enormous diversity of culturally patterned relationships between infants and adults. These relationships are known as *childhood training practices*. The feeding, cleaning, and handling of infants are culturally patterned activities that vary widely from one society to another. In many cultures, for example, infants are constrained by swaddling bandages or cradle boards that immobilize their limbs. Elsewhere, freedom of movement is encouraged. Similarly, nursing may be on demand at the first cry of hunger or at regular intervals at the convenience of the mother. Nursing at the mother's breast may last for a few months or several years, or not take place at all. Supplementary foods may be taken in the first few weeks; they may be stuffed into the baby's mouth, prechewed by the mother, or played with by the baby; or they may be omitted entirely.

Weaning may take place abruptly, as where the mother's nipples are painted with bitter substances; and it may or may not be associated with the birth of another child. In some cultures infants are kept next to their mother's skin and carried wherever the mother goes (Fig. 12.1); elsewhere, they may be left behind in the care of relatives. In some cultures infants are fondled, hugged, kissed, and fussed over by large groups of adoring chil-

dren and adults. In others they are kept relatively isolated and touched infrequently.

Toilet training may begin as early as 6 weeks or as late as 24 months. The mode of training may involve many different techniques, some based on intense forms of punishment, shame, and ridicule, and others involving suggestion, emulation, and no punishment.

Treatment of infant sexuality also varies widely. In many cultures mothers or fathers stroke their babies' genitals to soothe them and stop them from crying; elsewhere, even the baby is prevented from touching its own genitals and masturbation is severely punished.

Another series of variables relevant to personality formation consists of later childhood and adolescent experiences: numbers of siblings; their relationships and mutual responsibilities (Fig. 12.2); patterns of play; opportunities to observe adult intercourse; opportunities to engage in homosexual or heterosexual experimentation; incest restrictions; and type of threat and punishment used against culturally prohibited sexual practices (Weisner and Gallimore, 1977).

Figure 12.3 depicts one theory of how these childhood training practices may be related to personality and to other aspects of culture. The basic variables influencing childrearing patterns are influenced by the nature of the culture's domestic, social, political, and economic institutions. These in turn are influenced by the ecosystem. Childrearing practices are also constrained by the necessity of satisfying certain biologically determined

12.1 CARE OF CHILDREN
Cultures vary greatly in the amount of body contact between mother and infants. Top, Swazi mother and child. Bottom, Arunta mother and child. All-purpose carrying dish on head and digging stick in hand. [American Museum of Natural History

universal needs, drives, and capacities that all human infants share (e.g., oral, anal, and genital urges). The interaction between the childrearing practices and these biological needs, drives, and capacities molds personality; personality, in turn, expresses itself in *secondary* institutions; that is, roughly what we have been calling "superstructure" in this book.

Patterns and themes

Many other proposals have been made concerning how to treat the relationship between personality and culture. One popular option acknowledges the fact that culture and personality are two different ways of looking at the propensity to think, feel, and behave characteristic of a given population and uses psychological terms to characterize both personality and the cultural system. For example, Ruth Benedict in her famous book *Patterns of Culture* (1934) characterized the institution of the Kwakiutl potlatch (see Ch. 4) as a "megalomaniacal" performance—behavior dominated by fantasies of wealth and power. She saw potlatch as part of a *Dionysian* pattern that was characteristic of all the institutions of Kwakiutl culture. By Dionysian she meant the desire to achieve emotional excess, as in drunkenness or frenzy. Other cultures, such as that of the Pueblo Indians, she saw as *Appollonian*—given to moderation and the "middle of the road" in all things. Benedict's *patterns* were psychological elements reputedly found throughout a culture, "comparable to the chromosomes found in most of the cells of a body" (Wallace, 1970, p. 149). Most anthropologists have rejected such attempts to use one or two psychological terms to describe the different personalities and functionally distinct institutions that can be found in even the simplest cultures.

Some anthropologists attempt to identify dominant *themes* or *values* that express the es-

12.2 JAVANESE GIRL AND BROTHER
One way to free mother for work in the fields is to turn over the care of infants to 6-year-old sister. [United Nations]

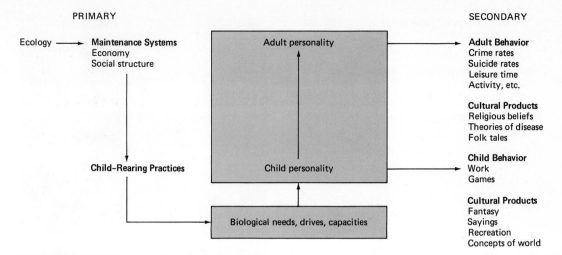

Ecology ⟶ **Maintenance Systems**
Economy
Social structure

Adult personality

Adult Behavior
Crime rates
Suicide rates
Leisure time
Activity, etc.

Cultural Products
Religious beliefs
Theories of disease
Folk tales

Child-Rearing Practices

Child personality

Child Behavior
Work
Games

Biological needs, drives, capacities

Cultural Products
Fantasy
Sayings
Recreation
Concepts of world

*12.3 THE RELATIONSHIP OF BASIC PERSONALITY
TO ECOLOGY, CHILD-REARING PRACTICES, AND
SECONDARY AND PROJECTIVE INSTITUTIONS*
[After LeVine 1973, p. 57]

sential or main thought and feeling of a particular culture. The "image of limited good" is one such theme (p. 166). Themes and values are readily translatable into personality traits. For example, the image of limited good reputedly produces personalities that are jealous, suspicious, secretive, and fearful. The culture of poverty also has its psychological components—improvidence, lack of future-time orientation, sexual promiscuity. An important theme in Hindu India is the "sacredness of life," and an important theme in the United States is "keeping up with the Joneses." The problem with attempts to portray cultures in terms of a few dominant values and attitudes is that contradictory values and attitudes can usually be identified in the same cultures and even in the same individuals. Thus, although Hindu farmers believe in the sacredness of life (Opler, 1968), they also believe in the necessity of having more bullocks than cows (see p. 218); and although many people in the United States believe in trying to keep up with the Joneses,

there are others who believe that conspicuous consumption is foolish and sinful.

Basic personality and national character

A somewhat different approach to culture and personality postulates that every culture produces a basic or deep personality structure that can be found in virtually every individual member of the culture. When the populations involved are organized into a state, the basic personality is often called *national character*. The notion of basic personality structure has always enjoyed considerable popularity among travelers to foreign lands as well as among scholars. One often hears it said that the English are "reserved," the Brazilians "carefree," the French "sexy," the Italians "uninhibited," the Japanese "orderly," the Americans "outgoing," and so forth. Gerardus Mercator, the Belgian father of mapmaking, wrote the following descriptions

of European basic personalities in the sixteenth century:

Franks Simple, blockish, furious

Bavarians Sumptuous, gluttons, brazen-
faced

Swedes Light, babblers, boasters

Saxons Dissemblers, double-hearted, opin-
ionative

Spaniards Disdainful, cautious, greedy

Belgians Good horsemen, tender, docile,
delicate

Modern scholarly versions of basic personality structure make use of more sophisticated
psychological concepts, most of which owe
something to the influence of Sigmund Freud
and psychoanalysis.

The concept of basic personality type must
not be permitted to obscure the fact that there
is a great range of personalities in every society and that the more populous, complex,
and stratified the society, the greater the variability. In every society many individuals
have personalities that deviate widely from
the *statistical mode* (most frequent type), and
the range of individual personalities produces
wide overlaps among different cultures. For
example, it would certainly be correct to
characterize the basic type of Plains native
American male personality as an aggressive,
independent, and fearless person. Yet it is
known from the institution called *berdache*
(Fig. 12.4) that there were always some young
men whose vision quests were doomed to failure and who found themselves temperamen-
tally unsuited to the warrior's calling. Don-
ning female dress and dedicating themselves
to female domestic and sexual specialties,
these men found acceptance among their
people.

Very little is actually known about the
amount of personality variance in different
societies. It is certain, however, that complex,
state-level populations consisting of millions
of people contain an enormous variety of
types (Fig. 12.5). Moreover, the more complex
the criteria used to define the basic personal-

12.4 BERDACHE
**Finds-Them-And-Kills-Them, last of the
Crow male homosexual transvestites.
[Museum of the American Indian, Heye
Foundation]**

12.5 PERSONALITY IN COMPLEX SOCIETIES
As this demonstration against the opening of the new Tokyo International Airport indicates, all Japanese can scarcely be described as having deferential and conformist personalities. [UPI]

ity, the more likely that the modal type of personality will be found in relatively few individuals. Anthony Wallace (1952), using twenty-one dimensions to define basic personality among the Iroquois, found that the modal type was shared by only 37 percent of the total sample.

Oedipus and personality

Within any given society, the most obvious and pervasive example of personality differences is the difference between men and women. In recent years, an intense debate has developed concerning the extent to which certain recurrent personality traits associated, respectively, with males and females express human nature or the effects of cultural conditioning.

Followers of Sigmund Freud have long held that the anatomical characteristics and reproductive roles of males and females predestine men and women to have fundamentally different personalities: men to be more "masculine"—that is, more active, aggressive, and violent; women to be more "feminine"—that is, more passive, meek, and peaceful. Freud saw the difference between masculinity and femininity as arising out of the different ways in which boys and girls related to their mothers and fathers from infancy to adolescence. According to Freud, a traumatic, universal, and unavoidable conflict takes place during the years preceding puberty. This is called the *Oedipus conflict*, and it is caused by biologically determined sexual strivings and jealousies within the nuclear family. The early sexual feelings of a young boy are directed first toward his mother. But he soon discovers that mother is the sexual object of his father, and he finds himself in competition with his father for sexual mastery of the same woman. The father, while providing protection, also provides stern discipline. He suppresses his son's attempt to express sexual love for his mother. The son is frustrated and fantasizes that he is strong enough to kill his father. This seething hostility and jealousy arouse fear and guilt in the young boy: fear, because the father in fact or in fancy threatens to cut off his penis and testicles; and guilt, because the father is not only hated but also loved. To resolve this conflict successfully, the young boy must redirect his sexuality toward females other than his mother and learn how to overcome his fear and how to express his hostility in constructive ways.

For the young girl, Freud envisioned a parallel but fundamentally different trauma. A girl's sexuality is also initially directed toward her mother, but at the phallic stage the little girl makes a fateful discovery: She lacks a penis. She blames her mother for this and redirects her sexual desires away from her mother and toward her father.

Why this takes place depends upon the girl's reaction of disappointment when she discovers that a boy possesses a protruding sex organ, the penis, while she has only a cavity. Several important consequences follow from this traumatic discovery. In the first place she holds her mother responsible for her castrated condition. . . . In the second place, she transfers her love to her father because he has the valued organ which she aspires to share with him. However, her love for the father and for other men as well is mixed with a feeling of envy because they possess something she lacks. Penis envy is the female counterpart of castration anxiety in the boy. (Hall and Lindzey, 1967, p. 18)

Girls are supposed to suffer the lifelong trauma of penis envy as a result of their discovery that they are anatomically "incomplete." In this fashion, Freud sought to ground the psychological supremacy of males in the unalterable facts of anatomy—hence the Freudian aphorism: "Anatomy is destiny." Freud thought that not having a penis "debases" women and dooms them to a passive and subordinate role—the role of the "second sex." Freud believed the best hope a woman has of overcoming her penis envy is to accept a passive, secondary role in life, develop her charm and sexual attractiveness, marry, and have male babies.

Her happiness is great if later on this wish for a baby finds fulfillment in reality, and quite especially so if the baby is a little boy who brings the longed-for penis with him. (Freud, in Millet, 1970, p. 185)

Alternative male and female personalities

Starting with Bronislaw Malinowski's (1927) research on the avunculocal Trobriand family (see Ch. 6), anthropologists have criticized the concept of the Oedipus complex on the grounds that it imposes on the rest of the world a definition of masculinity and femininity appropriate to nineteenth-century middle-class Vienna, where Freud practiced and developed his theories (Fig. 12.6).

Ethnographic research indicates that Freud's Viennese definition of ideal male and female temperaments is scarcely universal. Margaret Mead's (1950) study of three New Guinea tribes—the Arapesh, Mundugumor, and Tchambuli—is the classic anthropological work on the spectrum of cultural definitions of ideal masculine and feminine personalities. Mead discovered that among the Arapesh both men and women are expected to behave in a mild, sympathetic, and cooperative manner, reminiscent of what we expect from an ideal mother. Among the Mundugumor, men and women are expected to be equally fierce and aggressive, and both sexes satisfied Mead's criteria for being masculine. Among the Tchambuli, the women shave their heads, are prone to hearty laughter, show comradely solidarity, and are aggressively efficient as food providers. Tchambuli men, on the other hand, are preoccupied with art, spend a great deal of time on their hairdos, and are always gossiping about the opposite sex. Although Mead's interpretations have been challenged as too subjective, there is no doubt that marked contrasts in sex roles do exist in different cultures. In few parts of the world outside nineteenth-century Vienna can one find the precise configuration that Freud believed to be a universal ideal. For example, Mervyn Meggitt (1964) has proposed a classification of New Guinea highland cultures into two groups on the basis of the ex-

12.6 FREUD'S MILIEU
A turn-of-century middle-class father with his two sons. Stern but protective. [**The Bettmann Archive**]

tent to which they act like "prudes" or "lechers."

Among the Mae Enga, who are Meggitt's archetypical "prudes," men and women sleep apart. A man never enters the sleeping room at the rear of his wife's hut, and a woman never enters the men's house. Contact with menstrual blood can cause sickness and death for a Mae Enga man. Mae Enga men believe that intercourse is debilitating, and after intercourse they undergo purification by sitting in a smoky hut to protect themselves. Mae Enga bachelors swear sexual abstinence until they are married and feel uneasy and anxious if sex is discussed, especially if women are present. In contrast, the Kuma men, who are Meggitt's "lechers," share sleeping quarters, have no fear of female pollution, do not practice purification or initiation rites, and gain prestige through boasting of their conquests. Kuma girls attend courting parties at which they select sexual partners from among married and unmarried males. Intercourse is discussed openly by both sexes. Lorraine Sexton (1973) has suggested that these differences may be associated with the high population pressure being experienced by the Mae Enga and the relatively low population density of the Kuma, extreme prudery being a mechanism that cuts back on the frequency of intercourse and thus limits fertility.

A male supremacist complex?

Despite these deviations from the narrow definitions of masculine and feminine in Western society, there remains considerable evidence that males tend in the overwhelming majority of societies to be more aggressive and violent than females. Moreover, although the Oedipus complex as Freud envisioned it is not universal, sexually charged hostility between older-generation males and their sons or nephews does occur very widely (see Barnouw, 1973; Foster, 1972; A. Parsons, 1967; Roheim, 1950).

A great variety of evidence suggests that the relatively more aggressive masculine male personality is associated with a pervasive complex that accords males a more dominant role than females in many spheres of social life. The clearest manifestation of this complex is to be found in the sphere of political economy. From our previous discussion (Ch. 8) of the evolution of political organization, it is clear that males have always preempted the major centers of public power and control. Headmen rather than headwomen dominate both egalitarian and stratified forms of redistribution. The Semai and Mehinacu headmen; the Solomon Island *mumis,* and the New Guinea big men; the Nuer leopard skin chief; the Kwakiutl, Trobriand, and Tikopian chiefs; the Bunyoro Mukama; the Inca, the pharaohs, and the emperors of China and Japan all show the same male preeminence. If queens reign in Europe or Africa, it is always as temporary holders of power that belongs to the males of the lineage. Nothing more dramatically exposes the political subordination of women than the fact that among the members of the United Nations, only two effective heads of state—Margaret Thatcher and Indira Gandhi—are presently (1982) women.

It was formerly believed that political control by women or *matriarchy*—the opposite of patriarchy or political control by men—occurred as a regular stage in the evolution of social organization. Today virtually all anthropologists concur in rejecting the existence of any authentically matriarchal society. One exception is Ruby Rohrlich-Leavitt (1977, p. 57), who contends that in Minoan Crete "women participated at least equally with men in political decision making, while in religion and social life they were supreme." Rohrlich-Leavitt's contention, however, is based on inferences from archeological data that can be given contradictory interpretations. There is no doubt that Minoan Crete was matrilineal and that women enjoyed a relatively high status. However, the basis of Crete's economy was maritime trade and it was men, not women, who dominated this activity. Rohrlich-Leavitt contends that the Cretan matriarchy was made possible by the absence of warfare and a male military complex. However, it seems likely that military activities were focused on naval encounters that have left little archeologically retrievable evidence. There is no reason, therefore, not to accept the following generalization of Michelle Rosaldo and Louise Lamphere:

Whereas some anthropologists argue that there are, or have been truly egalitarian societies . . . and all agree that there are societies in which women have achieved considerable recognition and power, none has observed a society in which women have publicly recognized power and authority surpassing that of men. (1974, p. 3)

The idea that matriarchies once existed often arises from a confusion between matrilineality and matriarchy. Matrilineality does not mean that women reverse the male domination of politics and become dominant, as implied in the concept of matriarchy. At most, matrilineality brings about a greater degree of political equality between the sexes; it does not lead to female dominance. This can be seen in the case of the matrilineal Iroquois. Among the Iroquois, senior women had the power to raise and depose the male elders who were elected to the highest ruling body, called the council. Through a male representative on the council they could influence its decisions and exercise power over the conduct of war and the establishment of treaties. Eligibility for office passed through the female line, and it was the duty of women to nominate the men who served on the council. But women themselves could not serve on the council, and the incumbent males had a veto over the women's nomination. Judith Brown (1975, pp. 240–241) concludes that the Iroquois nation "was not a matriarchy as claimed by some."

Pollution and sexual politics

Males in many cultures believe they are spiritually superior to females and that females are dangerous and polluting, weak and untrustworthy. Some anthropologists have argued that women frequently share the same or similar views about men. The extent to which women share the defamatory stereotypes men try to lay on them is unknown (see Kaberry, 1970; Leacock, 1975; Minge-Kalman, 1974; Sacks, 1971). One must dismiss the notion that any subjugated group really accepts the reason the subjugators give for keeping them down (see pp. 181ff). But if men do, in fact, enjoy an etic power advantage over women with respect to access to strategic resources, then these stereotypes, whether or not shared by women, will in all likelihood be associated with etic behavioral deprivations and disadvantages.

This point has been stressed by Shirley Lindenbaum with respect to two strongly male-biased societies in which she has done fieldwork. In Bangladesh, Lindenbaum notes the existence of a pervasive symbolism of female pollution.

Men are associated with the right, preferred side of things, women with the left. Village practitioners state that a basic physiological difference between the sexes makes it necessary to register a man's pulse in his right wrist, a woman's in her left, and they invariably examine patients in this way. Most villagers wear amulets to avert illness caused by evil spirits; men tie the amulet to the right upper arm, women to the left. Similarly, palmists and spiritualists read the right hands of men and the left hands of women. In village dramas, where both male and female parts are played by male actors, the audience may identify men gesturing with the right arm, women with the left. During religious celebrations there are separate entrances at such public places as the tombs of Muslim saints or Hindu images, the right avenue being reserved for men and the left for women. In popular belief, girls are said to commence walking by placing the left foot forward first, men the right.

In some instances, this right-left association indicates more than the social recognition of physiological difference, carrying additional connotations of prestige, honour and authority. Women who wish to behave respectfully to their husbands say they should, ideally, remain to the left side while eating, sitting and lying in bed. The same mark of respect should be shown also to all social superiors: to the rich, and in present times to those who are well educated.

Thus, the right-left dichotomy denotes not only male-female but also authority-submission. It also has connotations of good-bad and purity-pollution. Muslims consider the right side to be the side of good augury, believing that angels dwell on the right shoulder to record good deeds in preparation for the Day of Judgment, while on the left side, devils record misdeeds. The left side is also associated with the concept of pollution. Islam decrees that the left hand be reserved for cleansing the anus after defecation. It must never, therefore, be used for conveying food to the mouth, or for rinsing the mouth with water before the proscribed daily prayers. (1977, p. 142)

Lindenbaum found similar notions of female pollution and inferiority among the Foré of highland New Guinea. Here a woman is confined to special seclusion huts during pregnancy and childbirth:

Her seclusion there is a sign of the half-wild condition brought on by the natural functions of her own body. Other women bring the food, for if she visited her gardens during this period of isolation she would blight all domesticated crops. Nor should she send food to her husband: ingesting food she had touched would make him feel weak, catch a cold, age prematurely. (Lindenbaum, 1979, p. 129)

If a Foré woman gives birth to a deformed or stillborn child, the women is held solely responsible. Her husband and the men of the hamlet denounce her, accuse her of trying to obstruct male authority, and kill one of her pigs. Among the Foré as among many other New Guinea cultures, men appropriate the best sources of animal protein for themselves. The men argue that women's sources of protein—frogs, small game, and insects—would make them sick. These prejudices can have lethal effects. Throughout New Guinea they are associated with much higher death rates for young girls than for young boys (Buchbinder, n.d.). The same lethal results are evident in Bangladesh:

The male child receives preferential nutrition. With his father he eats first, and if there is a choice, luxury foods or scarce foods are given to him rather than to his female siblings. The result is a Bengalese population with a preponderance of males, and a demographic picture in which the mortality rate for females under 5 years of age is in some years 50% higher than that for males. (Lindenbaum, 1977, p. 143)

Religion and sexual politics

Women are often excluded from tapping the principal sources of religious power. Even where individualistic rituals prevail, women tend to have less access to the supernatural than men. Women rarely participate in the vision quests that give males the confidence to be aggressive and to kill with impunity. Women are seldom permitted to take the hallucinogenic substances that give males direct knowledge of the reality that lies behind worldly appearances.

As the men ritually ingest the various hallucinogens that let them journey into the hidden world, women remain bystanders, baffled and terrorized by the personality transformations and strange antics of their brothers and husbands. Among the Yanomamo, for example, the men take a substance called *ebene* which, in addition to putting them in contact with the *hekura*, or invisible mountain demons, causes green mucus to flow out of their nostrils. They run about the village on all fours, snarl and grimace like wild animals, and brandish their clubs and spears at women and children who cross their path. The men administer the *ebene* by blowing it up each other's nostrils through 3-foot-long hollow tubes:

As the drug would be administered, each recipient would reel from the concussion of air, groan, and stagger off to some convenient post to vomit. Within ten minutes of taking the drug, the men would be bleary-eyed and wild, prancing around in front of their houses, stopping occasionally to vomit or to catch their breath. In each group there would be one man particularly adept at chanting to the hekura . . . while the others retired to the sidelines in a stupor, green slime dripping from their nostrils. (Chagnon, 1977, p. 109)

To the extent that shamanistic cults are dominated by persons who have access to and who know how to prepare and use hallucinogens, male control over these substances imposes a severe handicap upon women. Even where hallucinogens do not play an important role in the shamanistic complex, however, males usually maintain control over the knowledge necessary for achieving visions and trances and for carrying out acts of sleight of hand (Fig. 12.7).

Communal cults in general are also pervaded by male supremacist beliefs and rituals. One of the most widespread of all communal complexes has as its explicit aim the retention of a male monopoly on the myths and rituals of human origins and the nature of supernatural beings. This complex involves secret male initiation rites; male residence in a separate men's house (Fig. 12.8) from which women and children are excluded; masked

male dancers who impersonate the gods and other spiritual beings; the bullroarer, which is said to be the voice of the gods and which is whirled about in the bush or under cover of darkness to frighten the women and uninitiated boys (see p. 203); storage of the masks, bullroarer, and other sacred paraphernalia in the men's house; threat of death or actual execution of any woman who admits to knowing the secrets of the cult; and threat of death or execution of any man who reveals the secrets to women or uninitiated boys.

12.7 FEMALE SHAMAN
Piegan "medicine woman." Not all Shamans are men. [Museum of the American Indian, Heye Foundation]

12.8 INTERIOR OF MEN'S HOUSE, NEW GUINEA
The men use the masks to terrify the women and children. [American Museum of Natural History]

Religion and sexual politics   **251**

Finally, ecclesiastical types of religions are also characterized by a pervasive functional interconnection between male-dominated rituals and myths on the one hand, and male supremacy on the other. The established high priests of Rome, Greece, Mesopotamia, Egypt, ancient Israel, and the entire Muslim and Hindu world were men. Highranking priestesses with autonomous control over their own temples, as in Minoan Crete, are the exception, even when the ecclesiastical cults include female deities. Today males continue to dominate the ecclesiastical organization of all the major world religions. All three major religions of Western civilization—Christianity, Judaism, and Islam—stress the priority of the male principle in the formation of the world. They identify the creator god as "He," and to the extent that they recognize female deities, as in Catholicism, assign them a secondary role in myth and ritual. They all hold that men were created first, and women second, out of a piece of a man.

Sex Roles and Ethnography

In reviewing the evidence of male supremacy, it is important to guard against using advanced state-level stratified forms of political hierarchy as the model for all sexual politics. Moreover, we cannot go from the proposition that "women are subordinate as regards political authority in most societies" to "women are subordinate in all respects in all societies." As Eleanor Leacock (1978, p. 247) points out, the very notion of "equality" and "inequality" may represent an ethnocentric misunderstanding of the kind of sex roles that exist in many societies. Leacock (1978, p. 225) does not dispute the fact that when "unequal control over resources and subjugation by class and by sex developed," it was women who in general became subjugated to men (recognizing, of course, that the degree of subjugation varied depending on local ecological,

economic, and political conditions). But in the absence of classes and the state, Leacock argues that sex roles were merely different, not unequal. There is certainly much evidence to indicate that power of any sort, whether of men over men or men over women, was trivial or nonexistent in many (but not all) band and village societies, for reasons discussed in Chapter 4. And there is much new evidence, supplied principally by women ethnographers (Sacks, 1971; Sanday, 1981), that the etic power of women has been substantially underestimated or misconstrued by male anthropologists who until recently were the main sources of cross cultural data on sex roles.

Trobriands revisited

Even one of the greatest ethnographers, Bronislaw Malinowski, could fall short of providing a balanced view of sex roles in his classic study of the Trobriand Islanders. As we saw in Chapter 8, at harvest time in the Trobriands brothers give their sisters' husbands gifts of yams. These yams provide much of the material basis for the political power of the Trobriand chiefs. Malinowski viewed the harvest gift as a kind of annual tribute from the wife's family to her husband, and therefore as a means of enhancing and consolidating male power. Annette Weiner has shown, however, that the harvest yams are given in the name of the wife and are actually as much a means of bolstering up the value of being a woman as a means of conferring power on men. Malinowski overlooked the fact that the gift of yams had to be reciprocated, and that the countergift had to go not to a man's brother-in-law but to a man's wife. In return for the yams received in his wife's name, the Trobriand husband had to provide her with a distinct form of wealth consisting of women's skirts and bundles of pandanus and banana leaves used for making skirts. Much of a husband's economic activity is devoted to trading pigs and other valuables in order to supply his wife with large quantities of woman's wealth. The skirts and bundles of leaves are publicly displayed and given away at huge funeral ceremonies known as *sagali* (which Malinowski knew about but did not see fit to describe in detail). Weiner (1977, p. 118) states that the *sagali* is one of the most important public events in Trobriand life. "Nothing is so dramatic as women standing at a *sagali* surrounded by thousands of bundles. Nor can anything be more impressive than watching the deportment of women as they attend to the distribution. When women walk to the center (of the plaza) to throw down their wealth, they carry themselves with a pride as characteristic as that of any Melanesian big-man."

Failure of a husband to equip his wife with sufficient women's wealth to make a good showing at the *sagali* adversely affects his own prospects for becoming a big-man. His brothers-in-law may reduce or eliminate their yam harvest gift if their sister cannot display and give away large quantities of bundles and skirts to relatives of the deceased. In Weiner's account not only are men more dependent on women for their power than in Malinowski's account, but also women themselves emerge as having far more influence in their own right. She concludes that all too often anthropologists "have allowed 'politics by men' to structure our thinking about other societies . . . leading us to believe erroneously that if women are not dominant in the political sphere of interaction, their power, at best, remains peripheral" (Weiner, 1977, p. 228).

Machismo revisited

Male supremacist ideals in Latin American are known as *machismo*. Throughout Latin America men are expected to be *macho:* that is, brave, sexually agressive, virile, and domi-

nant over women. At home, they dole out money to their wives, eat first, expect instant obedience from their children, especially from their daughters, go and come as they please, and make decisions which the entire family must follow without discussion. They "wear the pants," or at least they think they do. But as May Diaz has shown in her study of Tonalá, a small town near Guadalajara, Mexico, there are significant discrepancies between *machismo* as a masculine ideal and *machismo* as it is actually practiced in the bosom of the family. While women overtly seem to acquiesce to being bossed about by their fathers, husbands, and older brothers, they possess certain strategies for overcoming male control and for getting their own way. One such strategy is to play a *macho* male off against another *macho* male. The case of Lupita, a young unmarried Tonalá woman, illustrates how this works. Lupita's married brother caught her in the act of talking to a young man through the front window of her house. The brother demanded to know who the young man was but Lupita refused to tell him, fearing that her brother would go to their father and convince him to put an end to Lupita's flirtation. Lupita decided to manipulate the rules of *machismo* in her own favor. While helping her mother prepare the evening meal, Lupita told her mother that her brother's wife was nagging him and making him butt into Lupita's affairs. She knew this would elicit a sympathetic response from her mother (more sympathetic than if she had complained about her brother directly). She knew that her mother was antagonistic toward her daughter-in-law who had gained much influence over Lupita's brother and had come between mother and son. That night, as soon as the father sat down for dinner, Lupita's mother began to scold him for letting his son take over his authority and for not wearing the pants in the family. This convinced the father not to listen to what his son wanted to tell him about Lupita and he left the house as soon as he finished eating without forbidding Lupita to continue with her plans to gain a suitor. So Lupita and her mother achieved their ends, despite their lack of power, by appealing to the very rule that supposedly deprived them of power—a father should be boss in his own house (Diaz, 1966, pp. 85–87).

The distribution of power between the sexes is seldom simply a matter of women being completely at the mercy of men (or vice versa). As the Trobriand and Tonalá studies show, male anthropologists in the past may not have grasped the more subtle aspects of sexual hierarchies. Yet we must not fall into the trap of minimizing the real power differences embodied in many sexual hierarchies by placing too great an emphasis on the ability of subordinates to manipulate the system in their favor. It is well-known that slaves can sometimes outwit masters, that privates can frustrate generals, and that children can get parents to wait on them like servants. The ability to buffer the effects of systemic inequality should not be confused with systemic equality.

Warfare and the male supremacist complex

One theory—still controversial—is that the widespread practice of warfare accounts for the male supremacist complex in preindustrial societies, including the ideal of a masculine male personality and the ideal of a feminine female personality. Warfare is linked to male supremacy because in preindustrial combat with hand-held weapons, victory belongs to the group that can put the largest number of the fiercest and brawniest warriors into combat. Men on the average have a physical advantage over women with respect to the force they can exert with a club, the distance they can throw a spear, shoot an arrow, throw a stone, or the speed with which they

can run short distances (see Table 12.1 and Fig. 12.9). This means the group that can put the largest number of male warriors into combat will have the best chance of victory under preindustrial modes of warfare. How is this to be achieved? In band, village, and chiefdom societies, ecological constraints drastically limit the growth of population. It is not only enemy warriors that threaten survival, but also overpopulation. The problem, therefore, is twofold: to maximize the number of male warriors and at the same time minimize the pressure of population on resources. The solution to this twofold problem is to rear boys preferentially over girls, as indicated in the correlation between warfare, high male sex ratios in the junior age bracket, female infanticide, preference for male children, higher rates of junior female mortality from neglect and nutritional deprivation, including protein deficiencies (see p. 136). In other words, wherever there is intense preindustrial warfare, groups that develop these aspects of the male supremacist complex are likely to rout and displace groups that do not.

There remains the question of how men are to be trained to be fierce and aggressive so they will risk their lives in combat. Since the preference for rearing males over females means there will be a shortage of women as marriage partners, one way to ensure that

TABLE 12.1 WORLD RECORDS (1982)

Event	Men (min:sec)		Women (min:sec)	
100-meter dash	0:09.95		0:10.88	
1 mile	3:48.80		4:21.68	
400-meter hurdle	0:47.13		0:48.60[a]	
	(ft)	(in)	(ft)	(in)
High jump	7	8¾	6	7

[a] Women's hurdles are set lower than men's.
Source: Guiness Book of World Records, 1982.

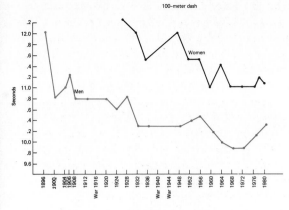

100-meter dash

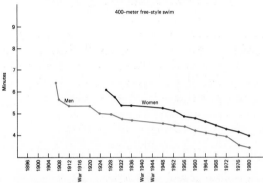

400-meter free-style swim

12.9 CAN THE GAP BE CLOSED?
Comparison of male and female Olympic records. It is possible that women may eventually surpass men in certain athletic performances, such as swimming, but not those most closely related to success in preindustrial warfare, such as running.

men will be aggressive in combat is to make sex and marriage contingent on being a fierce warrior. Logically, one might suppose that the solution to the problem of a shortage of women would be to have several men share a wife. But as we have seen, polyandry is extremely rare. Indeed, just the opposite occurs: In prestate societies practicing warfare there is a strong tendency for men to take several wives—that is, to be polygynous. Thus, instead of sharing women, men compete for

them, and the shortage of women is made even more severe by the fact that some men have two or three wives. This leads to much jealousy, adultery, and sexually charged antagonism between men and women, as well as hostility between men and men, especially junior "have nones" and senior "have severals" (Divale and Harris, 1976, 1978a, 1978b; Divale et al., 1978; see Howe, 1978; Lancaster and Lancaster, 1978; Norton, 1978).

Note that this theory relates the intensity of the preindustrial male supremacist complex to the intensity of warfare and of reproductive pressures. It predicts that wherever the intensity of warfare and reproductive pressure are low, the male supremacist complex will be weak or virtually absent. This prediction conforms to the widely held view that many hunter-gatherer band societies had both low levels of warfare and considerable sexual equality, and that both warfare and sexual inequality increased with the development of agriculture and the state. Moreover, it also accounts for the reported occurrences of strong male supremacist complexes in warlike hunter-gatherer band societies—as, for example, in Australia. Not all band societies confronted similar ecological conditions and similar degrees of reproductive pressure (Leacock, 1978).

Masculinity, war, and the Oedipus complex

The above theory reverses the causal arrows in Freudian explanations of warfare. Freud regarded the aggressivity and sexual jealousy of males to be instinctual. He saw both war and the Oedipus complex as products of this aggressive instinct. There is much evidence, however, to indicate that the aggressive and sexually jealous male personality is itself caused by warfare, whereas warfare itself is caused by ecological and political-economic stresses. Similarly, the Oedipus complex can be seen not as the cause of warfare, but as the consequence of having to train males to risk their lives in combat. Wherever the objective of childrearing institutions is to produce aggressive, manipulative, fearless, virile, and dominant males, some form of sexually charged hostility between the junior and senior males is inevitable. But this does not mean the Oedipus complex is an inevitable expression of human nature. Rather, it is a predictable outcome of training males to be combative and "masculine" (Fig. 12.10).

Male initiation, warfare, and sex roles

John Whiting (1969) and his associates have developed an interesting theory to account for variations in the severity of male puberty rites. These rites are defined as severe when they involve circumcision or other forms of mutilation, prolonged seclusion, beatings, and trials of courage and stamina. Whiting has shown that statistical correlations exist between such rites and other factors: (1) protein scarcities, (2) nursing of children for one or more years, (3) prohibition on sex relations between husband and wife for one or more years after the birth of their child, (4) polygyny, (5) domestic sleeping arrangements in which mother and child sleep together and father sleeps elsewhere, (6) child training by women, and (7) patrilocality.
Following our model, the following chain develops: Low protein availability and the risk of Kwashiorkor [a protein deficiency disease] were correlated with an extended postpartum sex taboo to allow the mother time to nurse the infant through the critical stage before becoming pregnant again. The postpartum sex taboo was significantly correlated with the institution of polygyny, providing alternate sexual outlets for the male. Polygyny, in turn, is associated with mother-child households, child training by women, resultant cross-sex identity, and where patrilocality is also present, with initiation rites to resolve the conflict

12.10 AGRESSIVE MALE GAMES
There is evidence of a close correlation between warfare and agressive male sports: Afghan game (above) requires daring feats of horsemanship; the gentle art of football, USA (below); on facing page, mock

combat in Indonesia (top left); boxing, USA (top right); the sporting life in England —rugby (bottom). [Eugene Gordon—p. 256, above and p. 257, top left; UPI—p. 256, below and p. 257, top right; George Gardner —p. 257, bottom]

and properly inculcate male identity. (*Harrington and Whiting, 1972, p. 491*)

"Cross-sex identity" refers to the psychodynamic process by which boys who are reared exclusively by their mothers and older women identify themselves with their mothers and other women. Where patrilocality is present, reasons Whiting, functional consistency demands that adult males must make a strong identification with their fathers and other males. Hence there is a conflict between what the male must do and think as an adult and what he is trained to do and think as an infant. Severe male initiation ceremonies are thus required to resolve this conflict by breaking the prepubescent identity. The functional-causal links in Whiting's model are diagrammed in Fig. 12.11.

Male initiation, warfare, and sex roles

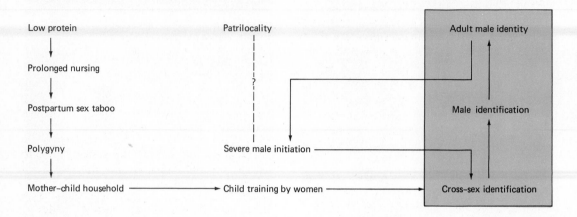

Varieties of sexual experience

Anatomy does not destine males and females to continue to display the personality characteristics of the past in the future. It is true that men are taller, heavier, and stronger than women; that men have higher levels of testosterone (the male sex hormone); that women menstruate, become pregnant, and lactate. Nonetheless, modern anthropology stands opposed to the view that anatomy is destiny. Males are not born with an innate tendency to be hunters or warriors or to be sexually and politically dominant over women. Nor are women born with an innate tendency to care for infants and children and to be sexually and politically subordinate. Rather, it has been the case that under a broad but finite set of cultural and natural conditions, certain sex-linked specialties have been selected for in many cultures. As demographic, technological, economic, and ecological conditions that underly these sex-linked roles change, new cultural definitions of sex-linked roles will emerge.

Anthropological research lends strong support to the view that the particular defini-

tions of masculinity and femininity found in many contemporary societies may be unnecessarily restrictive and unrealistically demanding. The prevalent fear of sexual deviance; the male's preoccupation with sexual potency; and the female's obsession with motherhood, sexual competence, and sexual attractiveness cannot be accounted for or justified by purely biological factors. Alternate standards of masculinity and femininity more responsive to individual differences are perfectly compatible with human nature (Hite, 1976; Murphy, 1976). Very little of a reliable nature is actually known about human sexuality in relation to culture. Anthropologists are certain, however, that knowledge about sexuality gained from the study of people living in one culture can never be taken as representative of human sexual behavior in general. All aspects of sexual relationships from infantile experiences through courtship and marriage exhibit an immense amount of cultural variation. Many different arrangements of Meggitt's "lechery" and "prudery" occur. For example, among the Mangaians of Polynesia, according to Donald Marshall (1971), boys and girls never hold hands and husbands and wives never embrace in public. Brothers and sisters must never even be seen together. Mothers and daughters and fathers and sons do not discuss sexual matters with one another. And yet both sexes engage in intercourse well before puberty. After puberty, both sexes enjoy an intense premarital sex life. Girls receive varied nightly suitors in the parents' house, and boys compete with their rivals to see how many orgasms they can achieve. Mangaian girls are not interested in romantic protestations, extensive petting, or foreplay. Sex is not a reward for masculine affection; rather, affection is the reward for sexual fulfillment:

> Sexual intimacy is not achieved by first demonstrating personal affection; the reverse is true. The Mangaian . . . girl takes an immediate demonstration of sexual virility and masculinity as the first test of her partner's desire for her and as the reflection of her own desirability. . . . Personal affection may or may not result from acts of sexual intimacy, but the latter are requisite to the former—exactly the reverse of the ideals of western society. (Marshall, 1971, p. 118)

According to a consensus reached by Marshall's informants, males sought to reach orgasm at least once every night, and women expected each episode to last at least 15 minutes. They agreed on the data presented in Table 12.2 as indicative of typical male sexual activity.

A very different attitude toward sexual activity appears to be characteristic of Hindu India. There is a widespread belief among

TABLE 12.3 AMERICAN AND HINDU SEXUALITY

Age group	White U.S. women	Hindu women
10–14	—	0.4
15–19	3.7	1.5
20–24	3.0	1.9
25–29	2.6	1.8
30–34	2.3	1.1
35–39	2.0	0.7
40–44	1.7	0.2
Over 44	1.3	0.3

Source: Adapted from Nag, 1972, p. 235.

Hindu men that semen is a source of strength and that it should not be squandered:

> Everyone knew that semen was not easily found; it takes forty days and forty drops of blood to make one drop of semen. . . . Everyone was agreed . . . that the semen is ultimately stored in a reservoir in the head, whose capacity is twenty tolas (6.8 ounces). . . . Celibacy was the first requirement of true fitness, because every sexual orgasm meant the loss of a quantity of semen, laboriously formed. (Carstairs, 1967; quoted in Nag, 1972, p. 235)

Contrary to popular stereotypes concerning Hindu eroticism (Fig. 12.12), there is evidence that coital frequency among Hindus is considerably less than among U.S. whites in comparable age groups. Moni Nag gives a summary (Table 12.3) of average weekly coital frequency for Hindu and white U.S. women. It is also clear, again contrary to popular impressions, that India's high level of fertility and population growth is not the result of sexual overindulgence caused by "not having anything else to do for entertainment at night."

TABLE 12.2 MANGAIAN SEXUALITY

Approximate age	Average number of orgasms per night	Average number of nights per week
18	3	7
28	2	5–6
38	1	3–4
48	1	2–3

Source: D. Marshall, 1971, p. 123.

Homosexuality

Attitudes toward homosexuality range from horror to chauvinistic enthusiasm. Knowledge of male homosexuality is more extensive than knowledge of female homosexuality. Several cultures studied by anthropologists incorporate male homosexuality into their

CHAPTER 12
Personality and sex

system for developing masculine male personalities. For example, the *berdache*, or feminized male of the Crow discussed earlier, performed sexual favors for great warriors without diminishing the latter's masculine status. On the contrary, to be served by a *berdache* was a proof of manliness. Similarly, among the Azande of the Sudan, renowned for their prowess in warfare, the unmarried warrior age grade, which lived apart from women for several years, had homosexual relations with the boys of the age grade of warrior apprentices. After their experiences with "boy-wives," the warriors graduated to the next age status, got married, and had many children (Evans-Pritchard, 1970).

Male homosexuality in New Guinea is highly institutionalized and closely associated with male supremacist attitudes and fear of pollution and witchcraft by women. These, in turn, are closely related to reproductive and ecological stress. Among the Etoro studied by Raymond Kelly (1976) men believe that semen is the substance that gives them life. Like the men of Hindu India, they believe that each man has only a limited supply of semen. When the supply is exhausted, a man dies. While coitus with one's wife is necessary to prevent the population from becoming too small, husbands stay away from wives most of the time. Indeed, sex is taboo between husband and wife for over 200 days per year. The Etoro males regard wives who want to break this taboo as witches. To complicate matters, the supply of semen is not something that a man is born with. Semen can be acquired only from another male. Etoro boys get their supply by having oral intercourse with older men. But it is forbidden for young boys to have intercourse with each other and, like the

oversexed wife, the oversexed adolescent boy is regarded as a witch and condemned for robbing his age-mates of their semen supply. Such wayward youths can be identified by the fact that they grow faster than ordinary boys. Although the Etoro have carried male homosexuality to a point that is unusual among cultures studied by anthropologists, they serve as a warning against confusing one's own culturally determined expressions of sexuality with human nature.

Sex roles in industrial society

Under industrial conditions, most of the male-dominated roles in agriculture, warfare, industry, and government cannot be said to need the extra musclepower associated with the male physique. Although menstruation, pregnancy, and lactation involve disadvantages in a few situations requiring rapid mobility or continuous effort under stress, modern governments and corporations are already adjusted to high levels of absenteeism and frequent change of personnel. With the long-range trend toward decreased fertility under industrial conditions, women are pregnant, on the average, less than 3 percent of their lives.

It is sometimes argued that menstruation interferes with the capacity of women to make rational decisions under stress, and hence that the exclusion of women from positions of industrial, governmental, or military leadership continues to be based upon a realistic adjustment to biological givens. However, the association between menstruation and irritability, depression, and physical pain is not necessarily a biological given. There is wide variation in the psychological states associated with menstruation among women in different cultures. An alternate hypothesis is that the folklore about menstrual disabilities

12.12 *HINDU EROTIC ART* (*facing page*)
Erotic themes are common in the sacred art of India. Shown, Lord Shiva and Parvati. [Sharma, DPI]

is itself at least in part a product of male supremacy rather than one of its causes.

Menstruation cannot be considered a barrier to sexual parity in positions of leadership and control. The top leadership of the U.S. military-industrial-educational establishment and of the equivalent groups in the Soviet Union and other contemporary great powers, consists of men who are chronologically well past their physical prime. Many of these leaders suffer from high blood pressure, diseases of the teeth and gums, poor digestion, failing eyesight, hearing losses, backaches, fallen arches, and other clinical syndromes associated with advancing age. Like menstruation, these disorders also frequently produce psychological stress. Healthy, premenopausal women certainly enjoy a biological edge over the typical male "elder statesman." As for older, postmenopausal women, they tend to be healthier than men and to live longer.

Sex roles for the future

One of the most remarkable trends of the twentieth century has been the rapid redefinition of sex roles and the restructuring of family life in the industrial nations. Everyone is aware of a profound change in attitude toward sexual experimentation and novel living arrangements. Couples are living together more often without being married; both men and women are getting married later; when they get married husband and wife are continuing to work; married couples are having fewer children, and they are getting divorced more often. One-child households, no-child households, single-parent households, and homosexual households are all on the increase (see Westoff, 1978).

What accounts for these changes? Wanda Minge-Kalman (1978a, b) suggests that many of these changes can be understood as a consequence of the rising costs and diminishing benefits of child labor. With industrialization, the cost of rearing children, especially after the introduction of child labor laws and compulsory education statutes, rose rapidly. The skills required for earning a living took longer to acquire. Hence parents had to wait longer before they could receive any economic benefits from their children. At the same time, the whole pattern of how people earned their living changed. Work ceased to be something done by family members on the family farm or in the family shop. Rather, people earned wages as individuals in factories and offices. What the family did together was to consume; its only product was children. The return flow of benefits from rearing children came to hinge more and more on their willingness to help out in the medical and financial crises that beset older people. But longer life spans and spiraling medical costs make it increasingly unrealistic for parents to expect such help from their children. Thus the industrial nations have increasingly been obliged to substitute old age and medical insurance and old age homes for the preindustrial system in which children took care of their aged parents.

Attempts to measure the actual cost of rearing a child to middle-class status in the U.S. and Canada are beset by methodological difficulties. But it is clear that the costs are rising fast. Family income required to feed, clothe, house, medicate, and educate a middle-class child from birth to 18 years of age is estimated to amount to $80,000. But this does not take into consideration the income the middle-class mother would have earned had she not stayed at home to take care of her child. This could easily amount to another $150,000. Small wonder, therefore, that in many industrial nations the fertility rate is now well below the 2.1 children per woman needed for replacement. With continuing inflation, high unemployment, and the need for two wage earners per family to maintain middle-class standards, one can predict that the fertility rate will drop still further and that it will continue to drop until the economic value of motherhood is recognized and paid for. For as Minge-Kalman concludes, the entire industrial labor force is now being produced by underpaid workers in that "cottage industry" we call the family. As long as this situation continues, more and more men and women will probably decide to have only one child or none, and more and more individuals will probably find that the traditional forms of family sexual and emotional togetherness are too expensive. We will return to the analysis of changing sex roles and family organization in the United States in Chapter 14.

Summary

Culture and personality are closely related concepts concerned with the patterning of thoughts, feelings, and behavior. Personality is primarily a characteristic of individuals; culture is primarily a characteristic of groups. Yet it is possible to speak of the personality of a group—of a basic, modal, or typical personality. The two approaches, however, use different technical vocabularies to describe the patterning of thought, feelings, and behavior.

Anthropologists who study personality generally accept the Freudian premise that personality is molded by childhood experiences. This has led to an interest in how adults interact with and relate to infants and young children, especially in such matters as toilet training, nursing, weaning, and sexual discipline. In some theories these experiences are seen as determining the nature of "secondary" institutions such as art and religion.

Other approaches to culture and personality attempt to characterize whole cultures in terms of central themes, patterns, basic personality, or national character. Care is necessary in order to avoid overgeneralizing the applicability of such concepts. A wide range of personality types is found in any large population.

Pervasive personality differences are associated with being male and female. Freudians emphasize the role of instincts and anatomy in the formation of the active, aggressive "masculine" personality and a passive, subordinate "feminine" personality. These differences reflect typical male versus female expressions of what Freud called the Oedipus complex. Freud's notions of typical male and female personalities have been challenged by anthropological data as being too ethnocentric. Nineteenth-century Viennese sex stereotypes cannot represent the ideal male or female personality in other cultures.

Nonetheless, a great variety of evidence suggests that in most societies males do have more aggressive and dominating personalities than females and that there is a residual core of truth in Freud's notions of antagonism between adjacent generations of males. The evidence in question consists first of the general preeminence of males in headship, redistribution, chieftainship, and monarchical and imperial political institutions on the one hand, and the absence of matriarchies on the other. Second, the pervasive male belief in the female as a focus of pollution and witchcraft reflects real power differences, regardless of whether females concur. Such beliefs, as in Bangladesh or among the Foré, are part of a system for depriving women of access to strategic resources (for example, animal protein) and do not enable women to achieve autonomy or a balance of power. Third, there is pervasive male control over the offices, rituals, and symbols of religion at all levels, from the shamanic to the ecclesiastical.

Anthropologists, however, have recently been sensitized to the possibility of exaggerating or misconstruing the extent and nature of male dominance. As illustrated in the elaborate female-run Trobriand funeral distributions, even the best of male ethnographers may overlook data relevant to women's status. And, as illustrated by Tonalá domestic life, even in strongly *macho* societies, women may get their own way by manipulating the "rules of the game."

In prestate societies the male supremacist complex can be explained by the pervasive need to rear maximum numbers of fierce, combat-ready males in overpopulated habitats. The theory predicts that the intensity of the male supremacist complex will vary directly with the intensity of warfare and reproductive stress. It also may explain why the Oedipus complex occurs, reversing Freud's causal arrows by viewing war as the cause rather than the effect of aggression and sexual jealousy. This shows that anatomy is not destiny. The role of cultural factors in male initiation, patrilocality, and polygyny, as discussed by John Whiting, also suggests that anatomy is not destiny. It is culture that determines how the anatomical differences between males and females are to be used in the definition of masculinity and femininity.

Anthropological studies lend support to the view that contemporary definitions of masculinity and femininity may be unnecessarily restrictive. Cross-cultural variations in sexual standards and sexual behavior prevent any single culture from serving as the model for what is natural in the realm of sex. Mangaian heterosexual standards contrast with those of Hindu India, which contrast with those of the contemporary industrial societies. Homosexuality also defies neat stereotyping, as can be seen in the examples of the Crow, Azande, and Etoro.

Sex roles in industrial society cannot be attributed to anatomical and physiological differences. As the technology of production has changed, so has the definition of ideal masculine and feminine roles. Industrialization has increased the costs of rearing children while lowering the benefits. It has therefore fundamentally altered marriage and domestic life. The continuation of these trends will further modify the ideal personalities of the man and woman of the future.

13

Applied Anthropology

This chapter explores the relationships between anthropological research and the achievement of practical goals by organizations that sponsor or use such research. A variety of cases illustrating the distinctive strong points of applied anthropology will be set forth and analyzed.

What is applied anthropology?

Since World War II, an increasing number of cultural anthropologists have become involved occasionally or regularly in research that has more or less immediate practical applications. They are known as practitioners of *applied anthropology.*

The core of applied anthropology consists of research commissioned by public or private organizations in the hope of achieving practical goals of interest to those organizations. Such organizations include federal, state, local, and international government bureaus and agencies, such as the U.S. Department of Agriculture, the Department of Defense, the National Park Service, the Agency for International Development, the Bureau of Indian Affairs, the World Bank, the World Health Organization, the Food and Agricultural Organization, various drug abuse agencies, education and urban planning departments of major cities, and municipal hospitals, to mention only a few. In addition, private organizations that have hired or contracted with anthropologists to carry out practical, goal-oriented research include major industrial corporations, foundations such as Planned Parenthood and the Population Council, and various branches of the Rockefeller and Ford Foundations' International Crops Research Institutes (Eddy and Partridge, 1978; Pitt, 1976).

It should be emphasized that cultural anthropologists do not have a monopoly on applied anthropology. Physical anthropology, archeology, and linguistics also have their applied aspects. But here we deal only with the applied aspects of cultural anthropology.

Research, theory, and action

Although the hallmark of applied anthropology is involvement in research aimed at achieving a specific practical result, the extent to which the applied anthropologist actually participates in bringing about the desired result varies from one assignment to another. At one extreme, the applied anthropologist may merely be charged with developing information the sponsoring organization needs to have in order to make decisions. In other instances, the applied anthropologist may be asked to evaluate the feasibility of a planned program or even to draw up a more or less detailed set of plans for achieving a desired goal (Husain, 1976). More rarely, the anthropologist, alone or as a member of a team, may be charged with planning, implementing, and evaluating a whole program from beginning to end. When anthropologists help to implement a program, they are spoken of as practicing *action anthropology* (see p. 283).

Note that the separation of applied from nonapplied anthropology shades off imperceptibly as theoretical and abstract interests come to dominate specific and concrete goals. It is often difficult to draw a line between applied and nonapplied research. Many anthropologists maintain that abstract theorizing can itself be construed as applied anthropology if it provides a general set of principles to which any action program must conform if it is to achieve success. For example, general theories about the causes of peasant backwardness and of urban poverty (see pp. 166 and 173) can have immense practical consequences even though the research behind their theories may not have been sponsored by organizations with the expressed goal of eliminating (or perpetuating) underdevelopment and urban poverty. Applied anthropology premised on weak or blatantly incorrect theory is misapplied anthropology.

Moreover, we must bear in mind that anthropologists who refrain from involvement in sponsored, practical, goal-oriented research may have practical ends in view for their descriptions and theories, but are unable to obtain support of suitable organizations for putting their findings to practical use. For example, the author of this book was sponsored by the Ford Foundation to carry out research on the nature of cultural change and race relations in what was then (1956–1957) the Portuguese colony of Moçambique. Although neither I nor the sponsoring foundation was explicitly concerned with a definite set of practical goals, I at least had the hope that the findings would be of some practical use in helping the people of Moçambique to achieve their independence from Portugal. I tried to render this help by publishing materials that documented the severely repressive and exploitative nature of Portugal's colonial system, the hope being that the U.S. State Department would therefore be persuaded to change its policy of endorsing and underwriting the perpetuation of Portuguese rule in Africa (Harris, 1958). Had the U.S. State Department been willing to implement a more enlightened policy with regard to Portuguese Africa, I would have been eager to participate in action programs aimed at decolonizing Moçambique.

Ironically, the founder of the Moçambique liberation movement, Dr. Eduardo Mondlane, was a sociologist-anthropologist who received his Ph.D. from Northwestern University. Mondlane can thus be said to have been involved in a form of action anthropology that has greatly influenced the course of events in southern Africa. He thought of himself both as a social scientist and as a political leader (Mondlane, 1969).

What do applied anthropologists have to offer?

The effectiveness of applied anthropology is enhanced by three distinctive attributes of general anthropology (see p. 4): (1) relative freedom from ethnocentrism and Western biases; (2) concern with holistic socio-cultural systems; (3) concern with ordinary etic behavioral events as well as with the emics of mental life.

1. Delineation of ethnocentrism The applied anthropologist can be of assistance to sponsoring organizations by exposing the ethnocentric, culture-bound assumptions that often characterize cross-cultural contacts and prevent change-oriented programs from achieving their goals. For example, Western-trained agricultural scientists tend to dismiss peasant forms of agriculture as backward and inefficient, thereby overlooking the cumulative wisdom embodied in age-old practices handed down from generation to generation. The attitude of Western experts toward the use of cattle in India is a case in point (see p. 216). Anthropologists are more likely to reserve judgment about a traditional practice such as using cattle to plow fields which a narrowly trained specialist might automatically wish to replace with tractors. Again, applied anthropologists are likely to see that the attempt to model a health care delivery system after those with which Western-trained doctors are familiar may represent nothing more than an attempt to replace the culturally unfamiliar with the culturally familiar. Expensive staffs, costly hospitals, and the latest electronic gadgetry, for example, are not necessarily the way to improve the quality of health services (Cattle, 1977, p. 38). The American notion that milk is the "perfect food" has led to much grief and dismay throughout the world, since many populations in less developed countries to which tons of surplus milk in powdered form were sent as nutritional supplements lacked the enzyme needed to digest lactose, the predominant form of sugar in milk. Western notions of hygiene automatically suggest that mothers must be persuaded not to chew food and then put it in their baby's mouth. Yet it was found that in the case of the Pijoan Indians of the U.S. Southwest that premastication of infant foods was an effective way to combat the iron-deficiency anemia to which the infants who are fed exclusively on mother's milk are subject (Freedman, 1977, p. 8).

2. A holistic view As industrial society becomes increasingly specialized and *technocratic* (that is, dominated by narrowly trained experts who have mastered techniques and the use of machines others do not understand), the need for anthropology's holistic view of social life becomes more urgent. In diverse fields (e.g., education, health, economic development), there has been a convergence toward using narrow sets of easily quantified variables in order to objectively verify the accomplishment or lack of accomplishment of an organization's goals. All too often, however, the gain in verifiability is accomplished at the expense of a loss in "validity" (or "meaningfulness"). Easily quantified variables may represent only a small part of a much bigger system whose larger set of difficult-to-measure variables has the capacity to cancel out the observed effects of the small set of variables (Bernard, 1981, p. 5). For example, after World War II the U.S. auto industry found it could earn more money by building heavier and more powerful cars without paying too much attention to the question of how long the cars would function without need of repairs. Other sets of variables, namely the ecological consequences of auto emission pollution, the political and military conditions that made it possible for the United States to enjoy low oil prices, and the perception by foreign auto producers that

there was a market for small, fuel-efficient, reliable, and long-lasting vehicles, were considered irrelevant to the task of maximizing the U.S. auto industry's profits. Hence what appeared in a narrow context to be a highly objective measure of success (high profits and domination of the U.S. auto market) turned out in a longer time frame to be devoid of validity.

Thus, in commonsense terms anthropological holism boils down to being aware of the long term as well as the short term, the distant as well as the near, parts other than the one being studied, and the whole as well as the parts. Without these perspectives, even the seemingly straightforward and simple project can end up as a disaster. Here is another example of what can go wrong when holistic principles are ignored.

Under the auspices of an international development program, experts from Australia tried to get the peasant Indians of Chimborazo Province in Ecuador to substitute high-yield Australian merino sheep for the traditional scrawny breeds the Indians owned. No one wanted the sheep, despite the offer to let them have them free if they used them for breeding purposes. Finally, one "progressive" Indian accepted the offer and successfully raised a flock of cross-bred merinos that were far woolier and heavier than the traditional Indian flocks. Unfortunately, the Indians of Chimborazo live in a caste-structured society. Non-Indian farmers who live in the lower valleys resented the attention being paid to the Indians; they began to fear that the Indians would be emboldened to press for additional economic and social gains, which would undermine their own position. The merinos caught someone's attention, and the whole flock was herded into a truck and stolen. The rustlers were well protected by public opinion, which regarded the animals as "too good for the Indians anyway." The "progressive" innovator was left as the only one in the village without sheep. Variables such as ethnic and class antagonisms, opportunities for theft, and the political subserviance of peasants are not part of the expertise of sheepbreeders, but they nonetheless proved to be essential to the achievement of their goals.

3. An etic view of organizations Technification and specialization are usually accompanied by the growth of bureaucracy. An essential component in bureaucracy is an emic plan by which the units within an organization are related to each other and according to which the individuals are expected to perform their tasks. As in most sociocultural systems, there is considerable likelihood that the etic behavioral substance of organizations and situations differs from the mental emics of the bureaucratic plan. Anthropologists who are trained to approach social life from the "ground up," and who are concerned with everyday events as they actually unfold, often can provide a view of organizations and situations that the bureaucracy lacks. Hospitals as studied by applied anthropologists, for example, are a rich source of jarring discrepancies between the emics of various staff specialists and the etics of patient care. From the point of view of the hospital bureaucracy, its various rules and regulations are designed to promote the health and well-being of patients. In fact, numerous studies have shown that the main effect of many rules and regulations is to shock and depersonalize the patients and to create in them a level of apprehension comparable to that which can be observed in an Ndembu boy awaiting the rite of circumcision in the "place of death" (see p. 203). On entering the hospital, patients are stripped of their clothing and their money. They become a case in a numbered room wearing a numbered bracelet for identification (the same way newborn babies are numbered). Groups of costumed personnel (some even wearing masks) speak to them in a strange new dialect: "Did you *void* this morning?" "When was your last B.M.?" (bowel movement). "You're going to have an EEG" (electroencephalogram). Patients are awakened, fed, and put to sleep according to a rigid schedule, and they are kept uninformed about their condition and what is happening to them (Fig. 13.1). One is forced to conclude that many hospital rules are primarily for the convenience of the staff and have an adverse effect on the health and well-being of the patients (Foster and Anderson, 1978, pp. 170–171).

The kind of work being done by applied anthropologists covers a range of cases far too broad to be surveyed in a single chapter. The following examples have been selected to illustrate the great diversity of problems that can benefit from an anthropological approach.

Development anthropology: Vicos

The Cornell-Peru Vicos project illustrates applied anthropology functioning over the entire range of research, planning, implementation, and evaluation. Vicos was a *hacienda*[1] in the Peruvian highlands inhabited by 373 economically serflike, depressed, and exploited families of Indian peasants (Fig. 13.2). Cornell University leased the *hacienda* in 1951 and turned it over to anthropologist Allen Holmberg with the objective of raising the Indians' standard of living and making them economically independent. At the time of intervention, the people of Vicos were unable to grow enough food to feed themselves; their farming lands were broken up into thousands of tiny scattered plots; their potato crop was subject to frequent failure; and they lacked motiva-

---

[1] A *hacienda* is a large farm on which a variety of crops is grown and which is worked by resident peasants.

tion for producing a surplus, since they were constantly in debt or at the beck and call of the landlords.

Under the feudal rules of the *hacienda* system, the peasants were required to labor on the owner's fields for three days per week. Holmberg decided to take advantage of this obligation by using it to familiarize the peasants with improved varieties of potatoes, fertilizers, fungicides, and insecticides. After seeing how successful the new seeds and methods were during their obligatory labor on the new boss's plot, the peasants were more willing to do the same on their own plots. This was facilitated by advancing the seeds and other materials on a sharecrop basis. Anthropologists and technicians carefully supervised the use of the new methods to ensure their success.

Meanwhile, other activities were underway: a full-scale education program; a hot school lunch program that introduced fruits and eggs, previously not part of the diet; a demonstration garden for growing leafy vegetables; and sewing machine lessons that enabled the women to make their own clothes. In addition, through frequent communal meetings and discussions, the peasants grad-

13.1 HOSPITAL SUBCULTURE
A patient, surrounded by unfamiliar machines and people talking a strange language, must not only cope with his disease, but with culture shock as well. [Seitz, Woodfin Camp]

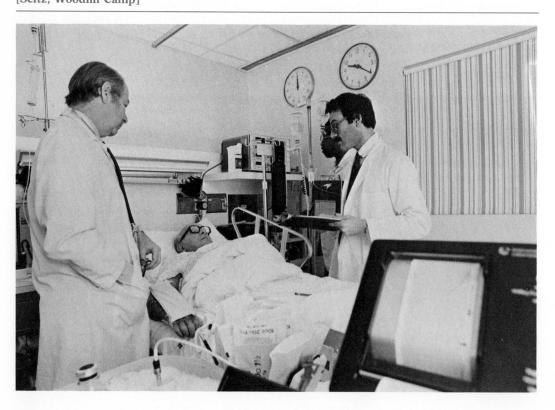

13.2 VICOS
**A community work party begins its potato
harvest. [Paul L. Doughty]**

ually came to place more trust in one another
and to seek cooperative, communal solutions
to their problems.

The culmination of all these changes was
the purchase of the *hacienda* by the families
living on it. This happened in 1962, and along
with higher incomes, better health, and literacy, was considered dramatic evidence of the
success of the project. The anthropologists'
intervention had avoided a forceful seizure of
the property; yet the land was not given to the
workers as a gift:

*They bought it; and instead of dividing the
land up into small holdings, the Vicosinos
[people of Vicos] elected to maintain the [hacienda] as a commercial production unit,
communally managed and worked for the
common good. (Dobyns, 1975, p. 201)*

No one doubts that the lives of the people of
Vicos were substantially improved as a result
of the intervention by Holmberg and other action anthropologists. As a model for developing the entire peasant sector of the Peruvian Andes, however, certain criticisms have
been expressed. The per capita cash outlays of
the Cornell-Peru project were quite modest in
comparison with those of other international
development efforts, yet there were hidden investment costs that are not likely to be duplicated on a scale large enough to affect a significant portion of the peasantry. These
hidden costs were the human and technical
capital poured into Vicos by highly trained,
honest, and relatively unselfish experts (including Holmberg) who worked diligently to

Development anthropology: Vicos   271

improve the lot of the peasants and whose livelihood was not based on profits or taxes taken out of the peasant's surplus production. (They were paid by universities and foundations, and many of them worked for next to nothing as graduate students hoping to be compensated by getting their Ph.D.s and making their careers in anthropology.) Although extremely interesting as a demonstration of what can be done by action anthropologists who had considerable power to boss the people in their charge, the Vicos project falls short of providing a more general solution to the problem of underdevelopment.

The not-so-green revolution

It is not often that anthropologists have a chance to initiate, implement, and evaluate a development program such as the Cornell-Peru project. A more typical role for the applied anthropologist is that of critic-observer of the change process. An important example of this role can be found in the anthropological critique of the "Green Revolution." This critique illustrates the importance of a holistic perspective for development projects.

The Green Revolution had its origin in the late 1950s in the dwarf varieties of "wonder wheat" developed by Nobel prizewinner plant geneticist Norman Borlaug at the Rockefeller Foundation's Ciudad Obregon research center in northwest Mexico. Designed to double and triple yields per acre, wonder wheat was soon followed by dwarf varieties of "miracle rice" engineered at a joint Rockefeller and Ford Foundation research center in the Phillipines. (The significance of the dwarfed forms is that short, thick stems can bear heavy loads of ripe grain without bending over.) On the basis of initial successes in Mexico and the Phillipines, the new seeds were hailed as the solution to the problem of feeding the expanding population of the underdeveloped world and were soon planted in vast areas of Pakistan, India, and Indonesia (Cioud, 1973). Although the new seeds have resulted in a definite increase in output per area, they have done so only at considerable economic and social cost. Moreover, this rate of increase has not been large enough to offset the rate of population growth, and hence per capita production of wheat and rice in most of Asia has remained stagnant (Wade, 1973). The main problem with the miracle seeds is that they were engineered to outperform native varieties of rice and wheat *only* if grown in fields heavily irrigated and treated with large inputs of chemical fertilizers, pesticides, insecticides, and fungicides. Without such inputs, the high-yield varieties perform little better than the native varieties, especially under adverse soil and weather conditions.

The question of how these inputs are to be obtained and how and to whom they are to be distributed immediately raises profound problems. Irrigated croplands form only 30 percent of Asian croplands (Wade, 1973). Most peasants in the underdeveloped world not only lack access to adequate amounts of irrigation water, but they are unable to pay for expensive chemical fertilizers and other chemical inputs. This means that unless extraordinary efforts are made by the governments of countries switching to the miracle seeds, the chief beneficiaries of the Green Revolution will be the richest farmers and merchants, who already occupy the irrigated lands and who are best able to pay for the chemical inputs (Cummings, 1978; Mencher, 1974a, 1978).

Anthropologist Richard Franke (1973, 1974) studied the Green Revolution in central Java. Despite the fact that yield increases of up to 70 percent were being obtained, in the village studied by Franke only 20 percent of the farming households had joined the program. The chief beneficiaries were the farmers who were already better off than average, owned the most land, and had adequate supplies of water. The poorest families did not

13.3 RICE HARVEST, JAVA
Harvesting (top) is done with a small hand-knife, known as the ani-ani. Each stalk is individually cut, but with the large supply of labor, a single morning is enough for all but the very largest plots to be harvested. The paddy is bound in bundles (bottom) and carried to the home of the owner where one-tenth portions are given to the harvesters. No other wage is paid. [Richard W. Franke]

adopt the new seeds. They make ends meet by working part-time for well-to-do farmers who lend them money to buy food (Fig. 13.3). The richer farmers prevented their part-time workers from adopting the new seeds. The richer farmers feared they would lose their supply of cheap labor, and the poor farmers feared that if they cut themselves off from their patrons, they would have no one to turn to in case of sickness or drought. Franke concludes that the theories behind the Green Revolution are primarily rationalizations for ruling elites trying to find a way to achieve economic development without the social and political transformation their societies need.

It should be pointed out that there can be considerable confusion regarding what is meant by a well-to-do farmer in underdeveloped countries. Some experts defend the Green Revolution against the criticism that it has primarily benefited well-to-do farmers by pointing out that most of the high-yield wheat farms in the Indian Punjab have less than 4 hectares (about 10 acres) and that Yaqui Valley wheat farms average only 69 hectares (Plucknett and Smith, 1982, p. 217). But throughout the underdeveloped world, any farmer who possesses as much as 2 or 3 hectares of *irrigated* land ranks among the top 10 percent of the rural population.

Why has there been so much public enthusiasm for miracle seeds that cannot be used by the great mass of ordinary peasants? From the point of view of the poor farmer, these seeds, with their water and chemical input requirements, might be described as *anti*miracles. If the seeds were miracles, they would require less water and fertilizer, not more. But the authorities and technicians responsible for promoting the Green Revolution originally sought to convert peasant farming into agribusiness systems modeled after high-energy agriculture in the developed countries (Cleaver, 1975). It was hoped that by stimulating the development of agribusiness in the tropics, the productivity of agriculture would be raised fast enough to catch up with the rate of population growth. This transformation obviously risks the virtual destruction of small peasant holdings—just as it has meant the destruction of the small family farm in the United States. There are penalties associated with this transformation even in the industrial nations, where the former farm population can be employed as car hops, meat packers, and tractor mechanics (see p. 51). But in the underdeveloped countries, where there are few jobs in the manufacturing and service sectors of the economy, migration to the cities cannot result in higher standards of living for hundreds of millions of underemployed peasants (Raj, 1977).

Much of the enthusiasm for the Green Revolution originated in the boardrooms of multinational corporations that sell the chemical inputs and the industrial hardware essential for agribusiness systems.

The association between the miracle seeds and agribusiness was present at the start of the Mexican wheat experiment. Ciudad Obregon in Sonora was the center of large wheat farms that depended upon extensive government irrigation projects in the Yaqui River Valley. The former peasant inhabitants of this valley—the Yaqui Indians—had been evicted from their lands in a series of military engagements, the last of which occurred in 1926 when the Yaquis tried unsuccessfully to kidnap Mexico's President Obregon (Spicer, 1954). The Yaquis were replaced by medium- and large-scale farmers who were the beneficiaries of $35 million of public funds expended on dams alone. The Mexican government subsidized the growth of the petrochemical industry, which supplied the fertilizers for the new seeds. Further subsidies were given to the miracle wheat producers in the form of government support prices pegged 33 percent above world market prices. It is true that the wonder wheat made Mexico into a wheat-exporting nation. Yet the price of Mexican wheat is so high that it must be exported—the average Mexican peasant cannot afford to eat it. Poor Mexicans eat corn and beans, which remain the basic Mexican staples. Meanwhile, in 1969 miracle wheat that had been produced at a cost of $73 a ton, the support price, was being sold at $49 a ton to foreign buyers. "Mexico thus lost $30.00 a ton, or 80¢ on each bushel exported" (Paddock and Paddock, 1973, p. 218). Cynthia Hewitt de Alcantara (1976, p. 320) has characterized the Green Revolution in Mexico as highly wasteful of natural and human resources and of the wealth created by government investments in irrigation facilities. "The ability of most rural people to satisfy their basic needs after thirty years of agricultural modernization is still in fact extraordinarily limited" (Hewitt de Alcantara, 1976, p. 135).

Recently, perhaps in part inspired by anthropological critiques, governments and foundations have recognized the importance of concentrating on helping poor farmers who depend on rainfall. For example, the International Crops Research Institute for the Semi-Arid Tropics, located in Hyderabad, India, has embarked upon a program to increase production of such dry farming crops as sorghum, millet, chickpeas, and peanuts, which are the staple foods of 500 million people in Asia and Africa (ICRISAT, n.d.). It remains to be seen whether substantial improvements in the yields of these crops can be achieved without expensive inputs.

The lesson of the Green Revolution is similar to that of the attempt to give merino sheep to the people of Chimborazo. In both cases, purely technological solutions fail to achieve their intended purpose because of the failure to take into account other and equally important parts of sociocultural systems.

Getting drunk in Denver

A similar lack of holistic perspective contributes to the widespread misunderstanding of the causal factors responsible for the failure of minority groups to work their way out of poverty (see p. 174). For example, Navajo men who migrate from their reservation to Denver in search of work frequently end up in jail on charges of drunken and disorderly behavior. A popular explanation for this behavior is that the migrants lack middle-class personality traits. Anthropologist Theodore Graves (1974) set out to test this notion by measuring the degree to which the possession of middle-class personality traits could be correlated with the rate of economic success and arrests for drunkenness among a sample of migrants. To determine which migrants possessed the strongest middle-class personalities and which the weakest, Graves devised three tests. The first test measured the migrants' future-time orientation by asking them to name five things they expected to do or expected to happen to them. They were then asked to say when they thought these events were going to occur—the average time cited in the future being the measure of their future-time orientation. The second test measured their degree of belief in their ability to control their own destiny by asking the migrants to choose from among paired statements that expressed feelings of fatalism or personal control. For example: "When I make plans, I am almost certain that I can make them work," versus "I have usually found that what is going to happen will happen regardless of my plans." Finally, in the third test, the migrants were shown six drawings of Navajos in everyday scenes and asked to tell what was happening in the pictures, what led up to it, what the people in it were thinking about or wanted, what would happen next, and how it would end. The answers were then rated for the extent to which they revealed a psychological concern with achievement, getting things done, and overcoming obstacles. The results of all three tests were then compared with data about how successful the migrants had been in getting jobs at various wage levels and at holding on to them. Only one of the success measures showed even a low positive correlation with the personality attributes, while half of the success measures showed correlations (statistically significant) in the direction opposite from that predicted by the first hypothesis. "We conclude that our data provide *no* empirical support for the thesis that an absence of middle class personality traits is contributing to Navajo marginality in the economic sphere" (Graves, 1974, p. 176).

Graves also found that future-time orientation and achievement motivation were indeed correlated with arrest rates, but in the opposite direction from that anticipated in the hypothesis. Those with middle-class traits get arrested more, not less frequently! Graves suggests that migrants who do poorly and have a future-time orientation tend to berate themselves and to be more anxious than those who live from day to day. Similarly, migrants who do poorly and have a high achievement drive feel their economic failure more keenly. Both types drink more often, which causes them to be arrested more often. Graves concludes:

A middle-class personality is adaptive only within a structural setting which permits the attainment of middle-class goals. Otherwise such psychological traits tend to be maladaptive *and to create additional adjustment problems for those who have acquired them.* (*1974, p. 83*)

This case not only illustrates the importance of a holistic anthropological perspective—the "structural setting" in Graves' words—but it also points up the need to challenge popular stereotypes by means of carefully designed empirical research.

Medical anthropology: marijuana

It has long been recognized that the mood, expectations, and personalities of drug users affect their reaction to psychoactive (mind-altering) drugs as much as the specific chemicals in the drugs themselves. Since culture denotes the total complex of behavioral and mental traditions surrounding individuals, one can expect that marked differences in reactions to psychoactive drugs will be found in different cultures. The study of the cultural component in drug-induced thoughts and behavior is therefore a source of essential information for anyone concerned with formulating or administering drug control policies.

Early in the 1970s a team of anthropologists and other behavioral and medical scientists led by Vera Rubin and Lambros Comitas (1975) undertook a cross-cultural study of marijuana use. Funds for the research were supplied by the National Institute of Mental Health's Center for Studies of Narcotic and Drug Abuse. Because they were interested in examining the long-term effects of marijuana on the health and well-being of chronic users, Rubin and Comitas selected the Caribbean island of Jamaica as the site for their study. Although marijuana is an illegal substance in Jamaica, Jamaicans are probably the most inveterate users of marijuana in the Western Hemisphere (Fig. 13.4). In the rural areas of the island, the researchers found that between 60 and 70 percent of working-class people use marijuana by smoking it, drinking it in tea, or eating it mixed with food. The most important difference between the marijuana complex in Jamaica and the marijuana complex in the United States is that working-class Jamaicans do not smoke marijuana to "turn on" or to achieve the hedonistic effects valued by middle class American users. Rather, the Jamaicans are motivated to smoke marijuana because they believe it helps them work better, and makes them healthier and stronger than nonusers.

Much of the opposition to the use of marijuana in the United States stems from the belief that marijuana deprives people of ambition and reduces their work drive. Although this may be true in the United States context, the Jamaican study suggests that apathy is not induced by the chemical, but by the cul-

13.4 *JAMAICAN RASTAFARIANS*
These two men are members of a movement in which the smoking of marijuana is viewed as a religions sacrament. [Peter Arnold]

tural conditions which surround its use. In Jamaica the primary reason given for smoking marijuana is that it helps one perform arduous and dull work. While weeding fields, for example, farmers said they were able to concentrate more on their task after smoking. Videotapes of farmers weeding with and without smoking suggested that their work was in fact more thorough and detailed after smoking. No evidence was found that those who smoked on the job worked less rapidly or less efficiently than those who did not. Rubin and Comitas conclude:

In all Jamaican settings observed, the workers [who smoke] are motivated to carry out difficult tasks with no decrease in heavy physical exertion, and their perception of increased output is a significant factor in bolstering their motivation to work. (1975, p. 75)

Many other aspects of the marijuana complex were studied. To assess the impact of chronic use on the health and personalities of users, a group of 30 smokers and a group of 30 nonsmokers with similar backgrounds and personal attributes were given a broad battery of clinical tests at the University Hospital in Jamaica (participation by both groups was completely voluntary). Aside from impairment of respiratory functions, which may be attributable to the fact that heavy marijuana smokers are also heavy tobacco smokers, the physical health of the Jamaican smokers was not significantly different from that of the nonsmokers. As for psychological states—intelligence, neurological fitness, sensory perception, memory, and attention, "There is no evidence that long-term use of cannabis [marijuana] is related to chronic impairment" (1975, p. 119). It must be emphasized that this finding need not be applicable to other cultures. It may very well be that in other cultural settings, such as the United States, the long-term use of marijuana does lead to impairments—the effects of cultural factors being no less real than those of physical or chemical factors.

Nonetheless, a second intensive cross-cultural study of marijuana smoking in a cultural setting different from Jamaica has led to conclusions similar to those drawn by Rubin and Comitas. This study was carried out in the Central American country of Costa Rica by a multidisciplinary team whose leaders included anthropologists William Carter (1980) and Paul Doughty. It employed a research design based on "matched pairs"—each of 41 male users was carefully paired with a male nonuser for age, marital status, education, oc-

cupation, alcohol consumption, and tobacco consumption. As a result of this design, all the above factors could be ruled out as causes of any of the observed differences in the behavior and physical condition of the users and nonusers.

Initially, the Costa Rican study seemed to corroborate the widely held view that long-term marijuana use leads to lack of motivation for work and economic advancement (Fig. 13.5). It was found that the users tended to have more part-time jobs, more unemployment, more job changes, and fewer material possessions than the nonusers. Yet there was an alternative explanation for these findings. It was possible that the users had become users because they were subject to greater economic and personal stress than the nonusers. If there was indeed a causal relation-

13.5 STREET SCENE, SAN JOSÉ, COSTA RICA
[Ann Hagen Griffiths]

ship leading to economic failure and apathy, corroboration could be found by showing that economic failure and apathy increased in direct proportion to the quantity of marijuana used. When comparisons within the user group were made, the results did not support the hypothesis that higher-dose levels were correlated with more marginal economic status. The reverse, in fact, was found to be the case. The more marijuana smoked, the more likely the user was to hold a steady, full-time job. Those who were working were smoking nearly twice as much marijuana per day as those who were unemployed. Those who had the shortest periods of unemployment were the heaviest users (Carter, 1980, 152ff).

Although some of the users in the Costa Rican study conformed to the stereotype of the unemployed, uncouth. streetwise vagrant, the majority of the users were more like Hector:

Hector is a laborer in a bakery where he has worked for the last three and a half years. He has a wife and two children for whom he is the only means of support. Hector never smokes at home or in the street or in public places. He does smoke, however, in the bathroom at the bakery, where he works from five in the afternoon until three in the morning. He claims that marijuana makes his work go faster and the night pass more quickly. (1980, p. 156)

Thus we can see that systematic cross-cultural comparisons are essential if we are to distinguish between cultural and physical-chemical aspects of psychoactive substances.

Getting drunk in Truk: "weekend warriors"

One implication of the marijuana studies and of Graves' Denver study is that behavior which appears to be deviant to the outsider may in fact represent a culturally sanctioned pattern for coping with the stresses and tensions of life as far as the insiders are concerned.

This point of view has been defended by anthropologist Mac Marshall (1978) in his study of drinking and brawling among the young men of Truk, an island in the eastern Caroline Islands of Micronesia (Fig. 13.6). Virtually all the able-bodied young men between 18 and 35 engage in daily or weekly bouts of drinking, accompanied by frequent outbursts of violent behavior usually directed at youths from other villages. The weekends are especially lively. In getting drunk, the young men sit in the bushes, laugh, sing, swap tales, and plan affairs with young women. Once drunk,

13.6 TRUK
A weekend warrior. [Mac Marshall]

they swagger, curse, utter ear-splitting war cries, break down doors, rush after women, intimidate friend and foe alike, and swing at each other with *nanchaku* (two sticks joined by a length of chain). Drunks are called "sardines," because like sardines in the can they have lost their heads.

Drunks are considered to be crazy, like animals, beyond the capacity of reasoning. However, they are seldom blamed for what they do when under the influence. All of this, claims Marshall, is not deviant but culturally expected behavior. It is deviant not to get drunk. On Truk young men should behave agressively, they should be preoccupied with proving their manliness, they should take risks, and they should engage in amorous pursuits:

Drinking and flamboyant drunken comportment are expected *of young men; in Truk the young man who abstains is "abnormal" not the other way around.* (Marshall, 1978, p. 67)

Getting drunk gives expression to the frustrations of not having one's opinions taken seriously and of having to show respect to one's elders. It is a way of venting pent-up aggressions that formerly were expressed in armed combat during military exploits. *Traditionally young men have been viewed as high spirited, irresponsible persons preoccupied with love affairs and image building. Young men are quite literally expected to engage in the proverbial "wine, women and song" in approximately that order. Their opinions are not sought on important lineage or community decisions."* . . . *Aboriginally, the major outlet through which young men could blow off steam . . . was by waging warfare. . . . Quite fortuitously as this outlet was closed off* [after colonial contact] *a new outlet was offered in drunkenness.* (Marshall, 1978, p. 125)

Mac Marshall's analysis warns us against assuming that drunken, rowdy, and disruptive behavior necessarily implies that a culture is breaking apart. Indeed, he sees getting drunk in Truk as an affirmation of cultural continuity rather than as disintegration. The practical implication of this analysis is that outsiders should not presume they are justified in trying to suppress the weekend warrior pattern as an absolute evil. The people of Truk themselves are best left to deal with this problem as they see fit.

Kuru: the case of the laughing sickness

Applied cultural anthropology has an important role to play in helping physical anthropologists and medical researchers understand the interaction between cultural and natural factors that cause people to become ill. The solution of the mystery of Kuru is a classic instance of how medical knowledge can be advanced by examining the interaction between cultural and natural causes of a deadly disease.

During the late 1950s reports that a previously unknown disease was rampant among the Foré peoples of Highland New Guinea suddenly made headlines around the world. Victims of the disease, called Kuru, were said to be laughing themselves to death. As reliable accounts began to replace rumor, Kuru turned out to be no laughing matter. Its victims progressively lost control over their central nervous system, including the nerves controlling their facial muscles, so that their faces were often contorted by ghastly grimaces and smiles. The disease was always fatal within a year or two of its first symptoms (Fig. 13.7).

Researchers led by Carleton Gajdusek found a puzzling *epidemiological* pattern (i.e., distribution and incidence of the disease in the population). Most of the victims were women and girls. Although a few young men came down with it, adult men never did. None of the neighboring tribespeople ever got Kuru, nor was it ever passed on to Europeans who were in close contact with the Foré.

The first solution was that the disease was genetic and passed on in family lines from generation to generation. But genetics could not explain the preponderance of female victims plus the occasional young man. Rejecting the genetic explanation, Gujdusek, who was trained both as a physical anthropologist and a virologist (one who studies viruses), began to explore the possibility that Kuru was caused by a type of virus known as a *slow virus*, whose existence in human beings had never been demonstrated but long suspected. Beginning in 1963, Gujdusek innoculated chimpanzees with brain extracts of Kuru victims. After long incubation periods, the chimpanzees began to show the Kuru symptoms. The demonstration that humans could harbor slow viruses has important implications for the study of many puzzling diseases, such as multiple sclerosis and certain forms of cancer. For his work, Gujdusak received the Nobel Prize for medicine in 1976.

It was left to two cultural anthropologists, Robert Glasse and Shirley Lindenbaum, however, to complete the explanation for the puzzling epidemiological pattern. Glasse and Lindenbaum drew attention to the fact that in years prior to the outbreak of Kuru, the Foré had begun to practice a form of cannibalism as part of their funeral rituals. Female relatives of the deceased consumed the dead person's brain. Since it was women who were always charged with the task of disposing of the dead, and never men, the Kuru virus never infected adult males. But what about the young men who also occasionally got Kuru? As in many cultures, the Foré's distinction between male and female roles was held less rigidly before puberty than after. Occasionally, therefore, a boy would be permitted to partake of what otherwise was defined as strictly female food. And some years later, this occasional youth would succumb to Kuru along with the much greater number of girls and women (Lindenbaum, 1979). Today, since the Foré have given up their cannibalistic

13.7 *YOUNG GIRL WITH ADVANCED KURU DISEASE*
[**From** *Edge of the Forrest: Sand, Childhood and Change in a New Guinea Protoagricultural Society,* **Smithsonian Institution Press, 1976. Photo by Dr. E. R. Sorenson**]

rites, Kuru has virtually ceased to exist among them.

The case of the vanishing associations

Villalta is a small town in the Dominican Republic with all the problems associated with life in an underdeveloped country: poverty, unemployment, illiteracy, and lowered life expectancy. Yet in one respect the town seems to be more "modernized" than others. It has a larger number of voluntary associations (or sodalites, see p. 131). Such associations are often interpreted as a sign of a community's progress in the direction of development.

But anthropologists Malcolm Walker and Jim Hanson (1978, pp. 64–68) found that these associations were disappearing or lapsing into disuse as fast as they were being created. During a short period the townspeople organized two adult education programs, cooking and sewing classes, a Red Cross chapter, a Youth for Reform association, a Girl Scout troop, a health clinic, a social club, and self-help programs for breeding rabbits, raising chickens, building bridges, and installing water pumps. But none of these projects or associations lasted more than a few days or weeks.

The circumstances surrounding the rise and fall of one of the adult education programs is typical of the rest. Members of the local elite called for a meeting to organize the program. Several outsiders were present, and an official from the Education Department gave a speech about the importance of adult education. The people at the meeting agreed and decided they would ask for volunteer teachers to teach evening classes in the schoolhouse. Another meeting was to be held in two weeks, at which time the teachers and classes would be organized.
Nothing in fact happened, and the follow up meeting was postponed indefinitely. The official was not heard of again. (Walker and Hanson, p. 66)

"If these associations are doomed to failure almost before the first meeting is over," asked Walker and Hanson, "why do the people of Villalta form them?" Their answer is that they are used by the local elites to give state officials the impression that Villalta is a thriving and forward-looking community responsive to the proposals of influential outsiders from whom the local elites hope to gain favors.
Through associations, the community can give the impression of its responsiveness and progressiveness; the community has its associations on stage, as it were, to put on a convincing performance before the audience of visiting officials. The performance itself is most important, not what happens after its conclusion and the departure of the audience. (Walker and Hanson, p. 67)

This case illustrates the importance of living in a community and of gaining a first-hand knowledge of its etic behavioral realities in order to distinguish between what people say they are doing and what they are actually doing. An investigator visiting Villalta for a short time might easily be impressed with the seeming responsiveness of its people to new ideas and its openness to change. While the community has changed, conclude Walker and Hanson, it is not necessarily for the better: "It has learned how to contrive performances and deceive outsiders" (p. 67).

The case of the unused clinic

During the 1970s, a series of community health centers was established by the Department of Health and Hospitals of a large northeastern city. These centers were located in poor neighborhoods and designed to provide health care for the local people. All but one of the centers was used to capacity. Anthropologist Delmos Jones (1976) was charged with the task of discovering why this particular facility was underused.

Jones proceeded on the assumption that the main reasons for the underutilization of the health center would be found not in the characteristics of the population it was designed to serve, but in certain characteristics of the center itself. Initial investigation showed that many people in the neighborhood did not know about the center's existence. Unlike the other centers, this one was located inside a hospital and could not be seen from the street. Moreover, among those who had heard about the center, few were aware of where it was or what it did. In addition, there were many people who had tried to use the center but had failed to do so. Probing further, Jones discovered that the neighborhood people had a negative image of the hospital in which the clinic was located. It had the reputation of being very "fancy" and not for poor people. This led to disbelief that somewhere inside the hospital there was a free clinic. Rumor had it that poor people were even turned away from the hospital's emergency room.

People who had persisted in trying to use the clinic reported that they couldn't find it. When they got to the hospital they couldn't find any signs telling them where to go. Even some of the hospital's receptionists didn't know where it was, or refused to say. Jones suspected the latter was the case because key members of the staff expressed displeasure at having a free clinic in their fancy hospital.

As at the other centers, this one had several neighborhood representatives. But these representatives had developed a defeatist attitude toward the client population and made little effort to contact people in the neighborhood. This apparently pleased the clinic's staff, who let it be known that they preferred to be underworked rather than overworked.

Jones set about correcting the situation. First, signs were placed in obvious spots to direct patients to the clinic. Second, receptionists were told where the clinic was. Third, leaflets were printed up and distributed throughout the neighborhood. Finally, new neighborhood representatives were hired who had a more positive attitude toward the population and the clinic. Attendance rose, but the story does not have a happy ending.

Although the new neighborhood representatives were initially enthusiastic, they began to perceive that the hospital staff continued to frown on having the clinic in the hospital, and they became increasingly hesitant to recommend the clinic to the neighborhood people.

Despite the fact that the reasons for the clinic's underuse seemed rather obvious, the hospital's administration refused to accept Jones's explanation. They preferred to continue to think that the problem lay with the attitudes of the neighborhood people. "I, the researcher," reports Jones, "became an advocate for my own research findings. . . . when policy makers don't listen, this could mean we are not telling them what they want to hear" (Jones, 1976, p. 227).

Advocacy as action anthropology

The fact that the implementation phase of a project is often controlled by administrators or politicians who will not accept the anthropologist's analysis or suggestions has led a number of applied anthropologists like Delmos Jones to adopt the role of advocate. Advocate anthropologists have fought to improve conditions in women's jails; lobbied in state legislatures for raising welfare allotments; submitted testimony before congressional committees in support of child health care programs; lobbied against the construction of dams and highways which would have an adverse effect on local communities; and engaged in many other consciousness-raising and political activities.

Some anthropologists hold the view that the only legitimate professional function of the applied anthropologist is to provide administrators, politicians, or lawyers with an objective analysis of a situation or organization, and that at most action should be limited to suggesting but not implementing a plan. In this way it is hoped that anthropology will be able to preserve its scientific standing, since it is clear that an all-out attempt to achieve a practical goal frequently involves rhetorical skills, cajolery, half-truths or outright deceptions, threats, and even violence.

Against this view, advocacy anthropologists insist that the objectivity of anthropology and the other social sciences is illusory and that failure to push for the implementation of a goal is in itself a form of advocacy. The objectivity is illusory, they argue, because political and personal biases control the commitment to study one situation rather than another (to study the poor rather than the wealthy, for example; see p. 295). And refraining from action is itself a form of action and therefore of advocacy because one's inaction assures that someone else's actions weigh more heavily in the final outcome. Anthropologists who do not use their skills and knowledge actively to bring about what they believe to be the solution to a problem simply make it easier for others with opposite beliefs to have their way. Such anthropologists are themselves part of the problem.

No consensus exists among anthropologists as to how to resolve these different views of the proper relationship between knowledge and the achievement of controversial practical goals. Perhaps the only resolution of this dilemma is the one that now exists: We must search our individual consciences and act accordingly.

Summary

Applied anthropology is concerned with research that has practical applications. Its core consists of research sponsored by organizations, public and private, with an interest in achieving practical goals. The role of the applied cultural anthropologist may consist merely in researching the possible means of achieving such goals; sometimes it includes drawing up plans and helping to implement them as well as evaluation of the results of implementation. Applied anthropologists involved in implementation are known as practitioners of action anthropology.

Beyond that core other forms of research may also be considered part of applied anthropology. Abstract theorizing often has important practical implications, as in the case of alternative theories about the causes of underdevelopment or urban poverty. Much research that is not sponsored by a particular organization with a definite goal in view may nonetheless be aimed at achieving such a goal, such as the independence of a colony or the development of a newly independent state.

Applied anthropology has three major distinctive contributions to make to the analysis and solution of urgent practical problems: (1) Exposure of ethnocentric biases. (2) A holistic viewpoint stressing the long term as well as the short term; the interconnectedness of the parts of sociocultural systems; and the whole of the system as well as its parts. (3) A commitment to distinguishing etic behavioral events from emic plans and ideologies. All too often the actual effects of an organization's plans and policies are sharply different from their actual everyday etic consequences.

The Cornell-Peru Vicos project illustrates applied anthropology functioning over the entire range of research, planning, implementation, and evaluation. This project substantially improved the standard of living of the serflike peasants who lived on Vicos *hacienda*. An important ingredient in this success was the use of the authoritarian powers of the new boss to introduce new forms of agriculture and other innovations. While successful in its own sphere, it is doubtful if Vicos provides a model for the development of the Peruvian highlands because of the hidden costs of the experts who guided the Vicosinos from day to day over a ten-year period.

The case of the not-so-green revolution illustrates the importance of a holistic perspective for development projects and the importance of the role of the applied anthropologist as critic rather than as change agent. Anthropologists have recurrently pointed out that high-yield miracle seeds benefit large landowners more than small poor farmers because the seeds require heavy inputs of water and chemicals. The cases of rice in Indonesia and wheat in Mexico point up the futility of seeking a purely technical solution to poverty and underdevelopment, since the effects of every technological innovation are modified by the total sociocultural context into which it is introduced.

The case of the Navajo migrants to Denver also illustrates the importance of placing a group's lack of economic success in the context of total life experience. Navajo drinking problems do not arise from a lack of motivation to succeed; they arise from the frustration of that motivation. This case also illustrates the importance of careful empirical research as a contribution of the applied anthropologist.

The studies of marijuana use in Jamaica and Costa Rica illustrate the importance of controlling for ethnocentric biases in research related to problems of health and welfare. Just as technological innovations must be seen in a definite sociocultural context, so too must the use of psychoactive drugs. The Jamaican and Costa Rican studies show that marijuana cannot be seen as a purely chemical-physiological problem. Its effects are different in different cultures. Unlike in the United States, marijuana is smoked in Jamaica and Costa Rica as a means of relieving the burden of work rather than as an escape from working.

The case of Truk's "weekend warriors" illustrates a similar point. A holistic and comparative view warns against the supposition that drunken, rowdy, and disruptive behavior necessarily means that a culture is breaking apart. It is at least arguable that this behavior is an affirmation of cultural vitality rather than a sign of its disintegration and hence that it should not be regarded as pathological behavior.

The case of Kuru illustrates the importance of knowing the cultural context in which diseases occur. Understanding the role of cannibalism in funerary rituals and the development of distinct dietary patterns among men and women provided the key to solving the disease's mysterious epidemiology.

The last two cases emphasize the discontinuity between the emics of bureaucratic plans and the etics of everyday behavior. In Villalta, a town in the Dominican Republic, the local elite enthusiastically sets up one association after another. Members typically meet for one session and then let the association lapse into limbo. From the ground-up, etic viewpoint of the applied anthropologist, this behavior becomes intelligible as an effort on the part of the local elite to curry favor with state officials. A similar discontinuity between plan and behavior characterizes the case of the underused clinic. The administrators in charge of the clinic program either do not recognize or will not admit the discrepancy between their stated plans and their own behavior. In such a situation, the administrators are the chief obstacle to implementation. This means that anthropologists who are committed to implementation—to action anthropology—must often assume an advocate role. No agreement exists as to whether professional anthropologists can assume an advocacy role as professionals without damaging the claim that anthropology is an objective, scientific discipline.

14

The Anthropology of the USA

This chapter attempts to provide a holistic account of contemporary United States culture. It draws upon the findings of anthropologists as well as experts in many different disciplines. It attempts to apply the distinction between emic and etic data to the description of U.S. society. It emphasizes the relationships among infrastructure, structure, and superstructure with respect to recent topics of concern, such as alienation from work, poverty, ethnic and race relations, crime, welfare, changing family structure, women's liberation, gay liberation, and religious cults and movements.

Mode of production

The USA can be characterized by its mode of production and its political economy. Its mode of production is industrialism. Its political economy is a blend of statism and oligopoly capitalism. Let us clarify these concepts. An industrial society is a society that relies on the *detailed division of labor* in combination with power-driven machinery to achieve mass production of goods and services. Detailed division of labor refers to the separation of production tasks into many tiny steps carried out by different workers.

The USA is indeed the top-ranking industrial manufacturing country in the world. Nonetheless, two-thirds of its work force is no longer engaged in manufacturing. Almost two-thirds of the U.S. labor force (not counting those who are engaged solely in unpaid household work) produce information and services rather than tangible objects. Most employed adult Americans work in offices, stores, restaurants, schools, clinics, and moving vehicles rather than factory assembly lines. They wait on customers, repair broken machines, keep accounts, write letters, transfer funds, and provide grooming, schooling, training, and information, counseling and therapy to students, clients, customers, and patients (Porat, 1979).

Farming, which once accounted for the vast majority of American workers, now occupies only 3 percent of the work force. With the industrialization and automation of agriculture, large numbers of workers were displaced. Migration from farm to city provided much of the labor supply for the growth of the manufacturing sector of the economy. But manufacturing peaked as an employer of labor in 1950. With the automation of factories, large numbers of workers were displaced and entered the service and information industries. Also, large numbers of service and information workers were recruited from the ranks of married housewives, with consequences to be discussed below.

The rise of the service and information sectors has led to the characterization of the USA as a "post-industrial society" (Bell, 1973). It would seem more appropriate, however, to call the USA a hyperindustrial[1] society rather than a postindustrial society, since the shift to service and information processing has merely resulted in extending the detailed division of labor and the use of mass-production machines into additional domains of production.

The modern office has come to resemble the factory and the distinction between blue-collar and white-collar workers has become increasingly blurred (Fig. 14.1). In the office, as in the factory, the detailed division of labor leads to the separation of mental from physical operations and of management from labor. Separate workers open mail, date and route orders, clear credit, check inventory, type invoices, calculate discounts and shipping fees, and dispatch items for shipment: *Just as in manufacturing processes . . . the work of the office is analyzed and parcelled out among a great many detail workers, who now lose all comprehension of the process as a whole and the policies which underlie it. The special privilege of the clerk of old, that of being witness to the operation of the enterprise as a whole . . . disappears. Each of the activities requiring intervention of policy or contact beyond the department or section becomes the province of a higher functionary.* (*Braverman, 1974, p. 314*)

State socialism

Although Americans think of the USA as being a capitalist country, its economy is actually best characterized as a mixture of socialist-like state enterprises and capitalist enterprises. Some 18 million people are directly employed by federal, state, and local govern-

[1] Hyper- means extra strong.

14.1 INFORMATION FACTORY
Accounting department of a large insurance company. Numbers and words instead of nuts and bolts but it's still an assembly line. Note the sex of workers. [Philip Jon Bailey]

ments. Another 35 million are largely dependent on government social security payments. Other forms of state, local, and federal pensions support an additional 2.5 million people. Welfare in the form of aid to dependent children, home relief, and aid to the handicapped supports about 14 million people. There are 2 million people in the armed forces. Then there are an estimated 6 million people whose jobs in private industry depend on government purchases of military equipment, construction contracts, government "bailout" loans to companies on the verge of bankruptcy, and assorted forms of government subsidies. Adding the dependents of these workers raises the total in this category to at least 10 million. By conservative estimate, therefore, over 80 million U.S. citizens are dependent on the redistribution of tax money rather than a share of profits made as a result of capitalist free enterprize. It can be said with a grain of truth that the USA is the third largest "socialist" state in the world after China and the Soviet Union.

Oligopoly capitalism

The essence of capitalist enterprise is the freedom to buy and sell in competitive price-making markets. Price-making markets exist where there are enough buyers and sellers so that buyers can compete with buyers, buyers can compete with sellers, and sellers can compete with sellers for the prices that best suit their respective interests. It has long been recognized that in order to preserve the free enterprise system, limitations must be placed on the ability of small groups of powerful buyers or sellers to gain control over a market to the extent that the prices they offer effectively determine the price that must be paid by anyone who wants a particular product or service. Early in this century, the U.S. Congress passed laws against the formation of monopolies and actively pursued the breakup of companies which then dominated the railroad, meat-packing, and petroleum industries. The antimonopoly laws stopped short, however, of prohibiting the formation of semimonopolies or *oligopolies*—that is, companies that control not all, but a major share of the market for a particular product.

The trend toward oligopoly was already well advanced in the earlier part of this century. But after the end of World War II, the pace of acquisitions and expansions quickened. As a result, by 1975 the 200 largest manufacturing companies had a greater share of all manufacturing, sales, employment, and assets than the largest 500 had in 1955. Today the 50 largest U.S. manufacturing corporations own 42 percent of all assets used in manufacturing, while the top 500 own 72 percent of these assets. Four or fewer companies dominate 99 percent of the domestic production of cars, 92 percent of flat glass, 90 percent of cereal breakfast foods, 90 percent of turbines and turbine engines, 90 percent of electric lamps, 85 percent of household refrigerators and freezers, 84 percent of cigarettes, 83 percent of television picture tubes, 79 percent of aluminum production, and 73 percent of tires and inner tubes (Galbraith, 1978; *The New York Times*, 28 August 1980).

Moreover, not only have fewer companies come to dominate more of the market for a particular product, but through mergers and acquisitions, an increasing share of all manufacturing is carried out by oligopolistic conglomerates that produce a variety of product lines ranging from tomatoes to oil, from green peas to luggage, and from aluminum to cigarettes. Many conglomerates have names few Americans have ever heard of. For example, Easy-Off Oven Cleaner, Brach's Milk Chocolate, Black Flag Ant Killer, Woolite, Anacin, and Chef Boy-Ar-Dee are well-known brand names. But not many consumers have heard of the American Home Products Corporation of 685 Third Avenue, New York City, which is the name of the conglomerate that manufactures all these items.

It is true that despite the growth of oligopoly, there remain millions of small-scale owner-operated companies in the USA. Many of these, however, are franchise operations in service and retail trades and in the gasoline and fast-food industries. Their policies, prices, and products are controlled by conglomerate parent companies. (Over half of the 4.4 million businesses that have payrolls are retail stores and service companies; U.S. Department of Commerce, 1977).

Industrial bureaucracy and alienation

The growth of government and oligopolistic corporations and the spread of industrialism to the information and service occupations has had far-reaching consequences for the quality of life and the orientation of personality in the USA since World War II. The majority of Americans now work for large-scale organizations governed by bureaucratic rules.

These organizations do not reward individual initiative or free enterprise so much as they reward the willingness of workers to perform standardized routine tasks. This has led to the appearance of what Karl Marx called "alienation" not only on the factory assembly line, but in offices, stores, hospitals, and shops. Workers in large bureaucratized enterprises, government or private, tend to become bored with their tasks, hostile to management, indifferent to the quality of their product, and disinterested in the welfare of the ultimate consumers of the goods and the services they help to produce.

The recent trend toward the industrialization of the information and service sector has intensified the problem of alienation by routinizing and bureaucratizing jobs that previously allowed for a considerable amount of individual style and self-expression. For example, as the fast-food chains take over the restaurant business, they do away with the need for qualified cooks and chefs, personalized menus, knowledgeable waiters, waitresses, and stewards. They use "equipment and products designed to be operated (or sold) by minimally trained, unskilled persons, of whom high turnover rates are expected," whose jobs consist of sorting out boxed uniform portions of food prepared and frozen off-premises (Job, 1980, p. 41).

Although some observers contend that the rapidly unfolding automation of the service and information sector will result in the elimination of many dull and alienating jobs, others fear that the "electronic office" will be a source of increased worker alienation (Fig. 14.2). There are indications that white-collar automation has already led to an increase in the detailed division of labor, to the elimination of many interesting and versatile secretarial positions, and to a further downgrading of skills and wages. A study of five large firms by sociologists Evelyn Glenn and Roslyn Feldberg (1977) concluded that automated clerical jobs were more mechanical and nar-

14.2 THE ELECTRONIC COCKPIT
**How will the spread of electronic data
processing affect the quality of office work
and the number of information and service
jobs in the future? [Herwig, Stock, Boston]**

row, and that "the main avenues for clerical
workers were either horizontal or downward." Karen Nussbaum (1980) of the National Association of Office Workers writes:
*Office automation as it is being introduced
today requires that a great many people te-
diously enter the data, push the right buttons,
fill out forms "for the computer" with perfect
accuracy, and feed the forms to the computer.
Each worker must discipline herself to the system imposed by the machine. Most often,
clericals work with computer terminals which
have been strictly programmed to perform only
one task. (p. 3)*

The new office machines themselves super-
vise and discipline their operators, virtually
eliminating contact and conversation with
other workers except those who perform similar functions nearby.

For typists, telephone operators, cashiers,
stock clerks, and mail sorters, automation
means progressively less to know and less to
think. By using optical scanning machines,
file clerks can dispense with knowing the sequence of the alphabet. Supermarket cashiers
no longer have to know how to add or sub-
tract. Airline reservationists no longer need to
know anything about timetables. Bank tell-
ers, in Harry Braverman's words (1974, p.
340), have become "mere check out clerks at a
money supermarket."

It seems likely that the alienation of U.S.
workers and of management itself is an im-

Industrial bureaucracy and alienation   **291**

portant cause of the decline in the quality of U.S. goods and services which became a focus of national concern in the 1980s.

Class stratification

Like all state-organized societies, the USA is a stratified society, and has a complex system of classes, minorities, and other hierarchical groups. Emic versions of U.S. stratification hierarchies differ from one class to another and bear little resemblance to etic accounts. James West (1945), who studied class relations in a small Midwestern community he called Plainville, concluded that there were different class hierarchies, depending on whether one took the viewpoint of the "upper crust," "good religious people," "non-church people," "all us good honest working people," Methodists, Baptists, and so on. At the bottom of all these hierarchies there was a category called "people who live like animals."

Lloyd Warner (1949) attempted to study the class structure of Yankee City (pseudonym for Newburyport, Massachusetts) by classifying people according to occupation, source of income, house type, and dwelling area. Warner's picture of Yankee City's classes (Fig. 14.3) represents a mixture of emic and etic criteria.

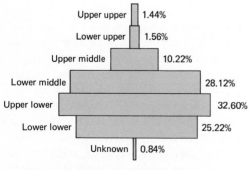

14.3 CLASS HIERARCHY—YANKEE CITY
[Adapted from Warner et al., 1949, p. 42]

There is no doubt that the USA is a highly stratified society. In terms of income, the poorest 5 percent of U.S. families account for only 0.5 percent of aggregate family income, while the wealthiest 5 percent account for 15.7 percent; the poorest 20 percent account for only 5.2 percent of aggregate family income while the highest 20 percent account for 41.6 percent (U.S. Department of Commerce, 1979, p. 31).

Is there a ruling class in the USA?

From both a practical and a theoretical point of view, the most important question that can be asked about class in the USA is whether or not there is a ruling class. Paradoxically, this is a subject about which relatively little is known.

The existence of a ruling class in the USA seems to be negated by the ability of the people as a whole to vote political power-holders in or out of office by secret ballot. Yet the fact that less than half of the voting-age population votes in presidential elections[2] suggests that the majority of citizens distrusts the candidates' promises or doubts that one candidate can do anything more than any other to make life significantly better (Hadley, 1978; Ladd, 1978). Moreover, it is well known that the actual selection of political candidates and the financing and conduct of election campaigns are controlled through special interest groups and political action committees rather than by the "people." Small coalitions of powerful individuals working through lobbyists, law firms, legislatures, the courts, executive and administra-

[2] In the 1980 presidential election, 49.5 percent of the voting-age population voted. This means that President Reagan, who received 50.7 percent of the popular vote, was actually elected by only 27.4 percent of the voting-age population (Election Research Center).

tive agencies, and the mass media can decisively influence the course of elections and of national affairs. The great bulk of the decision-making process consists of responses to pressures exerted by special interest groups (Aron, 1966; Dahl, 1961; Domhoff, 1970; Lundberg, 1968). In the campaigns for election to Congress, the candidate who spends the most money usually wins. In 1978, for example, the candidates who spent more than their rivals won 87 percent of the time in the House of Representatives and 85 percent of the time in the Senate (*The New York Times*, 1979).

Those who reject the notion that there is a ruling class in the United States base their claim on the multiplicity of special interest groups. They argue that power in the United States is dispersed among so many different contending blocs, lobbies, associations, clubs, industries, regions, income groups, ethnic groups, states, cities, age groups, legislatures, courts, and unions that no coalition powerful enough to dominate all the others can form. In the terminology of the economist John Kenneth Galbraith (1958, 1967), there is no ruling class; there is only "countervailing" power (Roach et al., 1969). But the crucial question is this: Is there a category of people who share a common set of underlying interests in the perpetuation of the status quo and who by virtue of their extreme wealth are able to set limits to the kinds of laws and executive policies that are enacted and followed out? The evidence for the existence of such a category of people consists largely of studies of the degree of concentration of wealth in giant corporations and wealthy families. This kind of data alone cannot prove the existence of a ruling class, since there remains the problem of linking the boards of directors of these powerful corporations and leaders of wealthy families with decisions on crucial matters such as the rate of inflation, unemployment, national health service, energy policy, tax structure, resource depletion, pollution, military spending, urban blight, and so forth. Nonetheless, as we will see in the next section, the extraordinary concentration of wealth and economic power in the USA strongly suggests that such linkages do exist (Roberts and Brintnall, 1982, p. 259).

The concentration of wealth

In a study of the concentration of wealth based on estate inheritance taxes filed with the Internal Revenue Service (Smith, Franklin, and Wion, 1973), it was found that the less than 5 percent of individual adults who have a net worth of $60,000 or more possess 35.6 percent of the nation's wealth. Average wealth per individual was $200,000. In contrast, 53 percent of the adult population would have been worth less than $3,000 if they sold all their possessions and paid all their debts:

Four percent of the population owned over a quarter of the nation's real estate, three-fifths of all privately held corporate stock, four-fifths of the state and local bonds, two-fifths of the business assets (excluding business real estate), a third of the cash and virtually all of the notes, mortgages and foreign and corporate bonds. After subtracting their debts, they were worth over a trillion dollars, enough to have purchased the entire national output of the United States plus the combined output of Switzerland, Denmark, Norway and Sweden in 1969. (J. Smith, 1973, p. 44)

The same study also showed that 1 percent of the richest adults—about 550,000 individuals—owned 21.2 percent of all the wealth, and that there were about 2,500 individuals who possessed more than $10 million, with an average of almost $20 million per head! Although these figures reveal more about class in the United States than do income studies, they still leave the structural significance of the concentration of wealth in doubt because they do not show the extent to which the top 1 percent of wealthy individuals are actually members of the same households, families, or personal networks. Despite the unprecedented decline in the value of stocks and bonds during the 1970s (of which the super-rich held a disproportionate share), the top 1 percent of wealth holders still held 19.5 percent of all personal wealth in 1975 (J. Smith, 1981).

Where the holdings of very rich families are identified as a unit, the degree of concentration of wealth can be quite astonishing. For example, the value of assets held by descendants of Thomas Mellon exceeds $5 billion. Although this wealth is held in separate trusts and accounts of about 50 living descendants (giving them an average of $100 million a head), a large block of it is managed by a single group of investment companies located in a skyscraper in Pittsburgh (Hersh, 1978; Koskoff, 1978). Mellon family interests control 23 percent of Mellon National Corporation, which controls 15 percent of the Gulf Oil Corporation, the tenth largest company in the world. This does not mean that all the Mellons think alike or conspire to influence corporate or public decisions as a unit. It does mean, however, that active key members of the family can forestall decisions adverse to their interests in the affairs of companies like Gulf Oil, Alcoa Alminum, and the Mellon National Bank.

The question of who controls the corporations in the United States is difficult to answer. The average individual stockholder owns only trivial amounts of stock compared with the top managers and the major stockholders. Fewer than 90,000 individuals—0.3 percent of all stockholders—own over 25 percent of all the stock in private hands. Fewer than 23,000 individuals—0.1 percent—own all the tax-free state and municipal bonds in private hands. The same top 1 percent of wealthy individuals own 40 percent of all treasury bills, notes, and mortgages. But about half of stocks and bonds are no longer owned by individuals; they are owned by so-called institutional investors who administer pension funds, trust funds, and insurance companies. It is the corporations, families, and people who control these institutional investors who have the greatest economic power.

According to a study carried out on voting rights in major corporations by the U.S. Senate Committee on Governmental Affairs (1978), power to vote stock in 122 of the largest corporations in America was concentrated in 21 institutional investors. These 122 corporations had a market value of about $500 billion, and they had 2259 subsidiaries and affiliates comprising the largest industrial, financial, transportation, insurance, utility, and retail firms in the country. The 21 top institutional investors consist mostly of banks and insurance companies such as Morgan Guaranty, Citicorp, Prudential Insurance, Bankamerica, Manufacturers Hanover, Bankers Trust, Equitable Life, and Chase Manhattan. Each of these banks is not only one of the five largest stockvoters in anywhere from 8 to 56 of the largest corporations, but as a group they are one another's largest stockvoters. Morgan Guaranty, which is the top stockvoter in 27 of the largest corporations, is also the top stockvoter in Citicorp, Manufacturers Hanover, Chemical New York, Bankers Trust, and Bankamerica. But the controllers and the controlled are really one and the same, because the largest institutional stockvoters in Morgan Guaranty are none other than Citicorp, Chase Manhattan, Manufacturers Hanover, and Bankers Trust (U.S. Senate Committee on Governmental Affairs, 1978, p. 3).

It is entirely possible, therefore, that a small group of individuals and families may in fact exert a decisive influence over the policies of this small but immensely powerful group of corporations. Some of the individuals and families involved are well known. Besides the Mellons, they include Rockefellers, Du Ponts, Fords, Hunts, Pews, and Gettys (Fig. 14.4). But it is a testament to the ability

14.4 MEMBERS OF THE RULING CLASS?
David Rockefeller (top, left). **Nelson Bunker
Hunt** (top, middle), **Paul Mellon** (top, right).
[UPI—left; Wide World—middle, right]

of the super-rich to live in a world apart that
the names of many other powerful families
are unknown to the general public. Anthropologists, with their many studies of people in
poverty, have been remiss in not studying the
corresponding patterns of thoughts and actions among the super-rich (Nader, 1972).

Poverty and upward mobility in the USA

Modern industrial democracies attribute
great importance to the achievement of mobility from the subordinate to the superordinate classes. In the United States, it was traditionally held that by diligent effort poor
people could work their way up from poverty
to riches within a lifetime. It is clear, however, that only a tiny fraction of the population can hope to move into the ruling class.
Moreover, the latecomer's chance for success
is always smaller than that of those who com-
peted for success in earlier times. The roster
of billionaires in the United States consists
overwhelmingly of people who inherited substantial wealth from their parents.

At the lower levels, the U.S. stratification
system is fairly open—but not as open as was
traditionally believed. The main factor that
determines a person's chances of upward mobility is the level at which one starts: "There
is much upward mobility in the United
States, but most of it involves very short social distances" (Blau and Duncan, 1967, p.
420).

According to official government standards,
a nonfarm family of four whose income was
$8,414 or less in 1980 was living in poverty.
By these criteria, 30 million Americans were
impoverished in 1980 (*The New York Times*, 21
August 1981). The adequacy of the government's definition of poverty remains in doubt,
however. At least one-third of a low-income
family's budget must be spent on food in
order to maintain minimum nutritional standards. Families of four with 1980 incomes
twice as high as the poverty cutoff (i.e.,
$17,000) were still too poor to enjoy a com-
fortable standard of living. The costs of food,
housing, education, transportation, and medical attention rose more rapidly than income,
and they had to contend with the declining
quality of goods, services, utilities, roads,

streets, public buildings, parks, and public transportation (Harrington, 1980).

What is the reason for the persistence of a large poverty class in a country whose aggregate wealth is greater than any other? Many people seek to understand this paradox by adopting Oscar Lewis's notion that the poor in the USA are victims of their own mental and behavioral shortcomings. But as we have seen (p. 174), the values said to be distinctive of the urban poor are actually shared by the middle class. For example, being suspicious of government, politicians, and organized religions is not an exclusive poverty class trait; nor is the tendency to spend above one's means. There is little evidence that the middle class as a whole lives within its income more effectively than poor people do. The only certainty is that when the poor mismanage their incomes, the consequences are much more serious. If the male head of a poor family yields to the temptation to buy nonessential items, his children may go hungry or his wife may be deprived of medical attention. But these consequences result from being poor, not from any demonstrable difference in the capacity to defer gratification.

The stereotype of the improvident poor masks an implicit belief that the impoverished segments of society ought to be more thrifty and more patient than the members of the middle class. Sometimes that belief is actually made explicit, as in George Gilder's book *Wealth and Poverty:*
The first principle is that in order to move up, the poor must not only work, they must work harder than the classes above them. (1981, p. 256)

Others maintain that it is conscience-saving to be able to attribute poverty to values for which the poor themselves can be held responsible (Piven and Cloward, 1971). According to Anthony Leeds (1970, p. 246), the poor in the USA are not victims of their own values; they are the victims

of certain kinds of labor markets which are structured by the condition of national technology, available capital resources, enterprise location, training institutions, relations to foreign and internal markets, balance-of-trade relations, and the nature of the profit system of capitalist societies. . . . These are not independent [characteristics] of some suppressed culture [of poverty] but characteristics or indices of certain kinds of total economic systems. (Leeds, 1970, p. 246)

What this boils down to is that due to factors beyond their control, even when poor try harder than the people above them, most of them are doomed to remain poor.

Streetcorner men, Washington, D.C.

The view that America's poor refuse to work hard and to save because of a culture of poverty fails to take into account the types of work and opportunities that are open to them. In his book *Tally's Corner* (1967), Elliot Liebow, an ethnographer who has studied the black streetcorner men of Washington, D.C., describes the conditions shaping the work patterns of the unskilled black male. The streetcorner men are full of contempt for the menial work they must perform, but this is not a result of any special tradition they acquire from the culture of poverty. Historically, the dregs of the job market in the United States have been left for blacks and other minorities—jobs whose conditions and prospects are the mark of failure, that are demeaned and ridiculed by the rest of the labor force and that do not pay enough for a man to get married and have a family; jobs that are dull—as in dishwashing or floor polishing; dirty—as in garbage collecting and washroom attending; or backbreaking—as in truck loading or furniture moving (Fig. 14.5).

The duller, dirtier, and more exhausting the work, the less likely that extra diligence and

14.5 BOTTOM OF THE LADDER
**Blacks cleaning out a sewer in a Washington,
D.C., suburb.** [Johnson, DeWys]

effort will be rewarded by anything but more of the same. There is no "track" leading from the night maid who cleans the executive's office to vice-president; from the dishwasher to the restaurant owner; from the unskilled, un-apprenticed construction worker to journeyman electrician or bricklayer. These jobs are dead ends from the beginning. As Liebow points out, no one is more explicit in expressing the worthlessness of the job than the boss who pays for it. The boss pays less than what is required to support a family. The rest of society, contradicting its professed values concerning the dignity of labor, also holds the job of dishwasher or janitor in low esteem.

So does the streetcorner man. He cannot do otherwise. He cannot draw from a job those social values which other people do not put into it. (Liebow, 1967, p. 59)

According to Liebow, an additional mark of the degradation involved in these jobs is that wages for menial work in hotels, restaurants, hospitals, office and apartment buildings take into account the likelihood that the workers will steal food, clothing, or other items in order to bring their take-home pay above subsistence. The employer then sets the wages so low that stealing must take place. Although implicitly acknowledging the need for theft, the employer nonetheless tries to prevent it and will call the police if someone is caught stealing.

Liebow tells the story of Richard, a black man in his twenties who had tried to support his family by extra jobs ranging from shoveling snow to picking peas and who had won the reputation of being one of the hardest-working men on the street. "I figure you got to get out there and try. You got to try before you can get anything," said Richard. But after five years of trying, Richard pointed to a shabby bed, a sofa, a couple of chairs, and a television set, and gave up:

I've been scuffling for five years from morning till night. And my children still don't have anything, my wife don't have anything, and I don't have anything. (1967, p. 67)

Liebow sums up the etic conditions regulating the work pattern of the streetcorner men as follows:

A man's chances for working regularly are good only if he is willing to work for less than he can live on, and sometimes not even then. On some jobs, the wage rate is deceptively higher than on others, but the higher the wage rate, the more difficult it is to get the job, and the less the job security. Higher paying construction work tends to be seasonal and, during the season, the amount of work available is highly sensitive to business and weather conditions and to the changing requirements of individual projects. Moreover, high-paying construction jobs are frequently beyond the physical capacity of some of the men, and some of the low-paying jobs are scaled down even lower in accordance with . . . the assumption that the man will steal part of his wages on the job. (pp. 50–52)

Ethnic chauvinism versus class consciousness

The intensity and clarity of racial and ethnic struggles in the USA present a counterpoint to the generally unconscious and confused nature of class relations. Racial and ethnic minorities and majorities rather than classes are the stratified groups that manifest a sense of their own identity, consciousness of a common destiny, and collective purpose. These phenomena are not unrelated. The persecution, segregation, and exploitation of minority enclaves by racial and ethnic majorities, and the activism of minorities on their own behalf, can be viewed as forms of political and economic struggle that preserve the overall pattern of class stratification. Instead of organizing to improve everyone's schools, neighborhoods, jobs, and health services, militant minorities seek to achieve their own ad-

vancement at one another's expense (Fig. 14.6). Ethnic chauvinism thus pits "have-nots" against "have-littles," and thereby allows the "haves" to maintain their wealth and power (see Bottomore, 1966; Perlo, 1976).

Once again the emic-etic distinction is vital to the comprehension of this situation. Ethnic pluralism in the United States has not arisen as the result of conscious, conspiratorial effort. The formation of ethnic and racial consciousness took precedence over the formation of class consciousness because of the relatively high rate of upward mobility enjoyed by white immigrants. Class consciousness did not develop because in the short run it was disadvantageous for the white working class, with its relatively high mobility, to

---

14.6 MINORITY AGAINST MINORITY
Victims of prejudice are not necessarily free of prejudice. Here black youths warn Puerto Ricans to stay out of their club's territory. [UPI]

make an alliance with the black working class. The blacks were abandoned (and actively persecuted) by working-class whites; they were left behind to suffer the worst effects of low wages, unemployment, and exploitation because by doing so large numbers of whites increased their own chances of rising to middle-class status. However, it can be argued that working-class whites have had to pay an enormous penalty for failing to unite with the black poverty and working classes. In her study of the working-class neighborhood of Greenpoint-Williamsburg in Brooklyn, N.Y., Ida Susser (1982, p. 208) found that racial divisions debilitated collective action and allowed elected officials and commercial developers a free hand that benefited middle- and upper-class whites. "So long as racial issues kept white voters loyal, elected officials could ignore the needs of a poor white working-class constituency."

One of the reasons for the limited success of the black power movement is that it provoked a reactive increase in the solidary sentiments and activities of the white cultural, racial, and ethnic groups in the United States. In response to real or imagined threats to their schools, neighborhoods, and jobs, "white ethnics"—people of Italian, Polish, Irish, and Jewish descent—fought back against black power. They mounted antibusing campaigns and created new private and public school systems based on segregated suburban residence patterns (Stein and Hill, 1977). As Orlando Patterson (1977) suggests, the time may come for both black and white minorities to rethink the consequences of "ethnic chauvinism."

Values and the matrifocal family: the Flats

One of the explanations for poverty in the urban ghettos[3] focuses attention on the problem of so-called fatherless, or *matrifocal*, families (see p. 91). In 1965, with the release of a report by Daniel P. Moynihan, then U.S. assistant secretary of labor, matrifocality received official recognition as the prime cause of the perpetuation of poverty among blacks in the United States. According to Moynihan, black youths are not properly motivated to take jobs that are actually available because of the absence of a male father figure in their family. They are reared in households where only the women are regularly employed. Adult males drift in and out of these households, and thus black youths grow up without the aid and inspiration of a stable male figure holding a steady job and providing comfort and security for wife and children. Moynihan proposed that matrifocality not only was a cause of poverty, but of crime and drug addiction as well.

Explanations of poverty that appeal to the enculturation experience within the matrifocal household must be rejected, because the phenomenon of matrifocality is itself a response to poverty. The main structural features of matrifocality are as follows: The domestic unit consists of a mother and her children by several different men. Some of the woman's coresident adult daughters may also have children. The fathers provide only temporary and partial support. Men who move in and out of the domestic unit are etically "married" to the mothers—they act out all the typical husband-father roles. Yet emically the relationship is distinguished from "true marriage," and the children are legally regarded as "illegitimate" (Gonzalez, 1970).

Like all domestic arrangements, the matrifocal family represents an adjustment to certain conditions that are beyond the control of its members. The conditions in question are these: (1) Both men and women lack access to strategic resources; that is, they own no sig-

[3] The most common explanation for black poverty continues to be racial inferiority. This explanation is discussed in the appendix, p. 326.

nificant property; (2) wage labor is available to both men and women; (3) women earn as much as or more than men; and (4) a man's wages are insufficient to provide subsistence for a dependent wife and children.

In the USA the official welfare policies of the government add to the tendency to form matrifocal families. Households that seek welfare support cannot contain able-bodied "fathers." Mothers whose husbands or children's fathers do not earn enough money to support the household can claim Aid to Families with Dependent Children (AFDC) welfare allotments, provided the fathers are not co-resident with their children. One of the reasons this expedient is built into the national and state welfare laws is that it is cheaper for the government to provide such payments than to establish a high-quality system of child day-care centers that would free mothers to go to work. Since fathers cannot stay home with their children and claim AFDC allotments, the law confers upon women an extra economic value that makes it inevitable that they will become the center of domestic organization as long as the men cannot earn enough to make the AFCD allotments unnecessary. Since it is the woman who is favored for AFDC payments, it is she who gets the lease in public housing projects and who controls (but does not own) the family's dwelling space (Fig. 14.7).

In her study of the Flats, a black ghetto in a midwestern city, Carol Stack (1974) provides an account of the strategies that poverty-level families follow in attempting to maximize

14.7 *MOTHER-CENTERED FAMILY*
Roxbury, Massachusetts [Herwig, Stock, Boston]

CHAPTER 14
The anthropology of the USA

their security and well-being in the face of the AFDC laws and the inadequate wages of the unskilled male. Nuclear families on the middle-class model do not exist in the Flats because the material conditions necessary for such families do not exist. Instead, the people of the Flats are organized into large female-centered networks of kinfolk and neighbors. The members of these networks engage in reciprocal economic exchanges, take care of one another's children, provide emergency shelter, and help one another in many ways not characteristic of middle-class domestic groups.

In the Flats the most important single factor that affects interpersonal relationships between men and women is unemployment, and the difficulty that men have in finding secure jobs.
Losing a job, or being unemployed month after month, debilitates one's self-importance and independence, and for men, necessitates that they sacrifice their role in the economic support of their families. Then they become unable to assume the masculine role as defined by American society. (Stack, 1974, p. 112)

Ironically, as Stack points out:
Attempts by those on welfare to formulate nuclear families are efficiently discouraged by welfare policy. In fact, welfare policy encourages the maintenance of non-coresidential cooperative domestic networks. (p. 127)

A woman can be cut off from welfare as soon as her husband gets out of the army or comes home from prison, or if she gets married. Thus, "Women come to realize that welfare benefits and ties with kin networks provide greater security for them and their children" (Stack, 1974, p. 113).

The crime connection

The USA has one of the highest rates of violent crime found among industrial nations. More than a fifth of the inhabitants of America's largest cities feel "very unsafe" when they have to go out at night in their own neighborhoods. Women and old people have the greatest fear. Over half of all U.S. women say that they are afraid to go out alone after dark. Senior citizens are afraid to leave their apartments during the day. People also feel insecure indoors: one-third of all U.S. households contain firearms purchased for protection against intruders (U.S. National Criminal Justice Information and Statistics Service, 1978). Crime victimization surveys indicate that annually there are over 4 million victims of assaults, a million victims of personal robberies (not including victims robbed in commercial establishments), 145,000 victims of rapes or attempted rape, and 150,000 victims of purse snatchings. According to the FBI's annual *Uniform Crime Report*, there are about 20,000 homicides per year.

There are proportionately 5 times more homicides, 10 times more rapes, and 17 times more robberies in the United States than in Japan; and there are proportionately 7 times more homicides, 12 times more rapes, and 8 times more robberies in the United States than in Great Britain. London and Tokyo have far less violent crime than less populous American cities such as Chicago, Philadelphia, or St. Louis. In 1979 there were 279 times as many robberies, 14 times as many rapes, and 12 times as many murders in New York City as in Tokyo (Ross and Benson, 1979).

One reason for the higher rate of violent crime in the USA is that U.S. citizens own far more pistols and rifles per capita than the Japanese or British. The right to "bear arms" is guaranteed by the U.S. Constitution. But the failure to pass stricter gun control laws itself reflects, in part at least, the pervasive, realistic fear of being robbed or attacked and the consequent desire to defend person and property. Hence, the cause of the high incidence of violent crimes must be sought at deeper levels of U.S. culture.

Much evidence links the unusually high rate of crime in the USA to the long-term, grinding poverty and economic hopelessness of America's inner-city minorities, especially of blacks and Hispanics. Although suburban crime is also on the rise, the principal locus of violent crime remains the inner cities. The FBI's *Uniform Crime Report* shows that blacks, who constitute 11 percent of the population, account for about 43 percent of all criminal offenders arrested for violent crimes. In two crucial categories of such crimes—homicides and robberies—black offenders actually outnumber whites on a nationwide basis, rural and urban areas included. But the disproportion is much larger in the cities where the incidence of violent crime is greatest (Hindelang, 1978).

One should note, however, that proportionately blacks themselves suffer more from violent crimes than do whites. Poor blacks are 25 times more likely than wealthy whites to be a victim of a robbery resulting in injury, and the ratio of black homicide victims to white homicide victims is 8 to 1. In fact, homicide is the ranking killer of black males between 15 and 24 years of age. More black males die from homicide than from motor vehicle accidents, diabetes, emphysema, or pneumonia. Two out of five black male children born in an American city in 1980 will not reach age 25.

The basic reason for all this crime is long-term chronic unemployment and poverty. During and after World War II, U.S. blacks migrated in unprecedented numbers from farms to cities in search of factory jobs just at the time when the economy was in rapid transition from goods production to service and information production. Today over half of America's blacks live in major cities, and over half of these—about 7.5 million people—live in the dirtiest and most dilapidated inner cores of these cities. During the 1970s in the large cities, while the number of central-city whites living in poverty declined by 5 percent, the number of central-city blacks living in poverty increased by 21 percent. In 1980 the median family income of whites was $21,900; that of blacks was $12,600 (*The New York Times*, 21 August 1981). The black unemployment rate was 16 percent as compared with 6.1 percent for whites (*Time*, 21 September 1981). But these figures include only people who were actively looking for work, or those who had part-time jobs and wanted full-time jobs.

Teenagers, both black and white, commit a disproportionate share of violent crimes. Ronald H. Brown of the National Urban League (1978) calculates that over half of all black teenagers are unemployed; and in ghettos like Harlem in New York City, the unemployment rate among young black youth may be as high as 86 percent (Fig. 14.8).

There is a body of scholarly opinion, which claims that poverty in general has little to do with the high rate of criminal violence in the United States and therefore that black unemployment and poverty are not sufficient in themselves to account for the high rates of U.S. crime. If one simply compares crime rates by states or cities, those with low per capita incomes do not necessarily have high rates of criminal violence. But the poverty of the black ghetto is different from the poverty of rural whites or of an earlier generation of urban ethnics. Unlike the rural poor, inner-city blacks have the opportunity as well as the motive to commit violent crimes. The city is an ideal setting for finding and surprising victims and successfully eluding the police. Most important, unlike the European immigrants of previous generations, with the passage of time blacks have become more and not less concentrated inside their ghettos (Fig. 14.9). Under these conditions, the benefits of criminal behavior outweigh the risks of getting caught and being sent to jail. John Conyers, himself a member of the black congressional caucus, writes:

When survival is at stake, it should not be surprising that criminal activity begins to resemble an opportunity rather than a cost, work rather than deviance, and a possibly

14.8 YOUTH ON A STOOP
The alternatives are dishwashing, floor polishing, truck loading. [Edwards, Monkmeyer]

profitable undertaking that is superior to a coerced existence directed by welfare bureaucrats. (1978, p. 678)

The welfare connection

A disproportionate share of violent urban crime in the USA is committed by black and Hispanic juveniles brought up in matrifocal families that receive AFDC allotments. This connection between juvenile delinquency and matrifocality reflects the fact that AFDC benefits are set below poverty-level incomes. Almost all inner-city AFDC women therefore count on supplementary incomes from husbands-in-hiding, coresident male consorts, or former consort fathers of their children.

Anthropologist Jagna Sharff (1981) found that all the mothers in a group of twenty-four Hispanic AFDC families living in New York City's Lower East Side had some kind of male consort. While few of the men in the house held regular full-time jobs, even those who were unemployed chipped in something toward food and rent from selling stolen goods, dealing in marijuana or cocaine, and from an occasional burglary or mugging. Some women had more than one consort,

14.9 PRUITT-IGOE
To avoid charges of coddling the poor for whom this huge high-rise project was built in
St. Louis, elevator exits were installed only on alternate floors and water pipes were run
through the corridors. Vandals broke the corridor windows, the pipes froze and burst, water
cascaded down the stairwells and then froze. This rendered the stairwells unusable and
trapped hundreds of people on alternate floors in waterless and heatless apartments. Plagued
by vandalism and crime and unable to obtain funds for security and maintenance, the
housing authority decided to dynamite the buildings and level the entire project despite the
acute shortage of low-income housing. [St. Louis Post-Dispatch]

while others picked up money and gifts through more casual relationships.

In their early teens, young inner-city boys make substantial contributions to their household's economic balance through their involvement in street crime and dope peddling. In addition, they confer an important benefit upon their mothers in the form of protection against the risk of rape, mugging, and various kinds of ripoffs to which the ghetto families are perpetually exposed.

Sharff found that AFDC mothers value sons for streetwise *macho* qualities, especially their ability to use knives or guns, which are needed to protect the family against unruly or predatory neighbors. While the AFDC mothers did not actively encourage their sons to enter the drug trade, everyone recognized that a successful drug dealer could become a very rich man. To get ahead in the drug business, one needs the same *macho* qualities that are useful in defending one's family. When a young man brings home his first drug profits, mothers have mixed feelings of pride and apprehension. Since young ghetto males have a 40 percent chance of dying by age 25, a ghetto mother has to have more than one son if she hopes to enjoy the protection of a streetwise male. In her sample of AFDC families, Sharff compiled this record of male homicides in the three-year period 1976 to 1979:

Victim's age	Immediate cause of death
25	Shot in drug-related incident
19	Shot in dispute in grocery store
21	Shot in drug-related incident
28	Stabbed in drug-related incident
32	"Suicide" in a police precinct house
30	Stabbed in drug-related incident
28	Poisoned by adulterated heroin
30	Arson victim
24	Shot in drug-related incident
19	Tortured and stabbed in drug-related incident

One must be careful not to conclude that every family on AFDC conforms to this pattern. For some mothers, AFDC represents a one-time emergency source of funds used in the aftermath of divorce or separation until they can find a job and arrange for child care. But several million inner-city women, mostly black and Hispanic, use AFDC not as a temporary crutch, but as a regular or recurrent source of subsistence. A hard core of such women—estimated by sociologists Martin Rein and Lee Rainwater (1977) to number about 750,000—stay on AFDC for as many as twelve years at a stretch. And a far larger number of inner-city women follow a pattern of going on and off AFDC as they move in and out of the labor market between pregnancies.

Domestic organization: the middle class

From colonial times to the present, the monogamous nuclear family has been the most common form of family in the USA. But with the transition to industrialism, the average size of nuclear families has steadily decreased and considerable numbers of Americans have come to spend a major portion of their lives living in childless families, single-parent families, consort pairs, and alone. In 1850 there were proportionately seven times as many families with four or more children as today. As for families with no children present, there are four times more today than in 1850. With the exception of the post-World War II baby boom, the birth rate per thousand women has declined during every decade since 1800.[4]

The declining size of the nuclear family is related to shifts in the cost-benefits of rearing children under urban-industrial conditions. In the predominantly rural America of colonial times, children cost relatively little to bring up because much of their food, shelter,

[4] Birth rates (per thousand women aged 15 to 44) increased between 1975 and 1980 as a result of the large bulge of women now in their prime reproductive years who were born during the post-World War II "baby boom."

and clothing was produced on the family farm. At the same time, they contributed to their own upkeep by starting to do valuable chores while they were still very young. Finally, as farm parents grew old and feeble, it was relatively easy for their children to "pay them back" by taking care of them. Farm families with large numbers of children tend to get ahead, whereas city families with large numbers of children get dragged down in the competition for economic improvement. On the cost side, all food, clothing, and shelter has to be purchased for city children. Furthermore, in order for city children to make a substantial contribution to household income, they have to go to school. The more schooling, the greater the potential return for both parents and child, but the greater the risk and expense. This means that on the benefit side, urban parents cannot expect even a modest return on their "investment" until middle age. Meanwhile, the expense of getting old and sick has steadily increased, partly because parents can expect to live longer as a result of desirable but costly medical intervention. By the mid-twentieth century the costs of old age could no longer be met even by relatively affluent children, and the burden of providing for aged and infirm people passed almost entirely from the family to the Social Security Administration, private medical insurance, pension funds, and assorted welfare programs, where it remains today.

The trend toward smaller nuclear families was also strengthened by improvements in the general health of the U.S. population and by reductions in infant mortality. In order to achieve a desired number of children, parents did not have to contend with the probability that many of their children would not live to adulthood, as is still true in less developed countries today.

Despite the steady decrease in the birth rate, the USA until recently had been a strongly pro-family and pro-natalist society, in conformity with the values of what can be called the marital and procreative imperative. According to this imperative, sex is supposed to be confined to marriage, everyone ideally has to get married, and every marriage is supposed to lead to reproduction. The function of marriage and sex, in other words, is to promote reproduction and childrearing as the primary duty and responsibility of anyone, male or female, who wants to experience sexual pleasure (Smith-Rosenberg, 1978, p. 238).

Of course these ideals were never universally obeyed, not even during the nineteenth century. We know from the warnings of doctors, preachers, politicians, and educators that masturbation, prostitution, and other kinds of "unnatural" sex flourished both in and out of the bonds of wedlock. We also know that men and women were making increasing use of contraceptive devices, that men refrained from getting married until they could support a wife, and that couples refrained from having children until they could afford them. Although there is no way we can reliably estimate the absolute degree of noncompliance with the marital and procreative imperative, the steadily falling birth rate suggests that the gap between values and behavior increased during the nineteenth and early twentieth centuries.

Women, work, and family

A corollary of the marital and procreative imperative is that once women get married, they have to stay home and take care of the children. During the early days of the factory system, England had experimented with the possibility of using married women as workers in factories. It was found that married women would accept lower pay than their husbands, but it soon became apparent that marriage, procreation, and the family itself were all threatened by that practice. The leaders of the

British Parliament feared that if the preference for hiring married women were allowed to run its course, there would soon be an end to the laboring classes, since women who worked all day were unwilling to marry and support unemployable husbands or rear children—at least not the kind of children who were likely to be suitable for employment in an industrializing economy (Minge, 1982).

All the industrializing nations found that the best way to preserve and increase the quantity and quality of their laboring classes was to prohibit or discourage the employment of married women in factory jobs. In the United States, the temptation to push married women into factory work was never as strong as in Europe because the great current of immigration into the New World provided ample numbers of qualified men, at least until the immigration laws were changed in the 1920s.

In 1890 only 14 percent of the women in the job force were married, and these women represented only 5 percent of working-age women. Most of these married working women were blacks and recent immigrants. For a married, native-born white woman to work outside the home for money was a phenomenal rarity: Only 2 percent of them did it. In contrast, 23 percent of married adult black women in 1890 (Brownlee, 1979) already held jobs.

Except for a tiny group of privileged women doctors, lawyers, college teachers, and other professionals, scarcely any native-born, married white women went to work unless their husbands died or abandoned them. A woman did not get married to a man who could not "support" her, which meant that many women had to postpone getting married and that many remained single for life. Although we think of the present feminist situation as characterized by a new tendency to delay marriage, the record for late marriages was actually achieved in 1900. Over 40 percent of American women that year between the ages of 20 and 29 had never had a husband (Raphael, 1979; Westoff, 1978).

Until World War II, therefore, the proportion of *married* women who participated in the U.S. work force remained small. In 1940, despite a sharp increase in working wives during the Great Depression, only 15 percent of married women who had a husband present held an outside job. But this was soon to change. By 1960, the proportion of employed married women with husbands present had risen to 30 percent, and by 1980 to about 50 percent. More than half of married women in the prime reproductive age 35 years or younger now hold jobs. As one might expect, the proportion of married women who go to work is highest among those who have no small children to take care of at home. This proportion has climbed to 80 percent among married women less than 35 years old. But the proportion of young married women who go to work even though (or because) they have small children to take care of is also high: 40 percent of those under 35 who have one or more children under 6; and over 60 percent of those who have a child at home between 6 and 18 (Smith, 1979; Kolko, 1979; Ryscavage, 1979).

The end of the marital and procreative imperative?

The traditional pro-natal system could tolerate increased participation by *unmarried women* in the labor force; but can it survive increased participation by *married women*? The fulfillment of the marital and procreative imperative hinged on women staying home in order to raise children. While one can easily think of alternative arrangements such as day-care centers that might resolve the contradiction between jobs and babies, no such arrangements were or are available on the requisite national scale. As married women poured into the labor force, the postwar baby boom collapsed and the fertility rate began its historic plunge, reaching zero-population-growth levels in 1972 and falling still further, to an average of 1.8 children per woman, by 1980. The idea that the baby boom collapsed because of the introduction of the "pill" can easily be dismissed, since the collapse began in 1957, while the pill was not released for public use until June 1960. As late as 1964, when fertility was falling with unprecedented speed, only 10 percent of married women of childbearing age were using the "pill" (Butz and Ward, 1979).

As all the polls and surveys of the 1950s showed, the baby-boom mothers at first had no intention of giving up their homebody role. At first, the married women who moved into the labor force were primarily housewives over 45 whose children had "left the nest." But a decisive break came in the early 1960s when younger married women, with children under 18, began to enter the labor force in droves.

By the early 1960s married women were finding it increasingly difficult to achieve or hold on to middle-class standards of consumption for themselves and their children, and the wife's job had begun to play a crucial role in the family finances. As the first of the baby-boom children approached college age, the burden of medical care, schooling, clothing, and housing for the average family increased far faster than the male breadwinner's salary. The onset of inflation in the early 1960s made these costs even more difficult to bear.

Pressures on married women to join the labor force have always existed, but married women had previously not yielded to them because there were simply no jobs they could or would take—no jobs they themselves and their husbands and the other partisans of the marital and procreative imperative regarded as suitable for married women. Suitable jobs —jobs compatible with the traditional goals of procreation and marriage—would allow women to work part-time or to move in and out of the work force in order to meet family needs. But if married women had to work, they should try not to compete with men and thereby cheapen the breadwinner's wages. They were supposed to work at occupations and industries in which women predominated.

Precisely these specifications characterize the jobs that became available for women workers after World War II as a result of the transition from manufacturing to service and information industrialism (see p. 288). The great bulk of the new jobs were of two types: information-processing jobs such as file clerks, secretaries, typists, and receptionists; and people-processing jobs such as nurses, primary school teachers, retail sales help, medical and dental assistants, guidance counselors, and social workers. These were woman-dominated occupations, mainly part-time, in-and-out, temporary, or dead-end. Hence the average employed woman in the United States makes only 58 percent of the average male's wages. Thus the entrance into the service and information sector represents a replay of the entrance of women into manufacturing early in the Industrial Revolution. But there is one crucial difference: This time the recruitment of women for employment outside the home does not threaten the livelihood of their husbands, since the kinds of jobs involved have long been dominated by women rather than men.

The male breadwinner finds it difficult to resist the new role society has prepared for him. While married men on the average still contribute about three times as much as their working wives to family income, wives' salaries now make the difference between just getting by or falling into poverty; or between a barely middle-class versus a workingman's family budget. As *The Wall Street Journal* (2 February 1976) put it: "The workingman breadwinner who doesn't have a wife on a payroll just may wind up not having enough bread."

The entrance of married women into the

labor force has brought about a rapid and probably irreversible restructuring of American domestic life. Although historian Carl Degler (1980) and sociologist Mary Jo Bane (1976) argue that the "family is here to stay," the family that remains is not the family of former times. It is not the lifetime male-dominated, two-parent, multichild, breadwinner family. Although it is true that most children will continue to be born into some kind of family situation, the kind of domestic unit involved and the typical pattern of life experiences with respect to residence, marriage, and childrearing that Americans can look forward to are fundamentally new additions to American culture.

Future family

As women struggle to achieve career parity with men and get ever more deeply involved in the job market, the historic downward trend in birth rates will probably continue for a long time to come. The first-time marriage rate has also been moving downward, falling from 90 per thousand single women in 1950 to about 65 in 1976. Most of this drop can be attributed to the aging baby-boom children who have been postponing marriage or not getting married at all. In 1960 only 28 percent of women between the ages of 20 and 24 were single; in 1974 the figure was 40 percent. And those who have gotten married have been getting divorced in unprecedented numbers. Between 1965 and 1978, the country's divorce rate more than doubled, with the highest frequency found again, significantly, among the younger, 20 to 24 age group. With one out of three marriages ending in divorce—an all-time high—it is far-fetched to point to a high rate of remarriage among older couples as evidence for the "preservation of the family." Along with the rise in the divorce rate, the postponement of marriage, and the fall in the birth rate, there has been an 81 percent increase in the number of families headed by

women—either separated, divorced, widowed, or never-married—since 1960. About 17 percent of all children now live in such families at any one time, and the odds that children born today will at one point be living in such families is well over 40 percent (Harrington, 1980, p. 85). As families grow smaller, as divorce rates rise, and as marriage and birth rates fall, more and more Americans will find themselves living alone for a good portion of their lives. The growth in the number of single persons in the age group 25 to 34 is probably a forecast of things to come. In 1950 only one out of twenty men and women in this age group was living alone; in 1976, one out of three was living alone! Among elderly widowed women (65 years and older), the frequency rose from one out of four to two out of three (NBER Reporter, 1979, p. 2). Only 6 percent of all American families fit the traditional pattern of full-time homebody wife and mother, breadwinner father and husband, and two or more dependent children (Wattenberg and Reinhardt, 1979, p. 460). Far more Americans are living alone or in single-parent, remarried, or childless families than in the traditional nuclear family into which the baby-boom generation was born.

According to the National Alliance for Optional Parenthood, in 1967 only 1 percent of wives between the ages of 18 and 24 did not expect to have a child. By 1977 this figure had changed to 5 percent, and 11 percent of all women between 18 and 34 now plan to remain childless.

Future sex

The entrance of married women into the labor force has ushered in an era of sexual liberation and experimentation in the USA. Patterns of sexual behavior that were once abominated, condemned, and regarded as criminal perversions have been widely adopted or tolerated in order to accommodate the growing percentage of men and women who are discouraged from getting married and having children by the rising cost of living and the need to have two wage earners per family. The separation of sex from procreation has led to the rapid rise in premarital and extramarital intercourse and to the flourishing of temporary consort unions in which the participating couples find no reason to get married since they do not intend to have children.

It is no accident, therefore, that along with the postponement of marriage, falling birth rate, high divorce rate, and increase of tem- porary consort unions, there has also been an increase in what previous generations of Americans regarded as degenerate or porno- graphic sexual commerce. From the pages of best-seller marriage manuals on the joys of sex to the centerfolds of *Penthouse*, *Playboy*, and *Playgirl*, Americans are being told that sex does not, need not, and should not lead to reproduction. There is a vast industry of X- rated movies designed for dates at the drive- ins and of films and videotape cassettes for private viewing. Survey reports of women's sex habits turn into best sellers, and there is a huge growth industry in massage parlors,

---

14.10 PORN
Making money out of sex is a big industry in the USA. [Johnson, DeWys]

CHAPTER 14
The anthropology of the USA

swinger clubs, escort services, live sex shows, and adult porno bookstores (Fig. 14.10).

The other side of the message that sex is for pleasure and not for reproduction is that parents have no fun. Americans now view the joys of parenthood with jaundiced eyes. According to a study carried out by the consumer research firm of Yankelovich, Skelly and White, Americans now rate new cars over children on the list of items deemed necessary for the good life.

Gay liberation

The rise in self-identified homosexuality typified by the call for gays to "come out of the closet" and by "gay pride" marches in the major U.S. cities can also be understood in relation to the weakening of the marital and procreative imperative (Fig. 14.11).

Anthropologist Dennis Werner (1979) has shown that societies which taboo homosexuality tend to be pro-natalist. Werner divided a sample of thirty-nine societies into two groups, pro-natalists and anti-natalists. The pro-natalists were societies that, like the USA, banned abortion and infanticide; the anti-natalists were societies that permitted abortion or infanticide for nonadulterous married women. Werner found that male homosexuality was frowned upon, ridiculed, scorned, or punished for all segments of the population in 75 percent of the pro-natalist societies and

14.11 OUT OF THE CLOSET
A gay rights march in New York City.
[Eagan, Woodfin Camp]

that it was permitted or encouraged for at least some people in 60 percent of the anti-natalist societies. Thus the aversion to homosexuality is greatest where the marital and procreative imperative is strongest.

Western society in the Judeo-Christian tradition fits this formula. The biblical injunction to multiply and fill the earth and subdue it has been spelled out in countless laws, repressive acts, and moral precepts directed not only against abortion, contraception, and infanticide, but against any form of nonprocreative sex—including homosexuality. It seems likely that the temptation for people to engage in homosexual forms of sex increases in direct proportion to the adverse balance of costs and benefits associated with the rearing of children; or in other words, when there is pressure on people to lower the birth rate. Note that this is not the same as saying that homosexuality or other forms of nonprocreative sex will occur *only* when there is such pressure. Some form or degree of homosexuality can be expected in almost any human society under a multitude of conditions (see p. 259). The point is that to the extent that homosexuality and other nonprocreative forms of sex are already present, their incidence and variety will tend to increase if people feel increasing pressure to reduce the number of their children.

In other words, gay liberation accompanied women's liberation because both movements represent facets of the collapse of the marital and procreative imperative and the male-dominated breadwinner family. Exclusionist homosexuals (i.e., homosexuals who reject heterosexuality) constitute the radical left wing of America's anti-natalist forces. The prominent role of lesbian activists in women's liberation makes this clear. Lesbians have repeatedly attacked heterosexual feminists for "collaborating with the enemy." According to the lesbian militants, men cannot help but be opposed to women's liberation and therefore women ought to sever all

intimate and supportive relationships with them, especially those involving sex, marriage, and reproduction. The antiparenthood theme in radical lesbian feminism aims to "demystify" women's reproductive functions. Pregnancy, "a temporary deformation of the body for the sake of the species," is an affliction of "fat ladies" caused by a "tenant," "parasite," or "uninvited guest." "Childbirth is painful and hideous. Motherhood is portrayed as a condition of terminal psychological and social decay, total self-abnegation and physical deterioration." Obviously only a small minority of feminists hold such extreme views (Elshtain, 1979, p. 498).

Despite their consciousness of themselves as people fighting for a sexual rather than a reproductive preference, America's gays are very much involved in the struggle to throw off the yoke of parenthood. Exclusive homosexuals enjoy contraceptive protection, no matter how relentless their search for sexual pleasure.

Religion

It might be supposed that as one of the world's technologically most advanced industrial societies, the United States would also be one of the societies in which the majority of citizens reject traditional forms of animism and animatism (see Ch. 10). Science is the principal source of modern technology, which in turn underlies the industrial mass production and consumption of goods, services, and information. While science is not necessarily opposed to a belief in souls, gods, or luck, scientific principles of knowledge do require that propositions based on faith, tradition, hunches, or visions be subjected to systematic logical and empirical tests. One might expect, therefore, that in a society in which science and scientific technology play a prominent role, most people would be agnostics, neither believing nor disbelieving in animism nor animatism, if not outright atheists.

Yet 94 percent of U.S. citizens profess a belief in God or a universal spirit, 89 percent say they pray, and 78 percent say they belong to some organized religious group (Princeton Religious Research Center, 1980, p. 17). True, only 57 percent say that their religious beliefs are "very important" to them and only 41 percent attend church during an average week (down from 49 percent in 1955). Nonetheless, this degree of belief and practice is far higher than in the non-Communist industrial societies of Western Europe and Japan (Princeton Religious Research Center, 1979). Moreover, there are signs that while the established U.S. churches are having difficulty holding their own (or are slowly losing influence), many novel forms of religious belief and practice seem to be taking their place.

Some observers detect signs of a large-scale religious "awakening." This awakening involves more than a reaffirmed belief in an active, personal deity. The forms of awakening range from weekend encounter groups to messianic prophets. As seen by sociologist Robert Bellah (1976), the most representative aspect of this awakening is the acceptance of "Asian spirituality" as an antidote for Western "utilitarian individualism." According to Bellah, aspects of Zen, Taoism, Buddhism, Hinduism, Sufism, and other Oriental religions first began to strike a responsive chord in the counterculture of the late sixties as Americans began to feel that the struggle to achieve material gains by and for individuals was hollow and meaningless. Helped along by drugs and meditation, the counterculture generation realized the "illusoriness of worldly striving." "Careerism and status-seeking, the sacrifice of present fulfillment for some ever-receding future goal, no longer seemed worthwhile" (Bellah, 1976, p. 341).

Recognizing that the United States had many unsolved material problems such as racism and poverty, Bellah nonetheless insists that the religious awakening was brought on as much by "the success of the society" and by the "realization that education and affluence did not bring happiness or fulfillment" as by its failures. Following this line of reasoning to its logical outcome, we are led to conclude that the basic cause of the religious awakening in the USA is a crisis of spirit and meaning rather than a crisis of practical material needs. Writes Bellah: "The deepest cause, no matter what particular factors contributed to the actual timing, was, in my opinion, the inability of utilitarian individualism to provide a meaningful pattern of personal and social existence" (p. 39).

It can be argued against this view, however, that the deepest and most characteristic impulse of America's religious awakening is not the search for ultimate meaning, but the search for solutions to America's unsolved economic and social problems. The role of "Asiatic" spirituality in the formation and propagation of new religious groups and rituals in the United States is easily exaggerated. The number of people involved in new cults, sects, and movements that have contemplation, withdrawal from worldly affairs, and other supposedly "Asiatic" motifs as their principal concern is actually quite small by comparison with the number involved in cults and sects and movements that have a definite program for mastering worldly problems and enhancing individual material welfare.

The point seems self-evident for those Americans who want to predict the future from horoscopes, cure illness through shamanic trances, or disable their boss or teacher by sticking pins in dolls. These are all techniques for mastering the world rather than retreating from it.

Utilitarian motives are also self-evident in the seemingly endless varieties of weekend encounter groups and mind-body therapies that are part of the "human-potential movement." Executives prescribe encounter groups and sensitivity training courses to improve relationships among employees and to step up sales.

In the more etherealized and spiritualized "trainings." the predominant, recurring theme is that of mind over matter. Not only do participants expect to control others by improving their control over themselves, but they expect to control physical happenings by the imposition of their thoughts on matter. Erhard Seminars Training (est), for example, claims that "nobody has to die unless he chooses to; all deaths are suicides, and there are no accidents. And you can fly if you allow yourself to know how" (Conway and Siegelman, 1978, p. 169). Similar extreme forms of mentalism—belief in the omnipotence of thought—characterize the principles and goals of the more "meditative" human potential disciplines. Scientology, for example, holds forth the promise of "not worrying and bogging myself down with a burden of problems"; "freedom from my compulsions"; "I no longer feel afraid of anything"; "ability to change body size"; "ability to see through walls"; and "ability to hear other people's thoughts" (Wallis, 1977, p. 121). Even cults such as the "Moonies" (The Unification Church), the "Hare Krishnas" (Fig. 14.12), and the Divine Light Mission have a definite worldly commitment—a yearning for control —which contradicts the notion that the current religious awakening in the USA is best understood as an Asian-inspired "critique of the expansion of wealth and power." Former "Moonie" Barbara Underwood, for example,

14.12 HARE KRISHNA
One of the Asian-derived cults which offer a life-style opposed to mainstream U.S. culture. [Hopker, Woodfin Camp]

confessed she wanted to make "millions of dollars" to purchase and maintain hotels, resorts, palatial residences from Chicago to New Orleans, training and living centers, college campuses, yachts, and even the Empire State and Pan Am Buildings. "Instilled in us was the firm belief that Moon must reclaim all ownership of money and land from Satan's stockpile." "Christians think that the Messiah must be poor and miserable," says a Unification Church training manual. "He did not come for this. Messiah must be the richest. Only He is qualified to have dominion over things. Otherwise, neither God nor Messiah can be happy" (Underwood and Underwood, 1979, p. 76; Welles, 1978, p. 255).

The electronic church

Whatever the balance may be between worldly and otherworldly themes in the cults that have adopted aspects of Asian religions, such cults are not representative of the main thrust of religious change in the United States today. Far more powerful are Protestant fundamentalism and the various born-again Christian movements that have been able to use television to expand membership and raise funds. These so-called "electronic churches" or "TV cults" to a large extent recruit their membership through a personal "gospel of wealth"—they promise material success and physical well-being to the true believer. Their message appeals especially to people who are sick, old, or isolated, impoverished by inflation, bewildered by the changes in sex mores and the family, and frightened by crime in the streets. According to TV preacher Jim Bakker, "The scripture says, 'Delight yourself in the Lord and he'll give you the desires of your heart.' . . . Give and it shall be given unto you." Bakker tells how one man prayed for a Winnebago mobile home, color brown, and got just that. Says Bakker: "Diamonds and gold aren't just for Satan—they're for Christians, too" (Bakker, 1976).

On his Old Time Gospel Hour, Moral Majority leader Jerry Falwell (Fig. 14.13) asks the faithful to turn over one-tenth of their income: "Christ has not captured a man's heart until He has your pocketbook." Two million potential contributors whose names and addresses are kept in a computer data bank receive frequent requests for money, one of which reads: "Maybe your financial situation seems impossible. Put Jesus first in your stewardship and allow him to bless you financially" (*Time*, 1 October 1979, p. 68).

Finding himself $50 million short of the funds needed to complete his City of Faith hospital complex near Tulsa, Oklahoma, video evangelist Oral Roberts raised money with the aid of swatches from a "miracle cloth." "My hands feel as if there is a supernatural heat in them," he declared. "My right hand is especially hot right now." Following God's instructions, Roberts began to turn out millions of swatches imprinted with his right hand. In return, those who acquire the cloth are promised "special miracles" (*Newsweek*, 10 September 1979). Another TV evangelist, Pat Robertson, recruits followers and raises funds through what he calls the Kingdom Principles: The Bible says the more you give to Jesus the more you will get back in return. And the harder it is to give, the greater will be the increase. Thus a woman in California who was on a limited income and in poor health:

decided to trust God and to step out in faith on the Kingdom Principles. She was already giving half her disability money to the 700 Club to spread the gospel of Jesus Christ. But just last week, she decided to go all the way, and to give God the money she spends for cancer medicine—$120 a month. And three days later—get this!—from an entirely unexpected source, she got a check for three thousand dollars! (Rifkind and Howard, 1979, p. 108)

14.13 THE ELECTRONIC CHURCH
**Jerry Falwells's "Old Time Gospel Hour"
being televised live from Lynchburg Virginia
to a network of 391 TV stations. Cameras can
be seen on the balcony and in the center of
the audience. [Wide World]**

Since all the other aspects of U.S. culture
are in flux, it is not surprising that religious
beliefs and practices are going through a period of change and ferment. The experience of
other cultures and historical epochs demonstrates that stresses brought on by rapid cultural change usually find expression in spiritual yearning, questing, and experimenting
which leads to an expansion and intensification of religious activity, broadly defined.

All the major world religions were born
during times of rapid cultural transformations. Buddhism and Hinduism arose in the
Ganges Valley of Northern India during an
epoch of deforestation, population increase,

and state formation. Judaism arose during
the prolonged migrations of the ancient Isra-
elites. Christianity arose in conjunction with
attempts to break the yoke of Roman imperi-
alism. Islam arose during the transition from
a life of pastoral nomadism to that of trade
and empires in Arabia and North Africa. Protestants split from Catholicism as feudalism
gave way to capitalism. As we have seen (Ch.
10), messianic and millennarian cults swept
across the Great Plains as the American Indians lost their lands and hunting grounds,
while in the wake of the European coloniza-
tion of New Guinea and Melanesia, hundreds
of cargo cults, devoted to acquiring worldly

wealth with the assistance of ancestors returned from the dead, spread from island to island.

There is reason to believe, therefore, that the rising intensity of religious activity in the USA constitutes an attempt to solve or to escape from the problems of malfunctioning consumerism, inflation, the upending of sex roles, breakup of the breadwinner family, alienation from work, oppressive government and corporate bureaucracies, feelings of isolation and loneliness, fear of crime, and bewilderment about the root cause of so many changes happening at once.

Summary

The USA's mode of production is industrialism, involving a detailed division of labor in conjunction with power-driven machinery and the mass production of goods, services, and information. As a result of the recent expansion of the service and information sectors, the USA is best described as a hyper-industrial society, since virtually all forms of economic activity now involve mass production, the detailed division of labor, and mechanical or electronic machinery.

Although from an emic perspective the political economy of the USA is said to be capitalism, from an etic perspective it is a mixture of socialism and capitalism. Again, from an emic perspective, the capitalist sector of the economy is viewed as being based on free enterprise price competition; etically, however, the degree of concentration of economic resources in the largest conglomerate corporations creates a situation of oligopoly that precludes the setting of prices through competitive market supply and demand.

The majority of Americans work for bureaucratized organizations that do not reward individual initiative so much as they reward the willingness of people to carry out routine, standardized tasks. As a consequence, there is widespread alienation not only on the assembly line, but in the information and service sectors as well. While some observers look to the automation of information and service jobs as a means of overcoming the problem, there is evidence that the electronic office of the future will further routinize and de-skill the labor force.

The emics and etics of the system of social stratification in the USA offer sharply contrasting views. Emic versions downgrade the degree of separation between the classes and deny the existence of a ruling class. From an etic perspective, however, there is considerable evidence that, despite countervailing sources of political influence, there is a ruling elite which decisively influences the overall shape of U.S. social, economic, and military policies. This evidence consists of the concentration of wealth in super-rich families and in the interlocking stockvoting powers of a handful of top institutional investors. In contrast to the many studies of the poor, however, very little is known about the super-rich; anthropologists have been remiss in not studying "up" as well as "down."

The persistence of a large poverty class again points to a serious split between emic and etic versions of U.S. life. Upward mobility is not as rapid or extensive as most Americans believe. There is a persistent tendency to blame the perpetuation of the poverty class on the victims of poverty, as can be seen in the popularity of Oscar Lewis's "culture of poverty" and in the demand that the poor must work harder than the affluent. The poor, however, share most values with the middle class, and there is little evidence that by trying harder the poor can overcome the structural conditions which lead to unemployment and underemployment. Evidence to the contrary can be seen in Elliot Liebow's account of Washington's streetcorner men.

In contrast to the emic blurring of class lines in the USA, racial and ethnic minorities and majorities consciously conceive of themselves as sharply defined and competitive groups. Ethnic and social chauvinism pits black "have-nots" against white "have littles" and thereby helps the "have-lots" maintain wealth and power. The "black power" movement has aided many privileged blacks, but it has further entrapped the majority of blacks in the nation's urban ghettos. The worsening plight of America's black underclass is often attributed to the allegedly pathological nature of the black matrifocal family. But matrifocality is itself a family form produced by poverty, unemployment, and the rules of the AFDC welfare program, as shown in Carol Stack's study of the Flats.

The USA pays a huge hidden cost for its failure to ameliorate the situation in which the black underclass finds itself. The long-term high unemployment of blacks and Hispanic ghetto males has created a situation of hopelessness and envy that has led a disproportionate percentage of blacks and Hispanics to make crime their career. America's racial and ethnic dilemma accounts to a large extent for the marked difference between rates of violent crime in the USA and the Western industrial nations and Japan. AFDC is also implicated in the high rates of violent crime in America's inner cities. As Jagna Sharff's study of Hispanic women on AFDC in New York shows, the AFDC stipends are set too low for families to live on, thereby encouraging young men to resort to criminal behavior to fill the gap in family budgets.

The development of the USA's hyper-industrial service and information economy has had a powerful effect on middle-class family life. After World War II, married women entered the labor force in unprecedented numbers, taking the rapidly expanding lower-paying service and information jobs. As inflation wiped out the possibility of achieving or maintaining middle-class status on their husbands' incomes, married women became locked into the labor force. Their role as wage earners conflicted with their role as mothers, subverted the traditional marital and procreative imperative, and undermined the male breadwinner family. It has also led to the separation of sex from reproduction, the spread of single-parent families, consensual trial unions, declining first-time marriage rates, and historically low fertility rates. The separation of sex from reproduction in turn has encouraged the expression of once-prohibited forms of sexuality, including homosexuality and pornographic movies, books, and videotapes.

The rapid pace of change and the problems induced by inflation; the bureaucratization, oligopolization, alienation, and feminization of the economy and the labor force; the challenge to the marital and procreative imperative; the prevalence of crime; and the persistence of poverty and sharp inequalities in wealth and power may supply the basic reasons for America's current religious awakening. The history of other cultures demonstrates that stresses brought on by rapid cultural change and social unrest usually find expression in spiritual yearning, questing, and experimenting which leads to an expansion and intensification of religious activity. Although some aspects of America's religious awakening can be attributed to an attempt to reject the material world, the center of religious ferment as seen in the video cults and human potential movement consists of attempts to overcome practical and mundane problems.

Appendix
History of Theories
of Culture

This appendix serves as a brief outline of the history of the development of anthropological theories. It presents the main research strategies employed by contemporary anthropologists and an examination of the evidence for racial determinism.

The impulse lying behind the development of cultural anthropology is probably as old as our species. Members of different human groups have always been curious about the customs and traditions of strangers. The fact that people who live in different societies build different kinds of shelters, wear different kinds of clothing, practice different kinds of marriages, worship different spirits and gods, and speak different languages has always been a source of puzzlement. The most ancient and still most common approach to these differences is to assume that one's own beliefs and practices are normal expressions of the true or right way of life, as justified by the teachings of one's ancestors and the commandments or instructions of supernatural beings. Most cultures have origin myths that set forth the sequence of events leading to the beginning of the world and of humanity and to the adoption of the group's way of life. The failure of other groups to share the same way of life can then be attributed to their failure to be true, real, or normal human beings.

The Enlightenment

As Europe entered the age of exploration and mercantile expansion, interest in describing and explaining cultural diversity increased. The discovery and exploration of a whole "New World"—the Americas—opened the eyes of philosophers, statesmen, theologians, and scientists to astonishing contrasts in the human condition.

Toward the middle of the eighteenth century, during the period known as the Enlightenment, the first systematic attempts to offer scientific theories of cultural differences began to emerge. The common theme of these theories was the idea of progress. It was held by scholars such as Adam Smith, Adam Ferguson, Jean Turgot, and Denis Diderot that cultures were different not because they expressed innate differences in human capacities or preferences, but because they expressed different levels of rational knowledge and achievement. It was believed that humankind, including Europe's ancestors, had at one time lived in an "uncivilized" condition, lacking a knowledge of farming and animal husbandry, laws and governments. Gradually, however, guided by the ever-expanding role of reason in human affairs, humankind progressed from a "state of nature" to a state of enlightened civilization. Cultural differences were thus largely a result of the different degrees of intellectual and moral progress achieved by different peoples.

Nineteenth-century evolutionism

The idea of cultural progress was the forerunner of the concept of cultural evolution that dominated theories of culture during the nineteenth century. Cultures were usually seen as moving through various stages of development, ending up with something resembling Euramerican life-styles. Auguste Comte postulated a progression from theological to metaphysical to postivistic (scientific) modes of thought. Friederick Hegel saw a movement from a time when only one man was free (the Asiatic tyrant) to a time when some were free (Greek city-states) to a time when all would be free (European constitutional monarchies). Others wrote of an evolution from status (such as slave, noble, or commoner) to contract (employee and employer, buyer and seller); from small communities of people who knew each other face to face to large, impersonal societies; from slave to military to industrial societies; from animism to polytheism to monotheism; from magic to science; from female-dominated horticultural societies to male-dominated agricultural societies, and from many other hypothetical earlier and simpler stages to later and more complex ones.

One of the most influential schemes was that proposed by the American anthropologist Lewis Henry Morgan in his book *Ancient Society*. Morgan divided the evolution of culture into three main stages; savagery, barbarism, and civilization. These stages had figured in evolutionary schemes as early as the sixteenth century, but Morgan subdivided them and filled them out in greater detail and with greater reference to ethnographic evidence than anyone else. (Morgan himself carried out a lifelong study of the Iroquois who lived near his home town of Rochester, New York.) Morgan held that "lower savagery" subsistence had been gained exclusively by gathering wild foods, that people mated promiscuously, and that the basic unit of society was the small nomadic "horde" which owned its resources communally. By "upper savagery," the bow and arrow had been invented, brother-sister marriage was prohibited, and descent was reckoned primarily through women. With the invention of pottery and the beginning of farming came the transition to barbarism. Incest prohibitions were extended to include all descendants in the female line, and clan and village became the basic units.

The development of metallurgy marked the upper phase of barbarism; descent shifted from the female to the male line, men married several women at one time (polygyny), and private property appeared. The invention of writing, the development of civil government, and the emergence of the monogamous family marked the beginning of "civilization."

Social Darwinism

In addition to the greater complexity and detail of the nineteenth-century evolutionary schemes, there was one fundamental difference between them and the eighteenth-century schemes of universal progress. Almost all the nineteenth-century schemes (with the conspicuous exception of Marxism) postulated that cultures evolved in conjunction with the evolution of human biological types and races. Not only were the cultures of modern-day Europe and America seen as the pinnacle of cultural progress, but the white race (especially its male half) was seen as the pinnacle of biological progress.

This fusion of biological evolutionism with cultural evolutionism is often but incorrectly attributed to the influence of Charles Darwin. In fact, however, the development of biological interpretations of culture evolution preceded the appearance of Darwin's *Origin of Species*, and Darwin was himself greatly influenced by social philosophers such as Thomas Malthus and Herbert Spencer. Malthus's notion that population growth led to an inevitable "struggle for existence" had been elaborated by Spencer into the idea of the "survival of the fittest" before Darwin published his theories of biological evolution.

The success of Darwin's theory of the survival of the fittest (he called it "natural selection") greatly enhanced the popularity of the view that cultural evolution was dependent on biological evolution. After the publication of Darwin's *Origin of Species*, there appeared a movement known as Social Darwinism based on the belief that cultural and biological progress were dependent on the free play of competitive forces in the struggle of individual against individual, nation against nation, and race against race. The most influential Social Darwinist was Herbert Spencer, who went so far as to advocate the end of all attempts to provide charity and relief for the unemployed and impoverished classes and the so-called backward races on the grounds that such assistance interfered with the operation of the so-called law of the survival of the fittest and merely prolonged the agony and deepened the misery of those who were "unfit." Spencer used Social Darwinism to justify the capitalist free enterprise system, and his influence continues to be felt among advocates of unrestrained capitalism as well as among advocates of white supremacy.

Marxist evolutionism

It is important to realize that while the writings and thoughts of Karl Marx were diametrically opposed to Social Darwinism, Marxism was also heavily influenced by the prevailing nineteenth-century notions of cultural evolution and progress. Marx saw cultures passing through the stages of primitive communism, slave society, feudalism, capitalism, and communism. Also, like many of his contemporaries, Marx stressed the importance of the role of struggle in achieving cultural evolution and progress. All history, according to Marx, was the outcome of the struggle between social classes for control over the means of production. The proletarian class, brought into existence by capitalism, was destined to abolish private property and bring about the final stage of history: communism. Upon reading Morgan's *Ancient Society*, Marx and his associate Frederick Engels thought they had found a confirmation of their idea that during the first stage of cultural evolution there was no private property and that the successive stages of cultural progress had been brought about by changes in the "mode of production"—as, for example, in the coincidence of the development of agriculture and the transition between savagery and barbarism in Morgan's scheme. Morgan's *Ancient Society* provided the basis for Engels' *The Origin of the Family, Private Property and the State* which, until the middle of the twentieth century, served as a cornerstone of Marxist anthropology.

The reaction to nineteenth-century evolutionism

Early in the twentieth century anthropologists took the lead in challenging the evolutionary schemes and doctrines of both the Social Darwinists and the Marxist Communists. In the United States, the dominant theoretical position was developed by Franz Boas and his students and is known as *historical particularism*. According to Boas, nineteenth-century attempts to discover the laws of cultural evolution and to schematize the stages of cultural progress were founded on insufficient empirical evidence. Boas argued that each culture has its own long and unique history. To understand or explain a particular culture, the best one can do is to reconstruct the unique path it had followed. This emphasis upon the uniqueness of each culture amounted to a denial of the prospects for a generalizing science of culture. Another important feature of historical particularism is the notion of *cultural relativism*, which holds that there are no higher or lower forms of culture. Terms like "savagery," "barbarism," and "civilization" merely express the ethnocentrism of people who think that their way of life is more normal than other people's ways of life.

To counter the speculative "armchair" theories and ethnocentrism of the evolutionists, Boas and his students also stressed the importance of carrying out ethnographic fieldwork among non-Western peoples. As the ethnographic reports and monographs produced by the historical particularists multiplied, it became clear that the evolutionists had indeed misrepresented or overlooked the complexities of so-called primitive cultures and that they had grossly underestimated the intelligence and ingenuity of the non-Caucasoid, non-European people of the world.

Boas's most important achievement was his demonstration that race, language, and culture were independent aspects of the human condition. Since both similar and dissimilar cultures and languages would be found among people of the same race, there was no basis for the Social Darwinist notion that biological and cultural evolution were part of a single process.

Diffusionism

Another early twentieth-century reaction to nineteenth-century evolutionism is known as *diffusionism.* According to its advocates, the principal source of cultural differences and similarities is not the inventiveness of the human mind, but the tendency of humans to imitate one another. Diffusionists see cultures as a patchwork of elements derived from a haphazard series of borrowings among near and distant peoples. In the critical case of the origin of American Indian civilizations, for example, diffusionists argued that the technology and architecture of the Inca of Peru and the Aztecs of Mexico were diffused from Egypt or from Southeast Asia, rather than invented independently (see p. 10 for a critique of diffusionism).

British functionalism and structural functionalism

In Great Britain, the dominant early twentieth-century research strategies are known as *functionalism* and *structural-functionalism.* According to the functionalists, the main task of cultural anthropology is to describe the recurrent *functions* of customs and institutions, rather than to explain the origins of cultural differences and similarities. According to one of the leading functionalists, Bronislaw Malinowski, the attempt to discover the origins of cultural elements was doomed to be speculative and unscientific because of the absence of written records. Once we have understood the function of an institution, argued Malinowski, then we have understood all we will ever understand about its orgins.

A. R. Radcliffe-Brown was the principal advocate of structural functionalism. According to Radcliffe-Brown, the main task of cultural anthropology was even narrower than that proposed by Malinowski. Whereas Malinowski emphasized the contribution of cultural elements to the biological and psychological welfare of individuals, Radcliffe-Brown and the structural-functionalists emphasized the contribution of the biological and psychological welfare of individuals to the maintenance of the social system. For the structural-functionalists, the function of maintaining the system took precedence over all others. But like Malinowski, the structural-functionalists labeled all attempts to find origins as speculative history.

Thus, the functionalists and structural-functionalists evaded the question of the general, recurrent causes of cultural differences, while emphasizing the general, recurrent functional reasons for similarities. This set the functionalists and structural-functionalists apart from the diffusionists as much as from the nineteenth-century evolutionists. Nor were the functionalists and structural-functionalists sympathetic to Boas's historical particularism. But like Boas and his students, the British functionalists and structural-functionalists stressed the importance of carrying out fieldwork, insisting that only after two or more years of being immersed in the language, thoughts, and events of another culture could anthropologists provide valid and reliable ethnographic descriptions.

Culture and personality

In turning away from the nineteenth-century notions of causality and evolution, many anthropologists, influenced by the writings of Sigmund Freud, attempted to interpret cultures in psychological terms. The writings of Freud and the anti-evolutionism of Boas set the stage for the development of the approach known as *culture and personality.* Two of Boas's most famous students, Ruth Benedict and Margaret Mead, pioneered in the development of culture and personality theories. Such theories in general may be described as psychological forms of functionalism that relate cultural beliefs and practices to individual personality and individual personality to cultural beliefs and practices. As we saw in Chapter 12, many advocates of the culture and personality approach stress the importance of early childhood experiences such as toilet training, breast feeding, and sex training in the formation of a basic or modal type of adult personality or national character. Some culture and personality theories attempt to explain cultural differences and similarities as a consequence of basic or modal personality. In general, however, culture and personality advocates do not deal with the problem of why the beliefs and practices that mold particular personality types or national characters occur in some cultures but not in others.

The new evolutionism

After World War II, increasing numbers of anthropologists became dissatisfied with the anti-evolutionism and lack of broad generalizations and causal explanations characteristic of the first half of the century. Under the influence of Leslie White, a broad effort was launched to reexamine the works of the nineteenth-century evolutionists such as Lewis Henry Morgan, to correct their ethnographic errors, and to identify their positive contribution to the development of a science of culture. White pioneered in postulating that the overall direction of cultural evolution was largely determined by the quantities of energy that could be captured and put to work per capita per year.

At the same time (about 1940 to 1950), Julian Steward laid the basis for the development of the approach known as *cultural ecology*, which stressed the role of the interaction of natural conditions such as soils, rainfall, and temperature with cultural factors such as technology and economy as the cause of both cultural differences and similarities.

The return to broad evolutionary points of view in the second half of the twentieth century among American cultural anthropologists was stimulated by archeological evidence that diffusion could not account for the remarkable similarities between the development of states and empires in the New and Old Worlds. The step-by-step process by which native American peoples in the Andean and Mesoamerican regions independently developed their own elaborate civilizations is now fairly well known, thanks to modern archeological research.

Julian Steward was especially impressed with the parallels in the evolution of the ancient civilizations of Peru, Mexico, Egypt, Mesopotamia, and China, and called for a renewed effort on the part of anthropologists to examine and explain these remarkable uniformities. Yet Steward was careful to distinguish his scheme of cultural evolution from the more extreme versions of nineteenth-century evolutionism. According to Steward, the problem with these evolutionists was that they postulated a single or "unilinear" set of stages for all cultures, whereas there are actually many or "multilinear" paths of development depending on initial environmental, technological, and other conditions.

Dialectical materialism

Both White and Steward were influenced by Marx and Engel's emphasis upon changes in the material aspects of modes of reproduction as the mainspring of cultural evolution. However, neither accepted the full set of Marxist propositions embodied in the point of view known as *dialectical materialism*, which gained considerable popularity among Western anthropologists for the first time in the 1960s and 1970s. Dialectical materialists hold that history has a determined direction—namely, that of the emergence of communism and of classless society. The sources of this movement are the internal contradictions of sociocultural systems. To understand the causes of sociocultural differences and similarities, social scientists must not only study these contradictions, but they must take part in the "dialectical" resolutions that lead to progress toward communism. The most important contradiction in all societies is that between the means of production (roughly, the technology) and the relations of production (who owns the means of production). In the words of Karl Marx: "The mode of production in material life determines the general character of the social, political, and spiritual processes of life. It is not the consciousness of men that determines their existence, but on the contrary, their social existence determines their consciousness" [1970 (1859), p. 21].

Cultural materialism

Further elaboration of the theoretical perspectives of Marx, White, and Steward has led to the appearance of the point of view known as *cultural materialism.* This is a research strategy which holds that the primary task of anthropology is to give causal explanations for the differences and similarities in thought and behavior found among human groups. Like dialectical materialists, cultural materialists hold that this task can best be carried out by studying the material constraints to which human existence is subjected. These constraints arise from the need to produce food, shelter, tools, and machines, and to reproduce human populations within limits set by biology and the environment. These are called *material* constraints or conditions in order to distinguish them from constraints or conditions imposed by ideas and other mental or spiritual aspects of human life such as values, religion, and art. For cultural materialists, the most likely causes of variation in the mental or spiritual aspects of human life are the variations in the material constraints affecting the way people cope with problems of satisfying basic needs in a particular habitat.

Cultural materialists differ from dialectical materialists mainly in their rejection of the notion that anthropology must become part of a political movement aimed at destroying capitalism and at furthering the interests of the proletariat. Cultural materialists allow for a diversity of political motivation among anthropologists united by a common commitment to the development of a science of culture. In addition, cultural materialists reject the notion that all important cultural changes result from the playing out of dialectical contradictions, holding that much of cultural evolution has resulted from the gradual accumulation of useful traits through a process of trial and error.

Structuralism

Not all post-World War II approaches to cultural theory are aimed at explaining the origin of cultural differences and similarities. In France, under the leadership of Claude Lévi-Strauss, the point of view known as *structuralism* has been widely accepted. Structuralism is concerned only with the psychological uniformities that underly apparent differences in thought and behavior. According to Lévi-Strauss, these uniformities arise from the structure of the human brain and of unconscious thought processes. The most important structural feature of the human mind is the tendency to dichotomize, or to think in terms of binary oppositions, and then to attempt to mediate this opposition by a third concept, which may serve as the basis for yet another opposition. A recurrent opposition present in many myths, for example, is culture: nature. From the structuralist point of view, the more cultures change, the more they remain the same, since they are all merely variations on the theme of recurrent oppositions and their resolutions. Structuralism, therefore, is concerned with explaining the similarities among cultures, but not with explaining the differences. See pages 235 to 237 for an example of a structuralist analysis.

Particularizing approaches

Mention must also be made of the fact that many anthropologists continue to reject all general causal viewpoints, holding that the chief aim of ethnography ought to be the study of the emics of different cultures—their world views, symbols, values, religions, philosophies, and systems of meanings—purely for their own sake, as a form of humanistic enlightenment.

Racial determinism

Despite the overwhelming evidence against the notion that sociocultural differences and similarities can be explained by genetic differences and similarities, racial deterministic theories continue to be offered. Although few anthropologists offer such theories, many psychologists and biologists continue to do so, and hence no survey of contemporary theories of culture can omit this viewpoint.

During the twentieth century, the dispute between the racial determinists and the cultural determinists was focused increasingly on the measurement of intelligence. Intelligence was at first regarded as a completely fixed essence or trait that could not be affected by life experience and culture. Karl Pearson, one of the most influential figures in the application of statistical measures to biological variation, wrote in 1924:

The mind of man is for the most part a congenital product, and the factors which determine it are racial and familial; we are not dealing with a mutable characteristic of being moulded by the doctor, the teacher, the parent or the home environment. (Pearson quoted in Hirsch, 1970, p. 92)

Various tests were devised to measure this fixed ingredient. Most of them, including the widely used Stanford-Binet IQ test, present in varying combinations tasks involving word meanings, verbal relationships, arithmetical reasoning, form classification, spatial relationships, and other abstract symbolic material (Thorndike, 1968, p. 424). Since these tasks are similar to the kinds of tasks by which general academic achievement is assessed, intelligence tests are good predictors of academic success.

The era of large-scale intelligence testing began when the United States entered World War I. To determine their military assignments, thousands of draftees were given so-called alpha and beta tests. After the war, psychologists arranged the results according to race, found the expected correlations between blacks and lower scores, and concluded that the innate intellectual inferiority of the blacks had been scientifically proven (Yerkes, 1921).

The army tests were scored by grades lettered A to E. The percentage distribution for 93,073 whites and 18,891 blacks on, above, and below the middle grade of C was as follows:

	Below C	C	Above C
Whites	24	64	12
Blacks	79	20	1

These results were seized upon to justify the maintenance of inferior social status for blacks in and out of the army. Subsequent analysis, however, showed that the scores were useless as measurements of the genetic factors governing intelligence (Bagley, 1924). They were useless because the tests had not distinguished between the assumed hereditary effects and the equally plausible effects of cultural and other nongenetic factors. The strength of these nongenetic factors became apparent when the scores of blacks from five northern states were compared with the scores of blacks from four southern states:

	Below C	C	Above C
Northern blacks	46	51	3
Southern blacks	86	14	0

The most plausible explanation for the superiority in the performance of northern over southern blacks is that the northerners had been exposed to cultural and other environmental conditions favorable to achieving higher test scores. Among such conditions would be quality and amount of schooling, experience with test situations, diet, and conditions of life in home and neighborhood. Further attempts to interpret the test results in terms of possible nongenetic effects showed that the differences between the races disappeared when the comparison was restricted to literate New York blacks and literate Alabama whites:

	Below C	C	Above C
New York blacks	72	28	0
Alabama whites	80	20	0

Some of the scientific racists proposed that the difference between New York and southern blacks could be explained genetically. They proposed that it was the more intelligent blacks who had migrated to the North. To counter this suggestion, Otto Klineberg (1935, 1944), an anthropologically trained social psychologist, studied the relationship between the length of time that southern black migrants had lived in the North and their IQs. Klineberg found that the scores of 12-year-old southern-born black girls improved proportionately to the number of years that had elapsed since they had left the South:

Years in New York City	Average IQ
1–2	72
3–4	76
5–6	84
7–9	92
Born in New York	92

As Klineberg's data indicated, the change in residence brought the IQs of southern black girls up to the level of northern blacks in seven to nine years. For the first time, it was now freely admitted by all concerned that IQ scores could be influenced by life experience. Obviously the gap between black and white IQ scores could be narrowed—but could it ever be closed? The IQs of southern migrants merely rose to the limit of the average black northerner's score, but the score remained some 10 points below the average of the northern white IQ. This difference between the northern black and northern white IQ persists to the present moment. If black and white IQs are compared on a national basis, the difference is still greater, amounting to about 15 points (McGurk, 1975; Shuey, 1966).

The still numerous and influential racial determinists in the field of psychology and genetics no longer propose that the entire 15-point difference between whites and blacks is due to innate, hereditary factors. It is now generally recognized that environmental influences are capable of raising or lowering a group's average. But by how much?

In the late 1960s, psychologists Arthur C. Jensen (1969), R. J. Herrnstein (1973), and H. J. Eysenck (1973) contended that there was proof that only about 3 points of the differences in IQ could be attributed to the environment. This held not only for IQ differences between blacks and whites, but for IQ differences between upper- and lower-class children of the same race. Intelligence, they claimed, had a "heritability" rating of 80 percent; that is, 80 percent of the *variance* (statistical dispersal around the mean) was due to hereditary and 20 percent was due to environment. This contention has not yet been proved.

How is the heritability figure of 80 percent arrived at? To measure "heritability," one must be able to observe the development of samples of individuals who have similar genotypes (see p. 20) but who are reared in dissimilar environments. This is easily done in the case of plants and laboratory animals, but it is difficult and immoral to do in the case of human beings. The closest one can get to the controlled conditions suitable for calculating heritability in humans is to see what happens when monozygotic twins (twins born of the same ovum and same sperm) are given to foster parents and reared apart in different families. Since monozygotic twins have the same heredity, any differences in IQ scores theoretically should be due to environmental factors. It is difficult to find and test a large sample of monozygotic twins who were for one reason or another reared apart in different families, so the IQs of dizygotic twins (same ovum, different sperm) and siblings reared apart have also been studied. It has generally been recognized that the IQs of the monozygotes are more similar than those of the dizygotes reared apart, who in turn have IQs that are more similar than siblings reared apart, whose scores in turn show more similarity than those of unrelated individuals. Thus the heritability value of 80 percent is based on the progressively similar IQ scores of the individuals who are progressively closer relatives.

The use of this method involves the assumption that the amount of difference in the home environment of twins and siblings is as great as the amount of difference in the home environment of unrelated children. This assumption has been called into question, however. Adoption agencies make a considerable effort to place siblings in foster homes that match the ethnic and socioeconomic characteristics of the parents, and they also attempt to place siblings in similar situations. The motivation and feasibility for such matching is probably greatest with identical twins and least with siblings in different age groups. Moreover, the difference between monozygotic twins and dizygotic twins is readily explicable by the fact that monozygotes are always the same sex, while half of the time dizygotes are a boy and a girl. Hence all existing estimates of the heritability of intelligence merit extreme skepticism (Kamin, 1974; see Osborne, 1978; Lochlin and Nichols, 1976).

Many of the conclusions of Jensen, Eysenck, Herrnstein, and other IQ hereditarians have also recently been thrown into doubt because of their reliance on the work of Sir Cyril Burt. This English psychologist was considered the world's leading authority on the distribution of IQs within families and classes. His studies showing the close resemblance of the IQs of twins and of the IQs of fathers and children within different classes were based on larger samples than anyone else's and held to be irrefutable evidence in favor of the hereditarian position. It is now clear that Burt not only fudged his numbers—changing results to suit his hereditarian convictions—but invented the data and signed the names of fictitious collaborators to his most revered publications (Dorfman, 1978, 1979; Hechinger, 1979; Hirsch, 1981; Kamin, 1974; McAskie and Clarke, 1976).

Even if one could have confidence in the claim that the heritability of intelligence is 80 percent, such a finding would have little significance for educational policy. At best, heritability is a valid predictor of intelligence only under a given set of environmental conditions. Heritability says nothing about what IQ scores or other heritable traits will be like under a different set of environmental conditions. And heritability does not define the limits of change. Even if IQ heritability is as high as the hereditarians claim, unknowably large changes in IQ scores could still be produced by altering the environment of low-IQ children. For "whatever the heritability of IQ (or, it should be added, of any characteristic), large phenotypic changes may be produced by creating appropriate, radically different environments never before encountered by [the] genotype" (Scarr-Salapatek, 1971a, p. 1224). This can best be seen by brief reference to the relationship between heritability and changed environment in the classic case of human stature. Identical twins tend to be very similar in height; so there is a high index of heritability for stature—90 percent. But this high value of heritability for stature has not prevented an increase in the average height of twins (and of everyone else) in the past few generations as a result of improved nutrition (J. Tanner, 1968). As Lee J. Cronback (1969, p. 342) has pointed out, although the term "heritability" is standard in genetics, it "is mischievous in public discussion, for it suggests to the unwary that it describes the limit to which environmental change *can be* influential." In the words of behavior geneticist Jerry Hirsch (1970, p. 101): "High or low heritability tells us absolutely nothing about how a given individual might have developed under conditions different from those in which he actually did develop." More recently, Hirsch (1981, p. 36) has condemned the preoccupation with measuring racial intelligence differences as scientifically "impossible (and thus worthless)."

The greater the amount of cultural difference between populations, the more trivial and futile the heritability measurements.

Thus, the highest recorded IQ gains in controlled studies are reported from populations with the greatest cultural contrasts. In Israel, for example, Jewish immigrants from Arab countries show a 20-point gain in one year (Bereiter and Engelmann, 1966, pp. 55–56).

When psychologists first began to recognize that the Stanford-Binet IQ test was "culture-bound," they attempted to develop substitutes that would be "culture-free" or "culture-fair" (Cattell, 1940). It is a contradiction in terms, however, to suppose that any enculturated human being can be approached in such a way as to overcome or cancel out the effects of enculturation (see Lynn, 1978). In the words of Paul Bohannan:

There is no possibility of any "intelligence" test not being culturally biased. The content of an intelligence test must have something to do with the ideas or with the muscle habits or with habitual modes of perception and action of the people who take the test. All these things are culturally mediated or influenced in human beings. . . . This is not a dictum or a definition—it is a recognition of the way in which cultural experience permeates everything human beings perceive and do. (1973, p. 115)

Bibliography

In the citation system used in the text, the names in parentheses are the authors of the publications mentioned, or of publications that support the descriptions or interpretations of matters being discussed. The year following the names is the year of publication and should be used to identify specific sources when more than one publication of the author is included. Letters following a date (e.g., 1972a) distinguish different publications of one author for the same year. "See" is used to refer to points of view opposed to those given in the text. Specific page numbers are provided only for direct quotes or controversial points.

Acheson, James M.

1972 "Limited Good or Limited Goods: Response to Economic Opportunity in a Tarascan Pueblo." *American Anthropologist* 74:1152–1169.

1974 "Reply to George Foster." *American Anthropologist* 76:57–62.

Adams, M., and J. V. Neil

1967 "The Children of Incest." *Pediatrics* 40:55–62.

Adams, Richard N.

1968 "An Inquiry into the Nature of the Family." In *Selected Studies in Marriage and Family*, R. F. Winch and L. W. Goodman, eds., pp. 45–57. New York: Holt, Rinehart and Winston.

1970 *Crucifixion by Power*. Austin: University of Texas Press.

Alexander, Richard

1974 "Evolution of Social Behavior." *Annual Review of Ecological Systems* 5:325–383.

1976 "Evolution: Human Behavior and Determinism." *PSA* 2:3–21.

1977 "Natural Selection and the Analysis of Human Sociology." *The Changing Scenes in the Natural Sciences, 1776–1976*, C. E. Goulden, ed., pp. 283–337. Academy of Natural Science. Special Publication 12.

Alland, Alexander

1977 *The Artistic Animal: An Inquiry into the Biological Roots of Art*. Garden City: N.Y.: Doubleday (Anchor Books).

Angel, Lawrence

1975 "Paleoecology, Paleodemography and Health." In *Population, Ecology and Social Evolution*, Steven Polgar, ed., pp. 167–190. The Hague: Mouton.

Armelagos, George, and A. McArdie

1975 "Population, Disease, and Evolution." *American Antiquity* 40:1–10.

Armstrong, Louise

1978 *Kiss Daddy Goodnight*. New York: Hawthorne.

Aron, Raymond

1966 "Social Class, Political Class, Ruling Class." In *Class, Status, and Power: Social Stratification in Comparative Perspective*, R. Bendix and S. M. Lipset, eds., pp. 201–210. New York: Free Press.

Bagley, William C.

1924 "The Army Tests and the Pro-Nordic Propaganda." *Educational Review* 67:179–187.

Bakker, Jim

1976 *Move That Mountain*. Plainfield, N.J.: Logos International.

Bane, Mary Jo

1976 *Here to Stay: American Families in the Twentieth Century*. New York: Basic Books.

Bao, Ruo-Wang (Jean Pasqualini), and Rudolph Chelminski

1973 *Prisoner of Mao*. New York: Coward, McCann & Geoghegan.

Barash, David

1977 *Sociobiology and Behavior.* New York: Elsevier.

Barber, Bernard

1968 "Social Mobility in Hindu India." In *Social Mobility in the Caste System*, J. Silverberg, ed., pp. 18–35. The Hague: Mouton.

Barnouw, Victor

1973 *Culture and Personality.* Homewood, Ill.: Dorsey Press.

Barnes, J. A.

1960 "Marriage and Residential Continuity." *American Anthropologist* 62:850–866.

Beattie, John

1960 *Bunyoro: An African Kingdom.* New York: Holt, Rinehart and Winston.

Bell, Daniel

1973 *The Coming of Post-Industrial Society: A Venture in Social Forecasting.* New York: Basic Books.

Bellah, Robert

1976 "New Religious Consciousness and the Crisis in Modernity." In *The New Religious Consciousness*, Robert Bellah and Charles Clock, eds., pp. 297–330. Berkeley: University of California Press.

Bender, Donald R.

1967 "A Refinement of the Concept of Household: Families, Co-residence, and Domestic Functions." *American Anthropologist* 69:493–503.

Bendix, Reinhard, and S. M. Lipset, eds.

1966 *Class, Status and Power: Social Stratification in Comparative Perspective.* New York: Free Press.

Benedict, Ruth

1934 *Patterns of Culture.* Boston: Houghton Mifflin.

1938 "Religion." In *General Anthropology*, F. Boas, ed., pp. 627–665. New York: Columbia University Press.

Bereiter, Carl, and S. Engelman

1966 *Teaching Disadvantaged Students in Pre-School.* Engelwood Cliffs, N.J.: Prentice-Hall.

Bernard, H. Russell

1981 "Issues in Training in Applied Anthropology," *Practicing Anthropology* 3 (Winter).

Berreman, Gerald D.

1966 "Caste in Cross-cultural Perspective." In *Japan's Invisible Race: Caste in Culture and Personality*, G. de Vos and H. Wagatsuma, eds., pp. 275–324. Berkeley: University of California Press.

1975 "Bazar Behavior: Social Identity and Social Interaction in Urban India." In *Ethnic Identity: Cultural Continuity and Change*, L. Romanucci-Ross and G. De Vos, eds., pp. 71–105. Palo Alto, Calif.: Mayfield.

Bettleheim, Charles

1978 "The Great Leap Backward." *Monthly Review* 30(3):37–130.

Bigelow, Robert

1975 "The Role of Competition and Cooperation in Human Evolution." In *War: Its Causes and Correlates*, M. Nettleship, R. D. Givens, and A. Nettleship, eds., pp. 235–261. The Hague: Mouton.

Birdsell, Joseph B.

1968 "Some Predictions for the Pleistocene Based on Equilibrium Systems among Recent Hunter-Gatherers." In *Man the Hunter*, R. Lee and I. Devore, eds., pp. 229–249. Chicago: Aldine.

1972 *Human Evolution: An Introduction to the New Physical Anthropology.* Chicago: Rand McNally.

Black, Francis

1975 "Infectious Disease in Primitive Societies." *Science* 187:515–518.

1961 *Family Structure in Jamaica: The Social Context of Reproduction.* New York: Free Press.

Blau, Peter, and O. D. Duncan

1967 *The American Occupational Structure.* New York: Wiley.

Bloch, Marc

1961 *Feudal Society.* Chicago: University of Chicago Press.

1964 "Feudalism as a Type of Society." In *Sociology and History: Theory and Research*, W. J. Cahnman and A. Boskoff, eds., pp. 163–170. New York: Free Press.

Bodley, John

1975 *Victims of Progress.* Menlo Park, Calif.: Cummings.

Bohannan, Paul

1973 "Rethinking Culture: A Project for Current Anthropologists." *Current Anthropology* 14: 357–372.

Boserup, Ester

1965 *The Condition of Agricultural Growth: The Economics of Agrarian Change under Population Pressure.* Chicago: Aldine.

Bottomore, T. B.

1966 *Classes in Modern Society.* New York: Random House (Vintage Books).

Boulding, Kenneth E.

1973 *The Economy of Love and Fear.* Belmont, Calif.: Wadsworth.

Braverman, Harry

1974 *Labor and Monopoly Capital: The Degrada-*

tion of Work in the Twentieth Century. New York: Monthly Review Press.

Bronson, Bennet

1972 "Farm Labor and the Evolution of Food Production." In *Population Growth: Anthropological Implications*, B. Spooner, ed., pp. 190–218. Cambridge, Mass.: MIT Press.

Brown, Judith K.

1975 "Iroquois Women: An Ethnohistoric Note." In *Toward an Anthropology of Women*, Rayna Reiter, ed., pp. 235–251. New York: Monthly Review Press.

Brown, Lester

1978 *The Global Economic Prospect: New Sources of Economic Stress*. Washington, D.C.: Worldwatch Institute. Worldwatch Paper 20.

Brown, Ronald

1978 Testimony: Hearings Before the Subcommittee on Crime, House of Representatives. Ninety-Fifth Congress, Serial No. 47. Washington D.C.: U.S. Government Printing Office.

Brownlee, W. Elliot

1979 "Household Values, Women's Work, and Economic Growth 1800–1930." *Journal of Economic History*. In *Sociology 80/81*, J. Scherer, ed., pp. 261–265. Guilford, Ct.: Dushkin.

Brunton, Ron

1975 "Why do the Trobriands Have Chiefs?" *Man* 10(4):545–550.

Buchbinder, Georgeda

In press *Nutrition and Population Dynamics: A Case Study from the New Guinea Highlands*. Queens, N.Y.: Spectrum.

Burton, Michael, Lilyan Brudner, and Douglas White

1977 "A Model of the Sexual Division of Labor." *American Ethnologist* 4(2):227–251.

Butz, William, and Michael Ward

1979 "Baby Boom and Baby Bust: A New View." *American Demographics Magazine*.

Carneiro, Robert

1970 "A Theory of the Origin of the State." *Science* 169:733–738.

1978 "Politician Expansion as an Expression of the Principle of Competitive Exclusion." In *Origins of the State*, Ronald Cohen and E. Service, eds., pp. 205–223. Philadelphia: ISHI.

Carroll, Lucy

1977 "'Sanskritization,' 'Westernization,' and 'Social Mobility': A Reappraisal of the Relevance of Anthropological Concepts to the Social Historian of Modern India." *Journal of Anthropological Research* 33(4):355–371.

Carstairs, G. M.

1967 *The Twice-born*. Bloomington: Indiana University Press.

Carter, William (ed.)

1980 *Cannabis in Costa Rica: A Study of Chronic Marihuana Use*. Philadelphia: ISHI.

Cattell, R. B.

1940 "A Culture-free Intelligence Test." *Journal of Educational Psychology* 31:161–179.

Cattle, Dorothy

1977 "An Alternative to Nutritional Particularism." In *Nutrition and Anthropology in Action*, Thomas Fitzgerald, ed., pp. 35–45. Amsterdam: Van Gorcum.

Chagnon, Napolean

1974 *Studying the Yanomamö*. New York: Holt, Rinehart and Winston.

1977 *Yanomamö: The Fierce People*. 2nd ed. New York: Holt, Rinehart and Winston.

Chagnon, Napoleon, and Raymond Haines

1979 "Protein Deficiency and Tribal Warfare in Amazonia: New Data." *Science* 203:910–913.

Clarke, William

1976 "Maintenance of Agriculture and Human Habitats within the Tropical Forest Ecosystem." *Human Ecology* 4(3):247–259.

Cleaver, Harry

1975 "Will the Green Revolution Turn Red?" In *The Trojan Horse: A Radical look at Foreign Aid*, Steve Weisman, ed., New York: Monthly Review Press: 171–200.

Cloud, Wallace

1973 "After the Green Revolution." *The Sciences* 13(8):6–12.

Cockburn, T. A.

1971 "Infectious Diseases in Ancient Populations." *Current Anthropology* 12:45–62.

Coe, Michael

1977 *Mexico*, 2nd ed., New York: Praeger.

Cohen, Mark N.

1977 *The Food Crisis in Prehistory*. New Haven, Conn.: Yale University Press.

Cohen, Myron

1976 *House United, House Divided*. New York: Columbia University Press.

Cohen, Ronald

1978a "State Origins: A Reappraisal." In *The Early State*, H. Claessen and P. Skalnik, eds., pp. 31–75. The Hague: Mouton.

1978b "Ethnicity." *Annual Review of Anthropology* 7:379–403.

Cohen, Yehudi

1978 "The Disappearance of the Incest Taboo." *Human Nature* 1(7)72–78.

Cohn, Bernard

1955 "Changing Status of a Depressed Caste." In *Village India: Studies in the Little Community*, M. Mariott, ed., 83:55–77. American Anthropological Memoirs.

Condominas, George

1957 *Nous avons mangé la foret de la Pérre-Genie Goo.* Paris.

1972 "From the Rice Field to the Miir." *Social Science Information* 11:41–62.

Conway, Flo, and Jim Siegelman

1978 *Snapping: America's Epidemic of Sudden Personality Change.* Philadelphia: Lippincott.

Conyers, John

1978 "Unemployment Is Cruel and Unusual Punishment." In Hearings Before the Subcommittee on Crime, House of Representatives. Ninety-Fifth Congress, Serial No. 47. Washington: D.C.: U.S. Government Printing Office, 674–679.

Craig, Daniel

1979 "Immortality through Kinship: The Vertical Transmission of Substance and Symbolic Estate." *American Anthropologist* 81:94–96.

Cronback, Lee J.

1969 "Heredity, Environment, and Educational Policy." *Harvard Educational Review* 39:338–339.

Cummings, R. C.

1978 "Agricultural Change in Vietnam's Floating Rice Region." *Human Organization* 37:235–245.

Curvin, Robert, and Bruce Porter

1978 "The Myth of Blackout Looters. . . ." *The New York Times* July 13, p. 21

Dahl, Robert

1961 *Who Governs? Democracy and Power in the American City.* New Haven, Conn.: Yale University Press.

Dalton, George

1965 "Primitive Money." *American Anthropologist* 67:44–65.

1969 "Theoretical Issues in Economic Anthropology." *Current Anthropology* 10:63–102.

1972 "Peasantries in Anthropology and History." *Current Anthropology* 13:385–416.

1974 "How Exactly Are Peasants Exploited?" *American Anthropologist* 76:553–561.

Davis, Shelton

1977 *Victims of the Miracle: Development and the Indians of Brazil.* New York: Cambridge University Press.

Degler, Carl

1980 *At Odds: Women and the Family in America from the Revolution to the Present.* New York: Cambridge University Press.

De Laguna, Frederica

1968 "Presidential Address: 1967." *American Anthropologist* 70:469–476.

De Loria, Vine

1969 *Custer Died for Your Sins.* London: Collier-Macmillan.

Demarest, William

1977 "Incest Avoidance among Human and Non-Human Primates." In *Primate Bio-Social Development: Biological, Social and Ecological Determinants*, S. Chevalier-Skolinikoff and F. Poirer, eds., pp. 323–342. New York: Garland.

Dentan, Robert

1968 *The Semai: A Non-Violent People of Malaya.* New York: Holt, Rinehart and Winston.

Despres, Leo

1975 "Ethnicity and Resource Competition in Guyanese Society." In *Ethnicity and Resource Competition in Plural Societies*, L. Despres, ed., pp. 87–117. The Hague: Mouton.

Devereux, George

1967 "A Typological Study of Abortion in 350 Primitive, Ancient, and Pre-Industrial Societies." In *Abortion in America*, H. Rosen, ed., pp. 95–152. Boston: Beacon Press.

Diaz, May

1966 *Tonalá: Conservatism, Responsibility and Authority in a Mexican Town.* Berkeley: The University of California Press.

Diener, Paul, and E. Robkin

1978 "Ecology, Evolution, and the Search for Cultural Origins: The Question of the Islamic Pig Prohibition." *Current Anthropology* 19:493–540.

Dillingham, Beth, and B. Isaac

1975 "Defining Marriage Cross-culturally." In *Being Female: Reproduction, Power and Change*, D. Raphael, ed., pp. 55–63. The Hague: Mouton.

Divale, William

1972 "Systematic Population Control in the Middle and Upper Paleolithic: Inferences Based on Contemporary Hunters and Gatherers." *World Archeology* 4:221–243.

1974 "Migration, External Warfare, and Matrilocal Residence." *Behavior Science Research* 9:75–133.

Divale, William, and Marvin Harris

1976 "Population, Warfare and the Male Supremacist Complex." *American Anthropologist* 78:521–538.

1978a "Reply to Lancaster and Lancaster." *American Anthropologist* 80:117–118.

1978b "The Male Supremacist Complex: Discovery of a Cultural Invention." *American Anthropologist* 80:668–671.

Divale, William, M. Harris, and D. Williams
1978 "On the Misuse of Statistics: A Reply to Hirschfield et al." *American Anthropologist* 80:379–386.

Dobyns, Henry
1966 "Estimating Aboriginal American Populations: An Appraisal of Technique with a New Hemisphere Estimate." *Current Anthropology* 7:395–449.
1972 "The Cornell-Peru Project: Experimental Intervention in Vicos." In *Contemporary Societies and Cultures of Latin America*, Dwight Heath, ed., pp. 201–210. New York: Random House.

Dole, Gertrude
1966 "Anarchy without Chaos: Alternatives to Political Authority among the Kui-Kuru." In *Political Anthropology*, M. J. Swartz, V. W. Turner and A. Tuden, eds., pp. 73–88. Chicago: Aldine.

Domhoff, G. William
1970 *The Higher Circles: The Governing Class in America*. New York: Random House.

Dorfman, D. D.
1978 "The Cyril Burt Question: New Findings." *Science* 201:1177–1186.
1979 Letter on "Burt's Tables." *Science* 204:246–255.

Drummond, Isabel
1953 *The Sex Paradox*. New York: Putnam.

Dumond, Don
1975 "The Limitation of Human Population: A Natural History." *Science* 187:713–721.

Dumont, Louis
1970 *Homo Hierarchicus: The Caste System and Its Implications*. Trans. Mark Sainsbury. Chicago: University of Chicago Press.

Eddy, Elizabeth, and William Partridge (eds.)
1978 *Applied Anthropology in America*. New York: Columbia University Press.

Efron, Edith
1972 *The News Twisters*. New York: Manor Books.

Eliade, M.
1958 *Birth and Rebirth: The Religious Meaning of Initiation in Human Culture*. New York: Harper & Row.

Ellul, Jacques
1965 *Propaganda: The Formation of Men's Attitudes*. Trans. K. Kellen and J. Lerner. New York: Knopf.

Elshtain, Jean
1979 "Feminists against the Family." *The Nation* November 17, pp. 481ff.

Ember, Carol, M. Ember, and B. Pasternak
1974 "On the Development of Unilineal Descent." *Journal of Anthropological Research* 30:69–94.

Ember, Melvin, and Carol R. Ember
1971 "The Conditions Favoring Matrifocal versus Patrifocal Residence." *American Anthropologist* 73:571–594.

Engels, Frederick
1972 (1884) *The Origin of the Family, Private Property, and the State*. New York: International Publishers.

Epstein, T. Scarlett
1968 *Capitalism, Primitive and Modern: Some Aspects of Tolai Economic Growth*. East Lansing: Michigan State University Press.

Evans-Pritchard, E. E.
1940 *The Nuer, A Description of the Modes of Livelihood and Political Institutions of a Nilotic People*. Oxford: Clarendon Press.
1970 "Sexual Inversion among the Azande." *American Anthropologist* 72:1428–1433.

Eysenck, H. J.
1973 *The Inequality of Man*. London: Temple Smith.

Fallers, Lloyd
1977 "Equality and Inequality in Human Societies." In *Horizons of Anthropology*, 2nd ed., S. Tax and L. Freeman, eds., pp. 257–268. Chicago: Aldine.

Fei, Hsiao-t'ung, and Chang chih-I
1947 *Earthbound China: A Study of Rural Economy in Yunnan*. Chicago: University of Chicago Press.

Ferguson, Brian
1979 "War and Redistribution on the Northwest Coast." Paper read at the meetings of the American Ethnological Association, Vancouver, B.C.

Firth, Raymond
1957 *We, The Tikopia: A Sociological Study of Kinship in Primitive Polynesia*. Boston: Beacon Press.

Fittkau, E. J., and H. Klinge
1973 "On Biomass and Tropic Structure of the Central Amazon Rain Forest Ecosystem." *Biotropica* 5:1–14.

Flannery, Kent
1972 "The Origin of the Village as a Settlement Type in Mesoamerica and the Near East: A Comparative Study." In *Man, Settlement and Urbanism*, P. J. Ucko, R. Tringham, and G. W. Dimbleby, eds., pp. 23–53. Cambridge, Mass.: Schenkman.

Fortes, Meyer
1969 *Kinship and the Social Order: The Legacy of Lewis Henry Morgan*. Chicago: Aldine.

Fortune, Reo
1965 *Manus Religion*. Lincoln: University of Nebraska Press.

Foster, George M.

1967 *Tzintzuntzan: Mexican Peasants in a Changing World*. Boston: Little, Brown.

1972 "The Anatomy of Envy: A Study in Symbolic Behavior." *Current Anthropology* 13: 165–202.

1974 "Limited Good or Limited Goods: Observations on Acheson." *American Anthropologist* 76:53–57.

Foster, George, and Barbara Anderson

1978 *Medical Anthropology*. New York: Wiley.

Franke, Richard W.

1973 "The Green Revolution in a Javanese Village." Ph.D. dissertation, Harvard University.

1974 "Miracle Seeds and Shattered Dreams." *Natural History* 83(1):10ff.

Frazer, James

1911–1915 *The Golden Bough*, 3rd ed. London: Macmillan.

Freedman, Robert

1977 "Nutritional Anthropology: An Overview." In *Nutrition and Anthropology in Action*, Thomas Fitzgerald, ed., pp. 1–23. Amsterdam: Van Gorcum.

Freire, Paulo

1973 *Pedagogy of the Oppressed*. New York: Seabury Press.

Fried, Morton H.

1967 *The Evolution of Political Society: An Essay in Political Anthropology*. New York: Random House.

1968 "The Need to End the Pseudoscientific Investigation of Race." In *Science and the Concept of Race*, M. Mead et al., eds., pp. 122–131. New York: Columbia University Press.

1972 *The Study of Anthropology*. New York: Crowell.

1975 *The Notion of Tribe*. Menlo Park, Calif.: Cummings.

1978 "The State, the Chicken, and the Egg: or What Came First?" In *Origins of the State*, Ronald Cohen and Elman Service, eds., pp. 35–47. Philadelphia: Institute for the Study of Human Issues.

Frisch, Rose

1978 "Reply to Trussel." *Science* 200:1509–1513.

Frisch, Rose, and Janet MacArthur

1974 "Menstrual Cycles: Fatness as a Determinant of Minimum Weight for Height Necessary for Their Maintenance or Onset." *Science* 185:949–951.

Fromm, Erich, and M. Maccoby

1970 *A Mexican Village: A Sociopsychoanalytic Study*. Englewood Cliffs, N.J.: Prentice-Hall.

Furstenberg, Frank, Theodore Hershberg, and John Medell

1975 "The Origins of the Female-Headed Black Family: The Impact of the Urban Experience." *Journal of Interdisciplinary History* 6(2): 211–233.

Galbraith, John K.

1958 *The Affluent Society*. Boston: Houghton Mifflin.

1967 *The New Industrial State*. Boston: Houghton Mifflin.

1978 *Almost Everyone's Guide to Economics*. Boston: Houghton Mifflin.

Gallup International

1980

Gandhi, Mohandas K.

1954 *How to Serve the Cow: Ahmedabad*. Navajivan Publishing House.

Gardner, B. T., and R. A. Gardner

1971 "Two-Way Communication with a Chimpanzee." In *Behavior of Non-Human Primates*, A Schrier and F. Stollnitz, eds., vol. 4, pp. 117–184. New York: Academic Press.

Gardner, R. A., and B. T. Gardner

1975 "Early Signs of Language in Child and Chimpanzee." *Science* 187:752–753.

Gearing, Fred, and B. A. Tindale

1973 "Anthropological Studies of the Educational Process." In *Annual Review of Anthropology*, vol. 1, B. J. Siegel, A. R. Beals, and S. A. Tyler, eds., pp. 95–105. Palo Alto, Calif.: Annual Reviews Press.

Glassow, Michael

1978 "The Concept of Carrying Capacity in the Study of Cultural Process." In *Advances in Archeological Theory and Method*, Michael Schiffler, ed., pp. 31–48. New York: Academic Press.

Gilder, George

1981 *Wealth and Property*. New York: Basic Books.

Glenn, Evelyn, and Roslyn Feldberg

1977 "Degraded and Deskilled: The Proletarianization of Clerical Work." *Social Problems* 25: 52–64.

Gluckman, Max

1955 *Custom and Conflict in Africa*. Oxford: Blackwell.

Goldschmidt, Walter (ed.)

1979 *The Uses of Anthropology*. Washington, D.C.: The American Anthropological Association. Special Publication No. 11.

González, Nancy L.

1970 "Towards a Definition of Matrilocality." In *Afro-American Anthropology: Contemporary Per-*

spectives, N. E. Whitten and J. F. Szwed, eds., pp. 231–243. New York: Free Press.

Good, Kenneth
n.d. Personal communication.

Goodall, Jane Van Lawick
1968 "A Preliminary Report on Expressive Movements and Communication in Gombe Stream Chimpanzees." In *Primates: Studies in Adaptation and Variability*, Phyllis Jay, ed., pp. 313–374. New York: Holt, Rinehart and Winston.
1979 "Life and Death at Gambe." *National Geographic* 155(5):592–620.

Goodenough, Ward H.
1970 *Description and Comparison in Cultural Anthropology*. Chicago: Aldine.

Goody, Jack
1976 *Production and Reproduction*. New York: Cambridge University Press.

Gough, E. Kathleen
1959 "Criterion of Caste Ranking in South India." *Man in India* 39:115–126.
1968 "The Nayars and the Definition of Marriage." In *Marriage, Family, and Residence*, P. Bohannan and J. Middleton, eds., pp. 49–71. Garden City, N.Y.: Natural History Press.
1978 "The Green Revolution in South India and North Vietnam." *Monthly Review* 29(8):10–21.

Gould, Harold
1971 "Caste and Class: A Comparative View." *Module* 11:1–24. Reading, Mass.: Addison-Wesley.

Gramby, Richard
1977 "Deerskins and Hunting Territories: Competition for a Scarce Resource of the Northeastern Woodlands." *American Antiquity* 42:601–605.

Graves, Theodore
1974 "Urban Indian Personality and the Culture of Poverty." *American Ethnologist* 1:65–86.

Greenberg, Joseph
1968 *Anthropological Linguistics: An Introduction.* New York: Random House.

Gregor, Thomas A.
1969 "Social Relations in a Small Society: A Study of the Mehinacu Indians of Central Brazil." Ph.D. dissertation, Columbia University.

Gross, Daniel R.
1975 "Protein Capture and Cultural Development in the Amazon Basin." *American Anthropologist* 77:526–549.
1981 "Reply to Beckerman." Mss.

Gujdusek, D. C.
1977 "Unconventional Viruses and the Origin and Disappearance of Kuru." *Science* 197:943–960.

Hadley, Arthur
1978 *The Empty Polling Booth*. Englewood Cliffs, N.J.: Prentice-Hall.

Hall, Calvin, and G. Lindzey
1967 "Freud's Psychoanalytic Theory of Personality." In *Personalities and Cultures: Readings in Psychological Anthropology*, Robert Hunt, ed., pp. 3–29. Garden City, N.Y.: Natural History Press.

Haller, John S.
1971 *Outcasts from Evolution*. Urbana: University of Illinois Press.

Hanks, Lucien
1972 *Rice and Man: Agricultural Ecology in Southeast Asia*. Chicago: Aldine.

Harner, Michael J.
1970 "Population Pressure and the Social Evolution of Agriculturalists." *Southwestern Journal of Anthropology* 26:67–86.
1972a "The Role of Hallucinogenic Plants in European Witchcraft." In *Hallucinogens and Shamanism*, Michael Harner, ed., pp. 127–150. New York: Oxford University Press.
1972b *The Jívaro: People of the Sacred Waterfalls*. Garden City, N.Y.: Natural History Press.
1977 "The Ecological Basis for Aztec Sacrifice." *American Ethnologist* 4:117–135.
1978 "Reply to Ortiz de Montallano." Paper read at the New York Academy of Sciences, November 17, 1978.

Harrington, Charles, and J. Whiting
1972 "Socialization Process and Personality." In *Psychological Anthropology*, Francis Hsu, ed., pp. 469–507. Cambridge, Mass.: Schenkman.

Harrington, Michael
1980 *Decade of Decision*. New York: Simon and Schuster.

Harris, Marvin
1958 *Portugal's African "Wards": A First Hand Report on Labour and Education in Mozambique*. New York: American Committee on Africa.
1968 *The Rise of Anthropological Theory*. New York: Crowell.
1974 *Cows, Pigs, Wars, and Witches: The Riddle of Culture*. New York: Random House.
1977 *Cannibals and Kings: The Origins of Cultures*. New York: Random House.
1979a "Comments on Simoons' Questions in the Sacred Cow Controversy." *Current Anthropology* 20:479–482.
1979b *Cultural Materialism: The Struggle for a Science of Culture*. New York: Random House.
1981 *America Now: The Anthropology of a Changing Culture*. New York: Simon and Schuster.

Harris, Marvin, and E. O. Wilson
1978 "The Envelope and the Twig." *The Sciences* 18(8):10–15, 27.

Hart, C. W. M., and A. R. Pilling
1960 *The Tiwi of North Australia.* New York: Holt, Rinehart and Winston.

Hassan, Fekri
1973 "On Mechanisms of Population Growth during the Neolithic." *Current Anthropology* 14: 535–540.
1978 "Demographic Archeology." In *Advances in Archeological Method and Theory*, Michael Schiffer, ed., pp. 49–103. New York: Academic Press.

Hazard, Thomas
1960 "On the Nature of the Numaym and Its Counterparts Elsewhere on the Northwest Coast." Paper presented to the 127th Annual Meeting of the American Association for the Advancement of Science, Denver.

Hechinger, Fred
1979 "Further Proof That I.Q. Data Were Fraudulent." *The New York Times* 30 January, p. C4.

Heider, Karl G.
1969 "Visiting Trading Institutions." *American Anthropologist* 71:462–471.
1972 *The Dani of West Iran.* Reading, Mass.: Addison-Wesley.

Heilbroner, Robert L.
1966 *The Limits of American Capitalism.* New York: Harper & Row.

Henry, Jules
1963 *Culture Against Man.* New York: Random House.

Herbers, John
1978 "Black-White Split Persists a Decade after Warning." *The New York Times* 26 February, p. 1ff.

Herrnstein, R. J.
1973 *I.Q. in the Meritocracy.* Boston: Little, Brown.

Hersh, Burton
1978 *The Mellon Family: A Fortune in History.* New York: William Morrow.

Herskovits, Melville J.
1938 *Dahomey, An Ancient West African Kingdom.* New York: J. J. Augustin.

Hewitt de Alcantara, Cynthia
1976 *Modernizing Mexican Agriculture.* Geneva: United Nations Research Institute for Social Development.

Hicks, David
1976 *Tetum Ghosts and Kin.* Palo Alto, Calif.: Mayfield.

Hill, Jane
1978 "Apes and Language." *Annual Review of Anthropology* 7:89–112.

Hindelang, Michael
1978 "Race and Involvement in Common Law Personal Crimes." *American Sociological Review* 43:93–109.

Hirsch, Jerry
1970 "Behavior-Genetic Analysis and Its Biosocial Consequences." *Seminars in Psychiatry* 2:89–105.
1981 "To Unfrock the Charlatans." *Sage Race Relations Abstracts* 6:1–67.

Hirschfeld, Lawrence, J. Howe, and B. Levin
1978 "Warfare, Infanticide and Statistical Inference: A Comment on Divale and Harris." *American Anthropologist* 80:110–115.

Hite, S.
1976 *The Hite Report: A Nationwide Study of Female Sexuality.* New York: Macmillan.

Hockett, Charles, and R. Ascher
1964 "The Human Revolution." *Current Anthropology* 5:135–147.

Hogbin, H. Ian
1964 *A Guadalcanal Society: The Kaoka Speakers.* New York: Holt, Rinehart and Winston.

Howe, James
1978 "Ninety-two Mythical Populations: A Reply to Divale et al." *American Anthropologist* 80:671–673.

Howell, Nancy
1976a "The Population of the Dobe Area !Kung." In *Kalahari Hunter-Gatherers*, Richard Lee and Irven De Vore, eds., pp. 137–151. Cambridge, Mass.: Harvard University Press.
1976b "Toward a Uniformitarian Theory of Human Paleodemography." In *The Demographic Evolution of Human Populations*, R. H. Ward and K. M. Weiss, eds., pp. 25–40. New York: Academic Press.

Huffman, Sandra, A. K. M. Chowdhury, and W. H. Mosley
1978 "Postpartum Amenorrhea: How Is It Affected by Maternal Nutritional Status?" *Science* 200:1155–1157.
1979 "Reply to Frisch." *Science* 203:922–923.

Husain, Tariq
1976 "The Use of Anthropologists in Project Appraisal by the World Bank." In *Development from Below: Anthropologists and Development Situations*, David Pitt, ed., pp. 71–81. The Hague: Mouton.

Ianni, F. A. J., and E. Story, eds.
1973 *Cultural Relevance and Educational Issues: A*

Reader in Anthropology and Education. Boston: Little, Brown.

ICRISAT
n.d. *This Is Icrisat*. ICRISAT: Hyderabad.

1961 "The Society of Japanese Monkeys." *Japan Quarterly* 8:421–430.

Itani, J., and A. Nishimura
1973 "The Study of Infra-Human Culture in Japan." In *Precultural Primate Behavior*, E. W. Menzell, ed., pp. 26–50. Basel: S. Karjer.

Janzen, Daniel
1973 "Tropical Agroecosystems." *Science* 182:1212–1219.

Jensen, Arthur
1969 "How much Can We Boost I.Q. and Scholastic Achievement?" *Harvard Educational Review* 29:1–123.

Jensen, Neal
1978 "Limits to Growth in World Food Production." *Science* 201:317–320.

Job, Barbara Cottman
1980 "Employment and Pay Trends in the Retail Trade Industry." *Monthly Labor Review* March, pp. 40–43.

Johnson, Allen W.
1974 "The Allocation of Time in a Machiguenga Community." Mimeographed.
1975 "Time Allocation in a Machiguenga Community." *Ethnology* 14:301–310.
1978 *Quantification in Cultural Anthropology*. Stanford: Stanford University Press.

Jones, Delmos
1976 "Applied Anthropology and the Application of Anthropological Knowledge." *Human Organization* 35:221–229.

Jorgenson, Joseph
1971 "On Ethnics and Anthropology," *Current Anthropology* 12(3):321–334.

Joseph, Suad
1978 "Muslim-Christian Conflicts in Lebanon: A Perspective on the Evolution of Sectarianism." In *Muslim-Christian Conflicts: Economic, Political and Social Origins*, S. Joseph and B. Pillsbury, eds., pp. 63–98. Boulder, Colo.: Westview Press.

Kaberry, Phyllis
1970 *Aboriginal Woman, Sacred and Profane*. London: Routledge. (Initially published 1939).

Kaeppler, Adrienne
1978 "Dance in Anthropological Perspective." *Annual Review of Anthropology* 7:31–49.

Kamin, L. J.
1974 *The Science and Politics of I.Q.* New York: Halstead Press.

Kay, Richard
1981 "The Nut-Crackers—A New Theory of the Adaptations of the Ramapithecinae." *American Journal of Physical Anthropology* 55:141–151.

Kelly, Raymond
1976 "Witchcraft and Sexual Relations." In *Man and Woman in the New Guinea Highlands*, P. Brown and G. Buchbinder, eds., pp. 36–53. Washington, D.C.: Special Publication No. 8, American Anthropological Association.

Kertzer, David
1978 "Theoretical Developments in the Study of Age Group Systems." *American Ethnologist* 5(2):368–374.

Key, Wilson
1976 *Media Sexploitation*. New York: Signet.

Klass, Morton
1979 *Caste: The Emergence of the South Asian Social System*. Philadelphia: ISHI.

Klineberg, Otto
1935 *Negro Intelligence and Selective Migration*. New York: Columbia University Press.
1944 *Characteristics of the American Negro*. New York: Harper & Row.

Knight, Rolf
1974 "Grey Owl's Return: Cultural Ecology and Canadian Indigenous Peoples." *Reviews in Anthropology* 1:349–359.

Kolko, Gabriel
1979 "The Structure of the Working Class and the Working Wife." In *The American Class: Prospects for the 1980s*, I. L. Horowitz et al., eds., pp. 95–113. New Brunswick, N.J.: Transaction Books.

Kortlant, A.
1967 "Experimentation with Chimpanzees in the Wild." In *Progress in Primatology*, D. Starck, R. Schneider, and H. Kuhn, eds. pp. 185–194. Stuttgart: Gustav Fischer.

Koskoff, David
1978 *The Mellons: The Chronicle of America's Richest Family*. New York: Crowell.

Kozol, Jonathon
1967 *Death at an Early Age: The Destruction of the Hearts and Minds of Negro Children in the Boston Public Schools*. Boston: Houghton Mifflin.

La Barre, Weston
1938 *The Peyote Cult*. Yale University Publications in Anthropology, No. 19. New Haven, Conn.: Yale University Press.

Ladd, Everett, Jr.
1978 *Where Have All the Voters Gone?* New York: Norton.

Lancaster, Chet, and J. B. Lancaster
1978 "On the Male Supremacist Complex: A

Reply to Divale and Harris." *American Anthropologist* 80:115–117.

Langdon, Steve
1979 "Comparative Tlingit and Haida Adaptation to the West Coast of the Prince of Wales Archipelago." *Ethnology* 18:101–119.

Lattimore, Owen
1962 *Inner Asian Frontiers of China.* Boston: Beacon Press.

Lawrence, Peter
1964 *Road Belong Cargo: A Study of the Cargo Movement in the Southern Madang District, New Guinea.* Manchester: University of Manchester.

Leach, Edmund R.
1968 "Polyandry, Inheritance, and the Definition of Marriage, with Particular Reference to Sinhalese Customary Law." In *Marriage, Family, and Residence,* P. Bohannan and J. Middleton, eds., pp. 73–83. Garden City, N.Y.: Natural History Press.

Leacock, Eleanor B.
1972 "Introduction" to F. Engels' *Origin of the Family, Private Property and the State,* pp. 7–67. New York: International Publishers.
1973 "The Montagnais-Naskapi Band." In *Cultural Ecology: Readings on the Canadian Indians and Eskimos,* B. Cox, ed., pp. 81–100. Toronto: McClelland and Stewart.
1975 "Class, Commodity, and the Status of Women." In *Women Cross-Culturally: Change and Challenge,* R. Leavitt, ed., pp. 601–616. The Hague: Mouton.
1978 "Woman's Status in Egalitarian Society: Implication for Social Evolution." *Current Anthropology* 19:247–275.

Lee, Richard B.
1968 "What Hunters Do for a Living, or How to Make Out on Scarce Resources." In *Man the Hunter,* R. B. Lee and I. DeVore, eds., pp. 30–43. Chicago: Aldine.
1969 "!Kung Bushman Subsistence: An Input-Output Analysis." In *Environment and Cultural Behavior: Ecological Studies in Cultural Anthropology,* A. P. Vayda, ed., pp. 47–79. Garden City, N.Y.: Natural History Press.
1979 *The !Kung San: Men, Women and Work in a Foraging Society.* New York: Cambridge University Press.

Leeds, Anthony
1970 "The Concept of the Culture of Poverty: Conceptual, Logical, and Empirical Problems, with Perspectives from Brazil and Peru." In *The Culture of Poverty: A Critique,* E. Leacock, ed., pp. 226–284. New York: Simon and Schuster.

Lees, Susan, and D. Bates
1974 "The Origins of Specialized Nomadic Pastoralism: A Systemic Model." *American Antiquity* 39:187–193.

Lenin, V. I.
1965 (1917) *The State and Revolution.* Peking: Foreign Language Press.

Leonard, Karen I.
1978 *Social History of an Indian Caste.* Berkeley: University of California Press.

Leroi-Gourhan, Arlette
1968 "The Evolution of Paleolithic Art." *Scientific American* 218(2):58–70.
1982 The Archaeology of Lascaux Cave." *Scientific American* 246(6):104–112.

Lesser, Alexander
1968 "War and the State." In *War: The Anthropology of Armed Conflict and Aggression,* M. Fried, M. Harris, and R. Murphy, eds., pp. 92–96. Garden City, N.Y.: Natural History Press.

Lévi-Strauss, Claude
1963a *Totemism.* Boston: Beacon Press.
1963b *Tristes Tropiques.* New York: Atheneum.

Lewis, Oscar
1961 *The Children of Sanchez: Autobiography of a Mexican Family.* New York: Random House.
1964 *Pedro Martinez: A Mexican Peasant and His Family.* New York: Random House.
1966 *La Vida: A Puerto Rican Family in the Culture of Poverty—San Juan and New York.* New York: Random House.

Lichtheim, George
1961 *Marxism: An Historical and Critical Study.* New York: Praeger.

Liebow, Elliot
1967 *Tally's Corner: A Study of Negro Street-Corner Men.* Boston: Little, Brown.

Lindenbaum, Shirley
1977 "The Last Course: Nutrition and Anthropology in Asia." In *Nutrition and Anthropology in Action,* Thomas Fitzgerald, ed., pp. 141–155. Atlantic Highlands, N.J.: Humanities Press.
1979 *Kuru Sorcery.* Palo Alto, Calif.: Mayfield.

Linton, Ralph
1959 "The Natural History of the Family." In *The Family: Its Function and Destiny,* R. Anshen, ed., pp. 30–52. New York: Harper & Row.

Livingstone, Frank B.
1968 "The Effects of Warfare on the Biology of the Human Species." In *War: The Anthropology of Armed Conflict and Aggression,* M. Fried, M. Harris, and R. Murphy, eds., pp. 3–15. Garden City, N.Y.: Doubleday.
1969 "Genetics, Ecology, and the Origins of Incest and Exogamy." *Current Anthropology* 10:45–62.

Lizot, Jaques
1977 "Population, Resources and Warfare among
the Yanomami." *Man* 12:497– 517.
1979 "On Food Taboos and Amazon Cultural
Ecology." *Current Anthropology* 20:150– 151.

Lochlin, J. C., and R. C. Nichols
1976 *Heredity, Environment and Personality.* Austin: University of Texas Press.

Lomax, Alan, ed.
1968 *Folksong Style and Culture.* Washington,
D.C.: American Association for the Advancement of Science, Publication 88.

Lomax, Alan, and Conrad Arensberg
1977 "A Worldwide Evolutionary Classification of
Cultures by Subsistence Systems." *Current Anthropology* 18:659– 708.

London, Miriam, and Ivan London
1979 "China's Victimized Youth." *The New York
Times* 10 February, p. 19.

Lowie, Robert
1920 *Primitive Society,* New York: Boni and
Liveright.
1948 *Primitive Religion.* New York: Liveright.
(Initially published 1924.)

Lundberg, Ferdinand
1968 *The Rich and the Super Rich.* New York:
Lyle Stuart.

Lynn, Richard
1978 "Ethnic and Racial Differences in Intelligence: International Comparisons." In *Human
Variation: The Biopsychology of Age, Race, and
Sex,* R. T. Osborne, C. Noble, and N. Weyl, eds.,
pp. 261– 286. New York: Academic Press.

MacLeish, Kenneth
1972 "The Tasadays: The Stone Age Cavemen of
Mindanao." *National Geographic* 142:219– 248.

MacNeish, Richard
n.d. "The Transition to Statehood (As Seen from
the Mouth of a Cave)." Unpublished paper.
1972 "The Evolution of Community Patterns in
the Tehuacán Valley of Mexico, and Specula-
tion about the Cultural Processes." In *Man, Settlement, and Urbanism,* P. J. Ucko, R. Tringham,
and G. W. Dimbleby, eds., pp. 67– 93. Cambridge, Mass.: Schenkman.
1978 *The Science of Archaeology?* Belmont, Calif.:
Duxbury Press.

Mair, Lucy
1969 *Witchcraft.* New York: McGraw-Hill.

Malinowski, Bronislaw
1920 "War and Weapons among the Natives of
the Trobriand Islands." *Man* 20:10– 12.
1922 *Argonauts of the Western Pacific.* New York:
Dutton.

1927 *Sex and Repression in Savage Society.* London: Routledge and Kegan Paul.
1935 *Coral Gradens and Their Magic* (2 vols.). London: Allen and Unwin.

Marett, Robert R.
1914 *The Threshold of Religion.* London: Methuen.

Marshall, Donald
1971 "Sexual Behavior on Mangaia." In *Human
Sexual Behavior,* D. Marshall and R. Suggs,
eds., pp. 103– 162. Englewood Cliffs, N.J.:
Prentice-Hall.

Marshall, Mac
1978 *Weekend Warriors: An Interpretation of
Drunkenness in Micronesia.* Palo Alto, Calif.:
Mayfield.

Marx, Karl
1970 (1859) *A Contribution to the Critique of Political Economy.* New York: International Publishers.

Marx, Karl, and F. Engels
1948 (1848) *The Communist Manifesto.* New York:
International Publishers. (Initially published
1848.)

Mason, Carol
1964 "Natchez Class Structure." *Ethnohistory*
11:120– 133.

Mason, J. Alden
1957 *The Ancient Civilizations of Peru.* Harmonds-
worth, Eng.: Penguin.

Mathur, Hari
1977 *Anthropology in the Development Process.*
New Delhi: Vikas.

Mead, Margaret
1949 *Male and Female.* New York: Morrow.
1950 *Sex and Temperament in Three Primitive Societies.* New York: Mentor.
1970 *Culture and Commitment.* Garden City, N.Y.:
Natural History Press.

Meggitt, Mervyn
1964 "Male-Female Relationships in the Highlands of Australian New Guinea." *American Anthropologist* 66:204– 224.

Mencher, Joan
1974a "Conflicts and Contradictions in the Green
Revolution: The Case of Tamil Nadu." *Economic and Political Weekly* 9:309– 323.
1974b "The Caste System Upside Down: Or, the
Not So Mysterious East." *Current Anthropology*
15:469– 478.
1978 *Agricultural and Social Structure in Tamil
Nadu.* New Delhi: Allied Publishers.

Millet, Kate
1970 *Sexual Politics.* Garden City, N.Y.: Doubleday.

Minge, Wanda
(In press) *The Rise of the Cost of Children: Family Economics in Historical Perspective.* Chicago: University of Chicago Press.

Minge-Kalman, Wanda
1978a "Household Economy during the Peasant-to-Worker Transition in the Swiss Alps." *Ethnology* 17(2):183–196.
1978b "The Institutionalization of the European Family: The Institutionalization of 'Childhood' as a Market for Family Labor." *Comparative Studies in Society and History* 20:454–468.

Minturn, Leigh, and John T. Hitchcock
1963 "The Rajputs of Khalapur, India." In *Six Cultures, Studies of Child Rearing*, B. B. Whiting, ed., pp. 203–361. New York: Wiley.

Miyadi, D.
1967 "The Differences in Social Behavior among Japanese Macaque Troops." In *Progress in Primatology*, D. Starck, R. Schneider, and H. Kuhn, eds. Stuttgart: Gustav Fischer.

Mondlane, Eduardo
1969 *The Struggle for Mozambique.* Baltimore: Penguin.

Mooney, James
1965 *The Ghost Dance Religion.* Chicago: University of Chicago Press. (Initially published 1896.)

Morgan, Lewis Henry
1877 *Ancient Society.* New York: Holt, Rinehart and Winston.

Morris, C.
1976 "Master Design of the Inca." *Natural History* 85(10):58–67.

Moynihan, Daniel P.
1965 *The Negro Family, the Case for National Action.* Washington, D.C.: U.S. Department of Labor.

Mullings, Leith
1978 "Ethnicity and Stratification in the Urban United States." *Annals of the N.Y. Academy of Science* 318:10–22.

Münzel, Mark
1973 *The Aché Indians: Genocide in Paraguay.* International Work Group for Indigenous Affairs (IWGIA), 11.

Murdock, George P.
1949 *Social Structure.* New York: Macmillan.
1967 *Ethnographic Atlas.* Pittsburgh: University of Pittsburgh Press.

Murphy, Robert
1956 "Matrilocality and Patrilineality in Mundurucu Society." *American Anthropologist* 58:414–434.
1976 "Man's Culture and Woman's Nature."

Annals of the New York Academy of Sciences 293:15–24.

McAskie, M., and A. M. Clarke
1976 "Parent-Offspring Resemblances in Intelligence; Theories and Evidence." *British Journal of Psychology* 67:243–273.

McEwen, Gordon, and D. B. Dickson
1978 "Was Huari a State?" *American Antiquity* 43:372–389.

McGrew, W. C.
1977 "Socialization and Object Manipulation of Wild Chimpanzees." In *Primate Bio-Social Development*, Susan Chevalier-Skolinkoff and Frank Poirier, eds., pp. 261–288. New York: Garland.

McGurk, F. C. J.
1975 "Race Differences Twenty Years Later." *Homo* 26:219–239.

Nadel, S. F.
1952 "Witchcraft in Four African Societies." *American Anthropologist* 54(1):18–29.

Nader, Laura
1972 "Up the Anthropologist—Perspectives Gained from Studying Up." In *Reinventing Anthropology*, Dell Hymes, ed., pp. 284–311. New York: Random House.

Nag, Moni
1972 "Sex, Culture, and Human Fertility: India and the United States." *Current Anthropology* 13:231–238.

Naroll, Raoul
1973 "Introduction" to *Main Currents in Anthropology*, R. Naroll and F. Naroll, eds., pp. 1–23. Englewood Cliffs, N.J.: Prentice-Hall.

Nash, Jil
1974 *Matriliny and Modernization: The Nagovisi of South Bougainville.* New Guinea Research Bulletin.

National Research Council
1974 *Agricultural Production Efficiency.* Washington, D.C.: National Academy of Sciences.

NBER (National Bureau of Economic Research)
1979 *Reporter* (Fall).

Neville, Gwen
1979 "Community Form and Ceremonial Life in Three Regions of Scotland." *American Ethnologist* 6:93–109.

Newcomer, Peter
1977 "Toward a Scientific Treatment of Exploitation: A Critique of Dalton." *American Anthropologist* 79:115–119.

Newman, Philip L.
1965 *Knowing the Gururumba.* New York: Holt, Rinehart and Winston.

Nishida, T.
1973 "The Ant-Gathering Behavior by the Use of Tools among Wild Chimpanzees of the Mahali Mountains." *Journal of Human Evolution* 2: 357–370.

Norton, Helen
1978 "The Male Supremacist Complex: Discovery or Invention?" *American Anthropologist* 80: 665–667.

Nurge, Ethel
1975 "Spontaneous and Induced Abortion in Human and Non-Human Primates." In *Being Female: Reproduction, Power, and Change*, D. Raphael, ed., pp. 25–35. The Hague: Mouton.

Nussbaum, Karen
1980 *Race Against Time*. Cleveland: National Association of Office Workers.

Odend'hal, Stuart
1972 "Energetics of Indian Cattle in Their Environment." *Journal of Human Ecology* 1:3–22.

Oliver, Douglas
1955 *A Solomon Island Society: Kinship and Leadership among the Sinai of Bouganville*. Cambridge, Mass.: Harvard University Press.

Onoge, Omafume
1979 "The Counter Revolutionary Tradition in African Studies: The Case of Applied Anthropology." In *The Politics of Anthropology: From Colonialism and Sepism toward a View from Below*, Gerrit Huizer and Bruce Mannheim, eds., pp. 45–66. The Hague, Mouton.

Opler, Morris
1968 "The Themal Approach in Cultural Anthropology and Its Application to North Indian Data." *Southwestern Journal of Anthropology* 24:215–227.

Orans, Martin
1968 "Maximizing in Jajmaniland: A Model of Caste Relations." *American Anthropologist* 70:875–897.

Osborne, R. T.
1978 "Race and Sex Differences in Heritability of Mental Test Performance: A Study of Negroid and Caucasoid Twins." In *Human Variation: The Biopsychology of Age, Race, and Sex*, R. T. Osborne, C. Noble, and N. Weyl, eds., pp. 137–169. New York: Academic Press.

Otterbein, Keith
1973 "The Anthropology of War." In *The Handbook of Social and Cultural Anthropology*, J. Honigman, ed., pp. 923–958. Chicago: Rand McNally.

Paddock, William, and E. Paddock
1973 *We Don't Know How: An Independent Audit of What They Call Success in Foreign Assistance*. Ames: Iowa State University Press.

Parker, Seymour, and R. Kleiner
1970 "The Culture of Poverty: An Adjustive Dimension." *American Anthropologist* 72:516–527.

Parsons, Anne
1967 "Is the Oedipus Complex Universal?" In *Personalities and Cultures: Readings in Psychological Anthropology*, Robert Hunt, ed., pp. 352–399. Garden City, N.Y.: Natural History Press.

Parson, Talcot
1970 "Equality and Inequality in Modern Society, or Social Stratification Revisited." In *Social Stratification: Research and Theory for the 1970's*, Edward Laumann, ed., pp. 13–72. New York: Bobbs-Merrill.

Pasternak, Burton, Carol Ember, and Melvin Ember
1976 "On the Conditions Favoring Extended Family Households." *Journal of Anthropological Research* 32(2):109–123.

Patterson, Orlando
1977 *Ethnic Chauvinism: The Reactionary Impulse*. New York: Stein and Day.

Peckman, Joseph, and B. Okner
1974 *Who Bears the Tax Burden?* Washington, D.C.: The Brookings Institution.

Pelto, Perttie, and Gretl Pelto
1973 "Ethnography: The Fieldwork Enterprise." In *Handbook of Social and Cultural Anthropology*, J. Honigman, ed., pp. 241–248. Chicago: Rand McNally.
1976 *The Human Adventure: An Introduction to Anthropology*. New York: Macmillan.

Perlo, Victor
1976 *Economics of Racism U.S.A.: Roots of Black Inequality*. New York: International Press.

Piddock, Stuart
1965 "The Potlatch System of the Southern Kwakiutl: A New Perspective." *Southwestern Journal of Anthropology* 21:244–264.

Piggott, Stuart
1966 *Ancient Europe*. Chicago: Aldine.

Pimentel, David, L. E. Hurd, A. C. Bellotti, and others
1973 "Food Production and Energy Crisis." *Science* 182:443–449.
1975 "Energy and Land Constraints in Food Protein Production." *Science* 190:754–761.

Pitt, David
1976 *The Social Dynamics of Development*. New York: Pergamon.

Piven, Frances, and R. Cloward
1971 *Regulating the Poor: The Functions of Public Welfare.* New York: Random House (Vintage).

Plucknett, D., and N. Smith
1982 "Agricultural Research and Third World Food Production." *Science* 217:215–220.

Polgar, Steven
1972 "Population History and Population Policies from an Anthropological Perspective." *Current Anthropology* 13:203–215.
1975 "Population, Evolution, and Theoretical Paradigms." In *Population, Ecology, and Social Evolution*, Steven Polgar, ed., pp. 1–25. The Hague: Mouton.

Porat, Marc
1979 "The Information Economy." Ph.D Dissertation. Stanford University.

Pospisil, Leopold
1963 *The Kapauku Papuans of West New Guinea.* New York: Holt, Rinehart and Winston.
1968 "Law and Order." In *Introduction to Cultural Anthropology*, J. Clifton, ed., pp. 200–224. Boston: Houghton Mifflin.

Premack, David
1971 "On the Assessment of Language Competence in the Chimpanzee." In *The Behavior of Nonhuman Primates*, vol. 4, A. M. Schrier and F. Stollnitz, eds., pp. 185–228. New York: Academic Press.
1976 *Intelligence in Ape and Man.* Hillsdale, N.J.: Erlbaum.

Price, Barbara
1977 "Shifts of Production and Organization: A Cluster-Interaction Model." *Current Anthropology* 18:209–233.
1979 "Turning States' Evidence: Problems in the Theory of State Formation." In *New Directions in Political Economy: An Approach from Anthropology*, M. B. Léons and F. Rothstein, eds., pp. 269–306. Westport, Conn.: Greenwood Press.

Princeton Religious Research Center
1979 *Emerging Trends.* Princeton, N.J.: 1 (March).
1980 *Religion In America 1979–1980.* Princeton, N.J.: Princeton Religious Research Institute.

Raj, K. N.
1977 "Poverty, Politics and Development." *Economic and Political Weekly* (Bombay), annual number, February, pp. 185–204.

Rambaugh, D. M.
1977 *Language Learning by a Chimpanzee: The Lana Project.* New York: Academic Press.

Raphael, Edna
1979 "Working Women and Their Membership in Labor Unions." In *The American Working Class: Prospects for the 1980's*, I. L. Horowitz et al.,

eds., pp. 95–113. New Brunswick: N.J.: Transaction Books.

Rappaport, Roy
1968 *Pigs for the Ancestors: Ritual in the Ecology of a New Guinea People.* New Haven, Conn.: Yale University Press.
1971a "Ritual, Sanctity, and Cybernetics." *American Anthropologist* 73:59–76.
1971b "The Sacred in Human Evolution." In *Explorations in Anthropology*, Morton Fried, ed., pp. 403–420. New York: Crowell.

Rasmussen, Knud
1929 *The Intellectual Culture of the Iglulik Eskimos.* Report of the 5th Thule Expedition, 1921–1924, vol. 7, no. 1. Translated by W. Worster. Copenhagen: Glydendal.

Rein, Martin, and Lee Rainwater
1977 "How Large Is the Welfare Class." *Change* September–October, pp. 20–23.

Renfrew, Collin
1973 *Before Civilization: The Radiocarbon Revolution and Prehistoric Europe.* New York: Knopf.

Ribeiro, Darcy
1971 *The Americas and Civilization.* New York: Dutton.

Richards, Paul
1973 "The Tropical Rain Forest." *Scientific American* 229:58–68.

Rifkind, Jeremy, and Ted Howard
1979 *The Emerging Order: God in the Age of Scarcity.* New York: Putnam.

Roach, Jack L., L. Gross, and O. R. Gursslin, eds.
1969 *Social Stratification in the United States.* Englewood Cliffs, N.J.: Prentice-Hall.

Roberts, Ron, and D. Brintnall
1982 *Reinventing Inequality.* Boston: Schenkman.

Roheim, Geza
1950 *Psychoanalysis and Anthropology.* New York: International University Press.

Rohner, Ronald
1969 *The Ethnography of Franz Boas.* Chicago: University of Chicago Press.

Rohrlich-Leavitt, Ruby
1977 "Women in Transition: Crete and Summer." In *Becoming Visible: Women in European History*, Renate Bridenthal and C. Koonz, eds., pp. 38–59. Boston: Houghton Mifflin.

Roper, Marilyn K.
1969 "A Survey of the Evidence for Intrahuman Killing in the Pleistocene." *Current Anthropology* 10:427–459.
1975 "Evidence of Warfare in the Near East from 10,000 to 4,300 B.C." In *War: Its Causes and Correlates*, W. Nettleship, R. D. Givens, and A.

Nettleship, eds., pp. 299–340. The Hague: Mouton.

Rosaldo, Michelle, and Louise Lamphere, eds.
1974 *Women, Culture, and Society.* Stanford: Stanford University Press.

Ross, Eric
1978 "Food Taboos, Diet, and Hunting Strategy: The Adaptation of Animals in Amazon Cultural Ecology." *Current Anthropology* 19:1–36.
1979 "Reply to Lizot." *Current Anthropology* 20:151–155.

Ross, Ruth, and G. Benson
1979 "Criminal Justice from East to West." *Crime and Delinquency* 25:76–86.

Roszak, Theodore
1975 *Unfinished Animal: The Aquarian Frontier and the Evolution of Consciousness.* New York: Harper & Row.

Rubin, Vera, and Lambros Comitas
1975 *Ganja In Jamaica: A Medical Anthropological Study of Chronic Marihuana Use.* The Hague: Mouton.

Ruyle, Eugene E.
1973 "Slavery, Surplus, and Stratification on the Northwest Coast: The Ethnoenergetics of an Incipient Stratification System." *Current Anthropology* 14:603–631.
1975 "Mode of Production and Mode of Exploitation: The Mechanical and the Dialectical." *Dialectical Anthropology* 1:7–23.

Ryscavage, Paul
1979 "More Wives in Labor Force Have Husbands with Above Average Incomes." *Monthly Labor Review* 102:40–42.

Sacks, Karen B.
1971 "Economic Bases of Sexual Equality: A Comparative Study of Four African Societies." Ph.D. dissertation, University of Michigan.

Safa, Helen I.
1967 *An Analysis of Upward Mobility in Lower Income Families: A Comparison of Family and Community Life among American Negro and Puerto Rican Poor.* Syracuse, N.Y.: Youth Development Center.
1968 "The Case for Negro Separatism: The Crisis of Identity in the Black Community." *Urban Affairs Quarterly* 4:45–63.

Sahlins, Marshall
1961 "The Segmentary Lineage: An Organization of Predatory Expansion." *American Anthropologist* 63:322–345.
1972 *Stone Age Economics.* Chicago: Aldine.
1978 "Culture as Protein and Profit." *The New York Review of Books* 23 November, pp. 45–53.

Salzman, Philip, ed.
1971 "Comparative Studies of Nomadism and Pastoralism." *Anthropological Quarterly* 44(3):104–210.
1978 "Does Complementary Opposition Exist?" *American Anthropologist* 80:53–70.

Sanday, Peggy
1973 "Toward a Theory of the Status of Women." *American Anthropologist* 75:1682–1700.
1981 *Female Power and Male Dominance: On the Origins of Sexual Inequality.* New York: Cambridge University Press.

Sanjek, Roger
1972 "Ghanian Networks: An Analysis of Interethnic Relations in Urban Situations." Ph.D. dissertation, Columbia University.
1977 "Cognitive Maps of the Ethnic Domain in Urban Ghana: Reflections on Variability and Change." *American Ethnologist* 4:603–622.

Scarr-Salapatek, S.
1971a "Unknowns in the I.Q. Equation." *Science* 174:1223–1228.
1971b "Race, Social Class, and I.Q." *Science* 174:1285–1295.

Scheffler, Harold
1973 "Kinship, Descent, and Alliance." In *Handbook of Social and Cultural Anthropology*, J. Honigman, ed., pp. 747–793. Chicago: Rand McNally.

Schermerhorn, R. A.
1970 *Comparative Ethnic Relations.* New York: Random House.

Schlegel, Alice
1972 *Male Dominance and Female Autonomy.* New Haven, Conn.: Human Relations Area Files.

Schlegel, Alice, and H. Barry
1979 "Adolescent Initiation Ceremonies: A Cross-Cultural Code." *Ethnology* 18:199–210.

Scrimshaw, Nevin
1977 "Through a Glass Darkly: Discerning the Practical Implications of Human Dietary Protein-Energy Interrelationships." *Nutrition Reviews* 35:321–337.

Scrimshaw, Susan
1978 "Infant Mortality and Behavior in the Control of Family Size." Paper presented at the Meetings of the American Association for the Advancement of Science, Washington, D.C., February.

Service, Elman R.
1975 *Origins of the State and Civilization: The Processes of Cultural Evolution.* New York: Norton.
1978 "Classical and Modern Theories of the Origin of Government." In *Origins of the State: The Anthropology of Political Evolution*, R. Cohen

and E. Service, eds., pp. 21–34. Philadelphia: ISHI.

Sexton, Lorraine
1973 "Sexual Interaction and Population Pressure in Highland New Guinea." Paper presented to the 72nd Annual Meeting of the American Anthropological Association, New Orleans, November 29–30.

Shabecoff, Philip
1977 "Why Blacks Still Don't Have Jobs." *The New York Times* 11 September, sec. 4. p. 4.

Sharff, Jagna
1980 *Life on Dolittle Street: How Poor People Purchase Immortality.* Final Report. Hispanic Study Project N. 9. Department of Anthropology, Columbia University.
1981 "Free Enterprise and the Ghetto Family." *Psychology Today*, March.

Shepher, J.
1971 "Mate Selection among Second Generation Kibbutz Adolescents and Adults." *Archives of Sexual Behavior* 1:293–307.

Shuey, Audrey M.
1966 *The Testing of Negro Intelligence.* New York: Social Science Press.

Simoons, Frederich
1979 "Questions in the Sacred Cow Controversy." *Current Anthropology* 20:467–493.

Simpson, George, and J. M. Yinger
1962 *Racial and Cultural Minorities.* 2nd ed. New York: Harper & Row.

Smith, C. T.
1970 "Depopulation of the Central Andes in the 16th Century." *Current Anthropology* 11: 453–460.

Smith, David
1974 *Who Rules the Universities? An Essay in Class Analysis.* New York: Monthly Review Press.

Smith, James D.
1973 *The Concentration of Personal Wealth in America.* Washington, D.C.: The Urban Institute.
1981 "Trends in the Concentration of Wealth in the United States." Paper presented at the Meeting of the International Association for Research on Income and Wealth. Chantilly, France, August 1981.

Smith, J. S. Franklin, and D. Wion
1973 *The Distribution of Financial Assets.* Washington, D.C.: The Urban Institute.

Smith, M. G.
1966 "A Survey of West Indian Family Studies." In *Man, Settlement, and Urbanism: West Indian Perspectives*, L. Comitas and D. Lowenthal, eds., pp. 365–408. Garden City, N.Y.: Anchor Books, 1973.
1968 "Secondary Marriage among Kadera and Kagoro." In *Marriage, Family, and Residence*, P. Bohannan and J. Middleton, eds., pp. 109–130. Garden City, N.Y.: Natural History Press.

Smith, Ralph
1979 "The Movement of Women into the Labor Force." In *The Subtle Revolution*, Ralph Smith, ed., Washington, D.C.: The Urban Institute.

Smith, Raymond T.
1973 "The Matrifocal Family." In *The Character of Kinship*, Jack Goody, ed., pp. 121–144. London: Cambridge University Press.

Smith-Rosenberg, Carroll
1978 "Sex as Symbol in Victorian Purity: An Ethnohistorical Analysis of Jacksonian America." In *Turning Points*, J. Demos and S. S. Boocock, eds. Supplement to the *American Journal of Sociology* 84.

Solzhenitsyn, Alexander
1974 *Gulag Archipelago.* New York: Harper & Row.

Sorenson, Richard
1972 "Socio-Ecological Change among the Foré of New Guinea." *Current Anthropology* 13: 349–383.

Sorenson, Richard, and P. E. Kenmore
1974 "Proto-Agricultural Movement in the Eastern Highlands of New Guinea." *Current Anthropology* 15:67–72,

Soustelle, Jacques
1970 *Daily Life of the Aztecs.* Stanford: Stanford University Press.

Speck, Frank
1915 "The Family Hunting Band as the Basis of the Algonkian Social Organization." *American Anthropologist* 17:289–305.

Spencer, Bladwin, and F. J. Gillen
1968 *The Native Tribes of Central Australia.* New York: Dover.

Spencer, P.
1965 *The Samburu: A Study of Gerontocracy in a Nomadic Tribe.* Berkeley: University of California Press.

Spengler, Joseph
1974 *Population Change, Modernization, and Welfare.* Englewood Cliffs, N.J.: Prentice-Hall.

Spicer, Edward
1954 *Potam: A Yaqui Village in Sonora.* Memoir 77, American Anthropological Association.

Spiro, Melford
1954 "Is the Family Universal?" *American Anthropologist* 56:839–846.

Srinivas, M. N.
1955 "The Social System of a Mysore Village." In *Village India: Studies in the Little Community*, M. Marriott, ed., pp. 1–35. Memoir 83, American Anthropological Association.

Stack, Carol
1974 *All Our Kin: Strategies for Survival in a Black Community*. New York: Harper & Row.

Stein, Howard, and R. F. Hill
1977 *The Ethnic Imperative: Examining the New White Ethnic Movement*. University Park: Pennsylvania State University Press.

Steinhart, John, and Carol Steinhart
1974 "Energy Use in the U.S. Food System." *Science* 184:307–317.

Stern, Curt
1973 *Principles of Human Genetics*. 3rd ed. San Francisco: Freeman.

Stewart, Omer C.
1948 *Ute Peyotyism*. University of Colorado Studies, Series in Antrhopology, No. 1. Boulder: University of Colorado Press.
1968 "Lorenz/Margolin on the Ute." In *Man and Aggression*, M. F. Ashley Montagu, ed., pp. 103–110. New York: Oxford University Press.

Street, John
1969 "An Evaluation of the Concept of Carrying Capacity." *Professional Geographer* 21(2): 104–107.

Sugiyama, Yukimaru
1969 "Social Behavior of Chimpanzees in the Budongo Forest, Uganda." *Primates* 10:197–225.

Susser, Ida
1982 *Norman Street*. New York: Oxford University Press.

Suttles, Wayne
1960 "Affinal Ties, Subsistence, and Prestige among the Coast Salish." *American Anthropologist* 62:296–305.

Swanson, Guy E.
1960 *The Birth of the Gods: The Origin of Primitive Beliefs*. Ann Arbor: University of Michigan Press.

Tanner, J. M.
1968 "Earlier Maturation in Man." *Scientific American* 218(1):21–27.

Tanner, Nancy
1974 "Matrifocality in Indonesia and Africa and among Black Americans." In *Woman, Culture and Society*, M. Rosaldo and L. Lamphere, eds., pp. 129–156. Stanford: Stanford University Press.

Terrace, Herbert
1979 "Is Problem Solving Language?" *Journal of the Experimental Analysis of Behavior* 31: 161–175.

Thorndike, R. L.
1968 "Intelligence and Intelligence Testing." *International Encyclopedia of the Social Sciences* 7:421–429.

Trigger, Bruce
1978 "Iroquois Matriling." *Pennsylvania Archeologist* 48:55–65.

Turner, Victor W.
1967 *The Forest of Symbols: Aspects of Ndembu Ritual*. Ithaca, N.Y.: Cornell University Press.

Tylor, Edward B.
1871 *Primitive Culture*. London: J. Murray.

Tyson, J. E., and A. Perez
1978 "The Maintenance of Infecundity in Post-Partum Women." In *Nutrition and Human Reproduction*, W. H. Mosley, ed., pp. 11–27. New York: Plenum.

Uberoi, J. P. Singh
1962 *Politics of the Kula Ring: An Analysis of the Findings of Bonislaw Malinowski*. Manchester: Manchester University Press.

Ucko, Peter J., and A. Rosenfeld
1967 *Paleolithic Cave Art*. London: Weidenfeld and Nicolson.

Underwood, Barbara, and Betty Underwood
1979 *Hostage to Heaven*. New York: Clarkson W. Potter.

U.S. Department of Commerce
1977 *General Report on Industrial Organization: 1977 Enterprise Statistics*. Washington, D.C.: Bureau of the Census, C3230.
1979 *Current Population Reports: Money Income of Family and Persons in the United States*. Washington, D.C.: Bureau of the Census.

U.S. National Criminal Justice Information and Statistics Service
1978 *Myths and Realities about Crime*. Washington, D.C.: U.S. Government Printing Office.

U.S. Senate Committee on Governmental Affairs
1978 *Voting Rights in Major Corporations*. 95th Congress, 1st Session. Washington, D.C.: U.S. Government Printing Office.

Vaidyanathan, A., N. Nair, and M. Harris
1982 "Bovine Sex and Age Ratios in India." *Current Anthropology* 23.

Vaillant, George C.
1966 *The Aztecs of Mexico*. Baltimore: Penguin. (Initially published 1941.)

Valentine, Charles
1970 *Culture and Poverty: Critique and Counterproposals*. Chicago: University of Chicago Press.

Wade, Nicholas
1973 "The World Food Situation: Pessimism

Comes Back into Vogue." *Science* 181: 634–638.

Wadel, Cato
1973 *Now, Who's Fault Is That?: The Struggle for Self-Esteem in the Face of Chronic Unemployment.* Institute of Social and Economic Research, Memorial University of Newfoundland.

Wagley, Charles
1943 "Tapirapé Shamanism." Boletim Do Museu Nacional (Rio De Janiero) *Antropología* 3:1–94.
1977 *Welcome of Tears: The Tapirapé Indians of Central Brazil.* New York: Columbia University Press.

Wagley, Charles, and M. Harris
1958 *Minorities in the New World.* New York: Columbia University Press.

Walker, Deward
1972 *The Emergent Native Americans.* Boston: Little, Brown.

Walker, Malcom, and Jim Hanson
1978 "The Voluntary Associations of Villalta." *Human Organization* 37:64–68.

Wallace, Anthony F. C.
1952 *The Modal Personality Structure of the Tuscarora Indians, as Revealed by the Rorschach Test.* Bulletin 150, Bureau of American Ethnology. Washington, D.C.: U.S. Government Printing Office.
1966 *Religion: An Anthropological View.* New York: Random House.
1970 *Culture and Personality.* 2nd ed. New York: Random House.

Wallis, Roy
1977 *The Road to Total Freedom: A Sociological Analysis of Scientology.* New York: Columbia University Press.

Warner, W. Lloyd, ed.
1963 *Yankee City.* New Haven, Conn.: Yale University Press.

Warner, W. Lloyd, M. Meeker, and K. Ellis
1949 *Social Class in America: A Manual for the Social Status.* Chicago: Chicago Research Association.

Watson, James
1977 "Pigs, Fodder, and the Jones Effect in Postipomean New Guinea." *Ethnology* 16:57–70.

Wattenberg, Esther, and Hazel Reinhardt
1979 "Female-Headed Families: Trends and Implications." *Social Work.* November, pp. 460–467.

Wax, Murray, S. Diamond, and F. O. Gearing
1971 *Anthropological Perspectives on Education.* New York: Basic Books.

Weiner, Annette
1976 *Women of Value, Men of Renown.* Austin: University of Texas Press.

Weisman, Steven
1978 "City Constructs Statistical Profile in Looting Cases." *The New York Times* 14 August, p. 1.

Weisner, Thomas, and Ronald Gilmore
1977 "My Brother's Keeper: Child and Sibling Caretaking." *Current Anthropology* 18:169–190.

Weiss, Gerald
1977a "The Problem of Development in the Non-Western World." *American Anthropologist* 79:887–893.
1977b "Rhetoric in Campa Narrative." *Journal of Latin American Lore* 3:169–182.

Welles, Chris
1978 "The Eclipse of Sun Myung Moon." In *Science, Sin and Scholarship,* Irving Horowitz, ed., pp. 243–258. Cambridge, Mass.: MIT Press.

Werner, Dennis
1979 "A Cross-Cultural Perspective on Theory and Research on Male Homosexuality." *Journal of Homosexuality* 4:345–362.

West, James
1945 *Plainville, U.S.A.* New York: Columbia University Press.

Westoff, Charles
1978 "Marriage and Fertility in the Developed Countries." *Scientific American* 239(6):51–57.

White, Douglas, et al.
1977 "Entailment Theory and Method: A Cross-Cultural Analysis of the Sexual Division of Labor." *Behavior Science Research* 12:1–24.

Whiting, John M.
1969 "Effects of Climate on Certain Cultural Practices." In *Environment and Cultural Behavior: Ecological Studies in Cultural Anthropology,* A. P. Vayda, ed., pp. 416–455. Garden City, N.Y.: Natural History Press.

Wilmsen, Edwin
1979 "Diet and Fertility among Kalahari Bushmen." African Studies Center, Boston University. Working Paper 14.

Wilson, E. O.
1975 *Sociobiology: The New Synthesis.* Cambridge, Mass.: Harvard University Press.
1977 "Biology and the Social Sciences." *Daedalus* 106(4):127–140.
1978 *Human Nature.* Cambridge, Mass.: Harvard University Press.

Wilson, Monica
1963 *Good Company: A Study of Nyakyusa Age-Villages.* Boston: Little, Brown.

Wittfogel, Karl A.
1957 *Oriental Despotism: A Comparative Study of Total Power.* New Haven, Conn.: Yale University Press.
1960 "A Stronger Oriental Despotism." *China Quarterly* January–March, pp. 32ff.

1979 Introduction to the 2nd English edition of *Oriental Despotism.*

Wolf, Arthur P.
1968 "Adopt a Daughter-in-Law, Marry a Sister: A Chinese Solution to the Problem of the Incest Taboo." *American Anthropologist* 70:864–874.
1974 "Marriage and Adoption in Northern Taiwan." In *Social Organization and the Applications of Anthropology: Essays in Honor of Lauristan Sharp*, Robert Smith, ed., pp. 128–160. Ithaca, N.Y.: Cornell University Press.

Wolf, Eric R.
1959 *Sons of the Shaking Earth.* Chicago: University of Chicago Press.
1966 *Peasants.* Englewood Cliffs, N.J.: Prentice-Hall.
1969 *Peasant Wars of the Twentieth Century.* New York: Harper & Row.

Wood, Corinne
1975 "New Evidence for the Late Introduction of Malaria into the New World." *Current Anthropology* 16:93–104.

Worsley, Peter
1968 *The Trumpet Shall Sound: A Study of "Cargo" Cults in Melanesia.* New York: Schocken.

Wright, Henry
1977 "Recent Research on the Origin of the State." *Annual Review of Anthropology* 6:379–397.

Yerkes, Robert
1921 *Psychological Examining in the United States Army.* National Academy of Science Memoirs No. 15. Washington, D.C.: National Academy of Science.

Index

Abortion, 56
Aché Indians, of eastern Paraguay, 157
Acheson, James, 169
Achieved statuses, 105
Achuara, 138
  food taboos of, 215
Action anthropology, 266
  advocacy as, 283–284
Adaptive capacity, 178
Adopted children, enculturation and, 33
Adultery, incest as, 99
Advocacy, as action anthropology, 283–284
Affinity, definition of, 104
Afghanistan, enculturation in, 7
Africa
  bride-price in, 96
  Dahomey of, 92
  European political development compared with, 148
  extended family in, 89
  money of, 75
  Portuguese rule in, 267
  scientific raciology in, 31
  witchcraft in, 127
African Ituri forest hunters, 12
Age-grade associations, 131
Age hierarchies, 161
Agency for International Development, 266
Age-set, 86
Aggresivity, 255
Agnostics, 312–313

Aid to Families with Dependent Children (AFDC), 300, 301
Alaska, technology in, 42
Albania, peasant of, 165, 166
Alcoa Aluminum, 294
Alexander, Richard, 34
Alland, Alexander, 222, 226
Alorese, of Indonesia, on descent, 104
Altamira, Spain, 229
Altruistic traits, 33–34
Amahuaca, food production of, 39
Amazon, Mundurucu of, 113
Amazon Basin, 137
  animal protein in, 215
  genocide in, 157
Ambilateral descent, 105, 106
Ambilocality, 110–111
American Legion, 133
Americans
  in Brazil, 33
  scientific raciology in, 31
Americas, European states in, 155
Amitalocality, 114–115
Ancient Society, 321, 322
Angel, Lawrence, 57
Animal biomass, 46–47
Animal protein
  in Amazon basin, 215
  warfare and, 137–139
Animatism, mana and, 187–188
Anthropological linguistics, 2–4
Anthropologists
  on human nature, 34
  nonacademic roles for, 5

Anthropology
  definition of, 2
  distinctive features of, 4
Antithesis, 235
Apaches, 12
Apes, displacement in, 29. *See also* Chimpanzees
Applied anthropology, 5, 16, 265–285
Appollonian culture, 242
Arabs, 50
Arapesh, 246
Arawak, 235
Archeology, 2–3
Argonauts of the Western Pacific (Malinowski), 65
Arishi-yama, monkeys of, 22
Arnheim, Australia, diffusion in, 11
Art, 221–238
  as cultural category, 222–225
  cultural patterning and, 227–229
  definition of, 222
  invention and, 226–227
  politics and, 230–233
  practicality versus, 225
  religion and, 229–230
Arunta
  art of, 230
  child care by, 241
  totemism of, 199
Arutam, 186, 187, 194
Ascribed statuses, 105
Ascription, 172